The Royal Navy in the Age of Austerity 1919–22

Bloomsbury Studies in Military History

Series Editor: Jeremy Black

Bloomsbury Studies in Military History offers up-to-date, scholarly accounts of war and military history. Unrestricted by period or geography, the series aims to provide free-standing works that are attuned to conceptual and historiographical developments in the field while being based on original scholarship.

Published:

The 56th Infantry Brigade and D-Day, Andrew Holborn
The RAF's French Foreign Legion, G.H. Bennett
Empire and Military Revolution in Eastern Europe, Brian Davies
Reinventing Warfare 1914–1918, Anthony Saunders
Fratricide in Battle, Charles Kirke
The Army in British India, Kaushik Roy
The 1711 Expedition to Quebec, Adam Lyons
Britain, Germany and the Battle of the Atlantic, Dennis Haslop
Military Transition in Early Modern Asia, 1400–1750, Kaushik Roy
The Role of the Royal Navy in South America, Jon Wise
Scotland and the British Army 1700–1750, Victoria Henshaw
War and State-Building in Modern Afghanistan, edited by Scott Gates and Kaushik Roy
Conflict and Soldiers' Literature in Early Modern Europe, Paul Scannell
Youth, Heroism and War Propaganda, D.A.B. Ronald
William Howe and the American War of Independence, David Smith
Postwar Japan as a Sea Power, Alessio Patalano
The D-Day Landing on Gold Beach, Andrew Holborn
Australian Soldiers in South Africa and Vietnam, Effie Karageorgos

Forthcoming:

Reassessing the British Way in Warfare, K.A.J. McLay
Australasian Propaganda and the Vietnam War, Caroline Page
English Landed Society and the Great War, Edward Bujak
General Lord Rawlinson, Rodney Atwood

The Royal Navy in the Age of Austerity 1919–22

Naval and Foreign Policy under Lloyd George

G. H. Bennett

BLOOMSBURY ACADEMIC
LONDON • NEW YORK • OXFORD • NEW DELHI • SYDNEY

BLOOMSBURY ACADEMIC
Bloomsbury Publishing Plc
50 Bedford Square, London, WC1B 3DP, UK

BLOOMSBURY, BLOOMSBURY ACADEMIC and the Diana logo
are trademarks of Bloomsbury Publishing Plc

First published in Great Britain 2016
Paperback edition first published 2018

Cover design: Sharon Mah
Cover image: Naval Offi cers of World War I by Sir Arthur Stockdale Cope
© National Portrait Gallery, London, UK

A catalogue record for this book is available from the British Library.

ISBN: HB: 978-1-4742-6838-7
PB: 978-1-3500-6711-0
ePDF: 978-1-4742-6840-0
ePub: 978-1-4742-6839-4

Library of Congress Cataloging-in-Publication Data
Names: Bennett, G.H. (George Henry), 1967 – author.
Title: The Royal Navy in the Age of Austerity 1919–22: Naval and Foreign Policy under Lloyd George/G.H. Bennett.
Description: New York: Bloomsbury Academic, an imprint of Bloomsbury Publishing PLC, 2016. | Series: Bloomsbury Studies in Military History | Includes bibliographical references and index.
Identifi ers: LCCN 2016012259 (print) | LCCN 2016012865 (ebook) | ISBN 9781474268387 (hardback) | ISBN 9781474268400 (ePDF) | ISBN 9781474268394 (ePub) | ISBN 9781474268394 (epub) | ISBN 9781474268400 (epdf)
Subjects: LCSH: Great Britain. Royal Navy–History–20th Century. | Lloyd George, David, 1863-1945–Infl uence. | Sea-power–Great Britain–History–20th Century. | Great Britain–Foreign Relations–1910-1936. | Great Britain–Military Policy.
Classifi cation: LCC DA89.B46 2016 (print) | LCC DA89 (ebook) | DDC 359/.03094109042–dc23
LC record available at http://lccn.loc.gov/2016012259
Series: Bloomsbury Studies in Military History

Typeset by Integra Software Services Pvt. Ltd.

To find out more about our authors and books visit www.bloomsbury.com and sign up for our newsletters.

For my father, who taught me to respect the Sea

Drake's Drum

DRAKE he's in his hammock an' a thousand miles away,
(Capten, art tha sleepin' there below?)
Slung atween the round shot in Nombre Dios Bay,
An' dreamin' arl the time O' Plymouth Hoe.
Yarnder lumes the Island, yarnder lie the ships,
Wi' sailor lads a-dancing' heel-an'-toe,
An' the shore-lights flashin', an' the night-tide dashin',
He see et arl so plainly as he saw et long ago.
Drake he was a Devon man, an' ruled the Devon seas,
(Capten, art tha' sleepin' there below?)

Roving' tho' his death fell, he went wi' heart at ease,
A' dreamin' arl the time o' Plymouth Hoe.
'Take my drum to England, hang et by the shore,
Strike et when your powder's runnin' low;
If the Dons sight Devon, I'll quit the port o' Heaven,
An' drum them up the Channel as we drumm'd them long ago'.
Drake he's in his hammock till the great Armadas come,
(Capten, art tha sleepin' there below?)

Slung atween the round shot, listenin' for the drum,
An' dreamin arl the time o' Plymouth Hoe.
Call him on the deep sea, call him up the Sound,
Call him when ye sail to meet the foe;
Where the old trade's plyin' an' the old flag flyin'
They shall find him ware and wakin', as they found him long ago!

Sir Henry Newbolt (1862–1938)

Contents

Preface

This book seeks to do three things: to advance, in the preface, a concept of the interconnectedness of naval policy; to propose, in the introduction, a potential case study focusing on naval policy in the period 1919–22; and then to explore that interconnectedness, as a means to demonstrate the concept, in subsequent chapters. It concludes with an examination of the repercussions of failure to successfully balance the different forces at play in naval policy and the importance of the relationships in the senior ranks of the Royal Navy between those who have to lead a service critically affected by British defence policy. The concept which this book seeks to advance stems from the processes, complexities and impacts of the building of complex warships as part of national defence. The building of warships depends on a network of relationships within the Royal Navy, between the naval service and government, between different branches of government, between the government and private sector and between the private sector and the communities which provide those employees. Those employees are, at the same time, voters and their political representatives have the capacity to affect government decision-making, while business leaders have the capacity to intercede with politicians, civil service and naval officers. Naval policy thus embraces both high and low politics, industrial relations and economic policy. The nexus of overlapping relationships at play in this field extends the importance, influence and impact of naval policy well beyond the realms of defence policy. The importance of naval policy as a significant force in wider national history has not been fully recognized by historians. The maritime element underpins the history of the British Isles and is indivisible from any wider historical analysis.

The elements of this concept of interconnectedness were fully evident in the defence policy of the Conservative–Liberal government headed by David Cameron from 2010 to 2015. On 17 July 2014 the 65,000-ton aircraft carrier HMS *Queen Elizabeth* left the dry dock at Rosyth, where her prefabricated sections had been brought together for final assembly. She had been officially named on 4 July by Queen Elizabeth II in a ceremony attended by David Cameron, the Prime Minister of the United Kingdom, and Alex Salmond, First Minister of Scotland and Leader of the Scottish Nationalist Party. With the dry dock clear, work would begin on the construction of HMS *Prince of Wales*, sister ship to HMS *Queen Elizabeth*. The prefabricated sections of the largest vessels ever built for the Royal Navy had been constructed at different yards around the United Kingdom to spread the economic benefits of the construction programme. Once in service HMS *Queen Elizabeth* would become the Royal Navy's capital ship for the twenty-first century: the largest and most effective weapons system in service with that force.

The politics of building the new generation of British aircraft carriers were particularly evident at the naming ceremony. Vital to British global power projection in the twenty-first century, the aircraft carriers would provide conventional military underpinning for national foreign policy. In the battle for government funding between the military services, the carriers represented an important success for the Royal Navy in securing long-term capabilities. On coming to office in the midst of an economic depression in 2010, the Conservative–Liberal coalition government had announced its desire to cancel the construction programme for at least one of the carriers, in the interests of national economy, only for it to emerge that the contracts for the ships had been structured in such a way as to make it less costly to proceed with their construction than fall foul of cancellation clauses. Other economic risks were also apparent. In 2010 Prime Minister Cameron was warned that cancelling one aircraft carrier would lead to the closure of three shipyards by 2013, the direct loss of 5,000 jobs and a considerably larger number of layoffs through indirect effects. Effectively, the outgoing Labour government of Gordon Brown had managed to tie the hands of the Cameron coalition to a programme that it otherwise felt it could not afford.[1]

A further level of political game playing around the new carriers was added by the prospect of a vote on Scottish independence from the United Kingdom in September 2014. Threatening the dissolution of a state that had survived two world wars, the importance to Rosyth and the wider Scottish economy of the contracts to build the aircraft carriers were key reference points in the political debate which began to grow as the first carrier neared completion. With the Royal Navy signalling that independence would rule out any future contracts for Scottish yards to provide its warships, the politics of shipbuilding were once again very evident. Warships required builders, bringing profits to firms, giving jobs to workers (directly and indirectly), building prosperity in towns and cities and ultimately bringing a political reward to the parties and governments which could take the credit for awarding contracts and supporting shipbuilding and allied trades. In their report of the naming ceremony the BBC estimated that some 10,000 workers, and over 100 companies, had worked on the building of HMS *Queen Elizabeth* and that the total value of the commercial contracts coming out of the aircraft carrier programme was worth an estimated £6.2 billion.[2] In stark economic terms the BBC drew attention to the essential set of relationships involved in naval policy and warship building.

The Financial Times, in its coverage of the naming ceremony, gave particular emphasis to the politics and symbolism at play in the event. Under the headline 'Warship sails into the defence of the UK', it revealed how during the ceremony dockyard workers had begun to boo when images of Alex Salmond (campaign leader for Scottish independence) appeared on a large video screen.[3] One dockyard worker was quoted as saying: 'They won't build complex warships outside UK sovereign territory... They haven't done that since the Second World War. If I voted for independence, I would be voting myself out of job. The majority of workers at the yard feel the same way.'[4] The potential social and economic damage to an independent Scotland of an end to building warships for the Royal Navy at Rosyth constituted a potent political threat to specific communities in an independent Scotland.

The launching of HMS *Queen Elizabeth* in 2014 was the first key stage in addressing a critical gap in national defences. That gap had opened up with the political games that had followed the advent of the Cameron government in 2010. It came into office amidst an international slump and economic difficulties at home. As the incoming government reviewed national security, the real priority of ministers was the state of the economy and a national deficit threatening bankruptcy.[5] Essential issues of national security were disregarded as politicians focused on political and economic imperatives. Under the 2010 Strategic Defence and Security Review (SDSR) ships, tanks and aircraft were sold for scrap value, military personnel fired and vital elements of Britain's defence capabilities dismantled in the rush for national economy.[6] Meanwhile, in a politically calculated move, state funding of free television licences, free bus passes and winter fuel allowances for Britain's senior citizens was retained.

One of the most significant aspects of SDSR 2010 was the scrapping of Britain's existing '*Invincible* class' aircraft carriers and the harrier aircraft that operated from them. Britain would have no aircraft carriers until the entry into service of HMS *Queen Elizabeth* and HMS *Prince of Wales*. Without carrier-borne aircraft, Britain would be forced to rely on good fortune that emergencies would not occur in parts of the world where the Royal Air Force would find it difficult to operate. It was a political gamble based on hope rather than realpolitik – the stupidity of which would soon be highlighted by the rise of

Islamic State in the Middle East, and a resurgent Russia able and willing to throw its weight around in international affairs. The decisions taken in 2010 constituted a serious military risk, condemning UK forces in the short and medium terms to have to conduct military operations without the potential for their own carrier support, including conducting large-scale operations against Islamic State and keeping Russian submarines out of UK territorial waters. Some, such as Geoffrey Till, considered that it was a gamble necessary to secure by the third decade of the twenty-first century a transformed and re-equipped Royal Navy in the front line of world navies.[7] Beyond potential terrorist threats from Islamic fundamentalist groups, the activities of organized crime and long-term dangers posed by climate change, ministers in 2010 saw no serious threats to UK national security requiring the deployment of large-scale conventional military forces. They therefore concluded that it was not essential to maintain those forces at existing levels.

Following SDSR 2010 as ministers argued over the need for HMS *Queen Elizabeth* and HMS *Prince of Wales*, the game of political football continued. Different ministers and departments, and external businesses, sought to influence the construction and kit that would go into the aircraft carriers and the lucrative contracts that would flow from them. In turn that led to changes, and then further changes, in their specification which increased their cost markedly and unnecessarily, and ensured that the Royal Navy would have less capable means of power projection at an inflated price.[8] SDSR 2010 and what followed from it were not good advertisements for the processes of Westminster government. SDSR 2015, unveiled in November of that year, had to quietly set about rebuilding the capabilities which had been jettisoned in 2010.[9]

To many observers of the history of the Royal Navy the 2010 process and its aftermath were reminiscent of Sir John Nott's infamous 'Defence Review' of 1981, which, with its plans for drastic cuts in the surface fleet, was publicly condemned by the Royal Navy as more about the economic imperatives of the Thatcher government than about the military needs of the country. Within twelve months of publication in June 1981 the review was being publicly and widely blamed as a contributory factor in Argentina's decision to seize British sovereign territory in South Georgia and the Falkland Islands. First Sea Lord Admiral Sir Henry Leach commented at the time of the resulting war that the Nott review had been 'done in a hurry, involved pre-judgement, and was driven by short term politico-economic expediency'.[10] The 1982 Falklands war cost the lives of 255 British service personnel, and the sweeping cuts to the Royal Navy's surface fleet were quietly halted in favour of a more gradual dwindling.

The same government which had helped to cause the war by its naval policy reaped the electoral fruits of victory with a landslide win in the 1983 general election.

The war did at least, as British singer Elvis Costello identified in his ironic hit 45 rpm record 'Shipbuilding', bring much needed relief to the British shipbuilding industry and its related communities hard hit by the Thatcher recession. With a record sleeve featuring images from Stanley Spencer's series of eight paintings *Shipbuilding on the Clyde*, depicting scenes from the Glasgow shipyards in the 1940s, the song rose to number 35 in the United Kingdom singles chart. The song was an ironic lament about the policies of the Thatcher government, and a reminder of the links between the fortunes of the Royal Navy, the industry which provided its ships and the working-class communities which built them. It also evoked the sense that those communities, and that industry, were as expendable as the sailors and soldiers called on to lay down their lives to redress the mistakes of politicians.[11] More than thirty years later, as the repercussions of SDSR 2010 became manifest, to some observers the song continued to retain its charge as the politicians continued to make avoidable mistakes, and to make decisions based on political considerations rather than what was in the security interests of the country.

Naval policy and the issues which flow from it are inherently and inextricably part of the political economy of the United Kingdom, and have been so for the past hundred years or more. That unchanging fact has been too easily overlooked by most maritime historians and those who might be called 'professional naval pundits'. Even those who use the term 'political economy' do not probe the full wealth of interconnections at play in decision-making about defence, but the connections are there to be traced and analysed. Those interconnections take the reach of naval policy well beyond the realms of the Ministry of Defence. It touches the economy, local and national politics, business, communities and a vast network of relationships. This book demonstrates this concept of interconnectedness by an analysis of naval policy in the period from 1919 to 1922, but it can be glimpsed across British history from the 1700s onwards.

For example, in December 1944, seventy years before the naming ceremony for HMS *Queen Elizabeth*, a young Princess Elizabeth had launched HMS *Vanguard* on the Clyde River.[12] The last of Britain's battleships, she had been the capital ship of her day. Like the launching of HMS *Queen Elizabeth* in 2014 the event combined international politics with naval policy, employment, regional prosperity and national politics all wrapped in symbolism. The launch took place on the day of Scotland's patron saint, St Andrew, with the future Queen's personal standard flying overhead. At the end of a long war, with hopes and fears for a future that would be dominated by cold war and nuclear threat, and with an electorate that had shifted firmly to the left, the launch was an affirmation of a set of relationships that had been tested by the Second World War in a generation, just as the launch of HMS *Queen Elizabeth* in 2014 would involve an assertion of the value of a relationship over three hundred years old.

For the working-class communities on the Clyde the unspoken backdrop to the launch of HMS *Vanguard* in 1945 and HMS *Queen Elizabeth* in 2014 was less happy days, in the aftermath of the First World War, when orders had declined for British shipbuilders on the Clyde, Tyneside and Merseyside. The lack of orders brought joblessness, dole and despair to families and destroyed whole communities. What started in the 1920s intensified in the early to mid-1930s and was only brought to an end by the approach of war after 1937. The events of the post-war period continue to cast long shadows on the shipbuilding industry and the regions which depend on it. The celebrations of 2014 and 1945 took place against the memories of leaner times, and concerns and hopes for the future evolution of British naval policy with its capacity to make or break the communities that live or die by shipbuilding.[13] In this most traditional industry the policy linkages, the high and low politics and patterns of business and regional boom and bust can be glimpsed repeating themselves across the past hundred years and beyond.

In this context, this book offers an analysis of naval policy in the period 1919–22: an earlier age of austerity than the one in which we find ourselves in the second decade of the twenty-first century. During the years after the First World War, as the Royal Navy identified Japan as its likely opponent in a future naval war, the British government was forced to 'tighten its belt' and cut back on naval expenditure in the interests of 'National Economy'. The central argument of the book is that the same kind of connections between naval and foreign policy (what a nation can and cannot do), the provision of ships for the Royal Navy, business and regional prosperity and employment were just as evident after the First World War as they are in the late twentieth or early twenty-first century. Furthermore, at a series of levels, naval policy was grist to the mill of politics: international politics between naval powers; Whitehall interdepartmental politics; the politics of coalition government, with Conservative and Liberal ministers vying with each other over budgets and influence; the politics of the English and Scottish regions; and the politics of prosperity and jobs. One hundred years on from the end of the First World War history, as least so far as naval policy is concerned, is to some extent repeating itself.

In covering its subject matter this book will engage with a series of important historiographical debates relating to: the history of the Royal Navy, the failures of British defence policy in the interwar period, the evolution of British foreign policy after 1919, British economic and industrial history and the nation's social and cultural history in the aftermath of the First World War. For example, one particularly important, and yet easily overlooked, aspect of Britain's external relations in the 1919 to 1922 period concerns the extent to which the political debate was influenced by concerns about the emergence of socialism as a political force, and the possibilities that the labour movement might grow into the main opposition to the Conservative Party. In *The Impact of Labour* Maurice Cowling has written that for the Conservative Party from early 1920 onwards the rise of the Labour Party, and what to do about it, was 'the major problem' in British politics.[14] That problem became increasingly central to every political calculation. The emergence of the modern Labour Party, the decline of the Liberals and the reinvention of the Conservative Party were vital political processes in play in the immediate aftermath of the First World War, but how far did this intrude into the field of defence politics? Was there some consideration and calculation about how naval policy might impact on the battle between the Conservative, Labour and Liberal parties in key regions and cities? Sound national finances, responsible and honest government and national security (with a strong Royal Navy) were the key elements in the identity of the Conservative Party as it struggled to redefine itself after almost twenty years in opposition or in coalition under a Liberal leader.[15] Also for the Conservative Party were there rather more nebulous and inchoate considerations about what kind of socialism might constitute their future opposition? Was it to be the potentially revolutionary politics of Red Clydeside or that of a moderate union movement and Labour Party?

Asking and answering questions such as these is an essential aspect of this book. It adopts a multifaceted approach rooted in political and naval history but opening up new and cutting-edge debates in other areas of historical study to transform traditional debates. As we have seen, history has a habit of repeating itself and the politics and political economy of British naval policy has scarcely changed in the century between 1914 and 2014. We have been here before, and we will be here again, unless we better understand the processes, personalities and politics at work in naval policy – this demands a joined-up approach, linking different areas of historical study. These linkages are starkly absent from much of the writing on naval history and British history in the 1919–22 period. As a discipline history excels in imposing divisions, or creating watertight compartments, within the overall passage of events. To the chronological divisions formed by the coming and going of different administrations in Westminster are added the disciplinary bulkheads of political, naval, military, economic, business, social, gender and labour history. The wider patterns and linkages are lost, and as much as this book is a contribution to the understanding of naval policy after the First World War, it is also a contribution to what might be labelled total history. Its significance is not only factual but methodological.

In terms of naval history as a sub-discipline it heeds Volker Berghahn's plea to reject the 'primacy of foreign policy' approach and to 'advance toward more sophisticated approaches that incorporate domestic factors'.[16] This book also accepts John Sumida's argument that navies 'are not only social entities but strategic, tactical, logistical, technical, economic, financial and administrative entities as well. Social and cultural factors might be the dominant factors in determining the outcome of a particular decision, but they are never the only agents at play'.[17] Similarly from the field of political science the book recognizes the validity of Samuel P. Huntingdon's complaint that 'analyses of strategy at times seem to assume that politics sets no limits on the military policies which the government can pursue.'[18] In accepting these points this book seeks to draw together the historiography and understandings from the sub-disciplines covering the history of this period in order to examine the interconnections at work in naval policy, and to highlight the repercussions over the course of the following twenty years of the decisions and understandings arrived at between 1919 and 1922. By bringing these strands together this book will offer an innovative reading of naval policy during this period, and offer a methodology for the reading of British defence policy in the twentieth century and beyond.

In respect of naval history, and especially because of the parallels which this book seeks to draw, one point in particular needs to be addressed at the outset. Playing an important role in the writing of modern naval history have been figures such as Captain S.W. Roskill, Samuel Eliot Morison and others with close associations to professional navies. Their work has sometimes been seen as history dressed in the form of a case for continued expenditure on navies. The same prejudices among the historical community have extended to the work of civilian academics who work in the field of War Studies, or establishments linked to the Ministry of Defence. Writers of naval history in the most humble and pacific universities can find themselves tarred with the same brush. For example, David Edgerton has charged Paul Kennedy in his narrative on *The Rise and Fall of British Naval Mastery* with wanting 'a navy kept at 1918 levels with 1914 levels of shipbuilding, rather than one adjusted to a peacetime standard devised in comparison with other navies'.[19] Such comments can be interpreted as value laden and indicative of a wider prejudice within academe.

It is remarkable, and a highly retrograde impulse, that in the early twenty-first century any part of human existence and endeavour might be considered to lie outside the purview of the historians. In an editorial in the *International Journal of Naval History* in 2009 Dr Gary Weir wrote as follows: 'Many university settings reject the study of military and naval history as characteristic of a violent aspect of our society that somehow promotes the armed forces rather than informs. It seems as if some places devoted to scholarship seek to study a world in which navies do not exist.'[20] Andrew Lambert, Laughton professor of Naval History, defined the problem in a British context: 'The key problem is that naval history operates in two distinct fields. Although developed to educate navies it has adopted and applied the methods of the historical profession. The close link with navies makes it an unwelcome presence in academic departments that equate the study of war with its promotion.'[21]

In writing naval history it does not automatically follow that by analysing and charting the decline of the Royal Navy one becomes a propagandist for naval arms and national navies. Nor does it follow that there is anything untoward if one considers that the personnel and material available to the Royal Navy leave it inadequate to the tasks placed upon it, or which might be placed upon it in the light of international events. Ships' crews are societies in miniature encased in wood or steel. Seamen and sea women are extensions of the larger society that they serve. The human tragedy of crews sent into combat in second-rate ships, or which are overwhelmed by the elements, breeds no militarism.

Likewise it is a geographical fact that Britain is an island, and that its national evolution has been deeply affected by the nation's relationship with the sea. The oceans contain the planet's most complex eco-systems and have been a place of scientific discovery and economic endeavour. Navies have played their role in that story. With two-thirds of the world's surface covered by water, and Britain dependent on the sea for 90 per cent of its imports, the Royal and Merchant Navies have been a vital part of British and international history. They remain so, and will continue to be so for the foreseeable future. Questions around the dilemmas which Britain faced a hundred years ago, and the impact of the decisions taken in response, remain remarkably current. Britain needs a critical naval history informed by the other sub-disciplines of history with which this book engages.

With the decision-making of politicians, civil servants and, indeed, admirals, the wisdom or error of their thoughts often becomes clear a decade or more later.

Today that time lag may be even longer. In 1919 a new capital ship was expected to have a life of twenty years: in the twenty-first century HMS *Queen Elizabeth* is considered good for half a century. The commanding officers of HMS *Queen Elizabeth* in her closing years in the latter twenty-first century have not yet been born. Decisions affecting naval policy thus cast long shadows across futures yet shrouded in darkness, and as Kipling noted in 1893 (echoed in sentiment by Elvis Costello in 1982), blood is the ultimate price of Admiralty when they go wrong.[22]

Acknowledgements

This book represents the culmination of more than twenty years' worth of research. Conversely the first draft was written at almost indecent speed during the summer of 2014. Prompted by the Daiwa Foundation's gracious decision to have Plymouth University host a symposium on Anglo-Japanese relations in September 2014, I volunteered to give a twenty-minute paper. Over that summer a twenty-minute paper grew into a 9,000-word article. That in turn grew into this book, as the subject matter forced me to make connections between disparate areas of research that I had investigated since starting a PhD in the 1980s. Diplomatic and military history would meet industrial and maritime history, political history would meet social and economic to try to come up with a broader, innovative and wide-reaching reading of Britain's strategic position, and naval policy, in the aftermath of the First World War.

In this endeavour there are many people and institutions that have assisted my research over the past twenty years. My colleagues at Plymouth University (those still active, those who are retired and those who are no longer with us) have invariably been a great help. In this context I would especially like to thank Dr Jonathan Mackintosh whose hard work and ideas led to Daiwa's decision to hold the symposium in Drake's hometown. Daiwa have been very supportive and I would also like to pay tribute to them and to the invaluable work that they do in bringing together two peoples on opposite sides of the globe.

The staff at libraries and archives great and small have never been less than outstandingly helpful including those at The National Archives UK; US National Archives; The National Maritime Museum (for giving permission to quote from the Beatty papers); Scottish Record Office; British Library; Britannia Royal Naval College Library; Plymouth, Exeter and Bristol University Libraries; Wirral Archives Service (for giving permission to quote from the Cammell Laird papers); Wiltshire and Swindon Archives (for giving permission to quote from the Long papers); and the Royal Archives (quotations from Beatty's Letter to King George V, 12 November 1921, appear by kind permission of Her Majesty Queen Elizabeth II).

In researching this book it has not been possible to trace the holders of copyright in every case. Publishers in particular seem noticeably less interested in responding to author queries than they were twenty years ago. In the case of any omission, if the copyright holder would like to contact me, care of the publisher, we will see that due acknowledgement is given in any future edition of the book.

On the maritime side I would like to express my thanks to Captain Michael Clapp, Julian Parker and the staff at the Maritime Foundation and to a range of characters at Southdown Quay in Cornwall who have given me (over several years) a grounding in the affairs of the commercial marine world. These include Nathan, Angry John, Big Chris, Spanner, Graham (the elder), Graham (the younger), Northern Dave, Chris and Marcia Rees, Café Paul, John Owles, Ben and Terry, and the owners, crews and residents of *Our Boys*, *Our Lizzie*, *Grayhound*, *Freya*, *Tectona*, *Le Drageur* and the *Phoenix*. They have continued the maritime education begun by my father almost fifty years ago.

At the level of individuals on the academic side I am indebted to Professor Gibson (for reading and critiquing the book), Professor Black, Professor Lambert, Dr Cummings, Dr Harrold, Dr Clarke, James Smith and Richard Porter. On the personal side, for keeping me grounded, I would like to express my thanks to John and Simon Harding, Tyler Hawke, Jason Clarke (King), Calum Caine, Dom, P.J. Jones, Danny and Mark Walsh, Maximo Jr and Jack Union, Terry and Alice Speller and the crews that surround them and the LEP and CPW 'families'.

Introduction

From 1919 to 1922 the makers of British naval policy faced particularly acute difficulties in struggling to balance the different and interconnected forces at play within it. In late 1919, at the end of a long and very costly war, the Royal Navy began to turn its attention to the next war – a war which would probably be fought in the Pacific with Japan as the likely opponent. It would be a war in which the Royal Navy would have quantitative and probably qualitative superiority, and the conflict would be decided not necessarily by a clash of main battle fleets, but rather by the economic strangulation of a Japanese economy heavily dependent on imports of raw materials, and the export of finished goods.[1] At the same time, the Royal Navy would maintain the freedom of the seas for British trade, or more particularly the strategic sea lanes which ran from North America to Britain, from Britain through the Eastern Mediterranean, from the Suez Canal to India and onwards into the Pacific to link Australia and New Zealand to the heart of the imperial superhighway across the oceans. Irrespective of war or peace, this was the highway which served to tie together a rather ramshackle and disparate Empire, and off from it branched connections to British possessions in Africa, the Pacific and the Far East. The Empire depended on a main maritime artery protected by the Royal Navy and by bastions such as Gibraltar, Alexandria and Trincomalee.

Naval dominance was a touchstone for the British imperial identity. Any power seeking to rival Britain on the high seas was a threat to that Empire and to British home islands equally as dependent as Japan on a continuing flow of imports and exports. With projections of a rapid increase in Japanese naval power after the First World War, it was inevitable that the Royal Navy should attempt to respond to a potential threat to the security of the Empire. As Christopher M. Bell has detailed, during the interwar period, planning for a future naval conflict against Japan would occupy the attention of the senior levels of the Senior Service far more than the threats from Germany, Italy and other nations.[2] The Royal Navy had a clear strategic vision of the war which was to come against the Japanese, but ironically when that conflict arrived in 1941, it lacked the means to execute its strategy and to prosecute the naval war against Japan. That would have to be left to the US Navy. Following the Japanese attack on Pearl Harbor on 7 December 1941, the unity of the British Empire would be undermined as the Royal Navy was driven from the East and Japanese forces would overrun large sections of the British Empire to leave the Japanese Army by 1942 contemplating invasions of Australia and India. It would not be until 1945 that a British Fleet in the Pacific, working with the Americans, would begin to carry the fight towards the Japanese home islands.

There were many reasons for the failure of British strategy against the Japanese which sought to contain and, if need be, strangle the Japanese naval threat to the Empire. These reasons included the slow pace of British rearmament in the late 1930s, and the fact that from mid-1940 to mid-1941 Britain stood alone in war against Nazi Germany and Fascist Italy. Nevertheless, the miscarrying of the strategy to deal with Japan was disastrous for those sailors, soldiers, airmen and civilians caught in the path of the Japanese military after 1941, and for an empire that was perhaps fatally compromised by the success of Japanese arms in 1941–42. The process of decolonization, of wholesale withdrawal from the Empire, would begin hard on the heels of Japanese defeat in 1945. It was scarce wonder that after 1945 the Empire broke up with astonishing speed. The protective shield of the Royal Navy was the principal benefit to the dominions and colonies of the imperial relationship, and the events of the war had fatally compromised the partnership. On this reading British naval policy in the interwar period assumes great significance. Did the problems begin in 1919, the point at which the Empire reached its apogee and the Royal Navy identified the Imperial Japanese Navy as its most likely next opponent in a major naval war? Was this the moment when naval dominance was sacrificed, when things went wrong in aligning the Royal Navy for 'The Shape of Things to Come', and the mother country failed in preparing the Empire for its gravest test?

This book examines the evolution of British naval and foreign policy in the period 1919–22 – the period of the Lloyd George coalition government. This is the point at which the need to contain Japan was identified, and the Royal Navy began to make its case to the government to secure the resources to effect an appropriate strategy to deal with that threat. How was this danger represented to the politicians? What assets did the Royal Navy possess in trying to secure Cabinet agreement on providing the resources to meet the threat? How did the public view the Royal Navy, the recent war and the challenges of the future? These are some of the questions which this book will address.

In doing so, this book seeks to contribute to the historiography on the Royal Navy, British defence policy and the outbreak of the Second World War, which has been dominated by perceptions that things really began to go badly wrong with British defence policy in the 1930s with the appeasement-inclined politicians of the National Government. Few historians have been prepared to go along wholly with Lord Chatfield's assessment that, by the end of the 1920s, the Admiralty, War Office and Air Ministry had been handed over by the politicians to the financial Gestapo constituted by the Treasury.[3] Against a post-war historiographical consensus framed by publication in 1940 of Cato's *Guilty Men*, which argued that Prime Minister Neville Chamberlain, Foreign Secretary Halifax and others were the architects of appeasement and national disgrace in the 1930s, Chatfield's comments made little impression until historians such as John Ferris and Christopher M. Bell re-examined defence policy of the 1920s.[4]

In 1919 conjuring up a threat of future war with a power which hitherto had been on friendly terms with Great Britain was the automatic response of a service which in the course of the hundred years between 1815 and 1919 had achieved and had slowly begun to lose naval supremacy: the ability to dominate the fleets of other powers on the surface of the world's oceans. Throughout that century the Royal Navy had maintained a close watch on the progress of the navies of rival powers. Britain's naval dominance was never as total, or as unproblematic, as British public opinion was ready to believe in the nineteenth century, and the Royal Navy maintained constant vigilance looking for the next threat to peace and assessing the balance of power at sea. No power on earth could ever truly dominate the oceans on a continuous basis, and on a number of occasions throughout the nineteenth century, rapid technological change had threatened the British battle fleet with immediate or projected obsolescence.

In 1919 threats, and potential threats, to Britain's maritime security could not and would not be taken for granted, and this was accepted by politicians. The Navy's prestige was invariably high: its superiority (material and human) was widely endorsed by a public to whom Nelson's victory at Trafalgar in 1805 was testament to British genius, pluck and god-granted fortune. The Navy received patronage and favour from the royal family, and Parliament, in the lead up to 1914, had been ready to vote the naval estimates to ensure the continuance of British maritime strength. Britain's naval power made her a state to be feared, to be courted and to be emulated. Victory over the Central Powers in the war of 1914–18 owed much to the ability of the Royal Navy to mount an economic blockade, and to bring to the land battle the resources of a global empire without interruption by enemy naval units that had been contained or destroyed. The surrender of the German High Seas Fleet in 1918, and its scuttling in Scapa Flow in 1919, seemed to affirm continued British dominance over the world's oceans. Only the Imperial Japanese and US navies could challenge the position of the Royal Navy as the guardian of the world's oceans. However, within three years of the scuttling of the Kaiser's fleet, the Royal Navy, or at least the British government, had agreed to surrender Britain's unqualified position as the premier naval power. How did this happen and what were the consequences?

During the years from 1919 to 1922, and in the naval and foreign policies of Lloyd George's peacetime government, there was a coming together into a perfect policy storm of a series of factors (long and short term) that forced decisions that would have far-reaching consequences for the Royal Navy and the nation it served. Those factors varied greatly and this book will range widely in terms of both their chronology and its composite themes. As Duncan Redford correctly observes, 'The complexities of British naval policy, operations, administration, technology and finance defy the tidy grouping of research into discrete chronological boundaries; in many ways the Navy's contemporary history can best be seen as the cumulative effect of previous successes and failures of naval and defence policy.'[5]

Britain's naval dominance had undoubtedly been a long time in the making, but it was a very short time in the ceding. The rise had been based on a series of long-term developments. The Industrial Revolution had provided a very advanced and prosperous economy, especially in such key industries as steel production, coalmining, engineering and shipbuilding. As an island nation, unencumbered by alliances, Britain had been able to invest in sea power rather than pay for the huge armies needed by continental powers to defend their borders. During the eighteenth and nineteenth centuries, the British Empire had extended into Africa and Asia. The Empire with its interconnecting trade routes provided a worldwide network of bases and coaling stations which provided the necessary infrastructure for Britain to project its power on a global basis through the Royal Navy. The Navy was backed by the world's largest merchant fleet which brought Britain such dominance in world trade that politicians, businesspersons and public opinion were all keenly aware of the importance of maritime matters. The merchant fleet also provided a large pool of experienced seamen who could be called upon in any emergency. As vital national assets the Empire and merchant fleets required protection and support in all parts of the world, and the Royal Navy had the capability and flexibility to deliver that protection and support wherever ships could navigate. Just as importantly, the lessons of history and national pride ensured that the Royal Navy enjoyed a considerable measure of prestige in British culture and the nation's affections.

Effectively there was work for the Royal Navy to do which could not be carried out by any other means, and the country had the industrial infrastructure to produce the necessary ships and keep up with new developments such as the transitions from sail to steam propulsion and from wood to steel construction. The British economy was prosperous enough to finance the high cost of the service, and public opinion (led by the socio-political elite of industrial society) was prepared to accept the cost. As the franchise steadily widened in Britain during the nineteenth century, this factor became steadily more important. Overall during the nineteenth century the cultural capital of the Royal Navy with the British voter and taxpayer remained high, but it was a fluctuating relationship that had its peaks and its troughs. The centenary anniversary of Trafalgar in 1905 (one of the peaks) underlined the public's powerful support for the Royal Navy, but by this stage some of the bases of British economic power, and the ability to sustain a strong Royal Navy, were coming under strain.

The signature of an Anglo-Japanese Alliance in 1902, and steadily closer relations with France in the face of an increasingly aggressive German foreign policy, highlighted growing British concerns in the Edwardian era about national security and the balance of power in Europe and Asia. Those factors which had given rise to Britain's naval dominance began to slip away in the approach to the outbreak of war in 1914. From maintaining a British Fleet capable of beating a combination of the next two largest fleets in the nineteenth century, the Royal Navy by 1914 was forced to accept a 60 per cent margin of superiority over the German Navy. By the end of a ruinous war that shook the Empire to its foundations, dislocating the production of staple industries (shipbuilding, steel and coal production), and leaving Britain massively in debt to the United States, Britain could not maintain the size of navy that imperial security and the rhetoric of empire appeared to demand.

The war had also raised industrial and political challenges that abutted the key issue of the size of the British Fleet. The effectiveness of submarines, mines and torpedoes had been demonstrated. Similarly the conflict had highlighted the potential of airpower (land-based and maritime). Some wondered by 1919 whether the battleship, the spiritual if not technological descendent of Nelson's flagship at Trafalgar, had had its day. Did the future belong to rapidly evolving and less costly weapons systems rather than the leviathans that had formed line of battle at Jutland? What might this mean for the future of warfare and the strategy of an island nation with its far-flung Empire? Building battleships required a major investment that Britain could ill-afford. To invest in a system on the verge of obsolescence was unthinkable. However, not to build battleships would further impact on the staple industries of iron and steel production and shipbuilding, which were seemingly in long-term inexorable decline. Without fresh orders firms would not maintain the specialist facilities for warship building, thereby decreasing the industrial potential of strategic British industries. This would, in turn, increase unemployment, particularly in the industrial North of England and in Scotland. Union militancy might increase, fuelling the growth of the Labour Party and more militant forms of socialism. The issue of the battleship and the strength of the Royal Navy touched a range of domestic issues as well as the culture and identity of the nation and empire.

There were also foreign policy implications. The Anglo-Japanese Alliance, signed in 1902, was once again up for renewal in 1921, and the American government was critically concerned about Japanese policies and intentions. During the war, both Japan and the United States had initiated large programmes for the building of warships. Those fleets threatened to outnumber and outclass the battleship fleet of the Royal Navy. Britain could not afford to compete with those programmes: likewise she could not afford to see her naval power simply eclipsed. The situation required action, but what action and at what cost? A series of policy dilemmas confronted the British government, and on the resolution of those dilemmas depended the future shape of British power and the evolution of the Empire. This book analyses those policy dilemmas and the Lloyd George government's attempts to understand and reconcile them.

The eventual means of resolving some of those problems came at the conferences held in Washington from 1921 to 1922. The outcomes of the conferences were several: a naval limitation treaty establishing overall parity of capital ships between the United States and Royal Navy (and Japanese preponderance in the Eastern Pacific); a multi-party treaty to uphold the territorial status quo in China; and a Four Power Pact by which Britain, the United States, Japan and France guaranteed to respect the integrity of each other's possessions in the Far East.[6] In practice the Four Power Pact meant little, but it did give the British a convenient reason to cancel the Anglo-Japanese Alliance in 1923 in a way which did not involve an outright insult to the Japanese government. The creation of the Alliance had been a significant moment in the lead up to the First World War, and its end arguably set Japan on the path that would lead to the outbreak of the Pacific War in December 1941. The abrogation of the alliance owed much to growing tensions and concerns within the Empire about imperial defence, and the eclipse of Britain's naval predominance would accelerate the process of imperial breakup as the dominions increasingly took their affairs into their own hands.[7] The process accelerated dramatically as a result of the war fought in the Pacific between 1941 and 1945. That war would also see the flowering of the Pax Anglo-Americana agreed at Washington in 1921 and 1922, and signalled by parity in capital ships.[8] However, the process had been less than easy and at several points in the 1920s a renewal of Anglo-American rivalry over naval armaments threatened to derail the development of the special relationship.

The different aspects of the policy dilemmas which emerged in the period after 1918 have been studied separately by diplomatic, naval, political, social, economic and cultural historians. What this study seeks to do is to combine these approaches to produce a more rounded and wider ranging analysis of this pivotal moment in the history of British power. The First World War had given rise to more questions than it had answered. How were Britain and the Royal Navy to respond to a series of critical challenges that impacted from Clydeside to Whitehall, to Tasmania, the Great Lakes and Caribbean? How could it deal with problems which ranged from balance sheets to naval design, the emergence of disruptive technologies to industrial policy, interstate diplomacy and the place of the Royal Navy in British society? After resolving the dilemmas of policy, how militarily strong was Great Britain in the interwar period?

The last of these issues has featured in the work of British historians who have viewed the steady reduction of the Royal Navy as part of the process of gradual national decline from weary imperial titan to middle-ranking, post-colonial member of the European Union. The story of the Royal Navy in the world wars, the barren years of the 1920s and 1930s, the Suez and Falklands Crises and the coalition government's SDSR 2010 provide effective illustrations of the narrative of national decline. David Edgerton does, however, remind us that the declinist literature that has dominated the UK national story can be taken too far. Before Britain was a welfare state it was a *warfare state* where the state, industry, armaments, armed forces and politicians were closely tied. National decline was neither inevitable nor necessarily gradual across the twentieth century. In the British state before and after the First World War, the armed forces provided much of the impetus for science, technology and manufacturing.[9] In a special issue of the *International History Review* in 1991 on 'The Decline of Great Britain' Keith Nielson, John Ferris and Brian McKercher challenged the declinist narrative of British military power in the interwar period.[10] Their collective argument was that the story of British military weakness in the years of appeasement has been overwritten and that the British state remained militarily strong in the early twentieth century. Yet such worthy revisionism has made little impact on the overall historiography of interwar Britain.

Meanwhile, diplomatic historians of the Anglo-American relationship have emphasized the need for all powers in the post-1918 period to try and resolve the differences between them to ensure the effective functioning of the League of Nations and the avoidance of rivalries and arms races which might lead to war. Erik Goldstein, for example, sees that in this period Britain confronted a succession of crises: diplomatic and imperial.[11] He points to fears of French ambitions to be the dominant military force in continental Europe as a key driver for British desires for a closer relationship with the United States.[12] While older historians view the 1920s as a period when Britain and the United States laid the foundations for the special relationship by resolving a series of key issues, Brian McKercher sees it as a defining period in a 'struggle for supremacy' between the two powers. While financial issues were significant, McKercher rightly argues that naval power 'stood as the most visible issue in the Anglo-American struggle for supremacy after 1918'.[13] Agreement over naval arms was vital to pave the way to an agreement with the American government over the repayment of Britain's war debts.

Anglo-Japanese and imperial historians have stressed the way in which the abrogation of the alliance with Japan revolved around concerns throughout the Empire. The Canadians in particular were opposed to the renewal of the Alliance because of American attitudes towards Japan.[14] Similarly the Australian government worried that the alliance was incompatible with its drive for a 'White Australia'. The views of the dominions on the question of renewing the alliance were fully expressed at the Imperial Conference held in London from 20 June to 5 August 1921. The conference helped to frame British policy towards the conferences which opened in Washington later that year. The outcomes of the Washington Conferences prevented a naval arms race between Britain, the United States and Japan. The Four Power Pact and the guarantee of China's territorial integrity safeguarded Britain's imperial interests in East Asia and, for a while, helped to maintain good relations with the Japanese. In the short term at least, the outcomes of the Washington Conferences were almost entirely positive for British diplomacy. In the medium term abrogation of the alliance set in play forces which would help to deliver the scenario of a naval war against the Japanese that the planners began to envisage in 1919.

The diplomatic and imperial facets of the dilemmas at the heart of the perfect policy storm of 1919–22 have tended to overshadow the relevant naval historiography, and Anthony Best reminds us that the Anglo-Japanese Alliance has been subject to extensive myth-making from the 1930s onwards by the British right, and after the Second World War by those who wished to portray the era of the alliance as a lost golden age of relations between Britain and Japan.[15] In this process the realpolitik considerations of diplomats, admirals and politicians in the 1919–22 period have perhaps become obscured. The work of naval historians, in particular, has not fully cross-fertilized the analyses put forward by diplomatic and imperial historians and vice versa. For example, none of the work on Anglo-Japanese relations by Ian Nish finds a place in the bibliography of Padfield's *Maritime Dominion and the Triumph of the Free World* or Wilmott's *Battleship*.[16] Nish in his ground-breaking 1972 study *Alliance in Decline* went further than most diplomatic historians by at least dipping into the Admiralty papers, and in referencing the work of Roskill.[17]

Thus the diversity of views on the alliance within the Royal Navy and the role of the Admiralty and the senior figures connected to it in the framing of policy towards the Far East have not been fully explored by the wider historical community. Likewise, the role of imperial and diplomatic issues in naval policy, and its intersection with other key problems facing the Royal Navy, has not been fully brought out by naval historians. Understanding the problems of existing historiography is actually vital to the creation of a rounded and accurate history of Britain's Navy in the twentieth century.

Considering the role of Volume 1 of Captain S.W. Roskill's *Naval Policy between the Wars* is particularly revealing.[18] A career naval officer, and official historian of the Royal Navy from 1949 to 1960, Roskill's histories were invariably written with ongoing struggles for the naval estimates in mind. Accessing a range of primary sources not available to most historians, *Naval Policy between the Wars* was semi-official, and a key underlying theme was the need for Anglo-American cooperation in policy.[19] The first volume examined the fight to maintain a one-power standard for the Royal Navy.[20] The threat to that standard is shown to be the building programmes of the US Navy.[21] The fact that Japanese programmes also posed a threat to that standard is acknowledged only in passing. Discussion of the Royal Navy's role in the abrogation of the Anglo-Japanese Naval Alliance features on just eight pages of a volume of over six hundred pages. As Gough comments, with 'immense pride' in 'the work of the Royal Navy', and 'a slight tendency to get off track', it was perhaps hard for Roskill to fully document the intricacies of a decision-making process that was to result in some of the darkest episodes in the history of the service during the Second World War.[22] Despite its deficiencies, Roskill's *Naval Policy between the Wars* remains highly influential and has cast a long shadow over the scholarship of the Royal Navy in the interwar period. As Christopher Bell has noted, 'The scope and seeming authority of this work have tended to stifle serious study of British naval history during this period. Recently, however, historians have begun to challenge orthodox views on this subject.'[23]

It is the contention of this book that in the aftermath of the First World War the Royal Navy faced a number of closely connected challenges which impacted the outlook of a service which was not of one voice or of one mind. The Anglo-Japanese Alliance and the danger of a future war with the Japanese intersected with a number of these problems, provoking heated debate within the Cabinet and the ranks of those responsible for British naval policy. Reluctantly in 1921 a consensus was arrived at whereby sacrificing the Anglo-Japanese Alliance, and living with the dangers of an antagonistic Japan, was seen as the least worst way to resolve a series of policy dilemmas. Contrary to Roskill's account of *Naval Policy between the Wars*, sacrificing the Anglo-Japanese Alliance was central to the evolution of naval policy in the immediate post-war period. The significance of these issues in driving the debate on the Anglo-Japanese Alliance in the period 1919–21 has not been fully explored by diplomatic and imperial historians. Effectively the examination of the vital intersection between naval, diplomatic and imperial policy which crystallized around the Anglo-Japanese Alliance in 1919–21 has fallen between the different subdisciplines of history. The full nexus of problems in naval and foreign policy facing the Lloyd George government after 1918 has been only partially revealed by earlier scholarship. This book addresses that problem.

1

The Navy and the Nation

The naval and diplomatic problems that were to crystallize in the aftermath of the First World War had long roots. Since the days of Elizabeth I, Britain's defensive shield was provided by the Royal Navy. Battleships were expensive items requiring considerable resources, skilled labour and increasingly specialized facilities for their construction. During the hundred years before 1918 Britain had found it steadily more difficult to afford the fleet necessary to ensure naval dominance against potential European rivals, to maintain the freedom of the seas to ensure the security of British imports and exports and to guarantee the security of a disparate empire spread across the globe. During the late nineteenth century the workshop of the world had seen its industrial lead, and dominance in world markets, steadily eroded. By the end of the nineteenth century Britain's staple industries (coal, cotton, steel and shipbuilding) were experiencing increasing competition from abroad, a lack of investment and innovation at home and a steady decline that was to unfold over the next century. To the statistics which underpinned this economic decline were added gloomy prognostications by British statespersons and the rising military potential of states not necessarily friendly towards Great Britain. Even though the historiographical consensus on Britain's long-term decline has been challenged over the past thirty years by John Ferris, Andrew Lambert and others, the arguments have revolved around the extent of that decline rather than its actuality.[1] Increasingly adverse economic statistics, and the worried comments of politicians, did hide underlying continuing strength, considerable overall military potential and the continuing utility and effectiveness of British sea power as a decisive strategic weapon. Perhaps what mattered more, though, and which hasn't fully filtered through into the historiography on the decline of British power from more specialized studies on technical change in the Royal Navy, was the possibility that technical innovations in the field of naval armaments might very suddenly render the British Fleet obsolescent, with the British state, and taxpayer, unable to sustain (because of a declining economy) the financial cost of meeting the challenge. This chapter examines the decline of

British naval power, and the threats from new naval technologies, which formed a vital backdrop to the formulation of naval policy after 1918. It further examines public attitudes towards the Royal Navy, which formed a vital underpinning for continued high levels of spending on naval defence.

When Napoleon fell from power following the Battle of Leipzig in October 1813, there was no doubt that the Royal Navy was the pre-eminent force on the world's oceans. In the period 1808 to 1809 the British Fleet had grown to 113 ships of the line (the forerunner of the battleship). This was in comparison to the French and Spanish Fleets (45 ships each) and the Russian and Danish Fleets (34 and 21 ships, respectively). Nelson's victory at Trafalgar in 1805 meant that in British society the Royal Navy enjoyed unprecedented prestige. Nelson represented the very embodiment of British national genius, and the service was celebrated from the lowest to the highest levels in British society. The Royal Navy was the chief protector of British national security. The service was also vital to the prosperity of a nation which depended on overseas trade to carry the products of a growing empire.

Britain's predominance owed much to the efficiency of crews rather than the material fabric of the fleet. In technical terms the sailing navy of Nelson's day was not vastly different to that which had defeated the Spanish Armada in 1588 – wooden-built sailing vessels carrying banks of cannon-firing broadsides. There was little to choose between a French or British ship of the line; indeed Spanish vessels were generally considered superior to those built by Britain because of Spain's access, via her Empire, to the tropical hardwoods of South America. However, the wealth of the British exchequer, thanks to the Industrial Revolution, meant that Britain could simply afford more ships than her naval rivals. Britain's naval predominance was unquestioned for the next forty years as the British economy flowered behind the protection of the wooden walls of the Royal Navy.

It was during the Crimean War (1853–56) that the first queries emerged about the security of those wooden walls. The vulnerability of British and French ships to fire from rifled artillery in Russian forts became very apparent. Three years after the end of the Crimean War, the French launched the *Gloire* – a revolutionary vessel, a steam-driven battleship, with an iron-clad hull, carrying rifled guns. Its armour had been designed to thwart direct fire from even the heaviest British naval guns. At a stroke it rendered every other naval vessel obsolete, ending Britain's naval supremacy. Fortunately the Royal Navy had begun to respond before the *Gloire* was launched, and in 1860 HMS *Warrior* (steam-driven, iron-clad hull, carrying rifled guns) was completed. With the completion of HMS *Black Prince* in 1861 Royal Navy supremacy was restored.

Britain had the largest fleet and the most technically advanced ships in the world. However, the *Gloire–Warrior* episode was instructive. In an era of rapid technological advances, innovation could remove Britain's naval supremacy at a stroke. Engineering and design innovation could render obsolete a fleet built at enormous expense. The threat of new technology affected every other area of British life in the mid- to late nineteenth century as other nations began to catch up to Britain's industrial lead.

The *Gloire–Warrior* episode underlines a central problem with the consensus narrative on the history of the Royal Navy. While Britain's navy was the foremost in the world, this did not prevent the public from perceiving problems, challenges and the spectre of imminent decline. Despite appearances to the contrary there was a growing uncertainty about Britain's naval capabilities in the late Victorian era. In his 1876 volume on *Naval Powers and their Policy* John Paget described a situation bordering on the catastrophic: 'Steam and Iron have for some years past been "levelling up" the maritime powers to such an extent that it behoves us to look to our laurels.'[2] Twenty years later similarly profound concerns about Britain's naval strength, in relation to other powers, were being raised by G.W. Steevens in his book *Naval Policy*.[3] He concluded on the question of the war-readiness of the Royal Navy: 'We have not the ships; we have not the men; we have not the guns. Our ships are inadequate to meet the two powers with which we might easily become embroiled.'[4] In hindsight, as Paul Kennedy has noted, the long lines of ships at the 1897 naval review to celebrate Queen Victoria's Diamond Jubilee 'did not denote the zenith of Britain's power [but] the defiant swan song of a nation becoming less and less complacent about the increasing threats to its world-wide interests'.[5]

Technological and other changes threatened British industrial and naval predominance. The emergence of new technologies such as mines and torpedoes subtly altered the strategic balance at sea. While most officers in the Royal Navy in the late nineteenth century discounted their effectiveness, in France officers of the Jeune Ecole of Admiral Aube were ready to embrace their potential value as a means to loosen the British stranglehold on the English Channel in time of war.[6] Growing tensions between the European nations forced the Royal Navy to focus on home waters, the North Atlantic and the Mediterranean. Only a token presence would be maintained in areas such as the Pacific and South Atlantic. Increasing closeness with the United States and the signature of the Anglo-Japanese in 1902 were diplomatic responses to declining British naval power, which became manifest in the increasingly small numbers of Royal Navy ships operating in the Caribbean, South Atlantic and Pacific.

A rapid acceleration of that decline began to emerge in the early twentieth century with the emergence of new technologies, but in 1906 the Royal Navy pre-empted the potential danger to British naval mastery by launching HMS *Dreadnought*. The battleship featured two revolutionary features: it was driven by steam turbines and was built around big gun armament instead of the medium-calibre guns which dominated battleship designs at the turn of the century. Ten 12-inch guns in rotating turrets could engage far distant targets. The dreadnought design rendered earlier naval vessels obsolescent, meaning that with the launch of HMS *Dreadnought* Britain's naval lead was back once again, as with the launch of HMS *Black Prince* in 1861, to just one vessel. Both the United States and Japan moved to embrace the new technologies at the same time, and they would launch their own dreadnought designs within months of HMS *Dreadnought* entering the water. Other countries would also embrace the opportunity to challenge British naval dominance.

The rise of Anglo-German naval rivalry, as the newly unified German state pursued a policy of *weltpolitik*, constituted a serious challenge to British naval dominance. Germany turned out dreadnoughts to force a redistribution of the European Empires in Africa and the Pacific. To respond effectively required vast government expenditure and, as other nations narrowed Britain's industrial lead and wealth, public finances were increasingly stretched. The Royal Navy (led by Admiral Sir John Fisher, First Sea Lord between 1904 and 1910) adopted a policy of scrapping more than 150 outdated ships which were considered unfit to face the modern vessels being built by Germany and other countries. Supported by the press and public, the government authorized ambitious naval-building programmes to preserve adequate superiority over the German Fleet. The cost of the Royal Navy rose inexorably. The naval estimates for 1889–90 had amounted to about £14.3 million. Ten years later it stood at £27.5 million.[7] As Andrew Lambert has argued as early as 1898, the rise in naval estimates was causing a financial crisis for the British exchequer.[8] As Britain engaged in a naval-building race with Germany, the figures on naval expenditure, and public borrowing, rose inexorably (Table 1.1).[9]

Table 1.1 Naval estimates 1907–14

1907–08	£31.25 million
1909–10	£35.73 million
1912–13	£45.07 million
1914–15	£50.69 million

Note: Massie, *Dreadnought*, p. 833. This figure, proposed by Winston Churchill as First Lord of the Admiralty in December 1913, was overtaken by the outbreak of the First World War in 1914.

The economic challenges facing the United Kingdom in the late nineteenth century, and the financial pressures of maintaining British naval supremacy, were to some extent undercut by vocal public support for spending money on the Royal Navy. As the British electoral franchise widened during the nineteenth century, and the price of maintaining British naval supremacy fell ever more heavily on the taxpayer, the relationship between the navy and the nation was thrown into ever sharper focus. Would the taxpayer be willing to maintain the levels of expenditure required to maintain the quantitative and qualitative edge of the Royal Navy over its naval opponents? What was the attitude of the British public towards the Royal Navy? What value did it attach to a rich naval past and a successful maritime sector? How was the Navy depicted in the British media, and within popular and elite culture? This emerging area of academic debate allows us to understand more fully the place of the Royal Navy in British society, its cultural influence and ability to secure the naval interest in political circles. As Greg Baer reminds us, 'Navies are... subordinate to governments, dependent on the nation for their rationale, legitimacy, and existence.'[10] Thus unless a society, or at least its leadership, recognizes the value and utility of sea power, democratic government is unlikely to view favourably calls for high naval expenditure. This chapter will now explore this central issue and the changing relationship between the Royal Navy and the British public.

It was a relationship in which there were certain key agents. In 1894 Henry Spenser Wilkinson, the defence correspondent for the *Manchester Guardian*, wrote a series of articles for the *Pall Mall Gazette* about the need to ensure a strong Royal Navy.[11] Wilkinson was not alone in his concerns. For some time, letters and articles had been appearing in the press expressing concern about 'our most sadly deficient and wanting navy'.[12] Some were written by anonymous Royal Navy officers and some by prominent figures in Victorian society such as Samuel W. Baker, explorer and army officer who urged that Britannia, as 'mistress of the sea', had to be 'supreme, absolutely paramount and superior to the whole world combined'.[13] Following Wilkinson's articles, on the suggestion of one anonymous letter writer, a meeting was held at the Westminster Palace Hotel on 11 December 1894. The meeting resulted in the formation of a Navy League to promote public awareness of Britain's dependence on the sea and the Royal Navy, to campaign for adequate naval expenditure and to operate on a non-partisan basis.[14] The formation of the League in 1894 pointed to growing worries about the decline of Britain's naval pre-eminence, and it was not the only sign.

The passing of the 1889 Naval Defence Act, voting significant funds to facilitate a naval-building programme, revealed rising British concerns about the extent to which British naval strength was under serious challenge in the late nineteenth century. In opposing the bill the radical Liberal MP Wilfrid Lawson asked: 'What is it for? Against whom is this proposed increase of our Navy directed? Avowedly against nations who are, we are told, most friendly to this country.'[15] Wilson was not alone in wondering why the international situation, and Britain's strategic position, merited the disbursement of millions of pounds for the purposes of a dramatic extension of naval armaments.

The Naval Defence Act formally enshrined the principle which successive British governments tried to operate by during the late nineteenth century: the idea of a two-power standard by which the Royal Navy would be larger than the combined size of the second- and third-ranked fleets in the world. The act contained a vote of more than £21.5 million to provide for the construction of 10 new battleships, 38 cruisers and supporting craft.[16] The government argued, in trying to overcome opposition particularly on grounds of cost, that it would create a level of deterrence which would persuade other powers (most notably Germany, France and Russia) to abandon their plans for naval expansion. This in turn would result in a saving to the British exchequer in the long term. The reality was that it simply fuelled an international arms race in the 1890s.[17] The Naval Defence Act, and the follow-up Spencer building programme of 1894, meant that during the 1890s expenditure on the Royal Navy more than doubled. As Ernest Protheroe noted twenty years later, 'In 1894 the Admiralty's programme for a single year was the largest that had ever been adopted. Seven first-class battleships, six second-class cruisers, and two smaller ships formed the British reply to the expansion of the various Continental fleets, and that of France in particular.'[18]

Championing this extension was the Navy League. Its members paid an annual subscription that was as low as one shilling to make the organization accessible to both middle and working classes. With offices in Victoria Street, London, it was ideally situated and had the necessary well-connected members to make its presence felt in government and political circles. The Navy League's journal (first published July 1895) became an important and influential platform for the naval lobby in Britain, especially as the organization's membership expanded from 14,000 to over 100,000 by 1914. On the date of the Battle of Trafalgar, the League dressed the area around Nelson's Column to draw public attention to the anniversary. At every turn the Navy League was a mass organization with significant presence in British political life.

The formation of the Navy League, the 1889 Naval Defence Act and the growth of spending on the Royal Navy in the 1890s point to two salient features of life in late Victorian Britain: that the Royal Navy appeared to enjoy substantial public and political support sufficient to sustain a doubling of the defence estimates during the decade; and that there were widespread perceptions that Britain's naval pre-eminence was under threat from the activities and ambitions of other powers in the late nineteenth century. In trying to understand the ramifications of the threats to the dominance of the Royal Navy, it is necessary to understand why the Navy was so valued by the British public and their politicians.

It would be easy to read into late Victorian culture a sense of a profound and widespread public understanding of Britain's strategic position as an island nation. The date of 1066, with the brutal and dramatic consequences resulting from the Norman Conquest, was one of the salient features of the history curriculum in private and public schools. In children's literature could be found titles such as W.J. Gordon's *A Chat about the Navy* with engaging illustrations and interesting stories and a clear political message: 'Our Navy is the finest fighting force on earth but there is not enough of it'.[19] Similarly Rear Admiral S. Eardley-Wilmot's *The British Navy Past and Present* was published in 1904 by the Navy League and dedicated to 'The Boys and Girls of the British Empire'.[20] This was part of a conscious effort on the part of navalists in the United Kingdom to overtly 'target children with propaganda'.[21]

In adult literature William Laird Clowes's *The Royal Navy: A History from the Earliest Times to the Present*, published from 1897 to 1903, would run to seven massive volumes (five were originally intended), with the preface to volume one reminding the following to its readers: 'It is upon the Navy that, under the good providence of God, the wealth, the prosperity, and the peace of these islands, and of the Empire, mainly depend.'[22] For the less affluent reader in the 1890s, there was the one-volume history of the Royal Navy such as Commander Charles N. Robinson's *The British Fleet: The Growth, Achievements and Duties of the Navy of the Empire* (1894).[23] Robinson, a serving Royal Navy officer, confidently asserted thus: 'It is now universally recognized that without the maritime arm as a defensive and fostering factor the British Empire can neither continue nor further grow.'[24]

Other books could 'sell' the Royal Navy in different ways. Titles such as Harry Williams's *The Steam Navy of England: Past, Present and Future* (1895) represented the Royal Navy as part of the beating heart of late Victorian innovation and science.[25] Yet even here the author could not help but express satisfaction at a 'healthy public opinion', with its insistence 'on the absolute necessity of keeping the Navy up to a strength as to enable it to meet fully and successfully the demands which would be made on it by a declaration of war against any two naval powers'.[26] Walter Wood's *Famous British Warships and Their Commanders* (1897) evidenced the extent to which successful senior naval officers from the Royal Navy's past had become icons of late Victorian Britain.[27] With the Empire a vital asset to the nation, writers such as Lieutenant Colonel Sir George Clark and James R. Thursfield were ready to tell their readers in *The Navy and the Nation* published in 1897 that control of the sealines of communication was a vital prerequisite for imperial defence.[28] Even a temporary failure for Britain to command the oceans would 'shake the foundations of the Empire'.[29] Making the point that Britain's naval supremacy was under threat were reference works such as *The Illustrated Guide to The Royal Navy and Foreign Navies*.[30] Published in 1896 the guide allowed its readers to compare the fleets of the leading naval powers. Its purpose was to ensure that 'the public should be roused to the fact that our Navy must be in a position to cope with any two foreign navies'.[31]

While Rudyard Kipling is popularly remembered for his creative writing around the theme of the British soldier in the late nineteenth and early twentieth centuries, he also used the Royal Navy, and its personnel, as a basis for some of his fictions. 'Judson and the Empire' published in 1893 followed the exploits of Lieutenant Judson on his journey by gunboat into Africa.[32] Between 1902 and 1904 Kipling published four stories in *Windsor Magazine* (later collected into the volume *Traffics and Discoveries* published in 1904).[33] The experiences of fictional Petty Officer Pyecroft were the primary focus of the stories, and they provided a means for the reader to explore the culture, heroism and technologies of the late Victorian/Edwardian Navy.

The value and history of the Royal Navy were similarly celebrated in other cultural forms from poetry to art to the music hall. Algernon Charles Swinburne's 1896 epic poem 'A Word for the Navy' was produced in popular version at a penny a copy.[34] The divine deliverance of 1589 as the Spanish Armada came to grief at the hands of Drake, Frobisher and Elizabeth's seadogs was amply celebrated in British art and literature. Likewise Nelson's victory at Trafalgar was a popular subject for some of the finest maritime artists of Edwardian Britain as the anniversary approached in 1905. William Wyllie's *Trafalgar, 2.30pm* showed the battle at its height, while William Overend's *The Hero of Trafalgar, 21 October 1805* depicted Nelson on the upper deck of HMS *Victory* in midst of the fighting. Overend's painting was later made available as a free print with *The Illustrated Sporting and Dramatic News* so that even the most humble household could celebrate Nelson's genius.[35] British culture was saturated with references to the Royal Navy's achievements over the past 300 years, and with an expanding electorate, that gave the naval lobby a degree of political leverage.

Strikingly, for the majority, the British public's level of understanding of maritime and naval issues did not rest on purely romantic notions of a maritime past, of naval heritage and history. For much of the mid- to late nineteenth century, the memory of Nelson (the saviour of the nation from Bonapartism in 1805) had languished. In 1904 *The Times* reflected on the success of the Navy League in shaping the public consciousness around Nelson and Trafalgar:

> The customary annual decoration of the Nelson column, under the management of the Royal Navy League, served to remind all who yesterday passed near Charing-cross of the great anniversary… which is becoming, every year, more and more sacred to Englishmen. The history of the celebration affords a highly interesting example of the success with which the League has striven to keep alive, or almost resuscitate, the memory of English naval heroism and of its greatest representative; for, so lately as twenty years ago, there were probably only a few persons in the country who could at once have mentioned the date of Nelson's crowning engagement.[36]

The public's lack of connection with the hero of 1805, the maritime identity of the nation and the command of the oceans which had marked the rise of British power following Trafalgar had been firmly evidenced by J.M.W. Turner's melancholic painting *The Fighting Temeraire*, and its public reception in 1839. That the painting attracted more attention than the scrapping of one of the British line of Battle in 1805 told its own story. When another of Nelson's ships, HMS *Foudroyant*, went aground on Blackpool Beach in June 1897, the level of public interest wasn't sufficient to secure the funds for her salvage. By 1900 the state of HMS *Victory*, Nelson's flagship at Trafalgar, which was still in service with the Royal Navy, was giving increasing cause for concern. Past glories and cultural relevance were no guarantee of ongoing public esteem and financial recognition as further evidenced by low pay rates in the late Victorian navy.[37]

If history and heritage had only limited impact in consciously defining and shaping the maritime aspect of Britain's national identity in late Victorian Britain, what probably mattered a good deal more was the sense that Britain's material prosperity depended on the sea. Britain was an exporting nation, relying on foreign markets to sustain a manufacturing base and easy passage of raw materials into the nation's factories via ports such as Liverpool. The sea carried the lifeblood of Britain's economy, and British ship owners and builders, insurers and managers grew wealthy off the trade. The sea was a place of profit and of jobs, with millions of people employed in maritime trades, or whose industries depended on those trades. Vital necessities of daily life from South American beef to loaves made with Canadian prairie wheat, and fresh eggs from Ireland, came via the sea. Occasional disruptions to the flow of trade served as powerful reminders to the working class of Britain's dependence on the sea. As the naval officer and politician Lord Charles Beresford noted in 1897, 'any dislocation of our imports of food supplies and raw materials would be first felt by the working man'.[38] The Royal Navy was the chief safeguard against such disruptions and the service consciously embraced that role. The majority of the British public, in being prepared to support high levels of public spending on the Royal Navy, did so on pragmatic grounds of cost and benefit, rather than the emotional and romantic grounds of history and heritage.

If the majority of the British public were prepared to lend their support to the issue of a strong Royal Navy, then they were encouraged in this view by powerful and influential vested interests. During the late nineteenth century, staple British industries such as iron and steel production, coal mining, shipbuilding and engineering began to come under growing competition from abroad, particularly from German producers. The antagonisms that this gave rise to naturally fed into public and political concerns about the rapid development of the German Navy and the Kaiser's increasingly erratic foreign policy, while at the same time emphasizing the importance of the domestic British market for the outputs of the staple industries. The Naval Defence Act of 1889 and the Spencer programme of 1894 came as vital relief to the captains of industries entering long-term decline as foreign competition increased. The doubling of expenditure on naval armaments during the 1890s more than simply sustained sectors of the economy otherwise declining: it ensured that they boomed. Profits rose, and share prices and share dividends increased. Employment remained high – artificially so.

The production of naval armaments was a highly lucrative business, more so than ordinary commercial work. The margin on contracts for the government was high, the Crown could be relied upon to pay promptly and rapid developments in naval technology ensured ongoing orders due to an increasing rate of obsolescence for the existing fleet and the systems which comprised its individual ships. In the lead up to the First World War the need for industrial success, jobs for the electorate and for taxes to pay for government expenditure created a symbiotic and circular relationship between government, naval policy and the staple industries. It also created a network of relationships that naval historian Arthur J. Marder traced in a 1938 article for the *Pacific Historical*

Review.[39] Members of Parliament held company directorships in armaments companies (12–15 in 1898 according to Marder) and the staple industries (24–30 in 1898 according to Marder), and industrial magnates represented constituencies in the industrial North East such as Jarrow, Sunderland and Gateshead.[40] There were suggestions that the names of many shareholders of the companies that made naval arms could also be found on membership list of the Navy League, and that the armaments companies supported the body with generous donations. Marder's 1938 article was shaped by the context of suspicions in the 1920s and 1930s that armaments manufacturers had played a malign influencing in shaping the policies of several nations in the run-up to the First World War, and he was able to suggest that there was no evidence to support particular claims such as those relating to the relationship between the Navy League and big business. However, he did successfully trace a network of mutual interests that helped to push spending on the Royal Navy in the quarter century before the outbreak of the First World War. That network was very considerable and, with hundreds of thousands of British jobs depending on naval expenditure, Lord Charles Beresford had some cause when he argued at a meeting of the Navy League in 1897 that 'every Britisher was interested in our Navy'.[41]

The German naval threat produced a form of military Keynesianism in the British economy during the late Victorian and Edwardian period. The 1898 publication in English of *The British Navy* by Captain A. Stenzel (German Navy, retired) suggested the need for constant vigilance and preparation against a potential enemy that had worked out that 'England's fate has always depended on the seas which wash her shores'.[42] While the Kaiser's High Seas Fleet remained a threat, the staple industries were relatively buoyant: when it was gone after 1919 there would be a reckoning. The long-term consequences on the staple industries were considerable as successive British governments after the First World War and, up until the 1980s, struggled with how to deal with foreign competition, structural problems and industrial decline in key sectors of the economy.

In conclusion, the causes of British naval decline had their origins in the mid-nineteenth century. Emergent technologies such as steam power, rifled guns and torpedoes could challenge Britain's naval mastery secured in the aftermath of the Battle of Trafalgar in 1805. Kennedy is right to point to the decline of the British economy as a key factor in the decline, but it was technological change allied to economic decline and other factors that really propelled British naval decline. Technological change could render valueless at a stroke, increasing heavy investment in Britain's battleships and cruisers. As British industry slowly lost its lead over its international competitors, the United Kingdom struggled to invest in national defence to the levels necessary to maintain the pre-eminence of the Royal Navy. In the early twentieth century, naval competition, and the threat of war with Germany, ensured that the politicians just about continued to meet the growing cost of maintaining Britain's maritime security. Public attitudes towards the Royal Navy formed the vital underpinning for the resolve of the politicians to meet the challenge to Britain's naval superiority, but that level of support was subject to fluctuations and, in time, would undergo significant changes. The electorate's attachment to an all-powerful Royal Navy, second to none, was questionable in many respects. The majority of the British working classes were prepared to accept high naval spending because it appeared to make sense in terms of national and imperial defence, seemed rational in terms of the national economy and because prominent figures in political and industrial circles were prepared to advocate it. British culture placed a rather romantic and sentimental veneer over the nation's relationship with the sea and its maritime past, massively inflating the historic achievements of the Royal Navy and the talents of its admirals. That was helpful in times of peace to sustain ongoing high levels of funding for the Royal Navy but, as the prospect of a naval clash with Germany loomed in the early twentieth century, it created levels of public expectation that would prove hard to sustain in the naval engagements of the First World War. Moreover, well before the outbreak of hostilities in 1914 growing British weakness, relative to other powers, was recognized if not publicly admitted by the signature of an alliance with Japan. The end of 'glorious isolation' constituted a recognition by the British government that, in an increasingly tense Europe, Britain needed to shore up her strength by turning to an emerging power in Asia.

2

Japan as a Factor in British Strategic Thinking

In the late Victorian period it became apparent that Britain could not afford simply to keep pouring money into military spending. However, through diplomacy Britain might offset some of the challenges that she was facing. The negotiation and signature of the Anglo-Japanese Alliance in 1902 marked a decisive move towards a more defensive policy, and away from the neo-imperial isolationism which had dominated British thinking during the late nineteenth century. The fact that Britain, for the first time in its history, had entered into a peacetime alliance, and with a non-European power to boot, was remarked on at the time and has echoed throughout the subsequent debate among historians.[1] While there has been some debate on the extent of British isolationism in the late Victorian period, there can be no doubt, as L.C.B. Seamen identifies, that signature of the alliance did mark a significant moment in the evolution of British foreign policy.[2] As Ian Nish reminds us, it was not a relationship that was entered into lightly or easily on either side and was preceded by considerable last-minute agonizing by both parties.[3] What has failed to register on the historiography is that right from its inception there was concern within British Parliamentary and imperial circles about just what an Anglo-Japanese Alliance might mean for Anglo-American relations and the situation in China.[4] Despite such questions, there was no question that Britain's relationship with Japan had become increasingly important to Britain's strategic interests in East Asia and the wider Pacific. As British power contracted, British possessions in East Asia became potentially vulnerable to attack by other powers. Under the alliance from 1902 onwards the Japanese would act as guardians of the British Empire in Asia. During the First World War Japan would give Britain considerable assistance. Thereafter, however, the Japanese would be transformed in the thinking of Royal Navy officers from guardian of the British Empire to the principal threat to its existence. This chapter explores the early stages of that process.

In many ways the post-1918 transformation in Anglo-Japanese relations was not surprising. Before the apparent harmony of the Anglo-Japanese Alliance from 1902 onwards relations had been problematic and unpredictable. In the 1840s, as the Royal Navy had forced China to open her ports to foreign trade, Japan remained nominally closed to the West. Japanese law for two centuries had made it crystal clear that foreign ships, foreign citizens, foreign religions and foreign trade were all to be rigorously excluded. This self-imposed isolationism had proved to be fairly effective, but it was never completely watertight. Contacts with the Chinese and Dutch had provided channels through which news of developments in the wider world had reached Japan and news of Japan could filter to the outside world. In an attempt to stiffen the official policy of isolation, an edict had been issued in 1825 ordering that any foreign vessels encroaching on Japanese waters should be fired on. British aggression against China in the 'Opium War' of 1839–42 forced China to cede Hong Kong and open five ports to foreign ships and traders, providing the Japanese with further reason to keep the West, and especially the Royal Navy, at arms' length.

It was, however, the US Navy which began the process of opening up Japan to foreign ships and foreign trade. A polite request delivered by Commodore Perry with four US Navy ships in 1853 was quietly left 'for consideration'. His return in 1854 to demand an answer was backed by eight ships and four thousand troops. The Japanese felt coerced into opening two ports where US vessels could call for water and provisions or to effect repairs. Whether visiting ships might take the opportunity to engage in trade was left rather vague. Other nations were not slow in demanding comparable access to Japanese ports. The pressure for greater privileges was relentless. The Japan–United States Treaty of Amity and Commerce signed on 29 July 1858 was followed within a month by similar treaties with France, Holland, Russia and Great Britain. Three ports had been opened to foreign shipping. Foreigners had been permitted to live and trade at these treaty ports; legations and consulates could be established; small bodies of foreign troops could be put ashore to serve as guards; and foreign citizens had been made answerable to their own consular officials, rather than to the Japanese legal system. This last provision, copied from the practice already established in China, had been particularly humiliating to the Japanese.

In the 1860s, as trade between Japan and the West grew, occasional diplomatic problems still arose, which produced a naval response on the part on the British and other powers. Foreign merchants may have been eager to establish themselves in new markets; the shogun and his advisers may have felt that they had no alternative but to give way in the face of the foreigners' dominant naval and military power; Japanese businesspersons may have rubbed their hands in expectation of profitable opportunities; but many of the leading *daimios* (feudal lords) and their samurai retainers hated foreigners, and felt that isolationism still offered the best protection for Japanese culture and Japanese values. In 1861 the British legation in Yedo (Tokyo) was attacked, and on 14 September 1862 a party of British riders was attacked in an encounter with the father of the daimio of Satsuma and his retinue on the highway. Affronted by some aspect of the British party's behaviour or demeanour, the dignitary's escort attacked them with swords. Charles Lennox Richardson, a British merchant, was killed and two others were seriously wounded, while a lady who was with them managed to escape unharmed. Lieutenant Colonel Edward Neale, *chargé d'affaires* at the British legation, patiently tried to calm the hotheads among the British residents while he negotiated with the Japanese. In due course he was directed by Earl Russell, the Foreign Secretary, to demand from the Japanese government an indemnity of £100,000 and a 'copious apology' for 'this barbarous attack', plus additional penalties to be imposed on the daimio of Satsuma.[5]

As xenophobic sentiment and hostile incidents mounted, the Japanese emperor himself made an almost unprecedented intervention to issue an edict in March and April 1863 for the expulsion of the 'barbarians'. The order was not communicated to foreign legations until June. Neale's response was forthright. Without waiting for instructions from London, he warned that Britain would take the strictest measures to maintain and enforce the treaty obligations affecting the Western presence in Japan. Moreover, he counselled the Japanese court against any measures that might amount to a declaration of war on all the treaty powers.[6] The arrival of seven Royal Navy vessels off Yokohama in August 1863, under the personal command of Vice Admiral Augustus Kuper, Commander-in-Chief of the China Station, was a direct response to the emperor's edit.

The Japanese, who were eager to slam the door once more in the face of foreigners, may have calculated that the great powers had their hands full elsewhere: the United States with their own civil war, Russia licking her wounds after the Crimean War, Britain and France coping with the Taiping rebellion in China, the French backing the Emperor Maximilian's cause in Mexico and the British fighting the Maoris in New Zealand. Nevertheless, in the middle of the nineteenth century Great Britain maintained by far the largest navy in the world to protect her imperial and commercial interests wherever they might be threatened. The Royal Navy had enough ships to protect those interests and support national policy, if required, in several parts of the world simultaneously. Some of Vice Admiral Kuper's ships mounted a number of the latest Armstrong breech-loading guns with rifled barrels.[7] All the ships were powered by steam engines. Six of them had been built in the last ten years and were fitted with screw propellers. Only one, the fourteen-year-old *Argus*, still relied on the less efficient paddle wheels. Kuper's Fleet did not consist of the largest first-rate ships fit to take their place in the line of battle. Such vessels were concentrated in home waters, the Mediterranean, the Caribbean and Indian waters, where Britain's most important interests and serious potential enemies were centred. The flagship HMS *Euryalus* mounted thirty-five guns, but only two other vessels, Pearl (21 guns) and Perseus (17), could be considered fairly powerful men-o'-war. Kuper tried to use his fleet to teach the daimio of Satsuma a lesson and to get compensation for the murder of Charles Lennox Richards and other members of his party, and to secure the arrest, trial and execution of the murderers.[8] While Kuper's Fleet achieved only a fraction of their aims and sustained heavy casualties in the process, the action against the daimio's forces did demonstrate the power of the Royal Navy.[9]

Naval force in the form of the Royal Navy and vessels of other navies continued to be used against the Japanese in defence of treaty rights.[10] In September 1864 a mixed international naval force bombarded to destruction the Japanese shore batteries that had closed the Strait of Shimonoseki to international maritime traffic.[11] The bombardments at Kagoshima and Shimonoseki had demonstrated to the powerful *daimios*, the shogun and the emperor that attempts to abrogate the treaties and expel the foreigners could prove very costly in face of foreign sea power, to which an island nation like Japan was very vulnerable. In 1865 the mere appearance of another multinational fleet (commanded by Admiral Sir George Vincent King in the huge British 73-gun battleship *Princess Royal*) was sufficient to persuade the emperor of Japan to ratify the various trade treaties and pay an indemnity for the closure of the Strait of Shimonoseki.

Anglo-Japanese relations improved steadily in the late nineteenth century with the Japanese very keen to develop a modern navy incorporating the skills, strategies, practices and material of the Royal Navy. From July 1873 and the arrival at the Japanese Naval Academy of a Royal Navy training mission, Britain provided the hand that guided the development of the Imperial Japanese Navy (IJN). This influence extended to the materiel of the Japanese Navy, with British shipyards receiving orders for designs from which Japan's warship builders could learn their trade. As Marder notes of the Imperial Japanese Fleet in 1882, nineteen of its twenty-eight major vessels had been constructed in British yards. Twelve years later of the eleven Japanese capital ships, seven were of British origin.[12] The growing relationship between the Royal Navy and their Japanese counterparts had particularly profitable outcomes for British warship builders.

That being said the British public in the 1880s and 1890s, as Israel Tarkow-Naamani identifies, knew comparatively little about Japan, which was portrayed in the British press as a strange and exotic land.[13] Reporting on Japanese affairs was dominated by stories of natural disasters with occasional features on Japanese ethnography, and some interest in the commercial value and potential of trade with Japan.[14] There was also some interest in Japan's relationship with the foreign powers, especially over the former's attempt to renegotiate or repeal the *Ansei* treaties effectively forced on Japan in 1858–59.[15] The 'unfair treaties' created a system of extra-territorial jurisdiction of consular courts for foreigners resident in Japan, and fixed import/export duties at a low level determined by the treaty powers. There was limited reporting on Japan's relations with her neighbours in Asia, but very little information on the development of Japan as a military power. One exception was *The Pall Mall Gazette* in 1885, which made claims striking enough to be picked up by the regional press:

> The arsenal of Koishikawa is Woolwich on a small scale, with 100 rifles and 70,000 cartridges for its day's work. The dockyard at Yokosaka is not behind Woolwich and Portsmouth in much except size, and first-rate torpedo-boats and the most elaborate modern ordnance are turned out there with the regularity of Armstrong or Krupp. The Armstrong cruisers lying off Tokio Bay are almost the finest vessels of their class afloat, and could make matchwood of any British vessels here except the flagship, and they are manned and officered entirely by Japanese seamen; while the War Department has at least 40,000 men under arms at this moment, and on a declaration of war could put 100,000 troops of all arms … in the field, with weapons equal to any carried today … Yet twenty-five years ago Japanese soldiers wore huge grotesque iron masks to frighten the enemy, chain and lacquer armour to turn his blows; their great shoulder-cannon would have been antiquated in England at the time of the Armada, and they were led by a man with a fan.[16]

The impression that Japan might be a power of some military potential was underlined in 1894 when Japan went to war with China following the outbreak of civil war in Korea. Japanese forces, including the Imperial Japanese Navy, proved more than a match for their Chinese opponents. The naval victories of the Sino-Japanese war of 1894–95 owed just as much to Chinese weakness as Japanese strength and suggestions by some historians that the IJN was 'state of the art' are somewhat wide of the mark.[17] Nevertheless, the naval engagements of the war, especially the Battle of the Yalu (17 September 1894), were studied closely by European naval officers eager to evaluate the effectiveness of new weapons such as the torpedo and the quick firing gun.

Japan's strategic and political position was transformed by the war, and the possibility of an Anglo-Japanese Alliance to contain Russia began to be advocated in some quarters in Britain such as the *St James Gazette*.[18] Such possibilities generated considerable concern in some parts of the Empire where there were worries about what such a relationship might mean for them in terms of security and trade.[19] De facto Japanese control was established over Korea (formally annexed 1910), and within Japanese political and social circles the prestige and influence of the military was enhanced by victory on the battlefield. Control of Korea encouraged the development of right-wing groups in Japanese society that were eager to champion military values, industrial expansion and territorial acquisition to give the Japanese population additional living space, and to assist national self-sufficiency in agricultural and industrial resources. Abroad, victory in Korea encouraged the great powers to view Japan in a rather different light. As Piotr Olender has written, the war strengthened Japan's position in Asia and the world, elevating Japan to the level of a Western power.[20]

At the same time the Sino-Japanese war further weakened the ramshackle Chinese state, deepening the power vacuum in mainland East Asia, thereby threatening to draw the major powers into conflict as they attempted to exploit the situation to gain trading and other rights inside China. In 1897 the German government used the murder of two missionaries to extort concessions from the Chinese government, which allowed the German government the use of the port of Tientsin and control of the railways on the Shantung Peninsula. In the same year the Russian government forced the Chinese government to grant a lease on the Liaodong peninsula, with the fine naval base at Port Arthur. As John Berryman has charted, the British government considered a potential military response to force the Russians to vacate the peninsula but refused to authorize it out of fears that the French might decide to support their ally.[21] The Franco-Russian axis meant serious potential difficulties for the British in trying to deal with either power in Europe or the Far East. It also posed a significant check on Japanese ambitions within China, and had already ensured that Japanese gains after the war of 1894–95 were not as fulsome as they might have been.

The Franco-Russian alliance meant that in the late nineteenth century British and Japanese strategic interests were brought into close proximity. The situation in China could make for some strange coalitions. In 1900 Britain and Germany resolved to use their influence to ensure an open door to trade throughout China. The Germans, sharing extensive land borders with the Russians, wanted to avoid possibilities that complications in the Far East could have ramifications in Europe. More strangely still, in the midst of the Boxer Rebellion in 1900, Britain cooperated with all the other European powers in China, plus the Americans and Japanese, to put together an international force to relieve the embassies besieged in Beijing.[22] The Chinese power vacuum, and increasing tensions between the European powers, made for a constantly shifting strategic balance.

It was still something of a surprise to the British public when on 30 January 1902 Lord Lansdowne (British Foreign Secretary) and Hayashi Tadasu (Japanese Ambassador in London) signed the papers creating an Anglo-Japanese Alliance. The possibilities of an alliance had been under consideration since 1895, but it was one of number of possibilities. Significantly, and overlooked in much of the historiography debate, were suggestions that Britain might look to conclude an agreement that embraced both Japan and the United States.[23] The possibility found some support in the *New York Times* and *New York Tribune* but rather less so in political circles, with the result that the agreement concluded between the British and the Japanese did not include the Americans.[24]

Japan's naval power was central to British considerations. As *The Penny Illustrated Paper and Illustrated Times* reported:

> It is mainly by means of her navy that Japan will in the future build up her power. The Navy comprises: First-class battleships, 6; third-class battleship, 1; first class cruisers, 7; second-class cruisers, 10; third-class cruisers, 6; first-class gun-boat, 1; torpedo gun-boats, 2; torpedo-boat destroyers, 20; first-class torpedo-boats, 50; officers and men, 19,000. Among these vessels are some of the finest battleships in the world. As a matter of fact, Japan is more up-to-date in naval matters than any Power, except perhaps Germany. Lord Charles Beresford thus described a Japanese man-of-war: 'She was in as good a condition as a man-of-war could be, and her ship's company were smart, well dressed and well disciplined'.[25]

Britain's naval needs were driving British foreign policy. An alliance with Japan was worth concluding precisely because of her naval strength. Events in China in the 1890s had drawn the foreign policy interests of Japan and Great Britain into closer orbit, but it was Britain's maritime security needs (and concerns that in a divided Europe Britain might find herself isolated) that gave shape to the eventual alliance.[26] Lord Selborne, First Lord of the Admiralty, had been the principal champion for the alliance, but it was Sir Michael Hicks Beach, the Chancellor of the Exchequer, who had played a surprising role in suggesting a diplomatic answer to the growing challenge to British naval power.[27] In rejecting Selborne's repeated calls to increase naval spending, Hicks Beach had urged the pursuit of diplomatic initiatives. The Anglo-Japanese Alliance was the eventual outcome of this suggestion. As Ian Nish has noted the Admiralty view was important in the conclusion of the alliance, but other factors were also involved. The Russian threats in Central Asia, and especially to British India, were also significant factors in the Cabinet's consideration of the potential value of the alliance.[28]

The provisions of the alliance signed in 1902 were limited: each signatory would observe strict neutrality if the other became involved in a war with a third power. If a combination of powers went to war with one of the signatories the other party was obligated to come to their assistance. Lord Salisbury, British Prime Minister, had wanted to avoid any agreement by which Britain could be easily catapulted into a war, and final signature of the alliance represented a triumph for Lord Lansdowne, the Foreign Secretary. The alliance was seen as a temporary expedient (signed for an initial term of five years) which was necessary to deal with growing Russian power in the East and the development of closer Franco-Russian relations. The growth of Russian and French naval power was causing concern within the Royal Navy, and a combination of the fleets of the two nations had the potential to pose an awkward threat to Britain's maritime security interests.

Under the alliance, both Britain and Japan renounced the pursuit of aggressive policies in China and Korea. The maintenance of Chinese territorial integrity was regarded as a British interest, and Russia was seen as a significant potential threat to those interests, and to the security of the British maritime empire. In the Russian danger the British and the Japanese found common purpose. The Japanese could safeguard the British Empire in Asia, while the British would prevent the French from coming to the assistance of their alliance partner Russia in the event of a Russo-Japanese clash. The signature of the alliance received little public debate, and this significant development in British foreign policy and Anglo-Japanese relations made little impact on the cultural and political consciousness of Edwardian Britain.[29]

The Russo-Japanese war of 1904–05, which saw the destruction and humiliation of Russian naval power, seemingly cemented the bond between the Imperial Japanese Navy and its British counterpart. The war was closely studied by naval strategists around the world as to the lessons it might provide about future naval conflicts.[30] During the war, as Vice Admiral Koda has detailed, the Imperial Japanese Navy learnt the lessons of modern naval warfare and put them to ever bigger and better effect, culminating in the victory at Tsushima.[31] The British were also on hand during the conflict to play a supportive and important role, as David Steeds has noted.[32] Six of the seven battleships (including the flagship *Mikasa*), and four out of the eight armoured cruisers, that wrought such havoc with the Russian Fleet at the Battle of Tsushima in 1905 were British-built. Tōgō Heihachirō, commander of the Japanese Fleet, had received Royal Navy training in England. For his victory, one hundred years since the Battle of Trafalgar the British press labelled him the 'Nelson of the East'.[33]

As Philip Towle has shown, the Royal Navy carefully scrutinized the naval aspects of the Russo-Japanese war to learn what lessons it could from the experience of its Japanese allies.[34] Meanwhile, the British public contented itself that the genius of its admirals and seamen had clearly been imparted to the Japanese by Royal Navy tutelage. *The Penny Illustrated Paper and Illustrated Times* proclaimed:

> Admiral Togo has won the most marvellous victory which has ever taken place upon the high seas. He has met an enemy considerably his superior in fighting strength and has not merely defeated, but has almost completely annihilated him. Admiral Rojdestvensky himself and his flagship and men have gone down fighting, and Admiral Nebogatoff, the commander of the third Baltic squadron, which only joined the fleet off Indo-China a week or two ago, is a prisoner on his flagship, and with him in the hands of the Japanese are several thousands of the Tsar's sailors. How many men lie underneath the waves is impossible to say. With the disappearance of the Baltic fleet disappears also Russia's power at sea for many years to come. Russia is reduced to the straits of Spain after her unsuccessful war with the United States and of Italy after the memorable sea fight at Lissa … Japan is now richer by several battleships and cruisers than she was at the beginning of the war. Port Arthur gave her several vessels, and the battle of the Korean Straits largely augments the list. On the other hand Russia has lost, at one blow, over ten million pounds' worth of war vessels, and her defeat has disrupted the famous balance of sea power which was for so many years held up as a bogey to frighten the British public.[35]

While Tsushima was an important symbol of the closeness of Anglo-Japanese relations in practical terms, it, to some extent, marked a parting of the ways. In the late nineteenth century the Japanese had called on the Royal Navy to provide it with the model, training and material on which to base the Imperial Japanese Navy. The victory of Tōgō Heihachirō's Fleet at Tsushima suggested that the Imperial Japanese Navy had learnt all that was necessary from the British. Since the Meiji restoration the government had supported a policy of *shokusan kogyo* (industrialization) in order to make Japan powerful and wealthy.[36] In May 1905 the keel of the first home-built battleship was laid down at the Yokosuka Navy Yard, and within two years Japanese admirals had settled on the need for a naval construction programme that would lead to a fleet of eight battleships and eight battlecruisers. Known as the 8:8 programme, the financial legacies of the Russo-Japanese war prevented its realization all the way up to the First World War. The Japanese diet was not about to sanction a large increase in public spending. However, the Japanese Navy's ambitions remained.

For the British while the Japanese victory was pleasing, the Russian threat was very quickly replaced by a naval challenge from the Kaiser's Germany. The value of concentrating the best units of the Royal Navy in home waters and the Mediterranean to meet the German threat saw the alliance renewed and expanded in scope in 1905. In June 1909 the Committee of Imperial Defence expressed its satisfaction: 'So long as the Anglo-Japanese alliance remains in force, the British possessions in the Far East are secure.'[37] Amidst this satisfaction was an undertow of suspicion and the committee also advised that if the government contemplated ending the alliance at any point, then the British Fleet in the Pacific should first be increased 'to neutralise the danger from a preponderant Japanese Fleet in the China Seas'.[38] In 1911, with Germany aggressively pursuing a policy of *weltpolitik* the alliance was again renewed.

In the creation and development of the alliance up until 1914, it was the politicians and diplomats that took the lead, rather than the British Admiralty and War Office. The alliance was, though, of enormous benefit to the Royal Navy, allowing a concentration of British ships in home waters and the Mediterranean. Quite what this 'pivot to European waters' might mean in the long term, especially in view of Britain's sizeable empire in the Pacific, was given little consideration. The possibility that the alliance might prove awkward in some ways for the British was discounted by the need for regular renewal and the provision that it would only come into operation in the event of one of the parties being attacked by two major powers. In the event it was to prove a serious underestimation by the British of the determination of the Japanese to prosecute foreign and military policies that might not find full favour in London.

3

The Impact of the First World War

Historians have charted the wide range of impacts of the First World War on Great Britain from profound social effects (Arthur Marwick and J.M. Winter), to industrial relations (McLean), to politics (Turner) and the armed services (Wohl).[1] Equally evident in the post-war period were the profound impacts of the conflict on British naval power, and on the strategic balance in European waters and beyond. To some extent, the First World War accelerated the pace of change from the emergence of new technologies which threatened the supremacy of the capital ship, through to the industrial decline which was eroding Britain's capacity to respond to those technologies. Cultural and political changes exacerbated those problems, limiting the capacity of the British government to respond to a substantial challenge to national security. In terms of the extant historiography on the Royal Navy, the technological challenges facing the Royal Navy as a result of the First World War have been emphasized at the expense of the contextual problems which impacted on the means and opportunities to respond to those issues. As a result the interconnectedness of naval policy in the post-war period has not been fully traced and understood.

When Britain went to war in August 1914 the Royal Navy could muster thirty-one modern capital ships to set against Germany's eighteen. Britain had a further sixteen under construction compared to Germany's ten.[2] The Royal Navy could still claim to be the largest in the world, but the margin of superiority had declined steadily since the 1880s. Then the Royal Navy could claim to be superior to the next three naval powers combined; for a time it aimed to be superior to any two possible rivals; by 1914 it had settled for maintaining 60 per cent superiority over Germany. Nevertheless, on paper, the Royal Navy's margin of superiority over its German rival at the outbreak of war appeared impressive. Ernest Protheroe at the end of 1914 assured his readers in *The British Navy: Its Making and Meaning*:

> If we compared the respective strengths of Britain and Germany, expressed in figures of broadside, and excluding guns under 6-inch, we had 347 guns to Germany's 143. If we took into account ships then building, we had it upon the authority of the First Lord of the Admiralty that during the twelve months following the outbreak of war the number of great ships to be completed for our country would be more than double the number completed for Germany, and the number of cruisers three or four times as great.[3]

Despite the assurances of naval propagandists and publications such as *The Navy from Within* and *The Navy of To-day* (1914), the hectic pace of new building, the emphasis on capital ships and the rate of technical innovation meant that, in many ways, the Royal Navy was ill-prepared for modern war.[4] The main fleet base at Scapa Flow was totally undefended at the outbreak of war. British capital ships were equipped with defective armour-piercing shells and poor ammunition-handling procedures, and their own ammunition magazines were inadequately armoured. Most importantly of all, as Roskill notes, in terms of the development of new weapons such as the mine and torpedo Britain lagged well behind Germany.[5]

On the outbreak of war there were high hopes that the new conflict would result in a repeat of Trafalgar and a reaffirmation of British naval dominance. As Bradley Cesario has noted, it wasn't until 1915 that the British public's anticipation of great naval victories began to decline.[6] Until that point, British culture (from magazines for boys to theatrical performances and the sale of patriotic goods) reminded the public that the officers of the Grand Fleet were the inheritors of Nelson's genius. As Jan Breemer has argued such high expectations were unreasonable in the extreme and were to prove a growing burden on the Royal Navy, which singularly failed to live up to its own self-image.[7] By the war's end those high hopes would remain unfulfilled, and on most assessments of the Royal Navy's performance from 1914 to 1918, the service had not had a good war. In 1915 an attempt to force the passage of the Dardanelles resulted in a failure that in turn led to the disastrous amphibious assault on the Gallipoli Peninsula later that year. The retired Lord Fisher of Kilverstone worried that the Royal Navy appeared to be missing opportunity after opportunity to establish its supremacy over the German Fleet.[8] In 1916 at Jutland the opportunity was possibly missed to secure the decisive naval victory over the German Fleet which would have been comparable with the victory over the French at Trafalgar. The British public were both pleased that the German Fleet had been brought properly to action, but rather mystified as to the outcome of the battle.[9] In the post-war period the battle of Jutland would be a subject of extensive and often heated controversy. In 1917 the development of the German U-boat campaign against merchant shipping came close to winning the war for the Kaiser. The dangers of the submarine, and the effectiveness of the countermeasures developed during 1917–18, would similarly be a dominant theme in post-war analyses of the course of the First World War.[10]

The success of the U-boat campaign underlined the vulnerability of the battleships which formed the measure of naval power for the Royal Navy. Losses of British ships at Jutland highlighted inadequacies in their design and build. In addition, significant failures elsewhere suggested that the mercurial British genius for naval strategy and warfare personified by Nelson might be slowly evaporating. In September 1914 a single U-boat had torpedoed and sunk three British armoured cruisers; at the same time the Royal Navy failed to find and sink the German warships *Goeben* and *Breslau* in the Mediterranean; in November 1914 Admiral Craddock's squadron was defeated at the Battle of Coronel; one month later the British East coast ports of Scarborough, Hartlepool and Whitby were shelled by the German High Seas Fleet. This was not a pattern of events which the British people expected, and it challenged deeply held assumptions about national security and the British genius for naval warfare.

To some extent, by war's end, the Royal Navy was satisfied that it had begun to get to grips with the U-boat through tactical innovations such as convoying, the use of aircraft in an anti-submarine role and the employment of innocent-looking, but heavily armed, Q-ships to act as deadly bait for passing U-boats. British science had also begun to tilt the balance back in favour of surface forces thanks to the development of submarine location equipment, such as sonar, and the perfection of the depth charge as powerful weapons in the prosecution of anti-submarine warfare. In addition, naval architects had begun to understand the lessons for future warship design emerging from the naval battles of the First World War. However, even within naval circles important questions remained about the submarine and the security of the battleship.

The British were further buoyed up by the fact that the Royal Navy could claim some genuine public successes, such as the destruction of von Spee's squadron near the Falkland Islands in December 1914; significant victories by British submarines in the Sea of Marmora and the Baltic and in 1918; and the Zeebrugge raid of 1918. Less publicly visible, but more important in strategic terms, the Royal Navy could also claim credit for four great strategic successes which made crucial contributions to winning the war: keeping open and protecting sea communications with the British Army in France, guaranteeing the British Isles against invasion, improvising (though belatedly) an effective convoy system which managed to keep open the Atlantic shipping routes and enforcing the naval blockade which eventually damaged Germany's ability to continue the war and led to mutiny in the German Fleet. These successes were not spectacular. They depended on applying sea power relentlessly, year after year, and ensuring that ships and persons needed for that task were not frittered away in pursuit of less important (but more eye-catching) enterprises. There was an uncomfortable gulf between the navy's achievements and the expectations of a nation brought up on the 'Nelson touch' and 'Rule, Britannia!' There was an even more heart-breaking contrast between the Grand Fleet swinging to its anchors in Scapa Flow and the fearful casualties and human suffering of the Somme, Vimy Ridge and Passchendaele.[11]

Within the Naval Service there was an acute understanding that the nature of the First World War might, given the prominence and casualties of the land campaign, displace the Royal Navy from its place in British society and culture.[12] Just three days after the armistice the First Sea Lord wrote to the commander of the Grand Fleet:

> There can be no naval officer who does not see the end of this war without a feeling of incompleteness … We feel it strongly at the Admiralty and realize how much more it must be the case with you and the Grand Fleet. The Navy has won a victory greater than Trafalgar, though less spectacular, and because of this lack of display it feels that the unthinking do not perhaps realize what the nation – indeed the whole world – owes the British Navy. The studied way in which the Navy is being ignored – in which Foch and his part are being exalted at its expense, both by the English Press and the politicians – I feel and resent as greatly as do you and the whole British Navy.[13]

The concerns implicit in Weymss's letter to Beatty about the long-term implications of the First World War on the place of the Royal Navy in British society, and its ability to maintain the backing of public and politicians for the continued maintenance of Britain's naval mastery, were made explicit at the signature of the Versailles Treaty. First Lord of the Admiralty Walter Long felt it necessary to personally expound the 'naval message', and to explain to the British public the vital role that the Royal Navy had played in securing victory:

> At last the Peace is signed, and the end of this great and terrible war has been reached. The part that the Navy has played in this gigantic conflict is perhaps not so apparent at first sight as it might well be – for indeed it is a truism to say that, had it not been for the Navy, it would have been impossible for our armies

> in any of the various theatres of war, to have successfully engaged and defeated our enemies. When it is thought that it was under escort by the Navy that troops, food, stores, munitions, were taken even across the narrow channel that separates France from England, it is evident that the task accomplished was a gigantic one. But when it is also remembered that the same duty was performed for all the forces fighting in many different parts of the world; that the Navy brought here thousands of troops from different parts of the British Dominions; escorted a very large proportion of the troops which came from the United States of America; and in addition, had to escort passenger and cargo steamers; it will be realised how tremendous was the work they performed, and how great a debt is due to them for the self-sacrifice, devotion and skill, with which this great task was accomplished. It must also not be forgotten that they had to watch the seas for torpedoes, to sweep them for mines, and to meet a large number of new devices for dealing death and destruction. They did not crown their work by another Trafalgar, but they fought several brilliant battles ... The Germans were defeated as completely at sea as they were on land. It is true, as I have already said, that there was no Battle of Trafalgar: but can the human mind picture a more wonderful spectacle, or a more complete defeat, than is to be found in the sullen passage across the North Sea of the German warships to be handed over on arrival off our shores, without demur or protest, to their victorious enemy.[14]

Despite the re-assurances of the effectiveness of British naval power between 1914 and 1918, Long's letter to *The Daily Express* contained considerable evidence of the growing sense of unease within naval circles about how the war might undermine the Royal Navy's position as the pre-eminent military arm in national affections and defence strategy. Long, echoing the concerns implicit in the First Sea Lord's letter of November 1918, referred to the lack of a modern Trafalgar not once but twice. The brilliant victory of 1805, which at the end of the nineteenth century had provided the Royal Navy with considerable political capital as it sought to increase naval spending, had now become the yardstick which it had failed to measure up against in the circumstances of the First World War. The repercussions of failing to live up to the expectations of public and politicians, no matter how unrealistic were those expectations, were always going to be considerable.

Despite the concerns felt at the way the war had ended, and the long-term implications for the Royal Navy, on the material side at least the Grand Fleet in 1919 remained formidable and imposing. During the course of the war the nation had continued to invest heavily in the Royal Navy. Those figures are an impressive testimony to the nation's determination to win the war, but naval expenditure had been very high indeed (Table 3.1).

Table 3.1 Naval expenditure 1915–19

1915–16	£205.73 million
1916–17	£209.88 million
1917–18	£227.39 million
1918–19	£325 million (estimate)

Note: Long to *Daily Express*, 18 June 1919, Long papers (Swindon and Wiltshire History Centre) 947/690.

Much of this was in the form of new construction. As Kenneth Warren has noted, 'During the four years preceding the war some £60 million was spent on new construction for the Royal Navy; in the four years of the war between £250 million and £300 million.'[15] This in turn had consequences for the British shipbuilding industry, which invested heavily in new facilities: 'In 1914 the UK had 580 shipbuilding berths greater than 250 feet. By 1920 there were 806.'[16] The flow of profitable orders did nothing, however, to encourage harmonious labour relations or innovation in practices and processes with the result that, despite the profits, the share of world construction of British yards fell during the war as Japanese and American yards made inroads into the market.

At war's end the Royal Navy could still claim to be the most powerful navy in the world. It then had in commission:

33 Dreadnought Battleships,
17 Pre-Dreadnought Battleships,
9 Battle cruisers,
109 Cruisers,
433 Flotilla Leaders and Destroyers,
137 Submarines,
19 Aircraft Carriers,
a great variety of other vessels.[17]

However, the war only accelerated the processes evident over the previous twenty years, producing accelerated naval decline. By 1918 the industrial pre-eminence of the mid-Victorian period had given way to businesses co-opted into the war effort and factories turned over to the weapons of war instead of goods for export. Markets in South America had been abandoned to American manufacturers as Britain struggled to maintain its importing capacity in the midst of unrestricted U-boat warfare. Most importantly, the national debt had risen to £7,435 million (almost twelve times the pre-war figure) and Britain owed £1,365 million to foreign creditors (mainly the United States).[18] Drastic economies were required and there could be no question of trying to maintain the fleet at anything approaching its wartime level. At the same time, Britain acquired responsibility for territory in Africa, the Middle East and the Pacific formerly controlled by Germany and the Ottoman Empire. That would stretch Britain's military forces still further.

In addition to the long-term threat to Britain's naval supremacy formed by a declining economy, in 1919 the British government faced a more immediate threat in the form of the potential fate of the German High Seas Fleet, which had been interned at Scapa Flow under Royal Naval supervision. With the politicians trying to work out the long-term security of Europe at the Paris Peace Conference, the fate of the Kaiser's Fleet loomed large in the thinking of the Royal Navy. This had two dimensions: human and material.

On the human side, British admirals in dealing with their German counterparts were struck by the sight of the officers of the Kaiser's former High Seas Fleet. With orders discussed, agreed and countersigned by sailors committees British officers were sympathetic to the plight of their former adversaries.[19] With considerable dissatisfaction in the lower ranks of the British Grand Fleet, the danger that an outbreak of revolution might take place on one of His Majesty's Ships was not out of the question. As discontent at the pace of demobilization and other difficulties manifested itself into strikes by soldiers, the police and, in some cases, sailors, in 1919, there was a keen appreciation within the Admiralty and officer class that, irrespective of financial or any other problems, something had to be done to alleviate the discontent and that meant improving about pay and conditions in the fleet.[20] Suspicions as to the complete loyalty of the lower decks, in the midst of a changing society and more politically active working class, refused to go away after 1918, and, although there had been mutinies and 'industrial grievances' across the history of the Royal Navy, division along what amounted to 'class lines' marked a new and potentially more difficult threat to an effective Royal Navy.

On the material side, the future of the ships of the German High Seas Fleet quickly became a bone of contention between Allies. The admirals of the Royal Navy and US Navy had no desire to incorporate German vessels into their battlefleets, with the attendant issues of fleet standardization, availability of spare parts and the difficulties of working between the metric and imperial systems.[21] Lloyd George also favoured a mass ceremonial scuttling of the vessels in the Atlantic as a signifier of Germany's defeat, but such hopes quickly foundered on inter-Allied wrangling on a range of issues, with the fate of the German Fleet drawn in as a key bargaining counter. The smaller naval powers in particular were also very eager to augment their own military strength. A redistribution of the fleet between the principal Allied powers on an equal basis could seriously affect the naval balance of power. Similarly redistribution on the basis of wartime losses could enhance the strength of the Royal Navy by a significant margin. In the event, the scuttling of most of the fleet by their skeleton crews in response to the punitive peace encapsulated by the Treaty of Versailles on 21 June fortunately removed this major issue that threatened inter-Allied discord and the predominance of the Royal Navy. The French were furious that the Royal Navy had allowed the scuttle to take place. First Sea Lord Wester Weymss was delighted that such a thorny and dangerous political and military question had been removed from the inter-Allied negotiating table.[22] A committee composed of five Admirals, from the British, French, American, Japanese and Italian Fleets, was left to come up with proposals for the remaining units of the Kaiser's Fleet.[23]

While the German naval menace had disappeared beneath the waters of Scapa Flow, the United States and Japan were emerging as powerful future rivals to Britain's naval pre-eminence. While the British Fleet had reached its peak in 1916, the American and Japanese Fleets would reach their apogee in the 1920s, thanks to construction programmes initiated during the war. A new naval arms race was in prospect and Britain's lead was rapidly being eroded by exponential advances in warship technology. In 1905 HMS *King Edward VII*, displacing 17,009 tons and carrying a main armament of 4 × 12-inch and 4 × 9.2-inch guns represented the state of the art in terms of naval construction. The groundbreaking HMS *Dreadnought*, of 1906, displaced 21,845 tons and carried a main armament of 10 × 12-inch guns. Ten years later, in the midst of the war, HMS *Royal Oak* was launched. She displaced 33,500 tons and carried a main armament of 8 × 15-inch guns. By the end of the war naval architects were planning battleships of almost 50,000 tons carrying 8 × 16-inch guns.[24] Bigger ships not only meant more expensive construction; they could also involve costs for such things as building new bases, deeper dredging of channels, bigger dry docks and widening of canals.

Britain could no longer afford a navy capable of defeating the next two largest navies, and the public was not as enthusiastic to support the Royal Navy through taxes as it had been one hundred years previously. The policy makers faced the distinct possibility that some new innovation or technical discovery might, with a single development, undermine British naval strength, leaving her without the financial means to regain her predominance.

If the war had undermined some of the basic supports in the United Kingdom which underpinned a large Royal Navy, then the process of erosion also extended to the British Empire. It was the existence of a large and scattered Empire which necessitated a large and powerful Royal Navy capable of global operations. In the aftermath of 1918 the British took the first hesitant steps towards decolonization just at the point at which the Empire reached its territorial apogee. Increasingly independent dominions would develop their own military capabilities, and in Africa, Asia and the Middle East the idea of home rule was increasingly accepted as the next logical step in the evolution of the Empire. The decline of Empire would mean the decline of the Royal Navy. The process of imperial withdrawal begun after 1918 would take a further forty years to manifest itself, and a further decade to accelerate the process of naval decline.

The process would be made more difficult because, despite the failure to secure a crushing Trafalgar-style victory at Jutland, the Royal Navy continued to enjoy high standing with the British public. As Andrew Gordon notes, the Royal Navy had done everything which could reasonably be expected of it.[25] The place of the service in the affections of the British public remained high, as evidenced by a steady stream of publications during and immediately after the First World War. Arthur Hungerford Pollen's *The British Navy in Battle* (1919) provided an excellent overview of the war at sea for an Anglo-American audience, while his *The Navy in Battle* (1918) proclaimed that with the exception of the U-boat threat the Royal Navy had enjoyed, control of the seas 'overwhelmingly established' and 'abjectly accepted' by the enemy.[26] The ubiquity of British sea power from the Danube to Dar-es-Salaam was celebrated by Conrad Cato's *The Navy Everywhere* (1919).[27] A romantic view of naval service was fostered by the likes of Bartimeus's *The Navy Eternal* (1918) and the young continued to be targeted by titles such as *The British Navy: The Navy Vigilant* (1918) with its advice to 'the boys and girls of the British commonwealth' to 'look after your moat'.[28] The Royal Navy remained an attractive career option despite the low pay. Taffrail's *The Sub* (1917) highlighted the excitements that might follow for an officer cadet in the Royal Navy.[29] To such celebratory books was added a steady stream of memoir accounts such as Admiral Sir Percy Scott's *Fifty Years in the Royal Navy* (1919), Lieutenant Gordon Maxwell's *Motor Launch Patrol* (1920) and Viscount Jellicoe of Scapa's *The Crisis of the Naval War* (1921).[30]

If the First World War generated considerable difficulties for the Royal Navy, then it also affected the wider strategic balance. With the end of the First World War in 1918, and especially after the German Fleet was scuttled at Scapa Flow the following year, the British began to turn their attention to an alliance that was due for renewal in 1921. The collapse of Russia into Bolshevism, and the imposition of the military clauses of the Versailles Treaty on Germany, removed the naval threats to Britain which had resulted in the signature of the alliance and then its renewal.[31] However, at the moment of naval apogee Britain faced a series of threats to its naval power. Owing billions to the United States in war debts, and with an economy dislocated by the war, Britain faced the very real prospect that her navy might be overtaken in size by that of the United States and/or Japan. Both nations were engaged in a programme of naval construction that had the potential to produce fleets to rival that of the Royal Navy. While the British had competed with Germany in a battleship-building race before 1914, the building of capital ships in British yards had come to a virtual halt during the First World War. In the post-war period, as the Americans and Japanese progressed their building programmes, the British were simply not in a position to respond (financially or in terms of the existing industrial infrastructure).

Potential complications or solutions to the problem lay at the imperial and diplomatic levels. The question of increased contributions by the dominions to imperial defence had been on the agenda since before the First World War as Nicholas Lambert has charted.[32] By 1918 four kinds of Empire naval cooperation had been established, as detailed in a post-war document:

(a) The provision, manning and maintenance of Dominion units or squadrons, e.g. the Royal Australian Navy.
(b) Payment for ships, e.g. the battle cruiser *New Zealand* by New Zealand, and the battleship *Malaya* by the Federated Malay States.
(c) The provision of men, e.g. the Newfoundland Naval Reserve, and the South African Naval Volunteer Reserve.
(d) Direct financial co-operation, e.g. New Zealand and South Africa.[33]

It was the growth of Empire naval units that increasingly looked like a way to relieve some of the burden on the Royal Navy. The Commonwealth of Australia had established its own naval forces on 1 March 1901. Nine years later the Naval Service of Canada had been founded. The following year King George V recognized their progress, by awarding the title Royal to the Royal Canadian Navy (RCN) and the Royal Australian Navy (RAN). In 1913 New Zealand Naval Forces were established as a local force under the command of the Commander-in-Chief China Station. Nevertheless, as Nicholas Tracy has shown, before the First World War the evolution of dominion naval forces was beset by political, financial and military concerns.[34] The war to some extent eased some of these concerns and by war's end the RCN had seven units at its disposal, and the RAN had established an impressive reputation by its operations in the Pacific, Mediterranean and home British waters. Even so, in 1917 the Imperial Conference had rejected the idea of a single navy for the Empire, agreeing, instead, to have common training standards for the Royal Navy and dominion naval units.[35] Two years later, at the Imperial Conference of 1919 the Admiralty suggested that Canada, New Zealand and South Africa should build up their own forces on the lines of the RAN.[36] In September 1919 the Admiralty began to investigate whether the dominions might be interested in acquiring some of the naval vessels that the Royal Navy was busy declaring surplus to its peacetime requirements.[37]

Even as they were doing this, however, the Admiralty remained convinced that an effective Empire navy required effective imperial government. Such a massive political leap in the evolution of the executive leadership of the Empire meant that the naval forces of the Royal Navy and Dominions would remain separate at least for the time being. The potential for an Empire navy and an effective pooling of resources would remain unrealized after the 1919 Imperial Conference, and there would not be another until 1921.

The growth of the dominion navies, or direct financial contributions from dominion government to British defence spending, represented possible solutions to the problems facing the British policy makers concerned to preserve Britain's naval predominance. Further potential solutions lay at the diplomatic level. The Anglo-Japanese Alliance potentially gave Britain some leverage over the Japanese, and also the Americans since they wished to see it terminated as a check on Japan's ambitions in the Far East. The potential for arms reduction, or arms limitation under the League of Nations created in 1919, opened another potential means to address the threat posed by the American and Japanese programmes. In any case, Britain and Japan's membership of the League of Nations, with its international obligations and emphasis on collective security arrangements, potentially raised awkward questions about discrete alliances.

As the British began to consider their attitude towards the strategic, diplomatic and military challenges facing them in the post-war world, attitudes within the Royal Navy towards the question of renewing the Anglo-Japanese Alliance continued to be shaped by the effectiveness of Japanese efforts in the First World War. From the military standpoint the Japanese had provided useful help as an operational partner capturing the German colonies at Tsingtao in China and in the Pacific. The Japanese had conducted operations against German cruisers in the Pacific and had helped to convoy Australian and New Zealand troops. In 1917 and 1918 the Japanese Navy had operated in the Mediterranean, from the Cape of Good Hope and from Honolulu and Singapore. They had also taken part in actions against Bolshevik Russia in the Far East. Timothy Saxon has good grounds for commenting in the year 2000 in *The Naval War College Review* that the Japanese Navy had strained its resources to the limit in aiding the British.[38]

Despite the realities, the Royal Navy after 1918 did not consider the Japanese to have been good alliance partners. During those periods of the war when Germany appeared ascendant, such as 1915 and late 1917, the Japanese were ready to push their territorial and economic ambitions in Asia.[39] Some Japanese newspapers such as the Tokyo-based *Jiji* and *Yordodzu* openly praised the efforts and successes of the German military. However, within the pages of the Japanese press could be found equally fervent expressions of loyalty to the cause of the Entente. For example, *The Tokyo Times* in 1916 published a pamphlet in English arguing that expressions of antagonism towards the British or demonstrations of pro-German sentiment were the work of a few malcontents or of spies loyal to Berlin.[40] The writer of the pamphlet concluded that it showed even 'to the meanest intelligence' that there was no question of an anti-British sentiment in Japan beyond: 'the essays of a few academic writers, sophomoric controversialists and a number of worthy people who may be depended on to "pick the wrong horse"'.[41]

To the officers of the Royal Navy, actions perhaps spoke louder than words, but here again was a problem. As the Commander-in-Chief China Station concluded in 1917, 'In general, it may be said that Japanese naval assistance in so far as it conformed to direct Japanese interests, was freely and willingly given. Where, however, the object to be attained did not especially further the policy of Japan, a certain amount of persuasion was necessary to induce her to undertake the required commitments.'[42] He further called attention to 'the particular traits' which rendered cooperation with the Imperial Japanese Navy 'a matter of extreme difficulty and requiring abnormal patience'.[43] Those traits included a 'failure to appreciate that we are in a state of war', an 'inability to act promptly' and an 'impression that it is derogatory to take orders or even act on requests from foreign officers'.[44]

By the end of the First World War the strategic balance was shifting against Britain in a number of respects. The economic and financial health of the nation was in long-term decline, and the emergence of disruptive technologies in the nineteenth and early twentieth centuries called into question Britain's traditional heavy investment in the Royal Navy as the chief guardian of national security. While the First World War saw the removal of the German naval threat, challenges were developing from the new naval powers of the United States and Japan. A naval threat from the latter was especially ironic given the relationship between Japan and Great Britain signified by the signature of the Anglo-Japanese Alliance in 1902 and its renewal thereafter. That alliance had been a means to offset the threat to Britain's naval predominance, but as the Japanese Navy expanded existing ally had to be considered potential future threat.

Such was the Royal Navy's prestige with the British public during the nineteenth century that the mixed fortunes of the service during the First World War led to profound disappointment. That in turn eventually fed through into British defence policy. The British government (and the British public) was no longer able, or willing to continue, to maintain the levels of investment in the Royal Navy necessary to secure its global pre-eminence. Moreover, with the prospect that some new technology might yet again emerge to render the Royal Navy obsolescent, the politicians turned to diplomatic means to preserve Britain's naval mastery for as long as possible. This was to prove remarkably effective with the Royal Navy remaining the largest fleet afloat until 1939. Ironically, despite the decline in comparative terms, in absolute terms the Royal Navy of 1918 was far more capable than the force which had emerged from the French wars. By 1918 the Royal Navy operated above and below the waves with aircraft and submarines as well as on them with battleships. The dreadnought-era battleship was faster; had longer range; and was more heavily armed, more manoeuvrable and vastly more capable than the ships of Nelson's day. Over the hundred years after 1813 the Royal Navy had lost its absolute supremacy, but it had developed its capabilities by investing in new technology within an ever smaller fleet.

Even so, from 1918 onwards the Royal Navy was locked into a process of decline. That decline was to see business contraction, growing unemployment and the steady destruction of the working-class communities, which had grown up in areas dependent on the staple industries. Combating the economic and social effects of the decline of Britain's staple industries formed a significant part of the economic and business policies of governments from Lloyd George's onwards. The decline of those industries was a pivotal factor in the growth of the Labour movement in Britain and the re-orientation of British politics along the lines of socialism versus anti-socialism. In 1919, as the thoughts of politicians, diplomats and naval officers turned to the question of the renewal of the Anglo-Japanese Alliance, the shipyards of the Clyde provided many socialists prepared to countenance extreme solutions to press their industrial demands. During the war shop stewards in yards such as Fairfields had demonstrated that their patriotism would not stand in the way of the pursuit of goals such as a forty hour week. The general strike called on Clydeside for 27 January 1919, which resulted in army units being called out to deal with serious public disorder with 40,000 workers on strike, was spearheaded by the shipyard unions.[45] Red Clydeside offered the Lloyd George government the prospect of other depressed areas in the industrial north turning towards the vision offered by Lenin and the Bolsheviks in Czarist Russia. The state of the economy provided the bottom line for all government policies from foreign policy to industrial policy and beyond. The question was whether the politicians and civil servants in the post-war period in Whitehall and beyond could find the means to revive the British economy, while ameliorating the worst effects of the decline.

4

Politics, Politicians and Whitehall

After 1918 the political contexts in which the policy makers would try to respond to the emergent challenges to British naval power were highly unstable, rendering more difficult the task of dealing with the critical issues in such a connected field of government policy. Those contexts have received considerable attention from historians and political scientists, but that scholarship has not impacted significantly on understandings of naval and diplomatic policy in the 1920s.[1] There has been little serious academic inquiry into the impact for the making and evolution of defence policies of a political system undergoing profound change. This is despite the gravity of the political and governmental changes being wrought as a result of the First World War on the political and governmental landscape of Great Britain.

The Liberal government had given way in May 1915 to a coalition involving the Conservatives. Prime Minister Herbert Henry Asquith slowly lost the support of his ministers, especially the leading Conservatives, over his handling of the war. In December 1916 Asquith resigned when faced with a plot hatched between Lloyd George, Liberal Secretary of State for War, and leading Conservatives to sideline the Prime Minister and run the war through a small committee. Lloyd George became the Prime Minister and the Liberal Party was split by the crisis: some supporting Lloyd George and others Asquith. In the interests of more efficient government Lloyd George revolutionized some key elements of government decision-making. From 1916 onwards, in the House of Commons Lloyd George was dependent on Conservative support. As peace approached in late 1918 Lloyd George determined to carry the coalition into the peace in order to meet the problems of peace-making and an unsettled post-war world. In truth he needed Conservative Party support to remain in power, and the Conservatives were nervous of standing against the 'Welsh Wizard' who had won the war for Britain. In effect, on both sides it was a temporary marriage of convenience.

To effect the continuation of the coalition into the peace, in the election that followed the armistice in late 1918 the Prime Minister issued those candidates considered loyal to him with a form of public endorsement. What followed was a landslide for Lloyd George as the coalition parties gained 525 of the 707 seats contested. Asquith's faction of the party was reduced to just thirty-three seats, with the party leader losing his seat.[2] The Labour Party, meanwhile, gained fifty-seven seats: an increase of fifteen over the previous Parliament. Most striking, however, was the rise in the Labour vote. In December 1910 Labour had gained just 7.1 per cent of the vote: in 1918 it more than tripled to 21.5 per cent. With the problems of the Liberals, the Labour Party was turning into a potential party of government. The appeal of the party to the working-class electorate in Britain's industrial heartlands was evident, and the 1918 Representation of the People Act (enfranchising women over thirty who met a minimum property qualification, giving the vote to all men over twenty-one and redistributing some seats to the larger industrial cities) increased the potential influence of that section of the electorate on the outcome of a general election. The party system was in flux after 1918 with the Conservatives struggling to find an identity after more than a decade out of power or in coalition, the Liberals beset by division and infighting and Labour struggling to build a national power base.

The rising power and influence of the working classes on British politics impacted firmly the political agenda. With a broad franchise, the political parties could not afford to ignore the central importance of jobs and social spending. What William Beveridge would later describe as the five giant evils of squalor, ignorance, want, idleness and disease were already shaping the programmes of the parties. Employment was seen as the central issue, impinging directly on the other four, by the Conservative and Liberal parties, which emphasized capitalist free market responses to the economy and towards social problems. The Labour Party, which had grown out of the Trade Union movement and socialist parties in the nineteenth century, was wedded to collective approaches towards common problems. Clause IV of the Party constitution adopted in 1918 enshrined the following as one of the principal goals of the party: 'To secure for the workers by hand or by brain the full fruits of their industry and the most equitable distribution thereof that may be possible upon the basis of the common ownership of the means of production, distribution and exchange.'[3] Such words held the promise of a brighter tomorrow for the British working classes.

At the centre of British politics from 1919 to 1922 stood Lloyd George: an enigmatic figure who has frustrated biographers and political scientists alike. The 'Welsh Wizard' who became Prime Minister in 1916 following plots to remove Asquith from leadership of a failing war effort remains a difficult subject to engage with. In terms of the sources upon which the historian must rely, Lloyd George left behind a plentiful archive, but offered no glimpses to outsiders of his inner motivations, thought processes and scruples. As Bentley Gilbert has noted Lloyd George was ready to talk to anyone about himself, but gave them little as to his private thoughts and motivations.[4] In a 1979 review article Gilbert highlighted the tendency of biographers to replicate each other's guesses on the forces at work in Lloyd George's character and mind.[5] They have in effect been 'colouring a shadow'.[6] Gilbert's suggestion that the real Lloyd George lay not in what he said but in the reforms and changes to Britain's political system that he introduced from 1906 to 1922 has much to commend it, but equally it is his quest to gain and retain power that defined him, his government and the lives of many of the other politicians he came into contact with. The idea of the coupon endorsement in the 1918 election may have been a device to ensure strong government into the peace, but equally it was a means for Lloyd George to maintain his hold on power. Retaining the Conservatives in coalition guaranteed him a majority, and ensured that the Asquithean Liberals and the Labour Party would be marginalized. For a Conservative Party concerned about its identity, and fearful of the electoral appeal of 'the man who won the war', maintaining the coalition into the peace made good political sense. Lloyd George was the dominating figure in British politics in the early twentieth century and he coupled brilliance with considerable charm. Most of the leading Conservatives of the day, including Conservative Party leader Andrew Bonar Law, respected, feared or were charmed by him in equal measure. Leading a coalition government from 1919 to 1922 the question of party fusion, to create a dominant force in the centre ground of British politics, continued to bubble away quietly beneath the surface. In the event Lloyd George squandered his opportunity to pursue that course, but that possibility underlined the extent of Lloyd George's political dominance from 1919 to early 1922, by which time events such as the sale of honours scandal had begun to dent his reputation.

Lloyd George's pursuit of power in the pre-war period saw him heavily involved as Chancellor of the Exchequer from 1908 to 1915 with domestic issues. However, in the aftermath of the terrible losses in the First World War, he concentrated on foreign affairs to the point where there were suspicions that the Foreign Office was being eclipsed by a Prime Minister determined to exercise personal control of key parts of Britain's external relations. In a 1976 article Alan Sharp described the Foreign Office as being in eclipse during the coalition government, and although the extent of the Prime Minister's dominance in foreign affairs has been contested by later historians, there can be no doubt of Lloyd George's presidential instincts on the foreign stage.[7] Seemingly not directly interested in the Royal Navy, his post-war foreign policy interventions brought Lloyd George into much greater association with naval policy. His earlier experiences as the Chancellor of the Exchequer, and at the Ministry of Munitions from 1915 to 1916, undoubtedly coloured his attitudes towards naval armaments. In his 'People's Budget' of 1909 Lloyd George had to find money for both welfare programmes and the provision of additional capital ships for the Royal Navy. The cost of naval armaments, the suggestion that the pre-war naval arms race had contributed to the outbreak of war in 1914 and the inherent tension between spending on welfare and the military were not lost on Lloyd George after 1918. The high levels of taxation in 1918, and a post-war economic slump, increased the urgency of securing reductions in government spending, especially in areas such as the naval estimates. Following the coupon election Lloyd George was determined to work with his Liberal and Conservative coalition colleagues in Cabinet to secure the peace of Europe, social progress at home and the country's long-term economic future.

The coalition cabinet which Lloyd George headed after 1918 had the benefit of reforms to government practice which he had overseen during the First World War. A Cabinet Secretariat supported and recorded the process by which ministers arrived at their decisions with an efficient system of memoranda and minutes. Via memoranda, and in discussion, the different government departments represented around the table in Cabinet had every opportunity to make their views clear on the issues of the day from taxation to naval policy, and then to arrive at collective decisions backed up the notion of collective responsibility. Lloyd George also had the benefit of a Prime Minister's Secretariat (often referred to as the 'garden suburb' after the collection of huts in the garden of 10 Downing Street which was its home). The Prime Minister's Secretariat had come into being in 1917 following Lloyd George's appointment as Prime Minister. The Prime Minister's Secretariat prepared papers for him and constituted an alternative source of advice to the Whitehall departments represented in Cabinet by their secretary of state. To all intents and purposes, however, in practice the Cabinet Secretariat represented just one more stream of information and opinion feeding through into the normal processes of Cabinet government. So far as the machinery of government was concerned naval policy, as least on paper, was to be determined by the 'normal' processes of debate, discussion and agreement that governed every other aspect of government policy. The critical question which Samuel P. Huntingdon poses in *The Common*

Defense: Strategic Programs in National Politics is whether 'normal' ways of government are best suited to producing effective policies for national security.[8] That question was not considered in British circles after the First World War and it remains to be considered in the twenty-first century.

Back in Cabinet in 1919 the Admiralty and Royal Navy were represented by the civilian First Lord of the Admiralty. The First Sea Lord (the military head of the service) also had access to the Cabinet and senior ministers. This dual civilian/military control of the Royal Navy was considered highly effective, but much depended on the personalities of the two men.[9] Both the First Lord and First Sea Lord possessed additional political leverage in that they could expect a potentially favourable audience from King George V. As Lady Lee of Fareham later noted in her diary, King George V was 'essentially a Naval officer' in the way he thought, talked and in his occasional use of the language of the forecastle.[10] 'Royal channels' pointed towards one of the other less visible constants of British politics, perhaps particularly visible in the 1915–22 period: unofficial, usually indefinable and constantly shifting groupings within the British elite to affect change and policy in one form or another. The cabal which brought down Asquith in 1915 was typical of the way in which business was transacted in and around Westminster. Tracing those networks through the associations between particular figures and the usually coded references in their surviving private papers is difficult, but not impossible in all cases.

The individuals who made up the Royal Navy's political representation in the post-war period, and who themselves might take part in such intrigues, were powerful and persuasive figures. The First Lord of the Admiralty who took up his appointment in January 1919 was the veteran Unionist politician Walter Long.[11] First elected in 1880, Long represented seven constituencies during a forty-year parliamentary career. In government from 1915 onwards, he was appointed First Lord of the Admiralty in 1918 with the express task of retrenching Royal Navy expenditure. In the circumstances of the Lloyd George coalition 1918–22, Long was not the kind of character whom the Prime Minister could routinely ignore. Long's health was a major issue even though up until 1920 Long was supported in the House of Commons by Parliamentary and Financial Secretary to the Admiralty Thomas MacNamara. The Liberal MP for Camberwell North West, MacNamara had held the post of Parliamentary and Financial Secretary to the Admiralty since 1908. With MacNamara's elevation to the post of Minister of Labour in 1920, Long lost an important support in the House of Commons. By late 1921 Lloyd George was increasingly concerned that Long was simply not up to the job of running a major department, and securing the economies in Admiralty expenditure necessary to help reduce the burden on the Exchequer.[12] Given the sensitivities of coalition government Lloyd George quietly shared his concerns with Andrew Bonar Law, leader of the Conservative Party. By the end of January 1921 Lloyd George judged that the situation was becoming urgent, probably in view of the need to frame the Naval Estimates for 1921–22.[13] In consequence, Lloyd George wrote to Bonar Law to ask him to talk to Long within the next week about stepping down.[14] A letter from the aged and ailing 66-year-old followed on 9 February.[15] Thereafter, Long and Bonar Law discussed the issue of a replacement with the choice eventually falling on Lord Lee of Fareham, Secretary of State for Agriculture, despite the fact that, as a peer, he would not be able to represent the Admiralty in the House of Commons.[16] Lee was initially hesitant to accept as he was not sure that he would be able to accept the lines of policy which the Prime Minister might wish to impose upon him. For example, Lee made clear that in framing policy at the Admiralty he would be unable to accept the possibility that Britain and the United States might find themselves on opposite sides in some future war.[17]

Agreement was eventually secured and on 18 February 1921 Lee of Fareham was appointed by Lloyd George with the understanding that he would continue Long's task of bearing down hard on the Royal Navy expenditure in the interests of the public finances. A former army officer in the late nineteenth century, Lee had daringly gathered intelligence at the Russian base at Vladivostock. Later he had served as British military attaché with US forces in the Spanish-American war. Present as Roosevelt's Rough Riders stormed up the San Juan Hill, he received the Spanish-American war medal. He was not unversed in the issue of great power politics in the Far East or in domestic American politics. Equally his grandfather had fought at the battles of St Vincent and the Nile as a junior officer.[18] Whatever Lloyd George's hopes, Lee of Fareham's memorandums to the Cabinet on naval matters were perhaps even more forceful than those of Walter Long.[19]

In volume one of *British Naval Policy between the Wars* Stephen Roskill is unkind to Lee of Fareham. Roskill emphasizes that Lee of Fareham had little understanding of naval policy or naval matters in general.[20] The Royal Navy's failure to secure a large post-war building programme is laid at his door, and he was seen as insufficiently vigorous in backing the Admiralty's attempt to secure from the RAF control over the Naval Air Service. Roskill's dislike of Lee of Fareham was a reflection of the Admiralty's opinion of a politician who believed in the art of the compromise. Considered by Roskill as perhaps the Civil Lord of the Admiralty held in the lowest esteem by the officers of the Navy Board,

Naval Policy between the Wars was to give scant attention to anything that Lee of Fareham might have achieved while in office.[21]

Supporting Lee of Fareham in the House of Commons from 1921 to 1922 was Parliamentary and Financial Secretary to the Admiralty Leo Amery, Conservative MP for Birmingham South. An ex-army officer and journalist, Amery would go on to become a Cabinet minister following the fall of Lloyd George.[22] Amery was well connected and equipped with acute political antennae. An ardent imperialist, he was regarded as one of the next generation of leaders for the Conservative Party.

Within the Lloyd George Cabinet were other members who saw themselves as unusually well positioned to speak on naval affairs. As a former First Lord of the Admiralty (1911–15), Churchill (successively Secretary of State for Air 1919–21 and Colonial Office 1921–22) had the connections and, as he saw it, the authority to occasionally trespass (usually in private) onto matters of naval policy. An ardent Americanist, Churchill was an equally firm supporter of British naval predominance. These were the two factors which militated against his support of the Anglo-Japanese Alliance. As he explained in the House of Commons, 'Let us never allow our sea power to fall to a point where we might be tempted to make, or be forced to make, compromises or entangling agreements in the desperate hope of supplementing our own exertions by the strength of others.'[23]

Two other former First Lords of the Admiralty sat in Cabinet. Eric Geddes had been First Lord from 1917 to 1919. Prior to this he had been Controller at the Admiralty with, in the midst of a growing sense of crisis over the number of merchant ships being sunk by U-boats, special responsibility for British shipbuilding. Following his move from the Admiralty in 1919, he was first a minister without portfolio and then Minister of Transport (1919–21). With his brother, Auckland Geddes, Ambassador to the United States after 1919, Eric was seemingly ideally equipped to play a leading role in shaping the naval and diplomatic agenda facing Britain in the post-war period. However, within naval and maritime circles Eric Geddes did not inspire confidence. Sir Archibald Hurd, naval correspondent to *The Daily Telegraph* and prolific maritime author, later wrote on the subject of Lloyd George's appointment of Geddes: 'No men more ignorant of naval affairs were ever associated together than the Prime Minister and Geddes.'[24]

Veteran Conservative politician Arthur James Balfour was another member of the Cabinet who could claim a certain amount of authority to speak on naval and diplomatic matters. Prime Minister between 1902 and 1905, Balfour had taken over as First Lord of the Admiralty following Churchill's resignation in 1915. He had held that post until he was appointed Foreign Secretary the following year. By 1919 Balfour was undoubtedly one of the elder statespersons of the Conservative Party, but age was taking a heavy toll on his capabilities. Increasingly deaf, Balfour found committee meetings at the Paris Peace Conference a considerable burden during 1919, and in October he stepped down as Foreign Secretary. His political value to Lloyd George as an elder statesperson of the Conservative Party ensured that he continued to sit in Cabinet as Lord President of the Council. By nature not a born meddler, Balfour was content to see himself as a repository of sage advice to be called upon by Lloyd George, and Bonar Law, the Conservative Party leader, as required.

In addition to those ministers who felt specially qualified by their earlier careers to talk about naval policy were others whose departmental briefs brought them into proximity, if not outright collision with the First Lord of the Admiralty. Given the cost of armaments, and the difficulties before 1914 of funding them, the Treasury had a particularly significant role to play in the evolution of British naval policy after the First World War. During the war, as Kathleen Burk has noted, the Treasury went through a dramatic reorganization and growth that enhanced its power considerably. Following the German armistice as the government faced a serious battle to reduce public expenditure as quickly as possible, and to obtain favourable terms for the repayment of British war debts to the United States, Lloyd George further concentrated power in the hands of the Treasury. Cutting government expenditure, reducing taxation, stimulating the economy and arriving at a reasonable settlement of war reparations from Germany, which would not cause economic collapse in Central Europe, were urgent priorities for the Treasury. On 19 July 1919 the Chancellor of the Exchequer, Austen Chamberlain, circulated a paper among his colleagues prophesying financial collapse unless government departments could find ways to drastically cut back their expenditure.[25] From this point on 'economy', 'reductions' and 'savings' became the mantra of ministers and civil servants.

The dislocation of British manufacturing after 1914 as peacetime production gave way to turning out war materials, the loss of overseas markets and the enormous losses of capital and material sustained by British businesses during the war added further levels of concern for the civil servants and ministers working in the Treasury building. In the eyes of the Treasury after 1918 the war was over, and another was highly unlikely within the foreseeable future. Indeed, this was backed by a working rule of thumb, accepted by the Cabinet on 15 August 1919, that there would be no war for at least ten years.[26] To the Treasury such an assurance was sufficient guarantee to make substantial cuts in military spending, and to resist any attempt to commence a large-scale programme of capital ship building to meet the naval challenges of the United States and Japan.

Also hoping for peace were the mandarins of the Foreign Office which was headed by Lord Balfour and later, from October 1919 to January 1924, by Lord Curzon of Kedleston. The diplomatic ramifications of the war were considerable with the map of world being remade. The British Empire reached the zenith of its size as former Turkish and German territories were placed, at least nominally under imperial control. The creation of a League of Nations, detailed in one of US president Woodrow Wilson's fourteen points of 1918, created a new factor in international relations: a collective security organization promoting peace, disarmament and economic and social progress. America's retreat into isolationism in 1919 robbed the organization of valuable prestige and the moral and economic force that came with support from the United States. The growth of the Empire, the disturbed state of world affairs after 1918, made impossible any attempt to achieve a balance between British foreign policy and the military capabilities required to support it. Moreover, as an arch imperialist and former Viceroy of India, Curzon was never going to be the kind of minister to champion a policy of retrenchment in foreign affairs.

Outside of the Cabinet, and working with the First Lord of the Admiralty was the First Sea Lord: the professional head of the Royal Navy. Responsible for every aspect of the Royal Navy, the incumbent was a powerful military and political figure, backed by a government department and by a global communications network. Naval attachés in British embassies around the globe were rich channels of information and a good source of overseas contacts. Every ship's captain on deployment overseas, and each commander-in-chief of particular stations (such as Commander-in-Chief China Station) was part British diplomat, part military leader and part envoy of the Royal Navy. The post of First Sea Lord carried weighty responsibilities and considerable power.

During 1919 there was a lengthy, and very public, controversy over the post of First Sea Lord. The episode had a potentially significant impact on naval policy after the end of the First World War and highlights the nature of power in Westminster and Whitehall circles in the early twentieth century. The incumbent First Sea Lord at the end of the war was Admiral Sir Rosslyn Weymss. In the period between late 1918 and early 1919 a misunderstanding arose between Weymss; Sir Eric Geddes, the outgoing First Lord of the Admiralty; and Admiral Beatty, Commander-in-Chief Grand Fleet. Weymss was ready to step down as First Sea Lord, and to let Beatty, who had commanded the battlecruisers at

Jutland, replace him in the post, providing that some other high (and presumably paying) post was available for the 55-year-old to move on to. Such a change was felt to be in the interest of a Royal Navy that needed to adjust itself back to peacetime conditions. Weymss's appointment as First Sea Lord in 1917 had been unexpected and not wholly popular within the naval service as he was 'not considered brainy'; nor did he have 'marked experience as an administrator'.[27] Even so, during the latter stages of the war, Weymss had proved his abilities in dealing with a range of problems including the intensification of the submarine war.

Weymss's conversation with Beatty and Geddes about hypothetical possibilities was taken by Beatty as a done deal and was reported to Long, the incoming First Lord of the Admiralty, who was happy to endorse Beatty's assumption of the post.[28] News of the appointment appeared in *The Times* in early 1919 just as Weymss was about to depart for the Peace Conference in Paris. Weymss was quick to deny the appointment and the Admiralty issued a firm denial.[29] Weymss asked the editor of *The Times* to see him, and the editor (without naming his source) explained that the story had been vouched 'on the highest authority'.[30] Weymss suspected Lloyd George as the source of 'the intrigue', although an indiscrete and well-connected Beatty was probably the more likely source of the information. Weymss's suspicion of Lloyd George is, however, telling. With the government keen to secure large reductions in the naval estimates, and the dangers of naval competition with the United States and Japan (which would involve a ruinously expensive naval war to maintain Britain's naval supremacy), a naval service politically crippled by a division between First Sea Lord and senior naval commander was convenient for the politicians.

The affair divided opinion in the country, Admiralty and Naval Service, and between Weymss, Beatty and Long (who was left to try to re-establish some sort of working relationship between the two men and himself). On 24 February Long wrote to Beatty to explain how the misunderstanding had occurred, to state that Weymss would continue in the post for the foreseeable future, and to stress that on Weymss's retirement Beatty would be invited to take up the post.[31] In the meantime, Long attempted to hasten the departure of Weymss. In March he discussed an idea with Lord Stamfordham by which Weymss would be appointed naval plenipotentiary to the Paris Peace Conference, leaving Beatty to take up the post of First Sea Lord. Stamfordham and King George V approved of the idea, and the latter let it be known that he was prepared to grant Weymss a peerage if it would secure his compliance.[32] On 7 March Long wrote to Lloyd George to enlist his support in affecting a speedy transition. This was his advice to the Prime Minister: 'I have satisfied myself that if a definite public announcement is not made in a very few days there will be a press campaign which will have the warm sympathy of the Navy and of the great majority of the public.'[33] On 9 March, as articles on the controversy appeared in the *London Evening Standard*, Lord Stamfordham met with Weymss to push the idea that he would take up the post of naval plenipotentiary.[34] Rather unexpectedly Weymss dug in his heels and tried to angle for an ambassadorship to Rome or Paris (which the Permanent Under-Secretary at the Foreign Office subsequently refused to consider as a possibility). A letter from Weymss to Long on 10 March also suggested that the First Sea Lord was not prepared to yield easily to make way for Beatty.[35] With ongoing controversy in the press, the following day Long wrote to Lloyd George to apologize for adding to the Prime Minister's burdens at such a difficult time. He sought to make up for it by reassuring Lloyd George saying, 'I am instilling need for rigorous cutting down and strict economy here.'[36] An apparent mistake in one part of the Royal Navy's business was to be redeemed by success in reducing the naval estimates. This helped to set the tone for much of the following century: the success of British naval policy was, in peacetime, based on how far the naval estimates and the fleet could be shrunk down in size.

With Weymss refusing to relinquish the post, Long felt compelled to defend him in private to leading political figures in order to try to draw a line under the press campaign that was being waged against the First Sea Lord. That campaign, principally by the Northcliffe press, was also intended to damage Long and the government. The defence of Weymss, however, may not have been a matter of simple political calculation on Long's part as it became apparent that the pro-Beatty camp was prepared to go to considerable lengths to secure his appointment as First Sea Lord. On 10 March Admiral Lord Charles Beresford, threatening to put down a motion in the House of Lords, wrote to Long to voice his support for Beatty.[37] The veteran naval officer (1859–1911) and Conservative politician (who, first elected in 1874, stood down as MP for Portsmouth in 1916) was an important figure within naval and nationalist circles where he was seen as a John Bull–like figure. In 1914 Beresford had played a key role in bringing down Prince Louis of Battenberg as First Sea Lord, and he was seen as a formidable opponent in political, naval and the social circles of the period. Beresford, whose affair with the Countess of Warwick had almost erupted into a public scandal when a letter between the two had fallen into the hands of Lady Beresford in 1891, gave Long the means to force the resignation of Weymss. Beresford advised Long to '"cherchez la femme" – which I am sure you know all about by now and which is known perfectly throughout the fleet.'[38] The retired Admiral also referred to a correspondence between the lady in question and the Overseas League of the Navy League, of which he was the president. Beresford went on to reveal that he had prevented plans for publication of the correspondence, which would have led to Weymss's resignation. He further offered to provide Long with copies of the letters. The inference was clear: Beresford was prepared to give Long the means to blackmail Weymss into resignation, while hinting darkly that he might release the correspondence for publication unless he got his way.

The public defence, with Weymss symbolically promoted to the rank of full Admiral on 12 March, did quiet the campaign to some extent as it was apparent that Weymss was not about to be hounded out of office, and the attack on the First Sea Lord by the Northcliffe press was leading Long and others to dig in their heels. Long was also using his connections to try and bring pressure on the leaders of the pro-Beatty camp. Commander Sir George Armstrong, with a remarkable background that spanned the Royal Navy, the Conservative Party and the press, wrote to Admiral Sir Charles Beresford, enclosing a copy to Long on 8 April 1919, to bring some pressure to bear.[39] Long and Armstrong were pre-war political associates and it seems likely that Armstrong's letter, on which Long's comments were invited before dispatch, was the result of some discussion between the two. Armstrong's letter casts considerable light on the divisions opening up in the Naval Service as a result of the affair. Armstrong referred to

> A vicious press campaign against Long and Weymss; social intrigues on behalf of Beatty; the dividing of the Service into two great camps, namely the Grand Fleet set, and the set who were not in the Grand Fleet; and the suggestion that the Navy contains only one man who is qualified for the position of First Sea Lord.[40]

The ostensible purpose of Armstrong's letter was seemingly to get Beresford not to proceed with a motion in the House of Lords. Armstrong argued that embroiling the Navy in controversy at a critical moment could only be counterproductive to the interests of the Royal Navy and country. By such efforts, and a public statement in the House of Commons by Long, saying that the First Sea Lord enjoyed the confidence of His Majesty's government, the campaign against Weymss was abated if not extinguished.[41]

The Weymss affair, however, took a fresh twist on 5 August 1919 with the publication of the 'War Honour's List'. There was no reward or thanks for Weymss despite a generous doling out of honours, and in spite of earlier conversations in which an honour had been hinted at as part of the price of his vacating the post of First Lord of the Admiralty. Weymss appeared heart-broken and angry at the public snub. Sensing further trouble Long apparently decided to force his hand, and in late August he apparently asked Weymss for his resignation, making reference to the subject of his 'own affairs'. Weymss referred to the conversation in a letter he sent to Long on 28 August. Enclosed with it was Weymss's resignation.[42] Interestingly, he reiterated his desire for an important post such as the Rome Embassy.

In his efforts to manage Weymss, Long may have benefited from the fact that the names of several other prominent Admirals did not appear in the honours list. Beatty wrote a note of protest to Long that the Navy had been badly done by in the honours list, and that potentially made it easier for Long to explain to Weymss that others were equally unhappy that their names did not feature in the post-war honours list.[43] Beresford's increasing infirmity and death on 6 September was another politically useful event in removing a potential complicating factor from the scene.

Long was not about to be messed around by Weymss and the correspondence between the two men took on a rather different tenor in the Autumn of 1919. Long was not about to let Weymss go immediately, but required him to go on 1 November to ensure an orderly transition to the Beatty era. That changed tenor can be glimpsed in a letter sent by Long to Weymss in October 1919: 'This letter has to be written. Your resignation must now be announced to take effect on November 1st on which date I have the King's assent to your promotion to be an Admiral of the Fleet.'[44] Weymss left office on that date without a further job to go to. In his letter to the King, Weymss revealed his anger at the way he had been treated and the lack of backing from the government when faced with 'intrigues' to 'oust me from my position of First Sea Lord'.[45] For nine critical months, as the Admiralty and Royal Navy had to come to grips with a series of life or death challenges to British naval mastery, the senior service was riven by divisions at its highest level of leadership. In those nine months Britain ceded that mastery to parity in fleet size between Britain and the United States.

Beatty's appointment as First Sea Lord was a natural progression for the most charismatic and celebrated British admiral since Nelson, or at least that is how Beatty thought about it.[46] For first nine months of 1919 his correspondence is marked by his personal anger at the situation with Weymss. Long attempted to distract him with committee work to inquire into some of the critical questions facing the Royal Navy in the post-war period.[47] Beatty in response said that there would be plenty of time to consider such questions after he became First Sea Lord.[48] This was undoubtedly unfortunate and would later give the politicians opportunities to stall the Admiralty on the question of issues of post-war naval construction.

To some extent this decision reflected Beatty's desire to construct a post-war Royal Navy in his own image. As Nicholas Rodger notes, Beatty was a man who 'inspired great devotion among his officers and men' by means of his 'tremendous and impressive personality'.[49] Andrew Lambert reminds us that, apart from his public image as a swashbuckling commander, the commander of the battlecruisers at Jutland was 'an educated and reflective officer, widely read and suitably instructed'.[50] In many ways a rather emotional man, Beatty viewed the Royal Navy as his navy, and he set about 'improving' the Admiralty by appointing men he trusted to key positions. That largely meant men who had recently served under him during his command of the Grand Fleet. The appointments of Vice Admiral Sir James Fergusson as Deputy Chief of the Naval Staff and Captain Alfred Ernle Chatfield as Fourth Sea Lord in 1919 were two of his key appointments.[51] Beatty undoubtedly wanted the fullest possible control over both the Admiralty and the Royal Navy, and before his appointment was made public Long had to specify in writing that the government would not entertain Beatty's suggestion that he be First Sea Lord and Commander-in-Chief.[52]

Whatever his personal outlook on the nations of the world (and Beatty was married to the rather unstable daughter of a Chicago chain-store magnate), the Royal Navy would not be relegated to secondary status on his watch. Thus in 1919 he wrote to the Admiralty calling for the German High Seas Fleet to be divided on the basis of war losses so as to ensure that the Royal Navy remained the largest in the world for the foreseeable future irrespective of the American 1916 building programme.[53] There were some obvious issues that he was prepared to engage with even before he became First Sea Lord.

As Stephen Roskill affirms, beyond the determination Beatty had a tremendous capacity for hard work and the ability to shut his mind to his personal problems. He was a figure capable of inspiring his subordinates.[54] Beatty believed in leading from the front and he had the social and the political skills to network efficiently and to get his way. This was a vital attribute for a First Lord of the Admiralty in early-twentieth-century Britain. The success of the Royal Navy depended on the ability of the First Lord and First Sea Lord to win the political battles to produce the fleet capable of winning the sea battles of the future. As Andrew Lambert has written, 'Beatty moved easily in government circles ... This was vital because his success was largely dependent on the ability of the First Lord and the Junior Civil Lord to win battles with the Treasury' and other Whitehall departments.[55] Celebrated by the media, Beatty was another man that Prime Minister Lloyd George could ill-afford to upset to the point of public outburst or resignation 'in a blaze of glory'.[56] Journalist ex-soldier Robert Barrington Ward at *The Observer* (later assistant editor at *The Times*) was a particularly strong supporter of the Admiral. In 1919 Winston Churchill, a former First Lord of the Admiralty, warned Lloyd George that once in post, Beatty would pursue the interests of the Admiralty with particular vigour.[57] Churchill recognized that in promoting the interests of that department Beatty would be unlikely to compromise or to see 'the bigger picture' of a government dealing with the difficulties of transition from war to peace. This would be further complicated by the fact that while Beatty had some excellent political skills and instincts, he was at the same time 'arrogant and politically naïve', to quote John Ferris.[58] His behaviour during the Weymss affair exhibited both traits to the full.

Despite Churchill's concerns about Beatty's pursuit of Admiralty interests, the Admiral was very much his own man and before 1919 he had criticized the Admiralty for various failings.[59] It took him several weeks after arriving in his new office to realize that reforms in the post-war period had largely transformed it into an efficient office whose advice and information he could trust.[60] On Far Eastern matters it also helped that Beatty understood something of the affairs of the East. He had spent the best part of two years on the China station and had been involved in fighting the Boxer Rebellion in 1900, fighting with the Japanese and other elements of the International Naval Brigade in defence of Tientsin.

Vital departmental backing to the First Sea Lord was given by the Admiralty, which was the government department responsible for the Royal Navy. The department had grown during the war and it had also suffered: one hundred and ten men of the civil staff of the Admiralty had been killed in action during the war.[61] The Admiralty was directed by a board composed of the civilian head of the service (First Lord) together with the Sea Lords. With an extensive staff (albeit one that contracted considerably in the 1919–22 period) the Admiralty represented a repository of expert knowledge and a powerful voice in government circles on naval policy.[62] With a British public susceptible to naval scares, and the national economy dependent on imports, the department was a fearsome potential opponent – a fact that was recognized within British political circles.[63]

A significant part of the Admiralty's political power came from the fact that as a department it had a sense of itself, of its past and its own importance. Tracing its origins back to Henry VIII's Council of Marine established in 1546, the Admiralty saw itself as one of the foundational elements of the modern British state in contrast to 'nouveau departments' such as the Foreign Office founded in 1782. The civil servants who worked for the Admiralty considered themselves as somewhat separate from the main body of the service. The Admiralty's sense of self can be glimpsed in one undated exchange between Oswyn Murray, Secretary to the Admiralty from 1917 to 1936, and MPs on the Public Accounts Committee of the House of Commons. Asked to confine himself to yes or no answers by one of the members of the committee, Murray refused on the grounds that he was there to give information to the committee and could not be expected to give one-word answers unless he felt that such an answer was an appropriate response to the question.[64]

Despite such self-assurance, throughout its history most naval officers operated under false prejudices when it came to the Admiralty. Most had little experience of the workings of the department, many regarding it as the place to which one would be sent for investigation and punishment after some perceived failure of duty on their part.[65] Things were particularly bad after the First World War. As Chatfield, Fourth Sea Lord (1919–20), explained in his memoirs, at the conclusion of the peace Admiralty and Royal Navy held each other in mutual suspicion.[66] Even in the lead up to the First World War, at the height of the naval-building fervour of the 1890s, the department had its critics.[67] The events of that conflict made matters worse. The division between Admiralty and Royal Navy was partly to do with structures and procedures. The Admiralty, like any other government department, was dominated by civil servants. A First Lord of the Admiralty, or Sea Lord, was rarely in post for more than two years and on coming to the job usually struggled to master their particular brief and the procedures of the department. Like most civil servants, those in the Admiralty had a close working relationship with their colleagues in the Treasury, often to the detriment of the interests of the Royal Navy (at least in the folklore of the Naval Staff).

A particular case in point that generated considerable hostility between the Admiralty and Royal Navy was the issue of pay. By the end of the war inflation and stagnant wage levels were producing considerable hardship for naval families. Prices had more than doubled as the government resorted to printing money to fund the cost of the war. Low levels of pay also posed a serious challenge to naval discipline on board ship. The growth of lower-deck benefit societies in the lead up to the First World War had caused concerns about the apparent spread of trades unionism to the Royal Navy.[68] During the First World War, with rising prices and stagnant pay, the benefit societies naturally became more prominent. That in turn led to rising levels of concern about the lower-deck benefit societies becoming a means to spread dissension or Bolshevism in the fleet. This was a potential problem which the Admiralty could ignore but which ship's officers could not. With the imminent arrival of Beatty and other officers from the Grand Fleet, the Admiralty grasped the nettle in early 1919. The Naval Estimates for 1919–20, calling for increased funds for naval pay and pensions, contained a frank admission that during the war, Royal Navy wages had declined in real terms, and in comparison to wages and salaries in the private sector.[69] The pay increases were accepted, but with such issues it was small wonder that there was 'a feeling in the Navy that the Admiralty Board was a thing apart from the sailor, a body that wore top-hats and was their permanent enemy'.[70]

The Admiralty was undoubtedly a conservative and bureaucratic institution. When Sir Oswyn Murray asked staff from one underperforming department for suggestions for reforms, the only idea forthcoming was 'that the Government should supply every clerk in that section with a fountain-pen and with "an allowance for its upkeep"'.[71] Almost inevitably outside the department, there was a perception that the different departments acted as 'largely watertight' compartments 'having no connection with one another. One Department did not know what the other Department was doing' and vice versa.[72] That conservatism extended to the reception of new technologies. In 1964 David Divine, defence correspondent for the *Sunday Times*, in writing about the creation of a Ministry of Defence, welcomed the demise of the Admiralty by declaring that the department had time and again stood opposed to the majority of the major technological changes that had transformed naval warfare since the nineteenth century.[73] Divine argued that it had taken maverick officers, pressures from politicians and industry and developments championed by other navies to force the Admiralty to engage with technological change over the previous century.[74] In effect, the Admiralty had held back the Royal Navy, rather than being its enlightened and forward-looking guardian.

The blame for the problems ascribed to the Admiralty by Divine undoubtedly deserved to be shared more widely. Conservatism was, to a large extent, forced on the Admiralty and Royal Navy by the Treasury and by politicians concerned by cost. The Director of Naval Construction in the post-war period describes in his memoirs how with the peace there was growing and unrelenting pressure, particularly from the Treasury, to cut costs.[75] Innovations in naval design were viewed with suspicion on the grounds of potential cost implications.[76] In an age of austerity the Treasury held the whip hand over other departments. The limited nature of the Admiralty's room for political manoeuvre was not always appreciated by the officers and men of the Royal Navy.

In the post-war period a number of reforms were introduced to address the division between the Admiralty and Royal Navy. The removal of the civilian secretaries to the Sea Lords, and their replacement with naval officers from the accountant branch, or men who had served as secretaries to flag officers, was seen as an important step forward. It created a buffer level between the civil servants and service chiefs through which the language, interests and values of the principal parties could pass and be translated into a form intelligible and acceptable to the other.[77] Allied to this, the post of Assistant Chief of the Naval Staff (ACNS), introduced during the First World War to deal with the expansion of military operations, was redefined to include supervision of the fighting efficiency of the fleet and to work closely with the controller of the Navy. The controller of the Navy, under whose office came the sections dealing with naval construction, naval engineering, scientific research, ordnance, mines and torpedoes, dockyards and everything else required to produce warships for the fleet, was second only to the First Sea Lord, in his ability to influence the direction and future of the Navy. The civil servants in those sections could remain in post for many years, while the naval officers appointed to work with them routinely rotated. Redefining the role of the ACNS gave the Navy, and in particular the First Sea Lord, greater leverage and influence over the sections of the Admiralty dealing with the material future of the fleet. In part, the change to the role of the ACNS was a reflection of concerns that the civil servants at the Admiralty were invariably slow to embrace technological developments (usually on the ground of cost or the slow pace of British bureaucracy). As one officer concluded, during the war the ships of the Royal Navy had proved deficient in a number of worrying respects.[78] Thus further reform at the Admiralty included disciplinary penalties on civil servants for unreasonable delay in progressing the papers (memoranda, proposals, reports) that were the lifeblood of any government department. One Sea Lord had found on his appointment in 1919 that papers could take months to proceed from one clerk, in one office to the clerk in the next.[79] Key issues could fall into administrative limbo as files proceeded on paperwork's equivalent of a grand tour of the Admiralty. The Edwardian period had demonstrated a quickening of the pace of technological change in naval warfare, and Jutland had demonstrated the outcomes in battle of one side's technological superiority over the other.

Beyond the Admiralty, First Lord of the Admiralty and the First Sea Lord, the Royal Navy had other means of applying pressure within Westminster. Even in retirement, former senior naval officers retained a good deal of authority and their opinions would be reported in the media or published in more extensive form. For example, Lord Jellicoe of Scapa, retired admiral of the fleet, used his volume on *The Crisis of the Naval War* published in the summer of 1920 to attack the Lloyd George Cabinet even though he was about to be appointed Governor General of New Zealand. Using the U-boat war to cite examples of where naval efficiency had been harmed by political meddling, he suggested that in the future the politicians should listen to the Royal Navy in their pursuit of economy:

> It would seem a matter of common sense that those who have not adopted the Navy as a profession should pay as much respect to the professional judgment of the naval officer as they would to that of the surgeon or the engineer or the lawyer, each in his own sphere. Governments are, of course, bound to be responsible for the policy of the country, and policy governs defence, but, both in peace and in war, I think it will be agreed that the work of governments in naval affairs should end at policy, and that the remainder should be left to the expert. That is the basis of real economy in association with efficiency, and victory in war goes to the nation which, under stress and strain, develops the highest efficiency in action.[80]

Jellicoe's message was not lost on the press in either the northern or southern hemispheres.[81]

After 1918 the House of Commons and House of Lords contained a number of distinguished and capable former naval officers ready to voice the concerns of the service on anything from the naval estimates through to relations with Japan. Connected by previous service and by social connections to senior figures in the Royal Navy, they remained interested and open to the Admiralty's view on the critical naval questions of the day.[82] In Unionist ranks sat men such as Rear Admiral Adair (Glasgow, Shettlestone), Commander Bellairs (Maidstone, Kent) and Commander Eyres-Monsell (Bolton). Among the Liberals sat equally distinguished former sailors such as Lieutenant-Commander Kenworthy (Hull) and Commander and Lieutenant Colonel Cecil L'Estrange Malone (East Leyton). In the Labour Party, Captain William Wedgwood Benn (Leith) had flown with the Royal Naval Air Service. Among the small number of independent MPs was Rear Admiral Sir Murray Sueter (Hertford), who won a by-election with 68.9 per cent of the vote in June 1921 on an 'Anti-Waste' ticket. A significant minority of MPs had served with the Royal Navy, and a similarly significant minority had served in other branches of the military. For example, Lieutenant Colonel William Wilfrid Ashley, the Conservative MP for Fylde, held an army rank, but equally he was one of the leading lights in the Navy League and a number of other pressure groups. Such MPs were not unsympathetic to the arguments of honourable and gallant members who had served with the Royal Navy. Beyond the ex-military MPs were a further tranche of members with vested interests in naval policy. Sir Clement Kinloch-Cooke and Viscountess Astor (respectively Unionist MPs for Plymouth Devonport, and Plymouth Sutton) were noteworthy members of this group. With much of the city's economy tied to the His Majesty's Royal Navy Dockyard Devonport, these constituency MPs took a very keen interest in all matters relating to the naval estimates.

The impact of this group of MPs after 1919 on naval and foreign policy is difficult to quantify. In no sense did it take its orders from the Admiralty, although Kenworthy had served in Whitehall during the war. Indeed, the naval lobby contained more than its fair share of people who had proved to be awkward square pegs in the neat round holes of the Royal Navy. Kenworthy in December 1917 had been part of the group of naval officers that had conspired to effect what Robert L. Davison has called the 'palace revolution', leading to Jellicoe's dismissal.[83] Sueter, who had played a leading role in the development of the Royal Naval Air Service, had been relieved of his command by their Lordships of the Admiralty in 1917 after writing to King George V. He considered that the battleship was rendered obsolete by the developments in airpower, and he considered the Admiralty a bastion of conservatism, bureaucracy and waste. His by-election victory was testament to the strength of public disquiet over high and growing levels of taxation, the apparent strength of the Anti-Waste political party founded by Lord Rothermere in 1921 and the growing unpopularity of high-spending government departments like the Admiralty. Cecil L'Estrange Malone sat at the other end of the political spectrum. Elected as a Coalition Liberal MP, Malone steadily drifted to the left, leading him into the Communist Party and a spell in gaol for appearing to advocate insurrection against the Crown. While Lloyd George could take little notice of Parliament, such was the scale of his majority after the 1918 khaki election, the unpredictability and volatility of men like Sueter, Malone and Kenworthy, and the fact that they did not see themselves as career politicians, ensured that their views were not unimportant. On occasion the naval lobby could provide useful supporting voices to those of the First Lord, the Admiralty and First Sea Lord.

With a voice in Cabinet, friends on the backbenches and the Admiralty as a bastion of expertise and authority in Whitehall, the Royal Navy after 1918 was effectively equipped to ensure that its needs and interests were adequately represented within the higher political circles of the British system of government. Most importantly of all, the Admiralty had important political and institutional weapons to meet the post-war challenge of a Treasury determined to get a grip of the post-war spending of all government departments. What was less apparent after 1918 was the extent to which the Royal Navy's political strength was being undermined by a sense of disappointment about the performance of the service during the war; a profound revulsion and rejection of war as an instrument of national policy; and the political and public priority to reduce government expenditure in the interests of national economy, reduced taxation and stable national finances.

5

The Need for Economy

The expansion of the Royal Navy in the nineteenth century had been underpinned by sound public finances and an economy transformed by the Industrial Revolution. The First World War saw a further and dramatic transformation of Britain's economic and financial position that was to have very negative effects on almost every aspect of government policy. As John Ramsden has recognized, the public finances, with high taxation, a massive national debt, industrial decline and stubbornly high unemployment sharply limited the Lloyd George government's scope for manoeuvre, and ability to deliver on the promises of 'homes fit for heroes' made during the coupon election of 1918.[1] In assessing naval policy in the period 1919–22, it is important to understand the profound financial and economic difficulties which the government was facing as a result of the war. It is also important to understand the international context, and domestic political contexts, which shaped and flowed from those difficulties. A set of economic relationships and political realities (taxpayers, workers, businesses, politicians, government and international relations) underpinned the connections at the heart of naval policy: a declining British economy, and disagreements about national strategy in the light of falling resources, made it difficult to respond to the technological and other challenges facing the Royal Navy.

The war had done enormous damage to the British economy, but it was the performance of the economy before the outbreak of hostilities that really conditioned the responses of policy makers to the nation's economic ills after 1918. As the Industrial Revolution had spread throughout Europe in the second half of the nineteenth century Britain had lost her dominance in manufactured goods. Powerful industrial rivals had emerged in the form of Germany and the United States, and, although on the outbreak of war Britain remained wealthy, she was slowly losing her market share of world trade in key manufacturing sectors. In 1880 Britain had accounted for 41.1 per cent of the world trade in manufactured goods. A decade later the figure stood at 40.7 per cent. During the

1890s the strength of German, American and other exporting rivals had forced the figure down to 32.5 per cent. In the last year of peace it fell still further to 29.9 per cent.[2] Within thirty-five years Britain's share of trade in world manufacturers had fallen by more than 25 per cent and the pace of decline appeared to be accelerating.

At the same time, the proportion of the gross national product (GNP) dependent on imports and exports was increasing. As Tim Rooth has calculated, in 1900 48.8 per cent of GNP was dependent on imports and exports: the figure had increased to 58.6 per cent by 1913.[3] The medium-term prognosis for the health of the economy of a small group of heavily populated islands did not look good in 1914. Britain had to export in order to pay her way in the world, and on the outbreak of war it looked as though that task was getting steadily harder. The U-boat campaign of 1917, when Britain's food stocks had fallen to just six weeks of essential needs, was a powerful reminder of the nation's vulnerability in the international economy. Any forward projection after 1918 of British economic performance based on pre-war GDP, and share of world trade figures, suggested the potential collapse of the British economy within a couple of generations. Thus after 1918, in addition to wrestling with the financial and economic fallout from the First World War, statespersons agonized over the long-term health and shape of the British economy.

What was also particularly problematic was that the war, and the peace settlement, had altered the international trading patterns which Britain needed to re-engage with, and to revive. War debts to the United States were a great burden on Britain, and it would take until 1923 to negotiate a settlement, but what was equally damaging to the British economy were the reparations payments imposed on Germany and the other defeated powers. For the purposes of trade, a strong British economy required a strong German economy. Economically enfeebled by the war, further weakened by the territorial clauses of the Treaty of Versailles, which took key industrial and agricultural areas away from Germany (albeit temporarily in the case of areas such as the Saar), the further requirement that the German government pay war reparations imposed a heavy burden on their economy. Political instability and threats from left and right created a lack of political, business and financial stability in Germany that culminated with hyper-inflation in 1922–23.

This had political consequences. British and French foreign policy diverged in 1919 at the Paris Peace Conference. Austen Chamberlain, Chancellor of the Exchequer in 1919, certainly believed in the idea that Germany would not be able to play her full part in the revival of the European economy as a result of reparations. A warning to that effect was delivered by John Maynard Keynes in his book *The Economic Consequences of the Peace*. In December 1919 Austen Chamberlain wrote to his sister to suggest that she buy the book as he found himself in agreement with Keynes's general conclusions and the bleak outlook it offered. In particular, he shared Keynes's concerns about Germany's ability to pay the level of reparations which had been imposed on her.[4]

From 1920 to 1922 the Lloyd George government tried to reach an accommodation with France that would pave the way for renegotiation of Germany's reparations debts, a revival of the Germany economy and stronger European trade to breathe life into the British economy. Such an agreement appeared tantalizingly close in early 1922, but ultimately it came to nothing, and with the fall of Lloyd George in October 1922 the Franco-British relationship fell apart. With Germany in the midst of hyper-inflation, professing herself unable to meet the schedule of reparation payments, the French occupied Germany's Ruhr industrial heartland with armed troops and proceeded to stay there until 1924. By mid-1923, with the French developing a powerful air arm, the British began to consider the consequences of a Franco-British war, and whether naval spending might need to be directed towards the Royal Air Force. Economic considerations could indeed cast long shadows over policy in strange and unexpected ways.

Economic considerations also affected the way in which the politicians viewed the Empire, the defence of which constituted the principal reason for a large Royal Navy. Britain's dependence on the Empire had been amply demonstrated during the war, and in the crisis of the U-boat campaign in 1917 the mother country had been willing to offer India and the Dominions significant political concessions, and greater freedoms, to ensure that the flow of aid was maximized. In the post-war period the policy makers had to make a difficult decision: Should free trade be abandoned in favour of protectionism which would turn the Empire into a powerful trading block? It might help to reverse the centrifugal forces that were pulling the Empire apart, and it would give British exporters a degree of security, but it would result in other countries replying in kind and shutting British manufacturers out of their markets. The choice and the dilemmas were never properly articulated to the electorate even in 1923 when a Conservative government went to the country with a protectionist manifesto. The outcome was a defeat for the Conservatives leaving the country to pursue a traditional role as a free-trading *laissez faire* economy with sterling returning to the gold standard in 1925 at the pre-war rate of $4.86 to the pound.[5] Within five years after the return to the gold standard, the possibility of an Empire economic policy, and tighter bonds between mother country and the dominions, had finally foundered on the repercussions of the Great Depression.

Beyond the medium- and long-term outlook for the British economy, the minds of politicians on economic and financial issues were concentrated by a short post-war boom followed by slump that had profound repercussions for the British economy, society and its politics. Between 1921 and 1922 the British economy suffered a dramatic contraction, with a range of economic indicators showing sharp downturn: the value of overseas trade fell (exports by 47.9 per cent and imports by 43.7 per cent); monthly production of pig-iron fell from 669,500 tons in 1920 to 217,600 tons in 1921; wage rates fell dramatically, wiping out three-quarters of the wartime increases.[6] By June 1921 the percentage of the insured population without a job had reached a post-war high of 17.8 per cent (2,171,288), and although it fell from this point, it still stood at 12.2 per cent in December 1922. The overall figure masked particular black spots on a regional and trade basis. Shipbuilding (36.1 per cent of insured persons) and iron and steel (36.7 per cent) were particularly badly affected as were shipbuilding districts (Scotland 21 per cent, Barrow-in-Furness 49 per cent, Jarrow 43 per cent).[7]

Signs of social strain were considerable. The formation of a National Unemployed Workers Union (NUWU) in 1921 by activists who made no secret of their communist leanings was one area of concern. Mass demonstrations in some of Britain's largest cities were another. The first of these took place in London in October 1920 when large numbers of unemployed men assembled in Whitehall to support a Labour deputation seeking an audience with the Prime Minister. Further demonstrations followed in London on 11 July and 4 October 1921, and similar protests were held in Dundee, Leicester, Cardiff and Bristol, and in cities particularly associated with the trades with the highest unemployment, namely Sheffield, Glasgow and Liverpool. Such protests could give rise to serious public disorder. For example, the demonstration in Liverpool on 13 September 1921 led to a riot involving a crowd of 5,000–6,000 people.[8] In the process the Walker Art Gallery was occupied as no hall was available for the speeches. Although none of the art was damaged, some of the buildings fixtures and fittings suffered and one hundred arrests were made.

The possibilities of relief through the placing of government orders, and the dangers that the slump might lead the working classes to turn their back on more moderate forms of socialism, were evident in some of the demonstrations. For example, on 12 September 1921 a Labour Party meeting at Woolwich Town Hall was broken up by bodies of men associated with the NUWU. During 1920 the situation became so bad in Woolwich Arsenal and the Dockyard that a movement to effect passive resistance to short-time working was formed.[9] Short hours turned to growing redundancies in due course. The September 1921 meeting had been called to develop practical proposals for the relief of the unemployed, and one of the ideas under discussion was calling on the government to place orders for munitions which could be produced at Woolwich Arsenal.[10] Protests at the level of unemployment took other forms. Prefiguring the Jarrow march of the 1930s in late 1922, a group of men walked all the way from Glasgow and other unemployment black spots arriving in London on 17 November 1922.[11] Concerns about the political nature of the protest were manifest in reports by *The Times*: 'The prevailing atmosphere was red: it appeared in the rosettes, in the banners, and in the legend on one banner showing a skull and crossbones and the words "Death better than starvation," … Many of the organizers held communistic views.'[12]

Unemployment created considerable costs for government, not least in terms of the cost of maintaining out-of-work labourers and their families. By the autumn of 1921 unemployment was the dominating issue in British politics.[13] In the face of the slump and growing unemployment, the government sought to cut expenditure to ensure that departments lived within their means. Falling unemployment meant falling tax revenue, generating the need for retrenchment in the public finances.

Within Parliament there was a considerable degree of consensus on Britain's financial and economic position in the post-war period. This consensus can be detected in speeches from the House of Commons to the House of Lords, from Secretaries to State to the humblest backbencher and from elder statespersons to the most recent arrivals in Parliament.

> Last year the quantity of our export trade was only 55 per cent of what it was before the war. The export trade of Germany was, I think about 25 per cent … The world is one trade unit … Trade is dependent on currency, the exchange and credit, and they are all broken down … Currency has gone adrift. It has broken from its moorings and is drifting helplessly.[14] David Lloyd George (Prime Minister)

> How is His Majesty's Government going either to restore the credit of the world or to make the labourers of all classes, brain workers, hand workers, or whoever they may be – the workers of the world – return to their pre-war rate of production? … We are struggling ourselves, struggling I am glad to say successfully, but not easily or lightly, with tremendous financial and productive problems of our own.[15] Arthur Balfour (Lord President of the Council)

> We have great economic and industrial disorganisation in this country. You have only merely to look at the papers to see a list of nearly 2,000,000 unemployed

> involving us in a cost of something like £2,000,000 per week. The whole country is groaning under a burden so heavy that it is materially diminishing our chance of recovery.[16] Lord Curzon (Foreign Secretary)

> If we cannot make our revenue pay our expenses what is the future of this country going to be? ... We have to bear a very heavy burden in this country for the cost of the war, but no one regrets that. It was the price of freedom; no one complains that it should be paid. But we have to bear a very heavy burden of expenditure owing to what has happened since the war ceased; and that to my mind is the price of folly.[17] Lord Buckmaster (Liberal Peer and Lord Chancellor 1915–16)

> The Prime Minister has said that we are the most heavily taxed nation in the world, and it seems to me that we have to pay taxes for all manner of things that happen throughout the whole of the civilised and uncivilised world. I protest, as a humble Member of this House, in the strongest possible manner ... I do not believe that British working men should pay a penny of this money. These ill-starred adventures, condemned in their initiation by the working classes of this country, should be opposed by every Member who believes in fair play for the British taxpayer.[18] (George Barker, Labour MP for Abertillery)

While Members of Parliament could identify the problems facing the nation, there was no overall agreement on how the challenges could be met, even in those domestic spheres more amenable to state action that the vagaries of international markets, or within the politics of the economic development of the Empire. The First World War had further eroded blind faith in *laissez faire*, as the shell scandal of 1915 and the performance of the Ministry of Munitions showed the need for and possibilities of state intervention.[19]

This consensus on the need to cut back, and the political pressure it constituted, exercised a subtle but strong and constant influence on naval policy. In its simplest expression, it increased the pressure to secure reductions in the yearly naval estimates. As Murray Sueter argued, 'For the two years since the Armistice ... we are spending an average of nearly 80 millions [on the Navy]. For what is this excessive expenditure. Whom are we going to fight.'[20] It certainly ensured a less-than-enthusiastic reception for any attempt to introduce supplementary naval estimates into the House of Commons for the purpose of naval construction programmes. Beyond this, the pressures for economy within the Admiralty and among senior naval ranks produced a range of responses ranging from grim acceptance to hostile resistance and thoughts of resignation.[21] Within the Admiralty the pressure to economise was debilitating, and it raised profound questions about the extent to which the leadership of the Royal Navy could accept the direction of the civilian government in making cuts below the levels which they considered necessary for the maritime security of Britain and the Empire. More than one admiral considered resignation in the face of the government's naval policy after August 1919.

One potential course to ameliorate the problem of public expenditure versus minimum security requirements manifested itself in a number of suggestions in Parliament about curbing British foreign and imperial policies to bring commitments and resources more into line. For example, some Members of Parliament were willing to call for the abandonment of most of Iraq, and concentration on the Basra vilayet, as a means of securing cuts in army expenditure. The escalating size of the national debt certainly played heavily on the mind of Robert Horne, the Chancellor of the Exchequer: 'The maximum figure reached by the dead weight National Debt of the country was on 31st December, 1919, when it amounted to the huge total of £7,998,000,000. By 31 March 1921, this figure had been reduced to £7,574,358,000. The corresponding figure on the 31 March 1922 was, as near as I can estimate it, £7,654,500,000.'[22]

Concerns about Britain's economic future, the levels of government spending and taxation found specific outlet in 1921 in the formation of an Anti-Waste League. The formation of the league was announced by the newspaper owner Lord Rothermere in *The Sunday Pictorial* in January 1921. Rothermere sincerely believed that the survival of the country was at stake if government expenditure was not reined in. He explained as follows:

> I wish to register my strong conviction that unless the world in general, and our own country in particular, grasps the true meaning of the ravages of the Great War, civilisation as we have known it cannot long survive. The Great War left the world immeasurably poorer, and its consequences have choked the channels of international trade and completely dislocated the international exchanges. We do not possess the wherewithal to begin a new and more spacious life. It will take all our energies and all our remaining resources to build up afresh what was best and most worth preserving in the old life which has gone. The fundamental economic factor is that even in pre-war days the world did not really produce sufficient for the needs of a very large proportion of its population. To-day production has undergone a great decline, and the situation is rendered worse because the world is unable to finance, distribute, and consume even its reduced production, and therefore the international movements of trade are slowing down towards a standstill. Starvation is an ugly word, but those nations which are industrial rather than agricultural are nearer starvation than appears upon the surface. We are primarily an industrial nation, and hardly any country in the world discloses a more perilous economic condition than that in which Great

> Britain now finds herself. If Labour realised the appalling dangers which are imminent, the word 'strike' would be erased from its vocabulary.
>
> We have drifted so near the point of economic collapse that even if the Government revise their policy of expenditure they may not now avert the risks which threaten us. Yet a beginning must be made somewhere, and after having devoted long and anxious thought and study to these tremendous problems I find myself still imbued with my original belief that the first step necessary for our economic salvation is a root-and-branch reduction of Government expenditure. If that is done, the rest may follow.[23]

In addition to stories in the press, especially *The Daily Mail*, the League contested by elections in order to put pressure on the Lloyd George government and to give it a voice in Parliament. The Anti-Waste League disbanded in 1922, but in the few short months of its existence, its presence was certainly felt in British political and naval circles. For example, Esmond Harmsworth (Rothermere's son) had been elected as Conservative MP for the Isle of Thanet in a by-election in 1919.[24] He was able to snipe at the government within Westminster, cooperating with independent MPs and independently minded Conservatives and Liberals. Following the end of Walter Long's tenure at the Admiralty in 1921, he was ennobled leading to a vacancy in his Westminster St George's seat. The Anti-Waste League contested the by-election securing its first MP in the form of James Erskine. A subsequent by-election at Hertford was won by Murray Sueter with the backing of Anti-Waste.[25] In some corners, as Adrian Bingham notes, the success of Anti-Waste at by-elections was seen as a reflection of the household concerns particularly of female voters, and evidence of a realignment of politics along gender lines, to go with the re-alignments taking place along the Socialism versus Anti-Socialism divide.[26]

As James Cronin identifies, Anti-Waste was perceived as dangerous by Lloyd George and other ministers because it provided a focus for wider concerns and agitation against the coalition.[27] It was the beneficiary of protest votes in by-elections and a rallying cry for dissident Conservatives. It was only following the 1922 budget that the Anti-Waste campaign really lost momentum. Thanks to the efforts of ministers, pushed by a Committee on National Expenditure headed by Sir Eric Geddes, and a follow-up committee headed by Churchill, government expenditure was trimmed from £1,136,000,000 in 1921 to £910,000,000 in 1922. This allowed the government to ease the burden of taxation with income tax cut from six shillings in the pound down to five, cuts in postal duty and taxes on tea.[28] With the end of the Coalition government in September–October 1922, and the opening up of clearblue water between the political parties, the

Anti-Waste activists joined the Conservatives in step behind the party leader Andrew Bonar Law.

The need for national economy was the dominating factor on the landscape of post-war politics. It influenced what government did and how it did it. It influenced the way in which individual politicians reacted to the politics of the moment. Winston Churchill was a particular case in point. As First Lord of the Admiralty before the First World War, he oversaw a large expansion in expenditure on the Navy. Out of office in the 1930s, he called for massive investment in naval armaments. But in office during the 1920s, especially as Chancellor of the Exchequer during the second Baldwin government, he was eager to reduce spending on the Royal Navy. Naval historians and Churchill's biographers have speculated on the apparent inconsistencies of view which could lead to such flipflopping on policy.[29] However, as Christopher M. Bell has demonstrated Churchill was entirely consistent in identifying what he considered to be the principal threat of the moment to the United Kingdom (national bankruptcy in the 1920s/aggression from Germany in the 1930s) and responding appropriately to the politics of the moment.[30]

In the financial circumstances prevailing after 1918, it was understandable that politicians would find it hard to sanction continued high levels of spending on the military. The public did not perceive any immediate danger of war, while the admirals and generals noted potential threats from the Pacific, to India, to the Near East, Turkey and North Africa. They also had to look to the medium and long term and the potential revival of tensions between the great powers. While the public and civil servants at the Treasury perceived a clear horizon, the military officers could see the potential for emergencies and brush-fire wars. They also understood the timescales involved in planning for war. With a capital ship taking four years to build, and probably a further year to work up to become fully effective, the Admiralty had to operate over a long timescale, and with a broader horizon than a Treasury and Cabinet, which focused on the latest economic and financial data and the next budget. It was tragic irony that neither party was wholly wrong or right in their approach, but effective government lies in building consensus and in planning for the longer term.

6

Washington, Tokyo and British Interests in the Pacific

Resolving the American and Japanese challenges to British naval power offered one very obvious means to address the issue of national economy and its contingent issues. If the threat to Britain's naval supremacy could be removed, ameliorated or negotiated away, then there was an opportunity to diminish the problems and knock on consequences, impacting through the set of connections involved in naval policy. At either end of the chain of connections lay the state of the economy and the international threat. If the scale of the threat could be aligned with the level of the economic resource base, or vice versa, then provision of resources (physical and human) through naval policy could be brought into equilibrium. In the circumstances of 1918 rebuilding the economy was a long-term project. Therefore, the Lloyd George government's best hope of resolving the naval crisis lay in some sort of treaty, arrangement or other diplomatic deal to remove the emerging threats from both Japan and the United States. That, however, was no easy matter.

As Andrew J. Williams, Alan P. Dobson and Donald J. Lisio, among others, have identified, the naval-building programme of 1916 with the goal of creating a two-ocean navy 'second to none' was one of a number of American challenges to Britain's world position, some of which predated the outbreak of war in 1914.[1] War debts to the United States, the growing threat to the British economy posed by American manufacture and trade, American opposition to Empire (especially in the case of the Irish independence movement and the desire to access markets and resources under imperial control) and American opposition to Britain's policy towards Asia (especially with regard to the Anglo-Japanese Alliance) raised complex questions about the future and security of Britain and her disparate Empire.[2] Within the British political and military elite, there were profound differences of opinion about how to respond. Donald Cameron Watt has identified clear groupings within the elite over policy towards the United States.[3] Old style imperialists, such as Lord Curzon, Foreign Secretary, regarded the United States as a challenger to Britain's pre-eminence in world affairs, to specific British interests and to the Empire in general. Americanophiles, of varying degrees, such as Winston Churchill, Minister of War, and Lord Lee of Fareham, First Lord of the Admiralty, considered that close relations with the United States were highly desirable. In the immediate post-war period many senior naval officers were firmly in the Americanophile camp such were the strong bonds of friendship that had been forged during the war between the Royal Navy and the US Navy. It was with some trepidation that Royal Navy officers had met their American counterparts for the first time in 1917 or 1918, but any tensions swiftly eased as senior officers of the US Navy proved genial and very eager to collaborate in the interests of defeating the Kaiser's High Seas Fleet.[4] The relationships which had emerged during the war were remarkably harmonious, effective and respectful. Combating the German submarine threat, and countering the threat from the Kaiser's High Seas Fleet, forged personal and professional relationships that were maintained into the peace.

Beyond the imperialists and the Americanophiles came the pragmatists who considered that a harmonious relationship with the United States, based on common interests, should be possible. This group was critically important. The views of the Americanophiles and imperialists were essentially fixed while those of the pragmatists fluctuated over time. Most importantly, during the immediate post-war period the views of many within this group became more negative. There was a sense that on a whole series of issues Britain and the United States were 'poles apart', and that American policy was in some senses hostile to British interests.

Equivalent kinds of fractures in opinion in the United States in 1919 were detected by Admiral Sir W.L. Grant. In 1915 Grant had been appointed Commander-in-Chief of the China Station. Later in the war he was appointed to the equivalent post covering North America and the West Indies. He was thus ideally qualified, on stepping down at the end of the war, to give Walter Long his thoughts on the developing political situation. In a letter of 25 February 1919 he described American public opinion as being divided along the lines of class and origin. The majority of the 'educated or wealthy classes' were described as being 'actively pro-British and as such actively endorses the British point of view as regards a predominant Navy'. The anti-British lobby in the United States was seen as predominantly of Irish and German extraction, while the majority of American voters were described as being 'not actively anti-British but blatantly pan-American' in their nationalist leanings.[5] Grant suggested that the British government should be careful not to antagonize majority opinion in the United

States and that many American politicians would probably be content to accept parity of naval arms with Britain.

The issues threatening to divide Britain and the United States were considerable. In part this was due to the personality and outlook of President Woodrow Wilson. A principled idealist, and an ardent internationalist, Wilson wished to change the world in ways directly threatening to British power and authority. The principle of self-determination, enshrined in Wilson's fourteen points of 1918, pointed at the heart of every European Empire made up of subject peoples. In his assessment of February 1919 Admiral Grant pointed to the president and Secretary of the Navy Josephus Daniels ('the pawn of the former') as key supporters of 'the large Navy idea'.[6] At the Paris Peace Conference Lloyd George had urged Woodrow Wilson to enter into discussions about limiting naval arms. When persuasion had failed, Lloyd George responded with threats that Britain might not be able to support the League of Nations unless an agreement was reached.[7] Wilson refused to be persuaded or browbeaten into talks with the result that during the second half of 1919 a diplomatic offensive was launched. It consisted of a special mission to the United States headed by Lord Grey, the former Liberal Foreign Secretary.[8]

Replacing the embassy of Lord Reading, Grey's mission lasted only from 13 August to 30 December 1919. Much to the surprise of the White House of Woodrow Wilson the announcement of the special embassy was made in the House of Commons without any prior signal to the State Department.[9] This led to a minor flurry of telegrams across the Atlantic. Grey arrived in Washington in the midst of the evolving battle to secure congressional ratification of the Treaty of Versailles by the two-thirds majority required by the American Constitution. It was a battle that President Wilson would ultimately lose, but on 9 September Lord Curzon in London wrote to Grey with a wide-ranging briefing on the current state of Anglo-American problems. The briefing contained an assurance that 'the strength of the British Navy next year will be based upon a standard of security that does not take account of the United States Navy as a possible enemy'.[10] It also expressed the hope of a longer-term working compromise between the British and the Americans on keeping their naval estimates in line so as to prevent a naval arms race. With the bitter fight over the Treaty of Versailles dominating political considerations in Washington, Grey found answers hard to come by, and on 25 November Curzon forwarded to Grey a personal request from Lloyd George to secure answers on American naval intentions as quickly as possible.[11] While Grey could provide facts and figures he could not provide any assurance about any changes to the 1916 building programme.

His suggestion was to secure reductions in the Navy estimates to encourage the Americans to do the same.[12] On 12 December Grey forwarded to Curzon more detailed figures on the American estimates and building programme.[13] By the end of the month the Grey mission had ended in failure. The hopes and good intentions of Grey yielded no results in a Washington beset by political crisis over the Treaty of Versailles. The papers of the mission demonstrate just how badly the British wanted to accommodate American opinion in the aftermath of the First World War. It was recognized that naval issues were a significant area of potential disagreement between the two powers. The Americanophiles wanted an understanding with Washington even if that meant a less-than-robust response to the threat to Britain's naval pre-eminence.

If Anglo-American relations were complex, then Anglo-Japanese relations were perhaps even more problematic. The Royal Navy had been integral to the development of that relationship over the previous fifty years. The growing self-sufficiency and ambition of the Japanese in their naval needs, which had become evident before 1914, was further enhanced during the First World War as the domestic steel, coal and shipbuilding industries expanded to fill the void left by European producers who had switched to meeting the war needs of their respective countries. In 1913 just five Japanese shipyards had the capabilities to produce steel vessels of 1,000 tons or more. By 1918 the figure had risen to forty-one.[14] This was a reflection of the fact that the First World War had provided a massive stimulus for Japanese industry. Foreign and domestic orders for Japanese firms increased massively, leading to major industrial expansion. A more prosperous economy meant increased tax receipts for the Japanese Treasury, and a greater willingness in the Japanese diet to support the ambitious construction plans of the admirals and Navy Ministry. American plans to create a navy second to none, made public in 1916, provided a powerful additional support to internal Japanese domestic arguments about the need for a large programme of naval construction. Thus in 1917 the politicians and diet were ready to support an 8:6 programme, and in the following year two battlecruisers were authorized to give effect to the full 8:8 programme desired by the Japanese Navy for the previous decade. Though impressive the Japanese programme paled in comparison with the American building programme of 1916. The Japanese government knew it, and there were genuine fears in Tokyo as to the purpose of the American military build-up. Try as they might the Japanese were in danger of being outbuilt by the Americans by a factor of up to 50 per cent.

In British circles, instead of seeing the Japanese programme of construction as being essentially defensive in nature, the development of the Japanese Navy was read in conjunction with the jingoistic pronouncements of politicians, military officers and sections of the national press. Japan made no secret of her imperial ambitions, and in some quarters there was a concern that those ambitions might not be limited to the Korean peninsula and to parts of Northern China. These suspicions formed a vital backdrop to the 1919 tour of Asia, the Far East and the Pacific by Admiral of the Fleet Lord Jellicoe.[15] Admiral of the Grand Fleet at Jutland in 1916, Jellicoe had been promoted to the post of First Sea Lord. Perceptions of a lack of vigour in dealing with the submarine threat in 1917 had led to his replacement in December of that year.[16] By marriage to Gwendoline Cayzer in 1902, and fraternal masonic ties to her father, the hero of Jutland was connected to shipping interests in Asia. Jellicoe's tour convinced him that following the conclusion of hostilities with Germany, there was a need for the Royal Navy to perform a strategic pivot to Asia to ensure the defence of the British Empire there. In his eyes, the Japanese represented a serious challenge to the security of the British Empire. However, before he arrived on the Canadian leg of his journey the Admiralty gave Jellicoe a stern rebuke for his suspicions of the Japanese, instructing him not to do anything which might inflame Canadian military opinion.[17] The Canadian naval staff had already come to the conclusion that Japan was a long-term threat to Canada, and Jellicoe (ignoring his instructions) was happy to confirm them in this view.[18] Thus in 1919 the Canadian government decided on the need to develop a larger naval force to preserve national interests especially in the Pacific.[19] Following Jellicoe's Asian tour the Admiralty did produce a memorandum anticipating the non-renewal of the alliance and suggesting that the Royal Navy would not be able to station sufficient naval forces in the Far East to overawe Japan. Some historians have perhaps been a little too quick to imply meaning to the Jellicoe mission and the October memorandum. As Ian Gow has put it, Jellicoe's suggestion meant that 'Japan ... had become the potential enemy in naval planning'.[20]

A close reading of Jellicoe's reports and papers shows that the Admiral was a good deal more circumspect in his approach to naval problems in the Far East than some have considered. In 1919 Jellicoe's mission was watched closely and interpreted (usually badly) in both American and imperial circles for what it might herald in terms of naval policy.[21] His four-volume report on the Australian leg of his tour contains some important caveats and qualifications on his approach to the problem. In volume IV he explained that all naval planning has to rely on the assumption of a potential enemy.[22] While he had considered Japan to be that possible enemy, on reflection he thought that omitting the US Navy from consideration had not been an entirely rational decision. Even if

Jellicoe had identified Japan as a possible enemy, it did not automatically follow that the Royal Navy had decided against the renewal of the alliance. Jellicoe had been instructed to keep his views to himself and the First Sea Lord, Admiral of the Fleet Wester Weymss wrote to Long to express his dissatisfaction with the report.[23] Perhaps more importantly the October memorandum was entitled the 'Naval Situation in the Far East'. Such a paper had to offer evaluations based on potential opponents in that region and, as a power with a global maritime reach, it did not automatically follow that an issue related to Asia and the Pacific would determine naval policy as a whole. The Royal Navy had to take a global view, not one based on the Asian theatre alone.

In developing post-war naval policy and foreign policy towards Japan and the United States, Britain's statespersons faced the difficulty of navigating a small labyrinth of agreements and obligations affecting the greater Pacific region. Maintaining the naval security of the British Isles and the Empire and pursuing British business interests in the Pacific region were obvious goals for policy makers. Those interests had been further extended as a result of the war. After 1918 the British Empire assumed mandates under the League of Nations to govern and develop former German colonies in the Pacific such as German Samoa and Nauru. Development of the military potential of the former German colonies was forbidden. Also prominent in the thinking of the policy makers were the requirements of the Anglo-Japanese Alliance which meant that Britain would have to come to Japan's assistance if she was engaged in a war with more than one power. Less prominent, but equally binding, were Britain's commitments to other powers in the region. Britain was under treaty obligation to come to Portugal's aid if her possessions in Timor and Macao were threatened. Under the Anglo-Chinese convention of 1846, Britain was required to defend the strategically important island of Chusan off the East coast of China and to restore it to Chinese sovereignty in the event of an attack. Britain had further obligations with regard to her policy towards Siam as a result of a joint Anglo-French Declaration of 1896, in which both powers agreed not to seek unique privileges or advantages in the country, or to move military forces into Siamese territory without the consent of the other party. Such agreements and obligations may not have loomed large in the thinking of politicians and admirals, but they very much mattered to the Foreign Office.[24] In developing policy towards the Pacific region, its principal powers and the question of Britain's naval power policy makers had to wrestle with the financial issues of the present, the technological and political issues of the future and diplomatic baggage that had accrued from the fourteenth century onwards.

If the diplomatic issues of the past featured in the thinking of British policy makers, then so did the potential problems of the future. The dangers posed to British naval power by the American and Japanese building programmes were considerable, but British statespersons recognized the potential dangers of growing antagonism between the two nations. The danger that this might lead to war was considered very real in the aftermath of the First World War. Politicians, naval strategists and diplomats speculated on the potential nature of any conflict arising in the Pacific and the outcomes for Britain and the Empire. The ultimate and best expression of these fears came in the form of a memorandum of October 1921 by Frank Ashton-Gwatkin, second secretary at the Foreign Office. Assigned to the Far Eastern desk at the Foreign Office on entering the diplomatic service in 1913, he married in Japan two years later. Deeply knowledgeable and fascinated by Japan, and with excellent writing skills and a powerful imagination, his memorandum summed up post-war fears about a Japanese–American conflict.[25] Arguing that the war would principally be a naval conflict in the waters of East Asia, the outcomes of a short war would be bad for Britain and the Empire:

> a) A very serious blow in China and in all Asia to the prestige of the white nations, not only the United States of America.
> b) The completing of the Japanese ring around the coasts of China and a decisive step towards Japan's ultimate domination of China.
> c) The bringing of the British and Japanese Empires into immediate neighbourhood of, and rivalry with, each other; Hong Kong and Singapore would be threatened, and our Australian dominions filled with dismay.
>
> A long war would be still more disastrous to us, for the following reasons:
>
> a) The ruin of two prosperous countries cannot in the long run advantage Great Britain or any other nation. It is an economic fallacy to think that we should be able to get any of our own back from the two nations who appeared to profit most from the European war.
> b) Our neutrality… would be increasingly difficult to maintain.
> c) The reaction of Asia, especially on China and India, would be a matter of increasing anxiety to Great Britain. The forces of nationalism and of anarchy would be developed to our disadvantage.
> d) An eventual victory of Japan would be a disaster to all the white races.
> e) Neither do we desire to see a crushing victory of the United States of America over Japan, with its effect on China and the elimination of Japan as a stable Asiatic country.[26]

The complexities and dangers inherent in the three-cornered relationship between Britain, Japan and the United States, and the issues at play in the naval and external policies of the three governments, were evident well beyond the confines of the British Foreign Office. Diplomatists, politicians and journalists in several countries put forward well-meaning contributions in the hope that the tensions and potential dangers could be alleviated. These ranged from the measured to the imaginative. The latter included the contribution of a radical Canadian Christian ex-Lieutenant Colonel under the title *The Destiny of Britain and America – With an Appendix Who Are the Japanese*. In 1920 he argued that the Japanese Samurai in fact were descended from one of the tribes of Israel and thus had more in common with the British and Americans that might be first supposed.[27] His biblically referenced narrative may have been bizarre but, like so many others to emerge in 1920 and 1921, it did contain interesting suggestions as to ways forward including the idea that the three principal naval powers of the Pacific should sign a collective agreement to stop the building of battleships.[28]

Such suggestions contributed to the whirl of ideas in 1919–20 as the British government considered its approach to renewal of the Anglo-Japanese alliance, and the issues related to it. In the consensus narrative that has emerged on the abrogation of the Anglo-Japanese naval alliance, there has perhaps been a tendency to overplay the post-1918 pro-American sympathies of the British in pondering future relations with Japan and the United States. The emergence of the special relationship after 1939 is perhaps partly responsible for this over-reading. While the Japanese had joined the war in 1914, the United States had not been so quick to join the conflict. Her businesses had profited nicely from neutrality, and in 1918 President Woodrow Wilson had sought significant influence in international affairs as part of the price of America's contribution to final victory. In 1915 Japan's presentation to China of twenty-one demands had been resented as an attempt to further weaken China's territorial integrity, while the attention of the European powers was turned elsewhere. Equally at issue in the post-war period were President Wilson's fourteen points of 1918. Dressed up as enlightened liberal principle, they still nevertheless threatened to rip up the British Empire and deprive the Royal Navy of the weapon of blockade by seeking self-determination and freedom of the seas. The failure of Congress to ratify the Treaty of Versailles, American attitudes towards the issue of Irish independence and the ambitious nature of the 1916 building programme were a matter of discussion not just in Westminster but 'in public places … in the streets … in the homes of all classes', as one Irish MP later described it.[29] For the British the First World War gave rise to issues with both Japan and the United States. The Admiralty had monitored with some alarm the unfolding of Japan's post-war building programme, with the Japanese Parliament seemingly ready to support a sustained capital ship building programme.[30] They viewed with perhaps even greater alarm the rapid development of the US Navy. On the diplomatic level the British government needed to come up with a deal to check the growing antagonisms between Britain, the United States and Japan. On the political level the Lloyd George government needed to come up with the means to appease the hard-pressed taxpayer. On a departmental level the Royal Navy needed a means to respond to the American–Japanese threat and the dangers of an ageing and unmodernized fleet.

7

Framing British Naval Policy

The set of challenges facing the maintenance of British power inevitably forced a series of reconsiderations of naval and foreign policy within the Admiralty and beyond. The connections inherent in naval policy would extend the debate on those challenges, and the issues emerging out of the Battle of Jutland, well beyond the confines of the Royal Navy and Westminster. Powered by a seemingly unceasing tide of comment and analysis on the war at sea, those issues continued to take shape long after the end of hostilities.[1] The controversy over Jutland would come to a head with the publication of Admiral Jellicoe's Official Dispatches on the Battle on 17 December 1920.[2] Comprising over 600 pages, the report would be eagerly scrutinized by the press and public: those interested in recent military history, and those more interested in deriving lessons for the future in terms of tactics, strategy and naval construction.[3] As Brian Ranft has pointed out, for Beatty it became an article of personal and professional faith that in 1916 Jellicoe had missed the chance to inflict a decisive defeat on Germany.[4] As First Sea Lord he pursued the controversy rather than accept the idea that battlefleets were no longer capable of Trafalgar or Tsushima style victories. The great victory had to have been lost, for to accept that the chance of it never existed would be to play into the hands of the advocates of the industrial war of attrition in which the Royal Navy was merely a facilitator of the decisive victory on land. In such a war smaller units would come to the fore and, instead of the clash of the battlefleets, the emphasis would be on trade protection, anti-submarine warfare and access denial. This was not the navy of Nelson, and Beatty was unwilling to overturn tradition and long-held thinking in the interest of a new strategy and a drastic realignment of the force structure of the Royal Navy. For Beatty in the post-war world, it was easier to maintain that Jutland was Jellicoe's failure rather than that of the service which he headed, or of a big fleet strategy potentially compromised by the changing nature and technologies of warfare. However, in framing British naval policy after 1918 additional forces were also at play. In the period 1919 to early 1921 their fluctuating and often erratic influences prevented the emergence of the kind of political/military consensus on which post-war naval policy could be built. That consensus required some sort of commonality of view on the future of British defence, a degree of certainty about the nation's finances and industrial future and the kind of political stability that had largely characterized Britain in the late nineteenth century. None of those factors were present in the 1919–21 period, resulting in degrees of turmoil within Whitehall and Westminster.

As the controversy over the Battle of Jutland developed after 1916, the imperative to cut government expenditure led to important and potentially far-reaching decisions. In late 1916 four admiral class battlecruisers had been laid down (HMS *Hood* at John Brown, HMS *Anson* at Armstrong, HMS *Howe* at Cammell Laird and HMS *Rodney* at Fairfield). In March 1917, with the U-boat campaign in full swing against Britain's sealines of communication, progress on the latter three had been stopped in order to prioritize merchant ship repair. While progress continued on HMS *Hood*, with the design specifications altered to take account of lessons learned from recent engagements, no further work took place on the other three ships and in February 1919 they were cancelled.[5] The decision made apparent sense in terms of public finance and naval policy. The three uncompleted battlecruisers were to a design now considered seriously dated. While HMS *Hood* was planned on that same design, she had been steadily modified during her construction and by February 1919 was substantially complete to the point that cancelling her would have made no financial sense. Nevertheless, the decision to cancel the three battlecruisers was not part of some carefully considered narrative on the future of Britain's defence: rather it was a rapid throwing of ballast to lighten the load on the national finances.

The decision to proceed with the construction of HMS *Hood* raised some additional issues for the Admiralty. Her modified design highlighted key questions about the future of the capital ship and whether the division between battleship (heavily armoured but slow) and battlecruiser (fast but lightly armoured) was now essentially redundant. An article in *The Naval Review*, taking its lead from a paper given by d'Eyncourt at the Institution of Naval Architects, on 24 March 1920 raised this question:

> What does the Hood as built represent? The weight of armour carried slightly exceeds that in the Queen Elizabeth, the main armament is the same but the speed is that of a battle cruiser. Although the description is clumsy, she can only be described as a battleship with the speed of a battle cruiser. We have, therefore, to consider whether the Hood represents a type of battleship which it is desirable to embody in future construction. The answer depends on the value of speed. If

the Hood is a battleship, as seems to be her correct designation, she should be compared with the Queen Elizabeth class rather than with R[oyal] Sovereigns.[6]

After 1918 the value and nature of the capital ship was under continuous review. In planning for the future, and developing a fleet and strategy to cope therewith, the Admiralty wanted time to consider the options and the state of naval power after the end of the First World War. As part of this process in October 1919 an internal Royal Navy Post-War Questions Committee, under the chairmanship of Vice Admiral Sir Richard Phillimore, began deliberating. The committee ranged widely in its inquiry, including consideration of the virtues of incorporating the Royal Naval Air Service into the Royal Air Force. The committee, guided by Eustace Tennyson d'Eynecourt, the Admiralty's Director of Construction, also examined detailed technical questions such as whether the German system of three propeller shafts was better than the system of four shafts which had been preferred by the British before 1914. The committee's most important findings, when it reported in March 1920, were that the capital ship remained the bedrock of naval power at sea, that the development of the mine, submarine and air-power had not seriously compromised the capital ship and that future designs of battlecruiser and battleship could incorporate features to further reduce the threat from these emerging technologies. Despite the prejudices of D'Eynecourt the committee supported the idea that the fast (but lightly armoured) battlecruiser and the slower (but more heavily armoured) battleship had very separate roles to play. The Director of Admiralty construction was very much in favour of a compromise design between the two forms.

No matter the opinions of the Admiralty and its Director of Naval Construction, within the officer corps of the Royal Navy the value of the capital ship, and the design of future battleships, remained under active debate. The principal forum for this debate was the pages of *The Naval Review*, where Royal Navy officers could publish opinion pieces anonymously. Launched in 1913 by a group of young naval officers *The Naval Review* sometimes ruffled the gold braid of senior officers, and in 1915 its publication had been stopped. Revived after the German Armistice, its pages from 1919 to 1921 featured impassioned assertions of the value of the big gun capital ship sitting alongside more measured analyses, and features on the submarine and airpower: 'As long as there is a sea to float upon, it is maintained that, by the power of the Capital Ship only, can a nation gain and hold that Command of the Sea which is vital to it.'[7] The consensus view was perhaps expressed by one un-named officer who reflected the following in 1920: 'the day of the battleship, as now conceived, is over, although as long as other nations compete in their production we shall have to do the same. She may take a generation to pass out of existence, but assuredly will become a thing of the past.'[8] In other words, within the officer corps of the Royal Navy there was a growing belief that the capital ship was obsolescent, but certainly not obsolete. In reality the prediction that the battleship might 'take a generation to pass out of existence' was to prove remarkably accurate, but during the interwar period, as Arthur Marder notes, the Admiralty would concentrate on the main battlefleet issues at the expense of anti-aircraft protection, convoying and the seemingly lesser issues of maritime defence.[9]

Despite the ongoing debate in the officer corps, the Admiralty, armed with the findings of the Post-War Questions Committee, felt ready to embark on a programme of reshaping the Royal Navy in the light of wartime lessons. The capital ship would be at the heart of the programme. The new construction would incorporate the lessons of Jutland in the material fabric of the service, allowing the Royal Navy to meet the challenges coming out of the American and Japanese building programmes. On 24 October 1919 the Admiralty produced a memorandum, signed by Long, on 'Naval Policy and Expenditure' which examined the threat posed by the Japanese and American building programmes.[10] It outlined two courses of action: either to consider building warships or to get the Americans to 'abandon or modify their 1916 programme'.[11] There was no call for a wider strategic reassessment of the strategic position of the British Empire in the Far East. The Royal Navy's emphasis, perhaps not surprisingly, was on ships. On 13 February 1920 the Admiralty circulated a memorandum to the Cabinet stating that parity with the US Navy (a 'one-power standard') was the minimum position which it was willing to accept. Demands for four ships to be laid down in 1920–21 and a further four in the following financial year were put forward by First Lord of the Admiralty, Walter Hulme Long. Long preceded his demands with a letter to Bonar Law, the leader of the Conservative Party, stressing concerns within the party at the coalition's apparent attitude towards the Royal Navy, and followed this up on 20 February with a letter expressing disappointments within the Admiralty that the Cabinet remained less than happy with the Naval Estimates for 1920–21.[12] Essentially Long was trying to exploit the political fault lines inherent in any coalition government in order to secure a new programme of building capital ships.

In presenting the Naval Estimates for 1920–21 (£84.5 million as opposed to £157.5 million on the 1919–20 estimates and supplementary appropriations), Long and the Admiralty went to some lengths to explain the difficulties that the Royal Navy was getting to grips with in the post-war world. Long commented:

> During the past year it has not been possible to frame a definite statement on Naval Policy owing to the changing situation, the necessity of keeping the fleet

> prepared for eventualities during the Armistice period, and the active operations imposed on the Navy in the Baltic. It is now possible to estimate more clearly and more closely the requirements of the future.[13]

Reflecting the outcomes of the Post-War Questions Committee, Long also commented on the capital ship controversy: 'In our opinion the capital ship remains the unit on which sea power is built up. So far from the late war having shown that the capital ship is doomed, it has on the contrary proved the necessity for that type.'[14] The presentation of the Naval Estimates for 1920–21 was intended to achieve two political objectives: first, to demonstrate that the Admiralty was a tightly run department, cutting down expenditure to an irreducible minimum, and second, to open the door to the building of new capital ships incorporating the lessons of Jutland. There was no question of a thorough strategic reassessment of Britain's position as a maritime nation in the light of political realities transformed by war. The battleship would remain because the strategy of the Trafalgar-style battle as the ultimate purpose of the navy remained central to thinking in the Royal Navy. That in turn counted in favour of a renewal of the Anglo-Japanese Alliance.

On the future of the alliance the Royal Navy's position in 1920 appeared to be supportive, at least in public. In June Beatty spoke at a dinner in London on the subject of Empire Naval Defence. His comments principally concerned dominion contributions to imperial naval security. When he touched upon the subject of the Anglo-Japanese Alliance his comments were noticeably diplomatic. He went out of his way to pay tribute to Japanese convoying in the Pacific during the First Word War and ascribed Japanese–American tensions to Japanese immigration into California. Finally he expressed the belief that it would be possible for 'two great countries' to find some arrangement.[15] Beatty's speech suggested ongoing Royal Navy support for the alliance.

However, the shifting balance between the Royal Navy, Imperial Japanese Navy and US Navy continued to force the evolution of Naval and Far Eastern Policy. One month after Beatty's speech, as the fruits of the American naval-building programme announced in 1916 began to arrive, Walter Hume Long warned the Cabinet that unless naval construction commenced in British yards the Royal Navy would be in 'a position of absolute and marked inferiority at sea by 1924'.[16] The Royal Navy faced the prospect of a naval-building race which the state of the public finances, in view of Britain's massive war debts, simply could not support. Interestingly, in 1920 through to early 1921 the naval lobby in Parliament drew little distinction between Japan and America: their principal concern was the threat to the Royal Navy's position as pre-eminent naval power. As Sir Clement Kinloch-Cooke, the MP for Plymouth (Devonport) put it, 'America and Japan … are building navies that can compare with ours. Both these countries have settled their programme for the next few years.'[17] While some members openly ruled out the thought of a future war between Britain and the United States, Sir Frederick Banbury (Unionist, City of London) voiced his suspicions of America: 'It is more likely that America is contemplating an attack upon Japan. That Japan is thinking about an attack upon America is unthinkable. If these are the facts, why is America suddenly going in for this large navy.'[18]

The prospect of Britain becoming the secondary power in terms of world navies was evident and a matter of concern in Parliament. However, for the Admiralty even the status of secondary naval power was under threat as a result of the relationship between the Royal Navy and private enterprise. As Hugh Lyon has demonstrated, in the late nineteenth century, with the transition from wood to iron and steel, the Royal Navy had turned to private shipbuilding yards and engineering companies to provide the ships, armament and machinery for the fleet.[19] The expertise of the Royal Dockyards lay in wood. To make good the leap to the new technologies, the Royal Navy turned to private enterprises that grew wealthy in the process (Table 7.1).

During the late nineteenth century this private–public partnership worked well. The Admiralty set the specifications and did the design of the hulls. The shipyards, engineering works and armaments firms found the means to give the Admiralty what it wanted in terms of the specifications, making a handsome profit in the process and with the opportunity to provide similar services to foreign navies such as the Japanese. In the good times up to and during the First World War, the partnership between Admiralty and the shipbuilding, engineering and armaments firms had worked well. The Admiralty got high-quality modern ships, without having to invest in the dockyard and other facilities necessary to produce them in the numbers, and at the speed, required by the British government.

After 1919, with the British government hesitant about naval building, the partnership between private enterprise and the Royal Navy suddenly became a serious potential problem. The main concern for the Royal Navy, highlighted by warnings from Sir Eustace H. Tennyson d'Eyncourt, Director of Naval Construction, lay at the deep structural level of Britain's naval shipbuilding capacity.[20] d'Eyncourt had done his apprenticeship as a naval architect with Armstrong Whitworth on the Tyne before moving to Fairfield Shipbuilding and Company on the Clyde. Holding the position of Director of Naval Construction from 1912 until returning to Armstrong Whitworth as a director in 1924,

Table 7.1 Major commercial sector firms involved in warship construction 1890-1914

Warship Producers before 1914
Armstrong Whitworth (Elswick and Walker)
Beardmore (Dalmuir)
John Brown (Clydebank)
Cammell Laird (Birkenhead)
Fairfield (Govan)
Palmers (Jarrow)
Scotts (Greenock)
Thames Iron Works (Blackwall)
Vickers and Sons & Maxim (Barrow-in-Furness)
Armour and Armament
Armstrong Whitworth
Ordnance: Armstrong (Elswick, Newcastle)
Armour and Forgings (Openshaw Works, Manchester)
Gun Mountings (Elswick Works)
Vickers
Ordnance River Don Works (Sheffield)
Armour and Forgings River Don Works
Gun Mountings Barrow
Beardmore
Ordnance Parkhead Works Glasgow
Armour and Forging Parkhead Works Glasgow
John Brown
Armour and Forgings Atlas Works Sheffield
Cammell Laird
Armour and Forgings: Grimethorp Works and Cyclops Works (Sheffield)

Note: Johnston, Ian, *Clydebank Battlecruisers: Forgotten Photographs from John Brown's Shipyard* (Barnsley: Seaforth, 2011), p. 10.

d'Eyncourt was acutely aware of the situation in Britain's shipyards and warship builders.[21] During the war most had concentrated on building smaller warships such as destroyers at the expense of constructing larger vessels. The building of battleships and battlecruisers had come to a virtual halt in 1916. At the end of 1920 the Admiralty, perhaps intentionally underplaying the ability of private yards to adapt to changing markets, advised the Cabinet that there were only four berths in the nation's shipyards now easily capable of the construction of the post-Jutland era of warships.[22] Even with investment in new berths (and some consideration was given to the lengthening of existing slips in the Royal Dockyards), the necessary skilled labour, armour plate and heavy-gun production facilities simply did not allow the building of more than four ships at a time.[23] For private enterprise firms involved with the armaments trade, peace and the promise that there would be no war for ten years was bad for business. In the free market, firms were not about to be sentimental in retaining facilities that cost money to maintain, and which might be redeveloped to make a profit in another line of business. In 1919 First Sea Lord Wester Weymss had presented a paper to the Admiralty on the need for the nationalization of armaments firms, but the Admiralty board tore it apart. One of the key parts of his paper pointed to the importance of the state 'keeping hold of the new warship building yards and suitable munition works, and refraining for the present from any precipitate action as to their disposal'.[24] One year later the scenario envisaged by Weymss was coming to pass as armaments and shipbuilding firms closed facility after facility.

The production of armour plate was a particular case in point. During the nineteenth century companies such as Vickers had developed special processes to produce plate armour for warships, beginning a metallurgical race between the steel producers of other countries as they competed to supply their navies with ever better protection. The processes to turn a steel ingot of around one hundred tons into armour plate were complex, involved and costly, as Bruce Taylor has amply detailed.[25] The high nickel and chromium content in armoured steel required high temperatures and repeated heating and working though hydraulic presses and rollers. Some especially hard steels might require three weeks in a furnace to ensure that sufficient carbon had been absorbed onto the face of the plate.

In the run up to the First World War, the production of steel, especially armour plate, became an extension of the competitive race between nations, and in 1905 the Vickers armour plate mill at Sheffield received a visit from Edward VII and Queen Alexandria so that the King could witness the processes for himself.[26] The war witnessed further research and development into the production of special process steel, but with the peace outside of Japan and the United States the market dried up. Merchant ships did not require armour plate, and with a market limited by a collapse in warship building, manufacturers had no incentive to maintain the facilities necessary for its production. Similar closures after 1918 of plant and production lines could be found in other areas of industry critical to the production of major warships.[27]

With a warship requiring fifteen to eighteen months of construction between keel-laying and launch, the decline in infrastructure constituted a serious long-term threat to the Royal Navy. On a best-case scenario with four ships being laid down in 1921–22 and a further four in 1922–23, the Royal Navy would cede its naval lead to the United States by the mid-1920s.[28] On a worst-case scenario with no ships being authorized in 1921–22, the Royal Navy would be pushed into third place by Japan by 1928. Given the relative states of the warship-building infrastructure in Britain, the United States and Japan, Beatty, d'Eyncourt and the Admiralty could see no way that the Royal Navy would ever be able to regain a lead in capital ships unless a renewal of capital shipbuilding could breathe new life into the partnership with private industry that had served the Royal Navy so well up until the end of the war. In 1919 d'Eyncourt wrote as follows:

> If the building of warships, gunmounting, etc should cease even for a few years, not only would all the skilled workmen accustomed to the higher class of work almost cease to exist, but the trained staffs, to some extent at the Dockyards, and completely at the Big Contractors, will be dispersed… Ship design is the only portion of our warship material which is completely worked out at the Admiralty.[29]

By 1920 the 'heavy gun, armour and gun mounting firms' were asking for a subsidy amounting to £500,000 per annum to keep their plant in existence. Beatty and d'Eyncourt simply did not contemplate the possibility that the public finances might rule out the ordering of any capital ships in 1921, 1922 and 1923. Beatty shared d'Eyncourt's concerns that any delay in placing orders for new construction was potentially 'disastrous to our chance of retaining our naval equality with the strongest Naval Power'.[30]

Within the warnings of Beatty and d'Eyncourt there was little concern about the overall impact on unemployment (beyond the loss of personnel with specialized trades). Warship building was a relatively small part of the shipbuilding market in 1919, although it was the most lucrative part of the trade. While overall unemployment in the immediate post-war period remained worryingly high, shipbuilding was in the midst of a boom. Driven by the need to replace merchant ship tonnage lost as a result of U-boat warfare, and the expectation of shipowners about a return to pre-war trade and profit levels, the shipyards were in the midst of a boom in 1919. *Lloyds Register of Shipping* in 1919 recorded that in the first quarter of 1919 the total amount of shipping under construction around the world stood at 7.75 million gross registered tons (mgrt), with 2.5 mgrt being built in Britain.[31] The previous record for world construction had stood at 3.5 mgrt in June 1913.[32] While the overall percentage of world tonnage under construction in British yards was falling, as other countries expanded their capacities, the yard owners in Britain could not see beyond their bulging order books. As Johnman and Murphy have noted, in the immediate post-war period John Brown's order books were bulging (including the construction of five liners) which filled the yard to capacity in 1919.[33] The order books for Farfield's (the best in thirty years) and Beardmore's (liners and refrigerated cargo ships) were similarly impressively full.

With yards elsewhere enjoying similar levels of demand, these were the best of times for British shipbuilding in the twentieth century. Beatty and d'Eyncourt in their warnings about warship building did not note it, but the real issue driving the decline of warship-building capacity was the buoyancy of merchant shipbuilding. The same companies that had built capital ships for the Royal Navy in the lead up to the First World War (John Brown, Fairfield, Beardmore's etc.) had no incentive, given the demand for merchant shipping, to allow specialist facilities to stand idle while turning away lucrative orders for new liners, refrigerated cargo vessels or other types of less sophisticated civilian vessel.

The building of merchant ships was a significantly less involved operation than the construction of warships. Ships tended to be simpler and smaller, and their design could be left to the yard instead of being overseen by the Department of Naval Construction. Likewise the process of contracting for new construction of merchant ships was rather easier than dealing with the Admiralty and Treasury. Lastly the workforce required to construct a merchant ship required a lower skill level than that required to build a new warship. Warships were, and remain, more complex in their systems and are generally designed to the higher set of engineering values necessary for some chance of survival in combat.[34] If yard owners in the early 1920s saw practical advantages in moving away from Admiralty building, then it also seems likely that the pre-war large margins on warship construction narrowed considerably as a result of pressure on the public purse. For example, John Brown's profit on the £6 million contract for the construction of HMS *Hood* (launched in 1918) was a mere £214,108.[35] It seems that between 1918 and 1921 the Royal Navy's reliance on a public–private partnership to supply its major warships was being undermined by market forces.

In addition to the infrastructure issues that were becoming apparent in 1919, within the Admiralty there was concern at the possibility that the Americans and Japanese might open up a significant technical lead over the Royal Navy and British shipyards. The defeat of the German High Seas Fleet had brought a number of technical windfalls into the Entente camp. As the First Lord of the Admiralty explained to the Cabinet in November 1920, the Royal Navy possessed only one ship (in the form of HMS *Hood*) which embodied what he called 'war experience'.[36] Post-war naval designs would incorporate some of the lessons of the First World War, and without a capital ship building programme British warship designers would not be able to capitalize. Without orders for British shipyards the Royal Navy could not stay at the cutting edge of warship design, and the long-term inadequacy of the infrastructure of warship building in Britain threatened the complete eclipse of her naval power. Beatty's concerns on the technical side certainly seem to have registered with Secretary of State for the Colonies Winston Churchill.[37] Without action and orders for capital ships the Royal Navy might in the medium term have to accept third power status in terms of the number of hulls and significant technical inferiority. In the longer term the Royal Navy might perhaps have to accept fleet parity with other European powers.

Ironically, the Japanese Navy immediately exacerbated the sense of crisis in Royal Navy circles. The placing of a large Japanese order for armour plate (7,600 tons) with the Vickers Company in December 1920 led to a sharp reaction on the part of the First Lord of the Admiralty.[38] The likelihood of an order being placed with Vickers had been signalled by the British Naval Attaché in Tokyo in October.[39] In his response to the development, Walter Long reminded the Cabinet that since August 1919 the Admiralty had been producing papers on post-war naval policy and construction without the government endorsing the service's professional opinion that it was necessary to start building battleships if a crisis in naval strength and capacity was to be avoided.[40] Instead, he advised the Cabinet that the maximum capital ship output per annum had fallen from four ships to three. He concluded that 'one of the main advantages that we have always possessed over other Naval powers, vizt., our ability to build quickly, is rapidly slipping away from us'.[41]

It is perhaps interesting that the order for armour plate was not looked upon in a more positive light. The order would at least mean the safeguarding of specialist facilities and British jobs. Armstrong was in the process of dismantling their Openshaw armour plant as Beatty noted in a memorandum dated 15 December: 'The armour plate plant had been dismantled. The only portion of the plant in use are the rolling mills which are being used to make railway material. The skilled workmen have been dispersed.'[42] Given the long history of British shipyards building vessels for the Imperial Japanese Navy, the order might have been taken as a signal that this export trade was about to undergo a renaissance. Indeed, reports of forthcoming foreign orders for warships continued to appear in the British press during 1920 and 1921.[43] However, the difficulties faced by Japanese shipyards were similar to those that challenged British warship manufacturers. By late 1920 the state of the economy meant that the Japanese government was eager not to place overseas orders. In any case they considered that Japanese yards could 'build men-of-war cheaper than they could buy abroad', and that private yards faced closure unless further orders were forthcoming.[44] The Japanese, like the British, were out to safeguard their shipbuilding industry.

In late 1920 the British had other specialist naval expertise that the Japanese wished to access. In September the Japanese government extended an invitation to the British to send a training mission of naval aviators to the Imperial Japanese Navy to teach the special skills involved in flying over sea.[45] The British ambassador in Tokyo Sir Charles Eliot endorsed the request on the grounds that it would be good in diplomatic terms and potentially good in terms of business relations between the two countries. With the future of the alliance under discussion, the Royal Navy demurred to provide the mission which would involve imparting 'our specially acquired knowledge without reservation'.[46] The Japanese ambassador was informed that such were the demands on the service that it would not be possible to dispatch an official British military mission. Instead, a civilian mission was offered and dispatched the following year under Sir William Francis Forbes-Semphill, who had previously flown with the Royal Navy Air Service.[47] The Semphill mission did nothing to ease American concerns over the development of Japanese military capabilities, or their suspicion of the Anglo-Japanese Alliance. The extent to which it did make a material contribution to the development of the Japanese naval air arm is open to speculation, but one keen observer of the Japanese scene in the 1920s later commented that the mission 'laid the foundations' for the emergence of a powerful Japanese air arm.[48]

Japanese actions in late 1920 suggested no slackening of the pace of their naval programme. Indeed, on 22 December the British Ambassador in Tokyo telegraphed London with details of Naval Estimates for 1921–22 showing increased expenditure on the Imperial Japanese Navy.[49] Signals meanwhile coming from the United States suggested some possibility of change in terms of American ambitions and intentions. The presidential election in November1920 resulted in a political hiatus as politics took precedence over policy. That hiatus continued until the reassembly of Congress on 4 December and the inauguration of Republican President Warren G. Harding on 4 March 1921. The election of Harding marked a decisive rejection by the American electorate of Wilsonian internationalism and the activist model of presidency which he had pursued during his administration.

Harding stood for a *laissez faire* approach towards the American economy, small government generally and the avoidance of foreign entanglements: they combined to place a large question mark over the future of the 1916 building programme. The best guess of the British naval attaché in November 1920, picking up on Harding's electoral promises of 'economy in armaments', was that the United States would proceed to complete the 1916 building programme but thereafter cut the naval budget back to a minimum.[50] It would take time to determine precisely what the naval policy of the new administration would constitute, and in the meantime the Admiralty had to assume a worst-case scenario in terms of the 1916 programme, as had the Naval attaché in Washington.

Despite the naval challenges posed by the United States and Japan, and the urgings of Long, the Cabinet were reluctant to take the decision in late 1920 to fund a substantial programme of capital ship construction. To enlist dominion support in maintaining British sea power, and perhaps to seek support from dominion governments in putting pressure on the Cabinet, on 3 December 1920 the Admiralty issued a paper entitled 'Empire Naval Policy and Co-operation'.[51] While stressing that the Royal Navy had 'neither lost sight of the existing Anglo-Japanese Alliance, or of the common obligations imposed on members of the League of Nations to effect a general reduction in armaments', the paper suggested that it was necessary to take practical steps in the interests of the naval defence of the Empire.[52] Reviewing the strategic situation, it laid bare the Royal Navy's difficulties in meeting the challenge of maintaining a one-power standard. It suggested that 'the worst situation with which the British Empire could be faced, from a naval point of view' would involve Japan seizing 'the opportunity of aggressive action in the Pacific at a time when the situation at home was threatened from another quarter'.[53] Although this situation was dismissed as 'improbable', the paper nevertheless defined the need for Empire naval forces capable of providing a fleet 'superior to that of any power or reasonable combination of Powers'.[54] While suggesting the need for the dominions to invest in their own naval defence, and to support the development of a network of naval bases and fuel reserves to support global operations by the Royal Navy, the paper did reassure its readers in the colonies that assistance from the main British Fleet could be expected to arrive within 'six weeks or at the most two months' after the outbreak of hostilities.

The paper was further evidence of the extent to which the state of the public purse was impinging on every aspect of post-war policy, but faced with the seriousness of the issues relating to naval defence, the government needed to do something, or at least to appear to be doing something. Its response, ignoring the earlier work and findings of the Post-War Questions Committee, was to set up a 'Sub-committee of the Committee of Imperial Defence [CID] on the question of the Capital Ship in the Navy' to investigate the extent to which the primacy of the capital ship had been challenged by technological developments in the field of naval warfare.[55] Interestingly, before this took place, in late 1920 the Admiralty considered revisiting the capital ship question using senior flag officers whose opinions might carry more weight than the naval officers of the Post-War Questions Committee.[56] It would, however, be left to the politicians on the Sub-Committee of the CID to hear the evidence of naval experts and come to their own conclusions. The sub-committee started its deliberations on 14 December 1920 and was chaired by Bonar Law.[57] Winston Churchill (Secretary of State for Air) and Eric Geddes (Minister of Transport) – both former First Lords of the Admiralty – together with Robert Horne (President of the Board of Trade) also sat on the Committee along with Walter Long (First Lord of the Admiralty) and Admiral Beatty (First Sea Lord). Illness would prevent Long from attending most of the sessions, leaving Beatty to fight the Admiralty's corner.[58]

In the week before the sub-committee commenced its investigation *The Times* ran a series of articles by Rear Admiral Sydney Stuart Hall which ensured that the debate on the future of the capital ship was held at the public level, as opposed to the narrowly governmental.[59] Hall had retired from the Royal Navy in September 1914 after a career of almost nineteen years as an officer in surface ships, submarines and in the Admiralty. In launching the series *The Times* commented, 'The most important subject now before the country is the question of the naval construction policy of the Admiralty. An invincible navy is the very life of the nation.'[60] Hall's articles, as *The Times* described, 'frankly and forcibly' expressed the 'misgivings of those who believe that security is no longer to be found in a bulwark of capital ships'.[61] The arguments put forward by Hall, and like-minded protagonists such as Sir Percy Scott, were further considered in the regional press during the winter of 1920–21.[62] This was evidence of the extent to which naval policy, through its cost, had become a political issue well beyond the dockyard towns, the shipbuilding centres and principal manning depot ports of the Royal Navy. It was made particularly evident in one report by a Dundee newspaper written in response to the emerging debate and HMS *Hood*'s sailing from John Brown's yard for Rosyth on 9 January 1920 to complete the process of fitting out. *The [Dundee] Courier and Argus* asked the following questions under the title 'Future of the Big Battleship':

> Does the completion of HMS *Hood*, the world's largest battleship herald the final tapping of the pockets of John Citizen for the wherewithal to construct

> super Dreadnoughts? Of the thousands who recently watched the leviathan glide majestically down the Clyde, how many, we wonder, realised that they had contributed to build the monster; that £6,025,000 of their money had been expended on what might have been the greatest acquisition to our Fleet had not the aeroplane now rendered it and its kin ludicrously vulnerable.[63]

Twelve months later media and public opinion remained acutely sensitive to the cost of battleship construction. 'Must we build battleships', asked an editorial in the *Yorkshire Evening Post* on 7 December 1920.[64]

The arguments for and against the capital ship were further examined by the Bonar Law Committee as it received memoranda from interested parties and interviewed a range of experts.[65] Beatty kept Long informed by letter about the developments.[66] The Admiralty's response to the concerns of Hall and those other opponents of the capital ship who testified before the sub-committee came in the form of a memorandum by Beatty which, after careful review, concluded this: 'We are still at a period in the world's history when all defensive, and a majority of offensive operations at sea can be carried out more efficiently by surface vessels than by submarines or aircraft. These conditions will certainly remain the same for the normal life of the ships for which the Admiralty are now asking the sanction of the Government.'[67] Undoubtedly, Beatty's belief in the capital ship was shared by most professional naval officers. Certainly, there were very few strategists prepared to believe that sea power had been fundamentally compromised by the new technologies. Even those prominent naval thinkers such as Raoul Castex and Admiral Sir Herbert Richmond, who reflected very fully on the experience of the First World War, were ready to believe that navies would simply absorb the new technologies into their existing line of battle, with the mine and torpedo becoming just another weapon in the arsenal.[68] If sea power remained supreme, then so did the capital ship. By early 1921, as Long prepared to step down from the Admiralty, the Royal Navy was convinced that it had made a solid case for the capital ship. Beyond the committee that case had also been made in public by various advocates of the naval cause, so much so that in January 1921 Sir Percy Scott felt moved to defend himself in a letter to the *London Evening Standard*. He complained:

> I know the trick the Admiralty are going to try to play on the country. They are going to say they have taken the opinion of all the higher ranks of officers in the Royal Navy, and that they are unanimous in their opinion that battleships should be built … At the present moment we have Beatty on the quarter deck of his battleship Popularity. He sounds the bugle call, and every naval officer rallies round him, and very properly they say: 'We will rot the Government that dares

> to take away from use the bread by which we live. Who is this horrible Percy Scott?' Oh poor me, poor me. But I am a Christian, and I will bear my cross. In this country the bureau of common sense is not closed to every one.[69]

Scott's sensitivity was powerful testimony of the public pressure which the naval lobby were able to bring to bear when it came to critical issues such as the future of the capital ship, but unfortunately, the political currents were still flowing against the Royal Navy in its pursuit of a naval-building programme. While Churchill, for example, was ready to envision a naval construction programme involving the laying down four capital ships a year for the next four or five years, others were less convinced. Roskill's conclusion in *Churchill & the Admirals* (1977) that, in the circumstances of the day, such a programme amounted to 'fiscal lunacy' would undoubtedly have found wide support if they had been known about outside of the Cabinet and Admiralty.[70] The Harmsworth press were continuing to lambast the government over its failure to rein back public expenditure. On 4 January the Cabinet Finance Committee had sent a minute to the Admiralty asking for the Naval Estimates for 1921–22 not to exceed £60 million. This was in reply to the Admiralty's sketch estimates presented in November/December 1920 of £97 million. The Finance Committee's request was supported by Lord Rothermere, who used the pages of *The Sunday Pictorial* to publish an attack on 'The Folly of the Big Battleship':

> Already there is ample evidence that most senior naval officers will struggle for the retention of the capital ship to their last gasp. They believe in it, just as some of their predecessors believed in sticks and strings instead of steam, in muzzle-loading guns instead of breech-loaders, in wooden ships instead of steel ships, in tank boilers instead of watertubes, in coal instead of oil, and in paint instead of gunnery. A very serious and grave conflict is impending in this matter. The whole weight of our armour-plate and naval construction interests will be thrown into the scale in favour of the capital ship. Yet the fight must be fought out, and in public, not behind the scenes. The agitation for more big battleships is not only the very worst form of squandermania, but from the naval and the political point of view approaches lunacy.
>
> I urge:
>
> (1) That we cannot afford to spend any money on naval construction at present.
>
> (2) That the next five years should be devoted to experimental research, and that meanwhile our existing naval resources, which might be greatly reduced in strength, are far more than adequate for our prospective needs.
>
> (3) That we should build no more battleships, because they are obsolete.

(4) That the United States and Japan are hurriedly building battleships for reasons of their own, and that their decision to pursue antiquated forms of warfare is no proof that the capital ship will survive.
(5) hat we need not be influenced by the example of the United States and Japan, whose interests do not conflict with ours.
(6) That even if the need arose, and if we had the ships, [we] could not operate with battle fleets on the other side of the Atlantic, still less in the Pacific.
(7) That the future of naval warfare lies in the development of submersibles, submarines both for the narrow and the open seas, skimmers/ naval aircraft, the improvement of the torpedo, the use of mines, provision against aerial attack, and the elaboration of harbour defences.
(8) That no nation is going to enjoy naval supremacy any more. This is a nasty pill, but we must swallow it.[71]

Rothermere's attack revealed the extent to which he was aware of the deliberations of the Bonar Law Committee and the debate taking place within government. It was also significant that the newspaper baron understood that the 'armour-plate and naval construction interests' were making significant contributions to the debate about the future of the capital ship. The potency of Rothermere's intervention was increased by the victory of an independent candidate, campaigning on a manifesto of 'ruthless economy'; in the Dover by-election in 12 January.[72] Sensing an opportunity, Harmsworth launched the Anti-Waste League, which would continue to try and harry the government over public expenditure. Rothermere's intervention and the events of mid-January 1921 meant that the capital ship had suddenly become a bone of political contention between the forces on the right of British politics, and within and without the government. As the Conservative Party was struggling to define its post-war identity in terms of its attitudes towards socialism and liberalism, and the continuation or abandonment of the coalition, various factions of the party were vying for the soul of the party from imperialists to navalists, anti-socialists to the industrial and financial lobbies. The battle would not be swiftly concluded.

In response to the Cabinet Finance Committee's urging to cut the naval estimates back to £60 million, on 25 January the Admiralty replied that, after very careful consideration, £85.5 million would be needed to meet minimum requirements.[73] Various possible proposals were put forward as a means of affecting further economies. Some of these were advanced because Long was aware that they would be politically unacceptable. The withdrawal of the South American squadron was firmly opposed by Curzon, the Foreign Secretary. The closure of Pembroke Dockyard could be guaranteed to cause Lloyd George political difficulties in one of the heartlands of liberalism. Cutting workforces in the royal dockyards by 25 per cent would affect a range of predominantly Conservative-held constituencies in cities such as Plymouth and Portsmouth and outrage the naval lobby in Parliament.

For his part, Rothermere considered the requirements of the Admiralty were hopelessly exorbitant. In a column in *The Sunday Pictorial* on 20 February he explained his opinion to his readers: 'In the same year, when the German High Sea Fleet was not at the bottom of the sea, we spent 48,000,000 on the Royal Navy. In my view 35,000,000 should now suffice for our naval protection.'[74] In his calculations Rothermere was ignoring wartime inflation, the post-1918 expansion of the British Empire and continuing instability around the globe which required forward deployment of forces in places such as the Black Sea and Eastern Mediterranean to meet potential threats arising from the revival of Turkish nationalism. To Rothermere's readers such caveats did not matter. Taxation was too high, and the government appeared to be wasting money. It was a potentially potent message especially to the middle classes, the wider electorate and key sections of the Conservative Party.

In putting forward politically awkward propositions such as the closure of the Pembroke Dockyard, along with a demand for naval estimates totalling £85.5 million, Long was undoubtedly playing Whitehall politics and political games within the Conservative Party and the Lloyd George coalition. But if Long was prepared to play politics, then so too were his Conservative counterparts on the capital ship sub-committee. In February 1921 Bonar Law, Horne and Geddes professed themselves unconvinced either way by the case for or against the capital ship. On that basis there was no clear case for an immediate programme of capital ship construction.[75] With Long's intransigence over further reductions to the naval estimates, there was a strong sense of 'tit for tat' internal politics at play within the government. However, the cricketing metaphor of 'kicking the ball into the long grass' was probably a more accurate representation of events. With concerns mounting over Rothermere's campaign, and the sudden threat of Anti-Waste candidates winning at by-elections, Bonar Law (as Conservative Party leader) together with Geddes and Horne wanted to delay a politically awkward decision on government expenditure. The opinion of three members of the capital ship committee, that the case had not been proven, created a political stalemate that would result in delay.

Beatty was both amazed and angry. He wrote to his wife saying, 'Bonar Law has cooked the report of the sub-committee to meet with political requirements.'[76] Within the Admiralty, there was further concern at the Bonar

Law group's understanding of the maritime security requirements of the Empire which underpinned their approach towards the enquiry. Their conclusion that on projections of naval strength by the middle years of the decade the Royal Navy and US Navies would fight each other to a standstill in the event of a war was ridiculed in the Admiralty. On the Admiralty's draft copy of the report in the National Archives, some unknown hand has commented that the stalemate 'wd. not prevent US from seizing West Indies & invading Canada'.[77]

Beatty, Long and Churchill wrote dissenting commentaries on the report, with the result that the outcome of the sub-committee was inconclusive either way.[78] Roskill has argued that, in writing his dissenting opinion, Long was effectively cajoled along by Beatty.[79] That is probably putting the case rather too strongly. Long had fought his departmental corner with considerable determination since his appointment and was not about to end his ministerial career on a low note. Either way with political stalemate the Royal Navy looked to the new First Lord of the Admiralty to finally secure agreement in Cabinet for the four battlecruisers to be built.

The Royal Navy were not the only ones expecting the new Secretary of State to secure orders for capital ships. The post-war boom in the shipbuilding industry collapsed during the winter of 1920–21. The expectations of the shipping companies had proved unfounded that it would be business as usual after the First World War in terms of freight rates and profits. As Johnman and Murphy have demonstrated, the price of building merchant ships in Britain escalated dramatically in 1920 as yard owners tried to exploit market conditions.[80] The result was a sudden drying up of new orders, and the cancellation of ships already contracted. By April 1921, *Lloyds Register of Shipping* reported that orders for 850,000 tons had been 'suspended or cancelled'.[81] A programme of construction for new capital ships could suddenly not come soon enough for yards whose order books in the spring of 1921 were getting suddenly and dramatically thinner. Given the lead times for ship construction ruin was a medium term rather than an immediate threat. Cammell Laird's profits declined from £303,005 in 1919 to £260,632 in 1920 and £170,487 in 1921.[82] With the drying up of orders came an increase in joblessness and rising poverty in those areas dependent on the trade. That in turn had a major impact on a Scottish economy suffering multiple assaults from the impact of prohibition in the United States on the whiskey trade, competition from the Antipodean colonies in the supply of wool and mutton and falling demand for fish from a wartime highpoint. As Tom Steel has noted, the heartland of post-war Scottish industry could be found around the River Clyde and its shipbuilding yards. Shipbuilding and its allied trade employed tens of thousands of workers, leaving Scottish industry as a whole highly exposed to the market forces in this one branch of engineering. In the early 1920s those market forces were very much in evidence as bust followed boom.[83]

By the end of the winter of 1920–21 British naval policy for the post-war period had still not taken any definite shape. The financial, industrial, political and strategic landscape had not stabilized after the upheavals of the First World War. This was not really the fault of the politicians. After the first major industrial war, the extent of the wartime dislocations and disruptions was beyond the comprehension of the society that had lived through it. Moreover, the First World War had not come to a neat end at 11 am on 11 November 1918. The collapse of the German and Russian Empires gave rise to a series of conflicts, and a network of potential flashpoints, from the Baltic to the frontiers of British India. British forces, including the Royal Navy, were caught up in these aftershocks from European waters to the Black Sea and the Caspian. It was all very well to impose the ten-year rule in late 1919, and expect major reductions in the naval estimates, but the realities of 'wars and rumours of war' required preparedness and the commitment of resources. However, the political realities of Eastern Europe, the Near East and Central Asia ran up sharply against the political realities of a war-weary Britain. The 'war to end all wars' had been fought to a successful conclusion by the forces of the entente powers: at least that is what the British electorate had been told in the coupon election of 1918. The complexities of the post-war period did not permit such easy catchphrase summation by the politicians. The British public did not have a realistic sense of the dangers of the post-war world, and the politicians saw no reason to try and educate them. Thus there was an increasing gulf between those required to furnish, via taxation, the means of military preparedness and those who might be required to fight against the forces of resurgent Turkish nationalism, an expansion of Bolshevik power or the repercussions of revolution in Germany. That gulf was the fault of the politicians who preferred to pay lip service to the ideals of the League of Nations and to defence through collective security.

8

Lee of Fareham's May Memorandum

As Lord Lee of Fareham took over as First Lord of the Admiralty on 18 February 1921, he was acutely aware of the need to make progress on the issue of naval policy. Already in January the Admiralty had produced a study of the possible effects of a war with either Japan or the United States, and in both cases it was clear that the effects would be considerable.[1] A war with the United States would be very unpopular across the Empire, and the Admiralty concluded that if war did break out, it would be in Britain's interests to conclude it as quickly as possible. Such considerations added to the urgency of the situation which confronted Lee of Fareham as he took office in February. In many respects a marginal figure in British politics, Lee of Fareham has not excited the interests of biographers or the writers of political history beyond Alan Clark's 1974 publication of an edited volume of Arthur Lee's papers and Ruth Lee's diary.[2] His time as First Lord of the Admiralty was relatively short, and also relatively short of drama, but in terms of the evolution of British Naval Policy in the interwar period, it was pivotal. For two years after 1918 Walter Long had tried and had largely failed to establish the lines of policy for the post-war Royal Navy. What strategy was it to pursue? How was it to deal with the challenges facing British naval power from the building programmes of the United States and Japan through to the Cabinet's unwillingness to fund a capital ship building programme to modernize the main battlefleet. Would a successful resolution of one of the issues break the chain of connected problems preventing the development of a rational and effective post-war naval policy?

Soon after his appointment in late February, Lee of Fareham wrote to Lloyd George to suggest that it was time to open direct discussions with the United States on the issue of naval arms.[3] While Lee of Fareham wished to avoid competition with the United States and Japan, he had concerns that Beatty was busy talking to the press behind the scenes as a means to lobby for a new programme of capital ship building.[4] Talk of such a programme might exacerbate tensions between the major naval powers, and Lee of Fareham knew the political realities that the

Cabinet were not about to approve expenditure on major programmes. Lee was convinced that there would have to be a diplomatic resolution to the challenge to the Royal Navy's pre-eminence. Without the danger of a naval arms race that Britain stood no chance of winning, the Cabinet might be willing to approve a limited programme of capital ship building in order to modernize the fleet.

A decisive influence on Lee of Fareham's thinking appears to have been developments in the United States. During late 1920 Senator William E. Borah of Idaho had developed the idea of an international conference on armaments. On 24 February 1921 he had proposed an amendment to the Navy Bill proposing that

> The President is authorized and requested to invite the Governments of Great Britain and Japan to send representatives to a conference which shall be charged with the duty of promptly entering into an understanding or agreement by which the naval building program of each of said Governments, to wit, the United States, Great Britain, land Japan, shall be substantially reduced during the next five years to such an extent and such terms as may be agreed upon, which understanding or agreement is to be reported to the respective Governments for approval.[5]

Washington watchers hoping to discern the naval policy of the new Harding administration could not have helped but notice the reference to naval arms in his inauguration address given just over a week later: 'We are ready to associate ourselves with the nations of the world, great and small, for conference, for counsel; to seek the expressed views of world opinion; to recommend a way to approximate disarmament and relieve the crushing burdens of military and naval establishments.'[6] Quite apart from the financial cost of the 1916 building programme, by 1921 the vulnerability of battleships to aerial attack was being debated in the United States just as it was in Great Britain. Aircraft carriers, rather than battleships, perhaps represented a better long-term investment in American naval power for the taxpayer. To Americanophiles such as Lee of Fareham the comments in Harding's inaugural address represented a potential crystallization of concerns over the 1916 programme at the political level in the United States, and a potential diplomatic opportunity.

A further set of signs may have come with the arrival in Britain in May of Admiral Sims of the US Navy.[7] Then serving as President of the US Naval War College at Newport, Rhode Island, in 1917, Sims had been appointed Commander-in-Chief of US Naval forces operating from Britain. In that position he had played a vital role in organizing the anti-U-boat offensive in the waters around the British Isles. Jellicoe had included a fulsome tribute to Sims for his 'intimate knowledge of gunnery, ... his attractive personality, charm of manner, keen sense of humour, and quick and accurate grasp of any problem with which he was confronted' in his 1920 book *The Crisis of the Naval War*.[8] The tribute was picked up in several press reviews at the time.[9] In May 1921 Sims returned to Britain for the award of an honorary degree by Cambridge University. The precise impact of the Sims visit on the development of British naval and foreign policy is difficult to quantify, but it did give rise to rumours in certain quarters that Sims had been involved in talks with the Admiralty.[10]

Those talks may have been on an entirely informal level, as the Admiral was warmly received by the British government and Royal Navy. Several dinners were organized in his honour, including one at 10 Downing Street.[11] Guests included senior military and civilian figures connected to the Admiralty and to the naval lobby in the House of Commons.[12] Remarks on the Irish problem by Sims at one of these dinners caused some controversy back in the United States. His very public defence of those remarks offers some support to the idea that the Anglophile Sims might have raised the naval issues at stake between the two countries in his conversation with British politicians and senior figures in the Admiralty: 'I have been advocating that we should keep together in decent companionship and brotherhood.'[13] Given this statement, the esteem with which Sims was held on both sides of the Atlantic, and the pressing nature of the issues dividing the two countries, it would have been remarkable if the Admiral had not been involved in lengthy discussions on current issues in the Anglo-American relationship with his dinner guests from the Royal Navy and world of British politics.

Borah's proposal for an international conference on disarmament and arms limitation, and the seeming reluctance of Congress to sanction high levels of naval spending, would have been an inevitable topic of the conversations taking place around Sims, and within the Royal Navy, there were officers who considered that arms limitation was in the interest of the service. Britain could not afford a capital ship building race, and arms limitation might (if appropriately handled) allow Britain to have a fleet capable of policing the Empire even within the reduced resources available after 1918. In other words smaller ships, with upper limits on tonnage and gun sizes set by international agreement, were one means by which Britain could afford a surface fleet large enough to provide imperial security. As one article in *The Naval Review* suggested, 'We may be sure that the solution does not lie in outbidding our rivals in size, gun calibres and speed; for there can be one ending only to such a competition – battleships so large that we cannot afford enough of them to execute the strategy essential for our security.'[14]

On 19 May 1921, Lee of Fareham visited the American Ambassador in London to indicate that he was willing to see parity between the Royal Navy and US Navy, and that he was not about to let the Anglo-Japanese Alliance damage relations between Britain and Japan. This personal, diplomatic approach has escaped the attention of most historians of the period except Phillips O'Brien, who identified the exchange using American diplomatic documents.[15]

Two days after his meeting with the American Ambassador, and presumably with some indication of the likely lines of American policy, Lee of Fareham came forward with a new memorandum for the Cabinet. His paper began by examining Britain's relations with both the United States and Japan. He was at pains to explain that there was simply no question of Britain and the United States going to war and that the ideal position in the eyes of the Royal Navy was 'to substitute an American for the Japanese Alliance', but that 'in the present temper of Congress, that would not be practical politics'.[16] The relationship with Japan was similarly problematic:

> For some years past the growth of social unrest, and even Communism, in Japan has greatly alarmed both the Government and the business community. So serious has it become, indeed, that the temptation to evoke a counter-wave of patriotism and national solidarity by plunging into war has played into the hands of the Jingoes and the very Prussian-minded military caste ... Their attitude towards the Anglo-Japanese Alliance is largely one of indifference; they know we would never help them in a war with United States, but they see a certain advantage in our enforced, if unsympathetic, neutrality.[17]

The May memorandum went on to call for the maintenance of a one power standard for the Royal Navy (and to begin a programme of naval construction to ensure that the US Navy, with its 1916 programme, did not surpass the British Fleet). Second, he suggested withdrawing from the Japanese Alliance under cover of 'some formal – possibly tripartite – agreement for the defence of our respective and legitimate interests in the Pacific'.[18] Effectively, the Royal Navy wanted to place orders for ships, modernizing the fleet and maintaining existing warship capacity, while avoiding issues with the United States. To realize these goals the Anglo-Japanese naval alliance would be traded as a diplomatic bargaining counter with the United States.

Lee of Fareham's paper had added significance in that he also rejected the desire of the Foreign Office and the Colonial Office to monopolize the political debate on the Anglo-Japanese Alliance: 'The renewal, or termination of the Alliance is ... not merely a Foreign Office question but an intimate concern of both the Admiralty and the Treasury.'[19] The First Lord of the

Admiralty was demanding that the Royal Navy's voice be heard, and for the Admiralty to play a significant role in making foreign policy on this issue. Lee of Fareham was convinced that his suggestion of rolling issues together offered the only way out of the policy impasse facing Britain at a military and diplomatic level.

The significance of the May memorandum was not lost on Lady Lee of Fareham, who recorded the following in her diary: 'A[rthur] has been very busy all day writing a memorandum for the Cabinet on the Anglo-Japanese Alliance. He thinks it would ease the Anglo-American situation, and incidentally the whole naval position, if the Alliance were not renewed. The Cabinet so far do not appear to have thought out this question at all.'[20] The significance of the memorandum and Lady Lee's comment finds no place in Roskill's *Naval Policy between the Wars*. Alan Clark's edition of Lee of Fareham's papers (previously published privately) came out five years after Roskill's first volume, and Roskill preferred Admiralty papers to cabinet memoranda and minutes as his primary source of choice. In any case, such was the odium that Lee of Fareham was held in by the Royal Navy that it was unlikely that Roskill (*semper fidelis* to the service) would easily have paid tribute to Lee's contribution to naval policy. However, in the eyes of Lee of Fareham and his wife, what was at stake with the question of renewing the Anglo-Japanese Alliance was nothing less than 'the whole naval position'.[21]

Lee of Fareham's paper represented a way forward for the Royal Navy and a potential way forward for the Empire. Within a week, at a dinner for Crown Prince Hirohito in London on an official visit, he made an appeal for Anglo-American-Japanese cooperation to find a way forward on naval and Far Eastern issues.[22] Hirohito's visit was a highly significant event, and showed the extent to which the Japanese were trying to demonstrate their commitment to the relationship with Britain. It was the first time 'that an heir to the Japanese throne had left his own country'.[23]

The discussions between Lee of Fareham and Beatty on the May memorandum cannot be directly evidenced by the available primary sources, but the results are evident in the extent to which the Admiralty began to pursue a joined-up policy of linking naval developments with the abrogation of the Anglo-Japanese Alliance. In May and June, in the Standing Defence Sub-Committee of the Committee of Imperial Defence, the Admiralty was busy trying to lay the groundwork for a successful Imperial Conference. The committee received papers covering the cooperation of the dominions in developing British Empire naval policy and the importance of developing a naval base at Singapore to support Far Eastern operations by the main fleet.[24] It also received an updated 'Strategic Assessment in the Event of the Anglo-Japanese Alliance Being Terminated' to underline the need for the dominions to contribute to imperial naval defence, especially with regard to the Far East.

The central message of these papers was evident in Beatty's speech to the Imperial Conference on 4 July 1921.[25] Beyond references to the United States in an opening survey of the strategic position of the Navy and the Empire, Beatty concentrated almost exclusively on Japan. The assumption throughout was that Japan constituted a threat to the British Empire, and in detail he presented an analysis of issues likely to arise in the event of war between Britain and Japan. It was a highly political speech in the form of a strategic assessment. Beatty's purpose was seemingly to give the hard sell to dominion governments of the line of policy proposed by Lee of Fareham's May memorandum, to press dominion governments into paying for the development of their own naval forces as part of the Royal Navy (reaffirmed in a separate meeting at the Admiralty one week later) and to pay for a network of naval bases suitable for the operation of a Far Eastern Fleet.[26] In short, Beatty hoped to enlist the dominion governments to support the lines of policy set out in the May memorandum and to accept the financial fallout which would result from the non-renewal of the Anglo-Japanese Alliance.

With the hard sell from Beatty the outcomes of the Imperial Conference were twofold. Dominion premiers (with the exception of Canada[27]) gave qualified support, at least for the time being, to the idea of renewing the Anglo-Japanese Alliance (in modified form to make it acceptable to the United States).[28] There was also support for the idea of an American-sponsored conference on the Pacific to realize the security arrangements outlined in the May memorandum. On 5 July, the day after Beatty's speech, Lord Curzon, the British Foreign Secretary, asked the American government to call a meeting to discuss Far Eastern security matters.[29] As W.R. Louis has identified, Curzon considered the alliance to be an excellent means of restraining the Japanese, and hoped that America might be persuaded to join the alliance in some form.[30] Two days later Curzon and the Japanese Ambassador in London notified the League of Nations that any continuation of the alliance would be in a form consistent with their membership of that international organization.[31] As plans for the conference developed over the summer of 1921, the foreign secretary was unhappy at the linking of issues of Far Eastern security and Naval Arms Limitation, but this was exactly what the Admiralty wanted and the basis of the policy put forward in the May memorandum. The Anglo-Japanese Alliance had become the diplomatic counter required to secure agreement with the US government on naval arms so as to maintain equality of size between the British and American Fleets. Given the state of the British economy, and the warship-building industry, it was easier to secure a diplomatic agreement with the United States to guarantee parity than to try to meet them in a naval-building race.

9

Next-Generation Battleships

During the spring-summer of 1921, as Lee of Fareham made progress in his attempt to bring naval and diplomatic policies into closer proximity, the connectedness of British naval policy meant it was still necessary to make progress, or at least to give an appearance of progress, on the issue of capital shipbuilding. The political and shipbuilding imperatives at play in naval policy are typically underplayed in most analyses of the period, and the building of British capital ships has been the preserve of popular rather than academic historians.[1] The shipbuilding issues pressing on the Admiralty required at least the preparation of contracts for the building of the next generation of capital ships that the Royal Navy wished to secure, even though Lee suspected that the Cabinet would not support a major building programme without a diplomatic agreement between the major naval powers. In April 1921 the Admiralty wrote to the Treasury to begin the process of contracting and to advise that it was imperative that 'preliminary action' was taken (involving some cost to the exchequer) so as not to cause later 'interruption' to the programme.[2] The Admiralty wished to build four new capital ships of the G-3 battlecruiser design. While the proposed G-3 battlecruiser programme has attracted the attention of technically minded naval historians, the associated battles in Whitehall over a class of ships that were never built have received scant attention from historians. Those battles, however, are revealing of relations between the Treasury and the Admiralty and the battles over naval policy being fought at the level of the civil service.

The new G-3 design, incorporating the lessons of Jutland, represented the best thinking of the Admiralty's research and design team. The Admiralty argued that it had the necessary go-ahead from the Cabinet and argued that any delay would lead to substantial increase in long-term costs. The reaction in the Treasury was sharply, and predictably, hostile. Sir George Barstow, controller of Supply services at the Treasury, was particularly outspoken in his reactions to the Admiralty's ambitions.[3] He wrote a minute for Robert Horne, the Chancellor of the Exchequer: 'One might suppose from the correspondence that the policy of HM Govt to begin building 4 capital ships is settled irrevocably and without possibility of reconsideration. If it is so settled … the Govt must make up their minds that there can be no saving on the navy estimates next year.' Barstow referred to his impression from a meeting of the Cabinet Finance Committee on 28 February, at which the naval estimates were discussed, that the decision to build the ships had not yet been taken and, indeed, that the possibility of an international agreement on naval arms might mean that they would never be required. He warned, 'you will realise that the Board of Admiralty far from entertaining any such hope are all for pressing on building new capital ships'. Interestingly and revealingly Barstow then went on to make a sweeping attack on Admiralty ambitions and, by implication, the naval and foreign policies of the Lloyd George government:

> The Admiralty found themselves on a Cabinet decision that the British fleet is not to be of less strength than any other naval power. The USA have for reasons of their own apparently decided that they must have the largest fleet in the world. Their resources are so much greater than our own that for every ship we lay down they can afford to put down two. Ostensibly I believe the USA only intend to have a fleet as large as that of any other power: but as the ships they lay down are new ships, there is no question of any balance between the two strengths, and we are to build in order to equal them and they in order to equal us. Apart from the national vanity of having the largest fleet, the USA are building with an eye to Japan, partly in view, it is alleged, of the Anglo-Japanese alliance in spite of the specific clause excepting the case of hostilities with the USA from those in which we should be called upon to assist them. Thus Japan in turn increases her navy and the Admiralty are able to say that unless we build more capital ships we shall sink to the position of third naval power. The whole proceeding is so ruinous and such a menace to civilisation that the most strenuous efforts are surely worthwhile to prevent the debacle which sooner or later must ensue … The Cabinet have recently been considering the Anglo-Japanese Alliance. If it is decided to continue it, the peace of the Pacific … would be secured. As regards the USA I have always believed that the proper course for Great Britain to take is to ignore her shipbuilding programme. This may sound paradoxical and 'ostrich' like. But in point of fact if we believe that the US Fleet will not in fact be used in war against us, it is the only sensible line to take … If anything could bring on war with the USA, it would be to compete with her in shipbuilding … while owing her 1,000 millions sterling. We are told not to 'run away' from the USA. I would not do so. I would ignore their shipbuilding. What can they do to us? They cannot invade us. They can invade Canada without a ship moving … I do

> not ignore the difficulties of the policy I venture to advocate. Government would have to face a 'jingo' press, a determined Board of Admiralty and a public vain of the big navy and easily stirred to emotion about it. If a middle course has to be adopted…I would build only 1 ship of the new type, not embark on 4 at once. But my strong opinion is that we ought to build none, and that the Admiralty are 'jockeying' the Government into the position of the opening of re-opening capital ship-building before a considered decision is taken.[4]

Within the confines of the Treasury building this was a remarkably outspoken attack on government policy, but it is illustrative of the tensions between the Admiralty and Treasury which had resurfaced after the end of the First World War. Big ticket items such as battleships were natural targets for a Treasury wrestling with issues of inter-Allied war debts and reparations, declining staple industries, high levels of post-war unemployment and taxation and the need to bring government spending under control. It made no sense to spend millions on technologies that might be verging on obsolescence, which the country (in the opinion of the Treasury) could not afford, and which might have to be scrapped as a consequence of an international agreement on arms limitation. Barstow's passionate denunciation of the government's naval and foreign policies, combined with the urgency of the financial situation, struck a chord with the Chancellor of the Exchequer. The Treasury refused the Admiralty's request to contract the preparatory work with the result that the issue had to be settled in Cabinet. In consequence, Lee of Fareham drew up a memorandum urging the Cabinet to decide the issue, and to authorize the initial steps for the building of four new capital ships of the G-3 battlecruiser design. This new design, incorporating the lessons of Jutland, represented the best thinking of the Admiralty's research and design team. The design represented a quantum leap in naval design, and the G-3 was considerably more advanced than the Japanese and American designs then being built. In his paper Lee of Fareham argued as follows: 'If…we alone stop building we shall enter the Conference stripped naked, so to speak, and with our future position hopelessly and permanently prejudiced.'[5] The First Lord of the Admiralty coupled this with a forwarding letter to the Prime Minister, highlighting the economies made by his department and rejecting the idea that naval expenditure might be trimmed a little further.[6]

Barstow was put in charge of the Treasury's response to the memorandum and he was forceful in making the case to Cabinet against the battlecruisers. He argued that the question which faced the Cabinet was of principle rather than of technical details associated with the building of the four ships: 'The question…is whether Great Britain embark upon an era of competitive naval shipbuilding.'[7] He described the question as 'a momentous one'. Barstow further questioned what the government's declared one-power standard actually meant: 'Does it mean that the British fleet is to be equal to that of any other power in British waters? Or in the selected area of operations of the rival power? Or finally is it to be equal on paper?'[8] The memorandum concluded that the one-power standard embodied 'a dangerous fallacy', and that strong finance formed stronger set of bonds for the empire than a strong fleet.

The Barstow memorandum was fascinating because it raised profound issues of principle rather than financial and contractual detail which might be expected from the Treasury, and in the event the Cabinet were more persuaded by Lee of Fareham's paper than that of Sir George Barstow. This left the government to bring forward in August naval estimates calling for the funds for the construction of the four new battlecruisers. The naval lobby in the House of Commons was ready to give its full support to the proposal, even though, with the conference on the horizon, there was a good chance that they would never be built. A debate on the naval estimates on 3 August 1921, extensively reported in the British media, produced a lengthy examination of the government's naval policy, with Leo Amery MP, Parliamentary Secretary to the Admiralty, asserting the continuing primacy in sea warfare of the capital ship.[9] Lady Astor reminded fellow members of their 'bounden duty to keep England a first-class naval power'.[10] Strikingly, the references to Japan, in contrast to the navy estimates debate in March 1921, were sharply critical, signalling the sea change in policy which had taken place with the May memorandum. Bellairs blamed Japan for the race in naval armaments arguing, 'It is obvious Japan saw an opportunity for creating a great navy, and that great navy is being built up with some object in the future.'[11] An opposition attempt to reduce the Navy vote was eventually defeated by 311 votes to 62.

Within the coalition the case for building the battlecruisers received further support in September from Hilton Young, the Lloyd George Liberal MP for Norwich. Appointed as Financial Secretary to the Treasury in April 1921, he was fascinated by the causes of high post-war unemployment. In September 1921 he wrote to Lloyd George giving his thoughts on the problem of unemployment. Summarizing the opinion of several bankers and industrialists (including shipbuilders W.L. Hichens of Cammell Laird and John Sampson of John Brown), he concluded that capital works programmes were an appropriate and effective response to mass unemployment.[12] Construction of the four battlecruisers could play a major role in alleviating unemployment and perhaps help to deliver key constituencies to the government at the next general election.

The levels of despair in some of the shipbuilding communities, and the extent to which building the G-3 battlecruisers represented the prospect of badly needed relief (especially with the prospect of a long, hard winter ahead), can be glimpsed in an 'off the record' briefing to a journalist by one of the directors of the firms that hoped to secure an order for one of the G-3 battlecruisers. In September 1921 one of the local Scottish newspapers reported the following:

> It is understood that the Admiralty is preparing to do all in its power to hasten work on the four new battleships in order to assist in providing employment during the winter. All the four ships will be built by private firms in England and Scotland, and the tenders for the ships have already been asked for. 'Ultimately each of the ships will employ directly something like 3000 men, but the benefit this winter will be felt indirectly among the large number of trades that make various machines and fittings for the ships.' said a director of one of the firms that had tendered for a contract. 'We have been preparing a list of the firms from whom we shall have to obtain various articles if we get the contract for one of these four ships. That list contains something like two hundred names. The first benefit, of course, will be in the steel trade. The moment the Admiralty lets the contract each of the successful firms will be able to put in hand large orders for steel plates. All sorts of firms, however, will receive sub-contracts.'[13]

Lloyd George was undoubtedly sensitive to the potential political impacts of the failure to restart capital shipbuilding, and the tone of the report in *The [Dundee] Evening Telegraph and Post* perhaps also raises questions about whether the Admiralty perhaps had some hand in leaking the information, while Lee of Fareham was still sidelined after a hernia operation on 22 August 1921.[14] Either way the potential political repercussions in certain constituencies of the failure to place fresh orders for capital ships were being considered within the ranks of the Labour Party. Leading Labour activist Beatrice Webb, whose husband, Sydney, had played a leading role in drafting the 1918 party constitution and who would contest the Seaham constituency in 1922, commented in her diary in October 1921 that in the industrial North East those involved in shipbuilding and mining were thoroughly disillusioned with the peace and felt a great sense of betrayal at the actions of the Lloyd George coalition.[15] Far from creating the conditions for revolutionary discontent, the depressed economy made the electorate apathetic, and more deferential and willing to accept the socio-economic status quo in case conditions might deteriorate further. In turn the Labour Party in its appeal to the electorate, and potential policies in government, would have to reflect that, making it a party of evolution rather than revolution.

The political impacts of naval policy, however, extended well beyond the Labour Party. In Plymouth, for example, which had a long-established tradition at general elections of penalising parties considered insufficiently responsive to the needs of the Royal Navy, there was considerable unease at unemployment and the failure to award new building contracts for the Royal Navy.[16] Naval policy could cost the coalition votes even in those areas which might be considered its strongholds.

Between October and the start of the Washington Conference in November, the Royal Navy placed orders for the four new battlecruisers with Swan Hunter, William Beardmore, Fairfield and John Brown.[17] It was estimated that the contract for each would yield £7 million, leading to the direct employment of 3,000 workers in each of the shipyards.[18] However, on 18 November 1922, without a single ship being laid down, the order was halted – outright cancellation being confirmed with the signature of the Washington Naval Treaty in February 1922. In truth, as John Jordan has identified, the G-3 battlecruisers, which were to prove remarkably influential on post-war capital ship design, were simply a 'bargaining chip' to bring the Americans and Japanese to the table at the Washington Conference.[19]

Both the nature of the design of the battlecruisers and the reasons for their suspension were reflections of the shipbuilding crisis threatening to engulf construction for the Royal Navy. With a planned displacement of 48,400 long tons, and mounting nine 16-inch guns as main armament, the battlecruisers embodied the lessons of Jutland and the latest technical advances that the Royal Navy was so keen to promote.[20] For example, the guns could elevate as high as 40 degrees and the turret design incorporated lessons learnt after the armistice from the study of German and American designs.[21] The main armament was mounted in three turrets, two forward and one between the superstructure amidships.[22] The secondary armament was installed in power-operated twin turrets, and the anti-aircraft weaponry (6 × 4.7-inch high-angle guns and 4 × 10-barrelled 2-pound pompom batteries) showed the extent to which the Department of Naval Construction was taking on-board the potential threat from the air.[23]

Capable of thirty-two knots the G-3 class battlecruiser, as John Jordan recognizes, had significantly improved armour protection over earlier designs (deck armour – 8–9-inch over magazines; armoured belt – 14-inch over magazines; 12-inch over machinery).[24] The Director of Naval Construction considered that the magazines were well protected – a key design feature after the loss of British battlecruisers at Jutland as a result of magazine explosions.[25]

The armouring of the vessels had also been designed to allow the vessel to withstand 'the explosion of a torpedo carrying a charge of 750-lbs', and a 7-foot deep double bottom was intended to prevent sinking as a result of a mine detonating under the vessel.[26] Counter-flooding gear would allow the vessel to be put on an even keel following any serious water ingress to the hull as a result of combat damage. The arrangements for the two forward torpedo tubes were influenced by study of the German battleship *Baden*.[27] The number of crew had been kept to a minimum so that the on-board facilities that they would enjoy were considerably better than other ships of the fleet. The only limiting factor on the design was the need for the battlecruisers to be able to pass through the Panama and Suez Canals and to be able to dock at Portsmouth and Rosyth. Able to cruise for 7,000 miles at sixteen knots, they were formidable vessels and represented a serious investment in the power and reach of the Royal Navy.[28] The British public was assured that these vessels would be 'markedly superior' to the ships of the existing fleet.[29] The design of the G-3 class was approved by the Admiralty on 12 August 1921, just nine days after the government had secured passage of the naval estimates in Parliament.

As the shipyards got to work on the early stages of constructing the G-3 battlecruisers, the Admiralty was ready with plans for a successor programme for four N3 class battleships (48,000 long tons, 9 × 18-inch main armament) in case there was a failure to reach agreement at the Washington Conference. Despite the hopes resting on the conference, the omens pointing towards success were not good. A groundbreaking multilateral deal on arms reduction/arms limitation seemed an unlikely outcome just two years after Congress and the American public had rejected the Treaty of Versailles, and thus President Wilson's vision of a United States at the heart of international policy-making and security.

The decision to award contracts for the four G-3 battlecruisers was essentially a bluff and a blind: a bluff to the Americans and Japanese that Britain was prepared to defend her position as the pre-eminent naval power if the Washington Conference failed to reach an agreement, and a blind to the shipbuilding industry and the shipbuilding towns to keep faith with the Royal Navy and naval policy. It had further political advantage in that a Labour Party and Trades Union movement increasingly wedded to pacificism and internationalism attacked the award of the contracts for the capital ships that would ease unemployment.[30] The September 1921 Trades Union Conference witnessed vigorous attacks on the coalition government's naval policy. That in turn drew a sharp response from some sections of the press. *The Western*

Table 9.1 G-3 specifications

G-3 Battlecruiser Design	
Dimensions	
Overall length	856 feet
Beam	106 feet
Draught (Fwd)	32.0 feet
Draught (Aft)	33.0 feet
Displacement (tons)	48,000 feet
Horsepower (shaft)	160,000
Speed	31–32 knots
Fuel	1,200 (tons)
Coal capacity	50 (tons)
Oil fuel capacity	5,000 (tons)
Crew	1,716 men
Armament	
Main	9 × 16-inch guns (3 turrets) with 80 rounds per gun (rpg)
Secondary	16 × 6-inch guns (8 turrets) with 150 fwd/95 aft rpg
	6 × 4.7-inch guns (high angle) with 200 rpg
	40 × pompon anti-aircraft gun (4 mountings) with 1225 rpg
	2 × torpedo tubes with 16 torpedoes
	2 × aircraft

Note: G-3 Specifications, TNA: ADM1/9232. See also ADM226/23 and 24.

Morning News, for example, commented the following: 'The vigorous criticism of the Government at the Labour Congress for their decision to build four new capital ships in the face of the existing unemployment seems to us to indicate confused thinking. If these ships are not built there will be a good deal more unemployment than there is at present.'[31]

Despite the sense of relief on Clydeside, Tyneside and Merseyside that orders for new ships had arrived and that unemployment could perhaps be brought under control, the Cabinet and the Treasury had every expectation of a successful agreement to limit naval arms at Washington and every intention of cancelling the ships at the earliest opportunity. From the moment that contracts were signed until the start of the Washington Conference, the four G-3 cruisers constituted the maritime equivalent of a stage army: impressive, a valuable convincer, representative of a larger threat and yet cheap and immediately disposable. The Admiralty was, no doubt, happy to allow the Cabinet to think in such terms on the basis that if the conference broke down it would be politically difficult for the government to rescind its decision to build them. Effectively, once the G-3 contracts had been issued, the Royal Navy would benefit from either an agreement on naval fleets at Washington or the construction of four of the most powerful and modern ships in the world. Despite this, the centrality of the G-3 battlecruisers to Britain's preparation for the Washington Conference is given little consideration in most accounts of the evolution of British policy in 1921.

10

Washington Conference

The Washington Conference was given considerable attention by journalists and other writers in the 1920s, and that trend has been continued by naval historians and by specialists in the field of international relations.[1] The conference, especially its outcomes, has been debated in a number of historiographical fields. In the debate on the decline of British power, Anne Orde argues that at Washington the British and Americans came to a mutual arrangement to embark on a programme of naval disarmament.[2] For Paul Kennedy this disarmament was the outcome of the reaction against war and armaments.[3] On the Anglo-Japanese Alliance, Orde and Malcolm Kennedy agree that the Anglo-Japanese Alliance was sacrificed for other considerations including naval disarmament (Orde) and war debts to the United States (Kennedy).[4] Philipps O'Brien sees the conference as a dignified means of bringing to an end an alliance which had reached the end of its life.[5]

The various approaches to the subject matter suggest the connectedness of naval policy at least at the international, rather than the domestic British, level. At the same time they have minimized the human story of what took place at the conference. That human story is, however, important: it coloured the outcomes of the conference, its perception by the public, and helped to condition relations between the major powers in its aftermath. The conference and its outcome depended to a certain extent on key sections of the set of personal relationships which helped to underpin the connectedness of naval policy. In the case of the British delegation the interpersonal dimension, between members of the delegation and Cabinet ministers back home, was particularly important.

In September 1921 Beatty and his American wife Ethel sailed for the United States in preparation for the Washington Conference, which would start in November. Beatty sailed in advance of the main British delegation as he intended to take a tour of the country as a guest of the American Legion. As Roskill relates, Beatty was feted wherever he went, including an official visit to the White House while he was in Washington DC.[6] Chicago, Kansas City, New

York and Philadelphia followed. Beatty sent a short report of his endeavours to King George V in November:

> Since my arrival in the United States I have indeed had a very busy time, mostly taken up with travelling, eating dinners and making speeches. The welcome accorded to me as the representative of Your Majesty's Navy has indeed been very warm and sincere, and the further West we went the more they appeared to appreciate the … Navy.[7]

At the same time as Beatty was trying to soften up the Americans with his gallant charm, personal appearances, fine speeches and American wife, a plethora of articles appeared in newspapers and journals showing the high level of public interest in Britain, Europe and the United States. In reviewing some of the recent literature in their November issues *The Naval Review* commented, 'At a time when all eyes are turned towards Washington and the newspapers are full of the Conference and of the various personalities attending it, … the appearance of' various publications on the naval problem in the Far East might be 'of interest' to readers of the *Naval Review*.[8] One of the publications considered by the Naval Review was Hector C. Bywater's *Sea-Power in the Pacific*.[9] British by birth before his family had emigrated to the United States, Bywater was a journalist and military writer. In *Sea-Power in the Pacific* he confidently predicted a naval war between Japan and the United States.

The main British Empire delegation journeyed to North America on the liner SS *Olympic* in late October. Among the delegation there was some trepidation at the task at hand. Rear Admiral Chatfield found the *Olympic* more than agreeable after his war years in the more Spartan conditions of a battlecruiser, but he was still troubled by the task facing the British Empire delegation. Hopeful that the naval officers of the different powers could find agreement, he was still worried about the possibilities of offending and alienating the Japanese or the Americans, or potentially both at the same time.[10] Chatfield and the British delegation reached Quebec on 8 November and journeyed onwards to Washington (with Sir Robert Borden, the former Canadian Prime Minister, as a representative of Dominion interests).

As the delegation travelled to its destination, the Admiralty gave detailed consideration to the likely post-conference strategic landscape. In a minute dated 3 November 1921 the Admiralty Director of Plans, Captain Barry Domville, emphasized that the likely ending of the Anglo-Japanese Alliance confronted Britain with the possibility that in some future war 'the main fleet would be permanently based thousands of miles from home waters'.[11] Preparing for that possibility would require substantial investment in fleet facilities at Singapore and a likely gap in capabilities 'for many years to come' until such time as those facilities were ready. The Singapore issue had been under discussion since the end of the First World War, but the potential outcomes of the conference meant that it was no longer an academic or minor issue: Britain's maritime security in the Far East might depend on the development of naval facilities at Singapore. Domville's minute demonstrates a growing realization that the policies which Lee of Fareham hoped to pursue at Washington and beyond would inevitably raise a fresh set of difficulties even as they resolved a set of older issues. So intractable had those difficulties appeared that there had seemingly been an air of unreality to earlier thinking about the repercussions which would follow from a deal on naval armaments and the dropping of the alliance in order to secure the cooperation of the Americans in the formation of a pax Anglo-Americana.

On 12 November the Conference on the Limitation of Armament opened. During the course of the conference the Cabinet was kept informed of developments by telegrams, and also by a series of personal letters which Maurice Hankey, Secretary to the Cabinet, wrote to Lloyd George.[12] The final Treaty on Naval Arms was signed on 6 February 1922.[13] The British delegation was headed by senior Conservative Arthur Balfour, Lord President of the Council, former Prime Minister and Foreign Secretary. Lee of Fareham as First Lord of the Admiralty was in attendance, as were Beatty and Auckland Geddes, British Ambassador to the United States. The dominions and India also sent representatives. The delegation of the United States was headed by Secretary of State Charles Evans Hughes and that of Japan by Baron Kato, Minister of the Navy.

In preparing for the conference Evans Hughes had become painfully aware of attitudes in the General Board of the US Navy. Composed of senior admirals the General Board had been established in 1900 as an advisory body. The opinion of the General Board in the lead up to the Washington Conference, no doubt true to the teachings of Alfred Thayer Mahan, was belligerently hardline: opposed to the suspected ambitions of both the Japanese and British and determined to press the case for a fleet second to none.[14] As Philipps O'Brien has argued Evans Hughes determined that it was necessary to keep the discussions firmly in his own hands, and to keep the US Navy firmly at arm's length from the negotiating table. Quite why he came to this conclusion is not clear, and the American approach was very different from that of the British as politicians and Royal Navy officers pulled together in a united effort.[15]

The British delegation were unsure of what the Americans would propose at the conference and rather more confident of their Japanese partner. In the lead up to the conference the journal *The Round Table* commented thus:

> The geographical fact, apparent enough to Japan, though less esteemed elsewhere, is that, while both for Britain and America the assurance of a free Pacific is of high importance, for Japan it is vital. Japan is wholly in the Pacific… Japan will welcome a naval understanding, as much to free her from apprehension, as from an intolerable financial burden.[16]

Four days later the Conference on the Limitation of Armament opened. After an opening address by President Harding, Secretary of State Charles Evans Hughes put forward a remarkably far-reaching set of proposals:

(1) That all capital shipbuilding programs, either actual or projected, should be abandoned;
(2) That further reductions should be made through the scrapping of certain of the older ships;
(3) That in general regard should be had to the existing naval strength of the Powers concerned;
(4) That the capital ship tonnage should be used as the measurement of strength for navies, and a proportionate allowance of auxiliary combatant craft prescribed.[17]

In the weeks that followed the wisdom and the means to effect the proposals would be debated as different governments vied with each other to protect their interests while at the same time effecting drastic measures of arms limitation.

Beatty and Lee of Fareham were ready to accept many of the proposals which the Americans put forward. They were, for example, prepared to accept the idea of a 5:5:3 ratio of capital ships to give practical effect to the principle of respecting 'the existing naval strength of the Powers'. They were not, however, prepared to accept the suggestion of a ten-year building holiday 'which would result in decay of naval-construction and armament industries, unless firms are heavily subsidised'.[18]

The American proposal, echoing Churchill's repeated calls for a naval-building holiday before the First World War, seems to have been carefully crafted to appeal to British sensibilities.[19] In practice, however, the Royal Navy with its aged fleet could not afford to wait ten years to begin replacing its fleet. Chatfield commented, 'We have got to safeguard our powers of building Navies at all costs… [A ten-year building holiday] would mean the extinction of British Sea

Power & we shall not budge on that point.'[20] At the end of a ten-year building holiday, it would need twelve capital ships to be laid down simultaneously for Britain to retain a relatively modern fleet. Given earlier concerns about the capacity of the shipyards, and the armaments companies, Beatty concluded that this was an unsustainable level of construction. British interests called for a steady and sustained programme of replacement. This issue quickly resolved itself into the key difference between the Americans and British, and also between the delegation in Washington and Lloyd George's Cabinet in London. Several members of the Cabinet were wholeheartedly in favour of agreeing to a ten-year building holiday because it would guarantee a deal with the Americans, and would demonstrate Britain's commitment to disarmament and world peace.[21] Beatty struggled to arrive as some sort of means to offset a naval-building holiday of ten years, such as the abolition of the submarine as a weapon of war, leading Lee of Fareham to make such a proposal to the conference. Ultimately it turned into something of a blind alley and a distraction.[22] There would be no deal on submarines to offset the fact that Britain, under the American proposals, would be left with an ageing fleet and an atrophied warship-building industry. Beatty expressed his thoughts on the alternatives in a telegram to the Admiralty on 15 November 1921:

> We are faced with the following alternatives for replacing capital ships.
>
> *Firstly*: To accept the US proposals for a 10 year holiday, with all its obvious impracticability.
>
> *Secondly*: To accept a policy of steady continuous replacement of laying down two ships every three years commencing immediately.
>
> *Thirdly*: To agree to a holiday of, say, three years, and then to proceed to lay down 2 ships every three years.
>
> Request you will consider these three alternatives and advise us with all dispatch, from the point of view on specialised warship construction.[23]

Beatty's behaviour at the conference, and that of Chatfield supporting the First Sea Lord, attracted some unwelcome comment from Churchill in London since it was felt in some quarters that Beatty and Chatfield had made common cause with their American counterparts against the machinations of the politicians. On 9 December Lloyd George wrote to Balfour to express the concerns.[24] This in turn drew an angry response from Beatty.[25] Churchill offered a half-hearted apology to the effect that no insult was intended which Beatty graciously accepted. Beatty undoubtedly recognized that Churchill was one of the members of the Cabinet who could be relied upon to give the Admiralty's opinion a fair hearing. He was also, no doubt, sensitive to the coming battle with the Committee on National Expenditure, chaired by Eric Geddes, that was examining ways of reducing the burden on the Exchequer. Shortly after the clash with Churchill, Beatty left the Washington Conference to deal with the Geddes Committee and the inevitable struggle for the naval estimates for 1922–23. The task of securing a favourable settlement was left to Balfour, Lee of Fareham and Chatfield.

Back in London Beatty was soon in fine form persuading and cajoling in equal measure members of the Cabinet to the reasonableness of the naval estimates. He also extended his offensive to the civil servants of the Treasury. In one meeting of the Committee of Imperial Defence, Beatty was heard to take Sir George Barstow aside to advise him that naval officers could show the mandarins of the Treasury how to make effective economies that would be more effective in the long term than a ten-year building holiday.[26] Beatty's return to London and the battles of Whitehall made good political sense. While Beatty was optimistic that the British delegation could secure a deal at Washington, he was fearful that it might not be accepted in the Cabinet.

If the British were having trouble in responding to the American proposals, then, as Sadao Asada has revealed, for the Japanese delegation the situation was even more problematic as a result of a profound disagreement between the military and the politicians. Vice Admiral Kato Kanji, senior naval officer in the Japanese delegation in Washington, had drawn the lesson from the First World War that Japan in peacetime required the greatest possible navy, because in the event of war with the United States American industry could quickly and easily outbuild Japanese shipyards.[27] Meanwhile Baron Kato Tomosaburo, the civilian Navy Minister, was more concerned with avoiding conflict and the health of the Japanese economy which he held to be the bedrock of national defence, insurance against Western influence and the best safeguard of Japan's future. Admiral Kato was determined that the delegation should not agree to accept a position of inferiority which harked back to the days of the unequal treaties which Japan had been forced to accept in the aftermath of the Perry mission in the 1850s. Kato Tomosaburo was equally determined to assert civilian control over Japan's destiny.

Back in Washington, the veteran Conservative politician Arthur James Balfour was putting in a highly effective performance. Although he was in the twilight of his career, having been Prime Minister from 1902 to 1905, at Washington he proved that he could still be charming, constructive and remarkably good at building bridges, particularly with the American, Japanese and French delegations. His status as an elder statesperson was used to good effect:

> It so happens I was head of the British administration which, twenty years ago, brought the first Anglo-Japanese Alliance into existence. It so happens that I was head of the British administration which brought into existence the entente between the British Empire and France. And through all my life I have been a constant, ardent and persistent advocate of intimate and friendly relations between the two great branches of the English-speaking race.[28]

Balfour was keen to secure a multinational agreement on naval armaments and Pacific questions. His attitude towards the former appears to have been influenced, at least to some extent, by the economic (and potentially political) windfalls that would result from such an agreement. He did not see this in terms of the support to the shipping industry which would result from even a limited programme of new naval construction. Rather he viewed it in terms of the wider benefit to the British economy if money was not being ploughed into naval armaments. Lower naval estimates would pave the way to tax cuts providing a powerful stimulus to the economy in the midst of depression. As he explained to the delegates on the question of cutting naval arms, 'It is easy to estimate in dollars, or in pounds, shillings and pence, the saving to the taxpayer of each of the nations concerned … It is easy to show that indirectly it will … greatly stimulate industry, national and international, and do much to diminish the difficulties under which every … government is … laboring.'[29] Thanks in no small part to Balfour's influence, and the resolution of Navy Minister Kato Tomosaburo in facing down Vice Admiral Kanji, the powers were able to come to a substantial measure of agreement on the limitation of naval arms by January 1922. It was only with the greatest reluctance that the Imperial Japanese Navy accepted a ratio of 70 per cent, which it regarded as the minimum level for maritime security.

Under the terms of the resulting treaty the powers agreed to 'abandon their respective capital ship building programs' so that 'no new capital ships' would be 'constructed or acquired by any of the Contracting Powers except replacement tonnage which may be constructed or acquired'.[30] Under Article IV of the treaty the total tonnage of the different national fleets was fixed: 'for the United States 525,000 tons (533,400 metric tons); for the British Empire 525,000 tons (533,400 metric tons); for France 175,000 tons (177,800 metric tons); for Italy 175,000 tons (177,800 metric tons); for Japan 315,000 tons (320,040 metric tons)'.[31] Under Articles V and VI the maximum tonnage of replacement vessels was fixed at 35,000 tons and the maximum calibre of main armament fixed at 16 inch.

In addition to the big gunships the treaty also set limits for the aircraft carriers of the respective fleets. The treaty stipulated that the aircraft carrier was not a capital ship, but an auxiliary required to support the operation of the battleships and battlecruisers of the main fleet. This was an interesting definitional point. Carrier-based naval aviation was seen as integral to fleet operation, even if they were not yet perceived as being sufficiently potent to be considered as capital ships. The tonnage allowance for aircraft carriers was generous: 'for the United States 135,000 tons (137,160 metric tons); for the British Empire 135,000 tons (137,160 metric tons); for France 60,000 tons (60,960 metric tons); for Italy 60,000 tons (60,960 metric tons); for Japan 81,000 tons (82,296 metric tons)'. In addition the size of new aircraft carriers was restricted under Article IX to '27,000 tons (27,432 metric tons)'.[32] Provision was, however, made for the powers to 'build not more than two aircraft carriers, each of a tonnage of not more than 33,000 tons (33,528 metric tons)', using 'any two of their ships, whether constructed or in course of construction, which would otherwise be scrapped under the provisions' of the Treaty.[33] Under Article XI the maximum size of cruisers was fixed at 10,000 tons (10,160 metric tons) and their armament restricted to a maximum 8-inch main armament. On the question of naval bases the British agreed not to develop a major base closer to Japan than Singapore and the American, the Hawaiian Islands.

Translating the 5:5:3 ratio into fleet realities was always going to present difficulties for all signatories. The Washington Conference would leave the Royal Navy with a force of twenty-one battleships and battlecruisers. Only one of them (HMS *Hood*) was considered modern, in that it incorporated the lessons of Jutland. Nineteen older ships were to be scrapped immediately, together with the four semi-completed G-3 battlecruisers.[34] To ensure there would be no ten-year holiday of British capital shipbuilding, in 1922 Britain would be allowed to lay down two new capital ships of a maximum 35,000 tons. Despite the provision for a limited programme of capital shipbuilding, Chatfield was bleak in his assessment of the likely effects on the armaments industry in Britain, Japan and America: 'Whatever happens… Armament Firms are going to be ruined as far as I can see & governments may have to take them over in part.'[35] The two new capital ships allowed under the Washington Conference would be completed by 1925, at which point a further four of the pre-Jutland capital ships would be scrapped.[36] At this point the battlefleet would consist of seventeen pre-Jutland ships and three post-1916 ships.[37] Two further capital ships would be laid down in 1931, a further two the following year and one more in 1933. In 1934 two further ships would be laid down, and the two laid down in 1931 would be completed. This in turn would lead to the scrapping of four of the pre-Jutland ships, with a further four going to the breakers yard in the following year as one more capital ship was laid down.[38] By the end of 1935, as the two ships laid down in 1932 were completed, the British Fleet would consist of thirteen pre- and five post-Jutland, capital ships. Two years later three further capital ships would be laid down, three more completed and four pre-Jutland ships withdrawn.[39] The last pre-Jutland ship would be scrapped in 1941 as HMS *Hood* and HMS *Ramilles* went to the breakers yard and Britain would be left with a fleet of fifteen post-Jutland warships.

The 5:5:3 ratio was also potentially significant in strategic and operational terms. Experience from the First World War suggested that in combat any fleet would require a margin of superiority of 50 per cent over the opposing force to secure a decisive victory.[40] Equality between the British and American Fleets, and Japanese predominance in East Asia, meant that it was unlikely that either of the three main fleets would be able to achieve a decisive victory in any theatre of operations. The British and Americans would always be compelled to divide their forces between two or more oceans, while the Japanese would be free to concentrate in the Eastern Pacific. This suggested that in any future war between two or more of the major naval powers, the result would be a strategic stalemate. In the event of war, under the 50 per cent rule, if valid and unaffected by other factors, none of the three powers would have the capability of launching naval operations capable of inflicting a decisive defeat on an opposing fleet. The prospect of operational and strategic stalemate created a form of strategic deterrence. Without the prospect of a decisive blow the likely outcome of any conflict was a long drawn-out war that would prove ruinous for the participants. There was little appetite after 1918 for the wars of the future to be fought on the basis of attrition.

Beyond signature of the Naval Treaty at Washington was a Four Power Treaty (13 December 1921) and a Nine Power Treaty (6 February 1922). Negotiation of those treaties was integral to the progression of the Naval Arms Treaty signed on 6 February 1922. As the American government had recognized in July 1921, 'It is manifest ... that the question of the limitation of armaments has a close relation to Pacific and Far Eastern problems'.[41] Under the terms of the Four Power Pact the signatories recognized the rights of the other parties with regard to their possessions in the Far East. It also established the idea of joint conferences on any future issues of dispute involving the respective national navies of the powers. It was understood that with the signature of the Four Power Pact the Anglo-Japanese Alliance would be allowed to lapse, and in the lead up to the conference some elements of the press had been ready to give their support to the idea of turning the alliance into a 'four cornered entente, under which everybody's rights were defined and secured under mutual guarantees'.[42] Under the Nine Power Treaty the signatories promised to respect the territorial integrity of China and to maintain her independence. This imposed a serious check on the potential imperial ambitions of all of the powers in China, but the blow was most keenly felt by the Japanese, who had the most to gain from the further disintegration of her near neighbour. Within Japanese nationalist circles there was grave disquiet at the checks imposed at Washington on what they saw as Japan's manifest destiny in Asia. Although Japan would continue to uphold the international order for several more years, the rot of Japanese democracy established itself firmly in the aftermath of the Washington Conference.[43]

British reactions to the Washington treaties varied considerably. In political circles there was considerable satisfaction that Britain had seemingly been able to square the circle: the preservation of a one-power naval standard while preserving good relations with both the United States and Japan (thus avoiding any issues with the dominions), and at the same time securing agreement on the status quo in the Far East and finding a means to help the government cut expenditure. Unsurprisingly, Balfour returned to London in mid-February 1922 to a rapturous welcome. As one of his biographers notes, Bonar Law found the public acclaim and newfound popularity almost an embarrassment. In the twilight of his career he was being feted by the Cabinet, and on the streets of London – something he had last experienced in the 1890s.[44] There was even talk of Lloyd George stepping down as Prime Minister and Balfour taking his place.

In Royal Navy circles there was some disquiet at the cancellation of the G-3 battlecruisers, but also some satisfaction. Beatty was able to reap some political capital out of the cancellation of the contracts since it would result in a substantial saving on the Naval Estimates for 1921–22.[45] In the circumstances of early 1922, with the Geddes committee scrutinizing every aspect of government expenditure, this could be represented as evidence that the Admiralty Board were doing their best to move towards the goal of drastic cuts in the naval estimates.[46]

In the shipyard towns there was no such split in opinion. There was a sense of near panic following the cancellation of the contracts for the G-3 battlecruisers, and overall the Washington Naval Treaty provided a fairly bleak prospect for the future. By January 1922 some of the towns affected had begun to mobilize to address the outcomes of the Washington Conference, and the economic and social effects of layoffs, in the midst of winter, following the cancellation of the battlecruiser contracts. The Lord Mayor of Newcastle met with the Lord Mayors and Town Clerks of Glasgow, Sheffield, Gateshead, South Shields, Jarrow, Tynemouth, Wallsend and Barrow-in-Furness to discuss coordinated action.[47] Their conclusion was that the situation was so serious that they should collectively lobby the Prime Minister for a meeting to discuss the local and regional issues arising from the government's naval policy and the impact of the Washington naval conference.[48]

Within the Royal Navy there was some division of opinion, but an overall satisfaction about what had been secured. Chatfield represented the vast majority of naval officers in his philosophical assessment of the Washington Conference that, from a weak position, Britain had been able to secure an agreement largely in line with national security.[49] His post-conference reflections on the details of the Washington Naval Treaty did, however, highlight the long-term problems arising from the agreement. He would have preferred a 25 per cent margin of British superiority over the United States to reflect the global nature of Britain's Empire, but recognised that the idea of equality had been accepted long before the conference. At least with a Japanese battlefleet set at nine ships it would take less investment in fleet infrastructure (port facilities and oil bunkering) at Singapore to enable the Royal Navy's main force to operate in time of war in the Far East. Given the state of government finances that investment could not be automatically assumed as a given, although that is exactly what Chatfield and other senior naval officers appeared to be have been ready to assume following the conference. Until such time as a fleet base at Singapore was fully operational, the Japanese, even with a reduced fleet, would be well placed to dominate the Eastern Pacific. The Washington Naval Treaty was effectively creating a gap in Britain's naval capabilities that would require additional government expenditure to close.

That gap and the flaws inherent in the Washington agreements have been recognized by post-war historians. Roskill concluded that the Washington Naval Treaty did prevent an arms race in capital ships between Britain and America, and did decrease tensions between the two states, if only temporarily.[50] Brian McKercher offers a rather bleaker assessment: 'The Washington Conference did not do what it was supposed to do in terms of relieving Anglo-American tensions. American Admirals were still suspicious of the Royal Navy – technical improvements in vessels and guns, the method of getting around the strictures imposed at Washington, as well as worry about protecting sea routes, were not eliminated.'[51] American historians have similarly not been appreciative of the achievements of the Harding administration in the field of naval policy.[52] Likewise, most historians of the Royal Navy, including Kennedy, Barnett and Marder, have concluded that the deal concluded at Washington was a poor one for Britain.[53] If the improvement in Anglo-American relations was short-lived the longer-term implications were even more serious. As Roskill commented in a sly dig at the failure of post-war politicians to fund the development of the Singapore base, the Washington agreements gave Japan strategic command of the Western Pacific, although this did not become fully apparent until 1942.[54]

11

Geddes and the Amery Memorandum

While the achievement of a naval arms agreement at Washington has been recognized by naval historians, and by international relations specialists, there has been comparatively little exploration of the post-conference period in which the Admiralty was forced to defend the Royal Navy from further cuts under the 'Geddes Axe'. The historiography on the 'Geddes Axe' is rather superficial, and Keith Grieves is right to challenge the consensus on Geddes, and to suggest that he was trying to implement a vision for Britain's financial future, rather than simply to cut government expenditure at any and every turn.[1] The problem for the Admiralty in trying to reconcile the different challenges facing the Royal Navy was that the Geddes proposals in 1922 amounted to a further cut in its resource base. The Washington Conference had played towards the vision of reduced government expenditure. This was a significant step in bringing into line the potential military threats to British naval power with the available level of the economic resource. But then the Geddes proposals threatened to alter the equation once again with the potential threat remaining the same, but with a further reduction in the finances available to meet it. The Washington proposals had amounted to deep cuts to the Royal Navy (easing pressure on the resource base), but they also fell hard on the US and Japanese navies (reducing the potential military threat). The Royal Navy would remain the largest afloat, and the construction of two new capital ships would help to preserve warship-building capacity and jobs. This constituted a rational and effective response to the policy dilemmas that had challenged Britain at the end of the First World War. The Geddes proposals then threatened to undermine the logic, in policy terms of the deal, that had been arrived at. The Admiralty, through British diplomacy, had no sooner begun to balance its books with the threat from the United States and Japan than Geddes, through the medium of Westminster politics, had arrived to tip the balance against it. Further unhelpful contributions for the sake of 'national finances' would follow, undermining the bases of the naval strategy which had begun to emerge following the Washington agreements.

In terms of the Empire, the goodwill of the United States, and hopefully Japan, could be counted on while Britain put in place the infrastructure required for its strategy of imperial defence in the Far East. That infrastructure would depend on the development of a major naval base at Singapore and the build-up of fleet-fuelling reserves at key points around the globe. During the interwar period it was believed, as a general rule of thumb, that a battle fleet lost 10 per cent of its fighting power for every 1,000 miles it had to operate away from its base.[2] Britain could afford only one fleet so it had to be highly mobile and be able to operate at any point where the interests of the British Crown were threatened. The 10 per cent rule made it even more vital that the Royal Navy should have a major fleet base available in the East to support fleet operations in the Pacific. As the conference began to wind down in February there was a feeling that the outcomes of the Washington Conferences represented a real achievement for the British delegation, but they also had long-term cost implications.

In August 1921 Lloyd George had appointed Sir Eric Geddes, a former First Lord of the Admiralty, to chair a committee to examine all aspects of government expenditure for the purposes of securing major reductions. In October the Admiralty received from the committee a questionnaire calling for a detailed explanation of each of the fifteen lines of expenditure contained in the naval estimates.[3] This was part of the committee's review process of every government department and by year's end the Geddes Committee had come forward with suggestions for reducing government expenditure to the tune of £87 million. The Cabinet, who first saw the proposals in December, accepted cuts of £52 million: the Admiralty Board was less enthusiastic when it considered the proposals in January.[4]

Under the proposals, spending on defence was expected to fall by more than one third, and Geddes had raised the prospect of a new Ministry of Defence to replace the ministries serving the three services. The Geddes proposals represented a wish list of cuts with no attempt, in the case of the military services, to balance allocations against duties and threats. The proposal to form a Ministry of Defence arose because the committee had formed the impression that each of the services was wasting money because of a lack of coordination between the three of them. It was also politically useful in that it threatened the Admiralty, War Office and Air Ministry, and potentially undermined, in the eyes of the public, any response to the proposals which they might mount on the grounds of 'national defence'. To argue against the Geddes proposals smacked of self-interest by some of the chief architects of 'squandermania'. To accept them would also reduce the authority of the service ministries, leaving them open to further 'reviews of national expenditure'. The proposal for a Ministry of Defence was thus a clever and direct threat to the service ministries, potentially increasing the ability of the Treasury to block or restrict spending on naval and other arms.

When the Geddes proposals, which swiftly became known as the Geddes axe, were made public, there were a range of responses. *The Times* gave a warm welcome to the proposal. The Saturday 11 February 1922 edition put the Geddes proposals squarely on the front page. The level of detail within the report was considerable, as was the newspaper's very public support for the cuts. Similarly enthusiastic responses by the print media to the Geddes cuts could be found in the Empire with the Sydney *Sunday Times* proclaiming, 'Economy Begins at Home.'[5] On the left of British politics there was equally firm support for the cutting of military expenditure.

However, from the Admiralty came a memorandum which, point-by-point, challenged the figures of the Geddes Committee, the nature of the calculation and the suggested extent of any saving. Remarkably this was released to the press. Stressing the Admiralty's commitment to reduce expenditure to the irreducible minimum, the memorandum cautioned as follows:

> Relying on the important agreements which the Government has entered into at Washington, the Admiralty have themselves produced very large reductions in the expenditure of the Navy which will affect personnel, dockyards, and all other services. Their object has been so to reduce the charge of the Navy as to inflict the least possible damage on those services which are most essential to the strength of the Fleet. They believe that these alternative reductions, amounting altogether to a total very little short of the quite unsubstantial round figure asked for by the Committee of National Expenditure, will not only in the result prove greater than could have been actually secured under the recommendations of that Committee, but that they will also avoid the impairment, and indeed almost complete destruction of, naval efficiency which would be involved in any attempt to translate these recommendations into action.[6]

The memorandum resulted in a flurry of public comment and criticism.[7] *The Times* commented on publication of the memorandum:

> Whether the Admiralty is right or wrong does not affect the question of the propriety of its opening its defence at this juncture and in this manner... A departmental rejoinder should be approved by the Cabinet and, if thought desirable, be given to the public... The question at the moment is not as to the soundness of the Admiralty's case, but as to the subordination of that Department to the Cabinet in a matter not yet judged.[8]

The local and regional press in Britain and throughout the Empire were just as exercised by the Admiralty's response to Geddes. The *Aberdeen Daily Journal* claimed that the memorandum showed that the department was 'up in arms' over the Geddes proposals.[9] *The [Dundee] Evening Telegraph and Post* described the Admiralty's reply as 'amazing'.[10] More pointedly *The Nottingham Evening Post* questioned the Admiralty's 'tact' in issuing the memorandum and questioned whether it constituted a 'grave breach of official discipline'.[11] Further afield *The Argus* in Melbourne, Victoria, carried a report on the memorandum under the heading 'Navy Challenges Report', and even the small-circulation provincial press in the Australian periphery thought the story serious enough to bring it to the attention of their readers.[12] Such widespread reportage demonstrates the extent to which Australian readers in particular appreciated how much imperial defence hinged on the Royal Navy.

Within naval circles there was some satisfaction at the robust nature of the Admiralty's response to the Geddes proposals.[13] In Cabinet on 18 February 1922 there was what Leo Amery later described in his diary as a 'first class tussle' between himself, Lee of Fareham and Robert Horne over the memorandum and the figures.[14] Seemingly in the interests of avoiding any possibility that Amery might be backed into a corner to the point of resignation, Lloyd George tried to build bridges between his Unionist colleagues. Amery's memorandum was dismissed as a minor matter, which was an unfortunate misunderstanding. In trying to address the substantive issue Lloyd George asked the Admiralty to see what else it might do in the interests of national economy. Following this, as the debate in government continued to revolve without either side giving ground, the Admiralty went on a public offensive drawing public attention to the extent of savings on the naval estimates since the armistice.[15] There was some public unease at the Admiralty's obvious unwillingness to work with the Geddes Committee as evidenced by one judge in the King's Bench Division. With a court case before him which involved the Admiralty's overpayment of £3,740 on a commercial contract to attack the department, the judge made a number of inflammatory remarks that were picked up in the press. Seeing the number of Admiralty officials in the court he commented. 'I suppose work at Whitehall has come to a standstill.'[16] Picking up on some of the judge's other criticisms of the Admiralty, one Dundee newspaper noted thus: 'This is the Department which spurned Sir Eric Geddes' Committee of distinguished business men as incompetent!'[17] Public sniping at the Admiralty continued in the newspapers for several weeks, with at least one local newspaper in March reporting Treasury criticisms of the Admiralty. Along with the publication of the final account for the Navy in the 1920–21 financial year, the Treasury released a letter from the Treasury to the Admiralty of 7 February 1922 calling attention to the fact that 'for the second year running naval expenditure has been under-estimated by very substantial sums [£1,632,990]'.[18] Nevertheless the Admiralty's intransigence continued, and eventually, the Geddes proposals were sent for review to a new committee under the chairmanship of Churchill where they were downgraded. Most importantly the Churchill committee concluded that there was no need to create a Ministry of Defence so long as the expenditure of each service was given detailed scrutiny. The key strategic battle had been won by the Royal Navy: the Admiralty would remain as a seat of power in Whitehall.[19] The extension of Treasury control had been resisted and the department, aided by the findings of the Churchill Committee that Geddes had not adequately factored inflation into his calculations of the requirements of the three services, could turn its attention back to the defence of the naval estimates. The Churchill Committee eventually concluded that naval estimates of £62 million were necessary for the Royal Navy to continue to operate on a one-power standard, in comparison to the £60 million put forward by Geddes. The Churchill Committee's suggested figure formed the basis for the naval estimates put forward to the House of Commons on 16 March.

The House of Commons during March 1922 revealed a number of reactions to the diplomatic and military outcomes of the Washington Conference, the threat of the Geddes Axe on British naval policy and Admiralty responses thereto. In the House of Commons on 16 March Leo Amery, carefully reiterating the critical points where the Geddes Committee had got their sums wrong, declared that the result of the Washington Conference was that

> without any dereliction from the one-power standard, the recognised minimum of security necessary for our existence as a free Power, we have been able to make far-reaching reductions in our naval organisation, and to effect economies, very substantial, when compared with the expenditure of the present year, and immense when compared with the future burdens that otherwise we should have had to shoulder.[20]

Lieutenant Colonel Burgoyne, the Unionist MP for North Kensington, picked up Amery's theme of burdens:

> The term 'naval supremacy' is wiped out of the British dictionary; we are finished in that line, and we can be rather proud of it, for what we have done is that we have announced to the world that we are prepared to go into partnership with the other great English-speaking race and are going to ask them in the future to bear something of the burdens and responsibilities of naval control.[21]

In a debate on voting an excess to the Naval Estimates for 1921–22, many MPs were ready to applaud the government's ambitions and actions at the Washington Conference, with the eventual vote being passed by 121 votes to 42.[22] In particular, Lieutenant Commander Kenworthy praised the British delegation for attempting to get the submarine abolished as a weapon of war.[23] Meanwhile Leo Amery, the Financial Secretary to the Admiralty, reassured the House that there was no question of planning for war with either Japan or the United States: 'If we were contemplating war with anyone, it would be our duty to this country to come to the House and ask for a measure of naval provision which would make the situation really secure. We depend absolutely for our life as a country and for our existence as an Empire on being able to hold the seas.'[24]

Despite some concern that over £533,000 of taxpayer's money had been wasted on the G-3 battlecruisers that were now to be scrapped under the Washington proposals, there was a widespread feeling that the Washington proposals and the Geddes cuts were part of the very same necessary process.[25] In any case, MPs were reassured that much of the expenditure had been on gun mountings that would be fitted to the two new battleships, and in other quarters there was an equally pressing concern to secure orders connected with the new building programme which would safeguard critical capacity in the armaments industry.[26]

In truth the Admiralty had 'pulled a fast one'. In the vigorous debate which had broken out between the Admiralty and Treasury in 1921 over the contracting for the G-3 battlecruisers, Sir George Barstow had insisted on the inclusion of cancellation clauses in the contracts with the four shipyards. Those clauses allowed the Admiralty to cancel the contracts in 1922 without serious financial repercussions for the Treasury. Understandably Barstow was somewhat upset when it emerged that cancellation clauses had not been inserted into the contracts for the machinery and armament that was to go into the hulls of the four ships. Revealingly in terms of the Treasury mind-set he was further irritated at having to come up with an appropriate accounting line and mechanism (under a separate subheading in the Navy appropriations) for money which had been lost to the Treasury by the Admiralty's oversight.[27] In an internal Treasury minute Barstow commented:

> I am exceedingly sorry that the Treasury did not make it clear without the possibility of evasion that in our view the question of a cancellation clause was a general question applying not merely to the hull and machinery contracts for the capital ships, but also the guns, gun mountings and armour. The emphasis with which we insisted on the necessity for a cancellation clause must have made it

> perfectly clear to the Admiralty that the Treasury at least regards the possibility of cancellation as not negligible: and if the Admiralty had not been so madly keen to commit the Govt. irrevocably to the building of these ships, they could not have ignored the implication of the Treasury request. [In point of fact I have reason to believe that the Admiralty decision not to have a cancellation clause in the gun, mountings and contracts was taken deliberately by the First Lord and First Sea Lord – overruling the argument put forward by their financial officers].[28]

In the debate on 24 March none of the Members of Parliament raised in public the kind of concerns being aired by Sir George Barstow in the private corridors of the Treasury. Many Conservatives were glad to avoid the cost of a ruinous arms race. Most of the naval lobby were ready to accept the realities of the situation. During the course of the debate, Lieutenant Colonel Ashley, one of the leading lights of the Navy League, concluded that 'We have got to cut our clothes according to our cloth. I would like to have a two-power standard, or I would like to have a three-power standard… But we must come down to realities.'[29] Left-wing members rejoiced in the achievement of a substantial measure of disarmament, but some radical members on both sides of the House wished the cuts could have gone further. Murray Sueter, for example, spoke against the building of two new battleships because of the obsolescence of the class:

> Why do we want to build two battleships in 1923?… I myself think that the capital ship is practically obsolete, though it may still have a potential value… By… most naval officers the usefulness of capital ships is regarded as problematical under existing naval and international conditions, and as still more problematical 10 years hence. Their retention appears to be due to a sort of megalomania and desire for window-dressing.[30]

Other MPs offered specific commentary on some of the Geddes proposals. Kenworthy, for example, stated that it was common knowledge in the Navy that it had been suggested to the Admiralty that if they did not insist on the closure of Pembroke Dockyard, they would be given an easy ride on other items. He further proposed the end of training junior officers of school age at Dartmouth and instead wanted them to be recruited directly from schools after completing their education.[31]

The issue of the Admiralty memorandum clearly troubled some MPs. On 16 March Leo Amery, during the debate on the Naval Estimates for 1922–23, was challenged over the publication of the memorandum. He responded by saying that it had been 'issued in pursuance of the Cabinet decision authorising Ministers to take such steps as might be required to rebut reflections made upon their Departments in the Report and that it neither discussed nor prejudged the issues of policy'.[32] One week later Amery again had to defend himself as Murray Sueter argued:

> The Geddes Report was issued on the Friday and on the following Sunday we were bombarded in the Press with such headlines as: 'The Admiralty torpedo the Geddes Report,' and 'Lord Beatty fires into the Report of the Geddes Committee.' That was most unpatriotic procedure, and the Admiralty were very ill-advised in issuing that Memorandum. If the Admiralty think fit to send such a Memorandum to the Press over the heads of Parliament and the Cabinet – I understand that the Lord Privy Seal said he had never seen that Memorandum until it was in the Press, and I believe the late Secretary for India also said it was not before the Cabinet – the Admiralty, which appealed to the public over the heads of Parliament and the Cabinet, have no right to break their own officers for appealing to Cæsar.[33]

The Amery memorandum caused a storm in 1922, and one which was slow to subside. However, that storm has been almost completely overlooked by historians of the period. The appearance of a government department publicly rejecting the suggestions of a Cabinet committee was striking as evidenced by Sueter's speech. Amery was not only unapologetic, but he also received no sanction for the publication of the memorandum. It was a remarkable episode, and, if nothing else, it demonstrated the Admiralty's confidence in responding to government proposals that it considered prejudicial to the maritime security of the United Kingdom.

12

Repercussions

We have reached the limit. Things have been scraped to the bone... We cannot go further unless, indeed, we abandon the one-power standard altogether, and drop to the rank of the second or third naval power – and if we drop once we shall do so for all time. We have no right to do that. We owe the maintenance of that standard to our fellow subjects in the Empire, with whom we formally, by resolution of the Empire Conference, agreed only last summer that the standard of equality with any other Power was our minimum. We have collaborated again with them at Washington in these last few months in re-affirming that standard and definitely fixing it in actual terms of ships and tonnage in the Naval Treaty. We owe it in trust to future generations of our people here and across the seas. All else in politics may change; one principle stands firm and beyond question. We live and move and have our being as a nation and as an empire by our power to keep open and free the highways of the sea. That power we can never surrender even to the best friend or the closest ally.[1]

Speaking in the House of Commons on 16 March 1922 Leo Amery, the Financial Secretary to the Admiralty, outlined the repercussions for the Royal Navy of the decision to accept a one-power standard, the deliberations and Washington Conference, and the further assault on naval spending which had emerged with the Geddes axe. In Amery's view if the Rubicon had not yet been crossed, the river had at least been reached and further naval cuts would raise profound dangers for Britain and the Empire. As Amery's biographer notes, he remained highly sceptical in private about the value of the agreement reached at Washington but in public he extoled its virtues and the statesmanship of President Harding.[2]

The economic and social repercussions of the decision to cancel the G-3 capital vessels were similarly apparent along part of the chain of connections involved in naval policy. The day before Amery's speech in the House of Commons senior ministers met with a deputation from the provinces eager to discuss the consequences of the cancellation. The deputation comprised Sir Samuel Roberts MP and the Lord Mayors of Sheffield, Newcastle, Barrow, Wallsend, Gateshead, Tynemouth, Jarrow and South Shields together with the Lord Provost of Glasgow. Roberts was Conservative member for Hereford, but had previously been Lord Mayor of Sheffield. His father was the MP for the Sheffield Ecclesall constituency as well as a director of Cammell Laird. The Board minutes for the Birkenhead shipbuilder show that he was regarded as a good friend of the business.[3] The deputation was received by Lee of Fareham and Robert Horne.

In opening the discussion Roberts outlined the position: 'The unemployment situation in the towns concerned, which… was already very serious before the cancellation of the orders, had been accentuated.'[4] The promise of two smaller capital ships was welcome news but the delay in their building until the end of the forthcoming financial year made for a serious situation in the cities represented in the deputation. The Lord Mayor of Sheffield reported that 50,000 men were unemployed in the city, amounting to 10 per cent of the workforce. Unemployment in Barrow had reached the level of 16 per cent and many of those in work were on short time. The Lord Provost of Glasgow gave the unemployment figure in the city as '76,000 unemployed and 9,500 on half time'.[5] In responding to the deputation, Lee of Fareham said that the government had been faced with no choice, but to cancel the orders for the four ships and that the delay in placing orders for the two 35,000 ton battleships was similarly inevitable as it would take time for the necessary design work to be concluded. The Chancellor of the Exchequer said that he would do what he could to ensure that the orders for the two new battleships came as quickly as possible.

Interestingly, within the Treasury files at the National Archives in Kew, there are two reports of the meeting. One version is intended for circulation within Whitehall, while the other is a rather longer document that seems to have been retained within the Treasury. The chief difference between the two papers concerns the remarks made by Sir Samuel Roberts MP to Lee of Fareham and Horne before the members of the delegation were brought into the room. Roberts went to considerable lengths to foreground the comments of the Lord Mayors by stressing the urgency of the situation and urging the need for 'instant relief'. He further stated, 'Quiet has been kept fairly well in these industrial centres, but there is a fear that discord may break out and trouble arise at any moment… There is no doubt that there is an undercurrent of feeling which might give rise to very serious trouble unless something is done for them to meet the immediate situation.'[6] In the circumstances of 1922 this was a clear warning

Table 12.1 John Brown's shipyard: employment and wages 1914–22

Year	Number employed	Average wages
1914	9,000–10,000	£1 16s. 8d.
1920	9,297	£4 2s.
1921	6,322	£3 13s. 5d.
1922	3,653	£2 14s.

Source: Figures drawn from Burton, Anthony, *The Rise and Fall of British Shipbuilding* (London: Constable, 1994), pp. 182–83.

that the cancellation of the order for the G-3 battlecruisers could reignite the spirit of Red Clydeside, spreading radical socialism to other areas.

What the deputation did not touch upon, but what remained of vital significance to the regions in which the ships were built, was that shipyard owners used high unemployment to cut wages. Thus the value to local economies of the men who still had jobs in the shipyards declined markedly, as can be seen from the figures for John Brown's (Table 12.1).

Despite the warnings, the Treasury remained resistant to any steps to hasten the building of the two new battleships. Sir George Barstow commented, 'Is their construction inevitable? I have no doubt of the Admiralty answer.'[7] He was willing to concede that there was perhaps some point in advancing the contracts to rather earlier in the financial year, if the decision to build them was irrevocable, so as to provide a 'form of outdoor relief' to some of the towns in Scotland and the north of England. His rationale was that it was 'better to build them during a period of unemployment and thus absorb labour which otherwise has to be supported from some form of public assistance'.[8] However, the Treasury was not prepared to go along with this line of policy before the department had tested whether or not the decision to order the ships was truly 'inevitable'.

Other departments also had designs on the money which the Admiralty hoped to spend on the two battleships. On 22 July Lee of Fareham wrote to Lloyd George to express his concern that lobbying was taking place on behalf of the Air Ministry to find funds for expansion by abandoning plans to build the two battleships.[9] His letter contained a thinly veiled threat of resignation should money for the battleships be put at the disposal of the Air Ministry. He also suggested that the Board of Admiralty would similarly find itself in an 'untenable' position.[10] On the day before sending the letter, Lee had remarked to Amery that 'the PM and Horne really mean to have a serious go at getting rid of the two capital ships and that he means to make it quite clear that the Board will stand no nonsense but will go out in a body rather than submit to that'.[11]

The Admiralty was not the only party to be deeply concerned at the wait to place orders for the new battleships. British shipbuilders, especially those who had lost contracts for the G-3 battlecruisers, were eager for news of the tendering process for the 35,000-ton vessels, and from the following press report from August 1921 'parliamentary representatives' in some of the concerned constituencies were eager to solicit information from governments sources:

> Shipbuilders concerned are hoping that at least one of the new battleship orders will be placed on the Clyde. Sir John Lindsay, town clerk of Glasgow, has received a communication on this subject from one of the city's Parliamentary representatives, who says that having made inquiry into the matter he has been given to understand unofficially that the tenders may be issued about October, and work under the contracts started towards the end of the year. The writer adds that, although it is not possible to make any prediction, the hope is entertained that one of the contracts will come to the Clyde.[12]

The battle between the Admiralty and the Treasury ensured that the matter would not be quickly resolved and by September the threat of an Anglo-Turkish war led to political crisis in Britain.

The fall of the Lloyd George government in October 1922, the resulting interregnum and the formation of a new Conservative administration under Andrew Bonar Law following the election on 15 November gave the Treasury a potential chance to reopen the debate on the two battleships. In early November Treasury solicitors were asked to give legal opinion on whether the stipulations of the Washington Treaty required the building of two new British capital ships in the current financial year. Opinion was also sought from the Attorney General who concluded that the Washington Treaty did not mean that Britain had to build the vessels, but that if they wished to proceed with construction then work had to begin before the end of 1922, and the ships launched before the end of 1925.[13] Leo Amery considered the opinion 'nonsense', but helpful in that it brought added pressure to lay the ships down before the end of the year.[14] The Admiralty's departmental response to the Treasury's concerns sought to enlist the support of the Foreign Office by suggesting that to unpick one part of the Washington Treaty would be to undermine the whole.[15]

With these opinions circulating in Whitehall, an internal review was prepared by the civil servants at the Treasury for Stanley Baldwin, the incoming Chancellor of the Exchequer. The review concluded that 'we neither need nor can afford these two ships, and that, as far as prestige is concerned, the moral effect of not building would tell greatly in our favour'.[16] The review was extensive and covered much of the ground of previous discussions about American and

Japanese intentions. On the latter the Treasury were fully content that 'There is nothing in Japan's record to justify the belief that she would be capable of an unprovoked attack on a Power which has hitherto been her best friend, or would incur the risk of bringing against her the two leading naval powers of the world'.[17] In framing the review, the Treasury strayed well beyond the facts and figures of the national balance sheet to engage in diplomatic and strategic readings better the province of the Foreign Office and Admiralty. The gifts of foresight that allowed the Treasury to predict that the Japanese attack on Pearl Harbor would never come, and that the British Empire in East Asia would not be overwhelmed, were in reality simply a ruse to cut national expenditure at any cost. The real goal of the Treasury was, in all probability, that the building of one of the ships (with attendant costs) might be deferred until a later date.

The Admiralty's response came in the form of an 'immediate and personal' letter to Baldwin from Leo Amery.[18] The letter, backed by supporting Admiralty papers analysing the issue of the capital ships, was indeed personal rather than departmental in its tone and contents. Amery emphasized the impact on unemployment relief if the ships were built (22,000 men employed, saving over £1 million a year). Amery appears to have had a good appreciation of his audience. Roy Jenkins has argued that Baldwin was concerned at the level of unemployment on both economic and political grounds.[19] High unemployment, in Baldwin's opinion, would make for a more radical Labour Party, and yet he could see few ways to affect reductions in the number of the jobless. Amery's immediate and personal level offered the new Chancellor of the Exchequer one potential means to make a reduction in unemployment.

Amery further argued in his letter to Baldwin that to fail to build the ships could undermine the Washington agreement. The effect of not building them, and the conclusion, that the Royal Navy had abandoned the one-power standard, would have a dramatic effect, or 'moral shock' as he put it, on the Empire.[20] Perhaps most critically of all, given recent political events when Conservative backbenchers and junior ministers had risen against the party hierarchy to bring down the Lloyd George coalition, Amery pointed to the political fallout from a failure to build the ships: 'As for public opinion here, that opinion, especially in the rank and file of our own Party, would be terribly shocked by the open avowal – and it would have to be an open and explicit avowal in Parliament – that we were no longer even approximately equal first among the sea powers'.[21] In addition, to the wider political issues of party identity and outlook, the specific issues of unemployment in staple industries affecting particular constituencies had not gone away. Despite the hopes expressed during the visit of the deputation of Lord Mayors on 15 March, the lack of improvement in the unemployment situation in those cities caused resentments to build during 1922. For example, in July the Lord Mayor of Sheffield had written to Sir Samuel Roberts to express his disappointment that the government had done nothing to advance the orders for the two ships, and to ask Roberts to arrange a meeting with the Prime Minister so that they might again put the case.[22]

The results of the 1922 general election were still being digested by the parties when Amery wrote to Baldwin to outline the Admiralty case. On the face of it the Conservative Party had done well, securing 55.93 per cent of the available seats (343), with the Labour Party far behind with 23.09 per cent (142). The Liberals, divided between those loyal to Asquith and those supporters of Lloyd George, managed to take just 18.70 per cent of the available seats (115). Over 50 per cent of the seats captured by the Lloyd George Liberals in 1918 changed hands in 1922. The outcome was a disaster for the Liberals and a significant breakthrough for Labour. The apparent decline of the Liberals and the divisions within them set alarm bells ringing for many Conservatives concerned by the rise of socialism. While the Conservatives were clear winners in terms of the numbers of seats gained, and would form the next government, any analysis of the popular vote for the 1922 general election pointed to a less emphatic victory: Conservatives (38.51%), Labour (29.65%) and the Liberals (18.92%). The Conservatives were massively over-represented in terms of their share of the popular vote, and 141 of the Conservative MPs elected had majorities of less than 1,500.[23] The results pointed to shifting electoral loyalties as the working classes in particular transferred their support from the Liberal Party to Labour. Liberal candidates did best when they were in straight fights against Conservative candidates. As Cook and Stevenson have written, the 1922 General Election transformed Labour's position from a minor party with an insecure base into that of potential party of government with key strongholds in Britain's industrial heartland.[24] Most importantly, in terms of the political warnings from Roberts and Amery to senior figures in the Conservative Party, came the constituency contests in areas such as Sheffield (critically affected by decisions on naval armaments). While some contests in the seven constituencies that covered the city indicated no change in terms of voter alignments, three (Attercliffe, Brightside and Hillsborough) demonstrated startling breakthroughs for Labour as workers abandoned the Liberals (Table 12.2).

The same pattern was also apparent on Clydeside and Tyneside, both critically affected by the decline of staple industries and by the lack of orders for British ships. In the Glasgow Govan Constituency, Labour turned a 1918 majority of 815

Table 12.2 Sheffield results showing seismic shifts towards the Labour Party in some constituencies (three Labour gains from the Liberals)

Sheffield Attercliffe		
1918	*Votes*	*Per cent*
Thomas Worrall Casey (Coalition Liberal)	12,308	65.3
William Crawford Anderson (Labour)	6,539	34.7
1922		
Cecil Henry Wilson (Labour)	16,206	68.2
Thomas Worrall Casey (National Liberal)	7,562	31.8
Sheffield Brightside		
1918		
John Tudor Walters (Liberal)	12,164	64.2
R.E. Jones (Labour)	6,781	35.8
1922		
Arthur Ponsonby (Labour)	16,692	60.4
John Tudor Walters (National Liberal)	10,949	39.6
Sheffield Hillsborough		
1918		
Arthur Neal (Coalition Liberal)	11,171	73.4
Arthur Lockwood (Co-operative Party)	4,050	26.6
1922		
A.V. Alexander (Labour Co-op)	15,130	56.2
Arthur Neal (National Liberal)	11,812	43.8

Note: 'The General Election', *The Times*, 16 November 1922, p. 6.

into one of 6,105 in 1922. In the city overall ten of the city's fifteen constituencies were gained by Labour with eight fresh gains (five from the Conservatives and three from the Lloyd George Liberals).[25] In Paisley Herbert Henry Asquith, Liberal Leader and former Prime Minister, saw his majority of 2,834 at the by-election of 1920 cut to just 316 in 1922. Asquith's daughter recorded in her diary how from the safety of a Glasgow hotel she and her father watched the results come in, while outside the crowd greeted every Labour victory with a deeply intimidating roar of approval.[26]

In the North East, South Shields saw 14.9 per cent swing to Labour with the Asquith Liberal candidate Edward Harney just winning the seat with a majority of thirty-five. Elsewhere on Tyneside, Gateshead was captured by Labour from the sitting Conservative, Jarrow was a Labour gain from the Liberals and Wallsend fell to Labour with a majority of 2,823 over the second-placed Conservative candidate. Similarly dramatic and, for the Conservatives, potentially worrying shifts in voter behaviour could be found in other constituencies potentially affected by the lack of naval orders. In Birkenhead, where employment was dominated by Cammell Laird, the withdrawal of the order for one of the G-3 battlecruisers helped to generate two interesting results in 1922. East Birkenhead was a rare Liberal gain from Alfred Bigland, the sitting Conservative MP, as the Labour Party declined to contest the constituency. In the neighbouring constituency (West Birkenhead) the Labour vote rose by 4,698, more than halving the majority of the sitting Conservative MP Lieutenant Colonel W.H. Stott. All told, fourteen of Labour's eighty-five gains at the 1922 general election came from areas directly affected by the failure to restart capital shipbuilding in the post war period.

As Iain McLean has noted about the 1922 general election, as a percentage of the electorate more people voted for Labour in Glasgow (41.6%) and Sheffield (42.5%) than in any other British city (Manchester was a distant third with 34.8%).[27] While it would be tempting to suppose a simple causal relationship between the cancellation of the G-3 battlecruisers and the outcomes of the constituency contests in Sheffield and Glasgow, the realities of the political life of both cities defy simple explanations. For example, in Glasgow while shipbuilding was the principal feature of the economies in areas south of the Clyde such as Fairfield, Govan and Kingston, other industries dominated life in the rest of the city. Analysis of the election literature put out by some of the Labour candidates in Glasgow in 1922 suggests unemployment and high rents as the issues on which the party was most keen to make its appeal to the voters. References to shipbuilding were few and far between, and Labour's commitment to the League of Nations and disarmament, if not outright pacifism, clearly limited party candidates in championing capital shipbuilding.[28] However, this could not disguise the fact that, with unemployment a key electoral issue, naval policy had the capacity to affect constituencies with shipyards employing thousands, across neighbouring constituencies that provided services to the shipyards and their workers and to places further afield, like Sheffield, that would supply the steel plate, machinery and semi-finished fabrications to build and outfit hulls.

In the aftermath of the election it was clear that securing orders that would underpin the local economies of constituencies hard hit by the long-term decline of staple industries was a means of safeguarding some sitting Conservative MPs in cities such as Sheffield, and a means of preventing the mass mobilization of working-class votes by the Labour Party: better a Conservative MP than a Liberal, but better a Liberal than a Labour member. Even in seats held by the Conservatives there were issues. In Plymouth, for example, aided by the July 1921 award of a contract to the Devonport Dockyard to build a cruiser minelayer, three sitting Conservative MPs had fought off strong challenges from Labour and the Liberals. At the time of the election the ship had still not been laid down and the issue of local unemployment was a factor in the election.

One man acutely aware of the dramatic swings to Labour was Conservative leader and Prime Minister Andrew Bonar Law, who, from his Glasgow Central constituency, had been ideally placed to witness Labour's dramatic victories. As Lord Blake, Bonar Law's biographer has noted, the leader of the Conservative Party was so concerned by the Labour tide sweeping Glasgow that he feared he might be defeated in his Glasgow Central constituency, and at least one Scottish newspaper had been prepared to speculate on that possibility in the closing hours of the election.[29] In the aftermath of the election *The Glasgow Herald* railed against those who had 'treated the menace of socialism with a degree of levity'.[30] A quarter of a million people had gathered in Glasgow city centre and at St Enoch railway station to send off the ten victorious Labour MPs as they departed for Westminster. On arrival at Westminister the Clydeside MPs made their presence immediately felt, helping to get Ramsay MacDonald elected as party leader. Although their radicalism was dulled and thwarted initially, they promised to radicalize the Labour Party. As Josiah Wedgwood noted, 'The coming of the Clydeside Socialists in 1922 was as the on-rush of a tidal wave. As was natural they had the poorest opinion of the old-stagers ... who had had all the limelight while they were building up a Socialist City Council in Glasgow, and a body of doctrine suitable for the soap-box at the street corner.'[31]

Remarkably for a politician, in the aftermath of the election Bonar Law continued to take little interest in the navy and the issue of shipbuilding. His thinking was dominated by other concerns of economy, business opportunity and honest government. In the midst of the election, as Bonar Law was preparing to give a speech in Glasgow, Tom Jones in the Cabinet Secretariat had been struck by Bonar Law's attachment to the ideology of business, personal responsibility and private enterprise. He was equally struck by his complete emotional failure to engage with the vital concerns of the Glasgow electorate. Begging the Conservative leader to make at least some gesture towards the plight of the Scottish working classes, Jones spoke of near starvation in the city and how birds could be seen nesting on the immobile cranes of the shipyards on the Clyde.[32]

In the aftermath of the election Bonar Law's 'sea blindness' continued to worry some of his closest supporters. Leo Amery, who had been rewarded with the post of First Lord of the Admiralty for his role in overthrowing Lloyd George, met with Bonar Law on 21 November 1922. Although, eight days later the keel of cruiser-minelayer HMS *Adventure* would be laid in the Devonport Dockyard in Plymouth, Amery confided in his diary that the meeting had not been wholly productive, as Bonar Law did not share his enthusiasm for the Royal Navy and remained sceptical about the value of the capital ship.[33] Rather than try and win over the Prime Minister, Amery hoped that the balance of opinion in Cabinet would support the Admiralty's position.

The approaching deadline of 31 December 1922 to lay down the two ships concentrated minds, and Leo Amery appears to have continued his campaign, stressing the strategic, economic (poor relief) and political case virtues of their construction. His letter to the Prime Minister on 5 December, which stated that contracts for the new construction and associated machinery were ready to go out, assured Bonar Law that he would find little objection in Parliament to the placing of the orders 'so substantial' was 'the employment involved'.[34] The following day in the House of Lords, Lee of Fareham, the former First Lord of the Admiralty, made a plea for the new ships in a way calculated to appeal to Conservative opinion: 'You cannot always expect to have the newest and the best, but there is this difference between the newest and less new in the case of capital ships. The post-Jutland capital ships possessed by the United States and Japan are capable of out ranging and capital ship which we possess.'[35] Thus on 11 December 1922 HMS *Nelson* was ordered from Armstrong Whitworth, and HMS *Rodney* from Cammell Laird at Birkenhead. With just three days left of the year, their keels were laid down on 28 December. This was both a political victory and a technical one. Faced with the cancellation of the G-3 battlecruisers and the need for a new design (built to treaty specifications, incorporating the lessons of the First World War, with the heaviest possible armament, and good and economical cruising range), the year had been a considerable challenge to the Director of Naval Construction and his team.[36]

By utilizing key elements, and those parts of the G-3 programme contracted without a cancellation clause, the Department of Naval Construction was able to produce an effective all round design that could be built within treaty specification and at a reasonable price. The weight was a particularly worrying issue, and Eustace Tennyson d'Eyncourt counselled the shipbuilders to make the

Table 12.3 Cammell Laird profit and loss in the 1920s

1920	+ £260,632
1921	+ £170,487
1922	+ £145,906
1923	+ £70,053
1924	+ £70,894
1925	- £36,381
1926	- £73,575
1927	- £112,046
1928	- £80,695

Note: Cammell Laird Annual Reports 1920–28, in Board Minutes, Cammell Laird papers ZCL5/44. See also Warren, *Steel, Ships and Men*, p. 204.

best ship possible while respecting the constraints on tonnage specified by the Washington Treaty.[37]

HMS *Nelson* (33,500 tons) was launched on 3 September 1925 and HMS *Rodney* (33,900 tons) on 17 December in the same year and in line with the date and tonnage stipulations of the Washington Treaty. The value of the contracts to their respective shipyards, in a difficult economic environment, can be glimpsed in the Annual Reports for Cammell Laird's in the 1920s (Table 12.3).

Nelson and *Rodney* were commissioned into the Royal Navy in late 1927 (15 August and 7 December, respectively), although some officers were less than enamoured of their design. As Stephen Roskill has commented, within the Royal Navy the Nelson class of battleship was disliked on aesthetic grounds.[38] The main thing, however, was that thanks to agreement at Washington, and thanks to a vigorous defence of the needs of the Royal Navy by Amery, there would be some shipbuilding, bringing relief to some communities and allowing a limited modernization of the surface fleet. It wasn't much, but it was better than nothing. HMS *Nelson* and HMS *Rodney* would breathe at least some life back into British capital shipbuilding. It would be a decade later, with war clouds firmly on the horizon, that British yards would begin the final programmes of battleship construction, to produce ships of rather greater aesthetic repute. Without the building of HMS *Nelson* and *Rodney* in the 1920s, it is doubtful whether British yards would have been able to undertake the ambitious battleship building programme of the late 1930s that provided some of the mainstays of the Royal Navy's wartime effort after 1940. It was a case of just enough and just in time to preserve necessary military capabilities and the industrial infrastructure of Great Britain.

13

Aftermath

The establishment of a Pax Anglo-Americana at Washington in 1921 and the agreement of the politicians, and a very reluctant Treasury, to build the two capital ships allowed under the Treaty were significant successes for the Admiralty and Royal Navy. The full significance of those successes has not been fully recognized by naval historians, at least in part because the Geddes Axe, the Treasury and the pursuit of 'national economy' over succeeding years turned them into hollow victories. British naval predominance had been surrendered in the interests of a diplomatic deal that went some way to balance British commitments and interests against the military and other realities of a power in economic decline. A costly naval-building race had been avoided and Britain remained on good terms with both the United States and Japan, even as the Anglo-Japanese Alliance was allowed to lapse in 1923. Unfortunately, in the years that followed, as this chapter demonstrates, this success was compromised at the political level.

In British political and naval circle there was some sorrow at the passing of the alliance and genuine sympathy towards Japan. In the House of Commons in March 1923, Philip Snowden, Labour Member of Parliament for Colne Valley, and a future Labour Chancellor of the Exchequer, described Japan as 'a country which is uncannily similar to our own, in its geographical configuration and its place in the northern latitudes, and a country which is rapidly developing as a great commercial nation'.[1] He expressed sympathy for her 'increasing population' as 'she looks across the narrow straits which divide her from the American Continent and … sees the words, "no yellow man may enter"'.[2]

Despite such sympathies the Royal Navy pushed ahead with the development of the strategic vision under-pinning naval policy following the Washington Conference. In addition to the building of new ships, that vision required the development of three other lines of policy: the development of a network of strategic oil-bunkering facilities to enable worldwide operations, the building of a major naval base at Singapore to support fleet operations in the Pacific and East Asia and the further development of the dominion navies to augment the forces of the main fleet. Within these three lines of policy was the need to prepare for the danger that Japan might turn hostile at some point in the future, leaving the British Empire in East Asia potentially vulnerable.

Delivering this strategic vision would take time, continuity of policy and stable resourcing: at least two of these three things were singularly absent from the policy of the government in the mid- to late 1920s. Economic and political considerations continued to intrude into naval policy, putting the brakes on the Admiralty's vision. Under Stanley Baldwin's short-lived first administration, policy remained largely on track, but only because political factors favoured the status quo. With foreign policy fixated by the French occupation of the Ruhr in January 1923, and Bonar Law's illness and eventual resignation as Prime Minister in May 1923, there was little scope or time for fundamental change in naval policy. Baldwin was in office for little more than six months before he decided that the economy and unemployment situation, especially in the staple industries of coal, iron, steel and shipbuilding, required him to go to the country on a programme of tariff protection. As Andrew Lambert has argued, in advance of the 1923 general election Baldwin was very much alive to the value of orders for naval construction, and the Admiralty speedily came forward with a programme for the construction of cruisers.[3]

The defeat of the Conservatives in the 1923 election, as the Labour Party increased its number of Scottish MPs from twenty-nine in 1922 to thirty-five in 1923 (despite anti-socialist pacts between the two other main parties in some constituencies), allowed the Labour Party to form its first minority administration.[4] Ramsay MacDonald's surprise choice as First Sea Lord was Lord Chelmsford, former Viceroy of India, and a Conservative. His appointment, as Lieutenant Commander Kenworthy later claimed, was a politically motivated sop to Conservative and Liberal opinion.[5] Certainly the peer only accepted the job after securing concessions from the Prime Minister which obligated the Labour Party to continue to support key elements (cruisers and development of the Singapore base) of the First Sea Lord's strategic vision. Chelmsford understood the political situation of January 1924 only too well: without his acceptance of the post of First Lord of the Admiralty, MacDonald would not be able to secure the agreed quota for secretaries of state in the House of Lords.[6] MacDonald would, therefore, be unable to form a government. In other words, without Labour support for the Admiralty's programme the first Labour government could not have been formed. In the event the Labour government proved rather more supportive of the construction of replacement cruisers than development of Singapore, but under the second Baldwin ministry, formed after an election in late 1924, even the cruiser programme came under growing scrutiny.

In detail, the strategic programme which was developed between 1919 and 1922, and which began to lose its way in 1924, was based on a simple rationale: Britain could afford only one fleet and that had to be based in the North Atlantic and Mediterranean. However, that fleet could continue to exercise military force on a global basis, ensuring the security and uniting the Empire, providing its mobility and operational effectiveness were maximized. In effect the fleet had to be able to go anywhere and conduct offensive operations in any ocean. Dominion naval forces could provide local defence and join with the main fleet on its arrival. The development of strategic fleet facilities across an empire dispersed across the continents, together with a powerful cruiser force, made strategic sense in terms of the Royal Navy, and it also had the potential to help the Empire make sense of itself as a global seaborne Empire rather than a set of widely dispersed territories scattered across the continents. The war, and its senseless waste of almost a million lives from across the British Empire, had raised profound questions about the relationship between the dominions and the mother country which had declared war on behalf of the whole Empire in August 1914. The development of an imperial naval strategy could provide a powerful corrective force to those which were pulling the Empire in different directions, as evidenced by the debate on the Anglo-Japanese Alliance in the run up to, and at, the 1921 Imperial Conference.

While the Royal Navy would get its two new capital ships, the development of oil and base facilities to support the global operations of the fleet became a victim of the continuing drive for economy and the ten-year rule imposed in August 1919. Roskill saw the ten-year rule as one of the dominating influences over naval strategy in the 1920s, while John Ferris has argued that it was really only after 1925 that the ten-year rule truly began to bite.[7] Either way, with the assurance that there would be no war for ten years, the politicians were reluctant to spend any money.

The idea of an Admiralty fuel reserve divided between home and foreign bases had been accepted in principle by the Standing Defence Sub-Committee of the CID on July 1921.[8] The Admiralty considered that a reserve of eight million tons (4.5 at home, 3.5 at overseas bases) would be required to support global fleet operations in time of war. This would insulate Britain from dislocations in the flow of oil on the outbreak of war, and any short-term shortage of tankers as ships were taken up from trade. This reserve would be accumulated over a number of years, at a rate of 500,000 tons per annum, to spread the cost, but by 1930 the reserve would be ready to support operations. In July 1921 while the CID was ready to accept the wisdom of the Admiralty's proposal, they were not ready to agree the cost or the timetable. Thus the cost and timescale for an Admiralty fuel reserve were queried by the Geddes Committee in 1921–22 and by the Churchill Committee, which followed it. Churchill, generally supportive of Admiralty policy, asked for the timescale to be adjusted so that completion of the oil reserve would take until 1933.[9] One member of the naval lobby in Parliament, Viscount Curzon, the Member for Battersea South, attacked the government for its delay in building up the oil reserve: 'You are economising in oil. You are not having the fuel stations that the Admiralty and the staff consider necessary. You are cutting down in the interests of economy, but that it a most serious economy to make.'[10]

During MacDonald's first Labour government, the Chancellor of the Exchequer tried to further delay the timescale and to cut back the size of the total to five million tons divided equally between home and foreign bases.[11] The Admiralty, with Lord Chelmsford as First Lord, fought its corner, but the financial imperatives counted against the Royal Navy. The assault on the fuel reserve was renewed under Baldwin's second government, and between 1926 and 1928 the rate of accumulation, which had been cut to 330,000 tons per annum, reduced still further to 100,000 tons.[12] With the advent of MacDonald's second ministry in 1929, accumulation was stopped altogether, such was the state of the national finances. At each turn chancellors of the Exchequer were happy, indeed eager, to tell the Royal Navy that its reading of strategy in the event of war with Japan was misguided, wrong or simply made up. In the mid-1920s Churchill was ready to accuse the Admiralty of making up the prospect of a war with the Japanese as a means to get its way on the oil reserve and on new cruisers.[13]

The danger of a war in the Far East could be ignored or discounted in ways in which European conflict could not. The distances involved, the time delays in reporting and levels of public awareness of Far Eastern regional issues (as opposed to European – especially after the Great War) meant that problems with Germany, Italy and France were more newsworthy and politically sensitive than difficulties with Japan and China. The Admiralty's suggestion in 1921 that the oil reserve should be completed by 1930 was remarkably good judgement, in view of the evolution of Japan's policies towards China in the 1930s. However, it was only with the evolution of German foreign policy in Europe in the 1930s that the National Government became more ready to fund the oil reserve. By 1937 a total fuel reserve of seven million tons had been agreed and 5,375,000 had been bunkered.[14]

The same pattern of delay on financial grounds, prevarication and politicians questioning the naval strategy of Admirals was apparent in policy towards the Singapore naval base. Having acceded to the Royal Navy's demands for two new capital ships in 1922, the Cabinet was less than eager to fund the development of the Singapore naval base – the key to the Royal Navy being able to operate in the Far East. At that location would be developed the fleet infrastructure to support the operations of the Royal Navy in the Far East in time of war. For much of the time the Royal Navy would have only a token presence at the base as the main fleet concentrated in home waters and the Mediterranean. At the outbreak of hostilities the base had to be prepared to defend itself before the arrival of the relief from the home fleet and/or Mediterranean. That period before the arrival of elements of the main fleet was estimated at seventy days, with a voyage time to Singapore from British waters of twenty-eight to forty-five days (Suez Canal route twenty-eight days – Cape of Good Hope route forty-five days).[15] Safe and secure facilities at Singapore were vital to the post–Washington Conference evolution of British strategy to meet the threat of a war in the Pacific.

The meeting of the Cabinet on 21 February 1923 considered a paper drawn up by Maurice Hankey, Secretary to the Cabinet, on the history of the Singapore naval base. Addressed by the First Sea Lord on the importance and likely cost of developing a fleet base at Singapore, the Cabinet concluded that 'a naval base should be established at Singapore on the understanding that no considerable expenditure need be incurred during the financial year 1923–24, and only a moderate expenditure during the financial year 1924–25'.[16] Progress on the construction of the base remained slow during the 1920s. All work on the project stopped during Ramsay MacDonald's first ministry, only to recommence under Stanley Baldwin's second ministry from 1924 to 1929.[17]

The outcome of the 1924 election cemented Labour's claim to have supplanted the Liberals as one of the two potential parties of government in a two-party system.[18] This was despite the fact that the Labour Party was labouring under significant problems, most especially the electoral fallout from the publication of the Zinoviev letter. The election further emphasized 'moderation and sound national finances' as the basis of the Conservative Party's electoral appeal. Thus progress on the Singapore base remained as limited as the flow of funds to support its development, although the sum of £1,294,000 for the development of the base was forthcoming from Hong Kong (£250,000), the Federated Malay States (£864,000) and New Zealand (£180,000).

In 1929 the incoming Labour government under Ramsay MacDonald once again stopped the project as a gesture towards the process of international disarmament. The stop-start nature of the building programme, and overlapping controversies about the wisdom of constructing a naval base at Singapore, led one commentator in 1932 to write:

> The project of constructing a naval base at Singapore large enough to accommodate the largest warships afloat, ever since it was first decided upon, has been the subject of the liveliest controversy. It has been denounced as a needless affront and provocation to Japan and as out of harmony with the modern tone in international relations and the conciliatory temper of the times; it has been attacked because of the great expense involved; it has been condemned on strategic no less than on political grounds. On the other side, one authority after another has stood forth in defence of what is described as a measure of ordinary Imperial necessity.[19]

However, by the time of the article's publication the Japanese seizure of Manchuria in 1931, combined with the economic downturn and formation of a National Government, had at last resolved the differences between the parties in the House of Commons on the issue of Singapore. With the threat of a hostile Japan, the pace of construction quickened in, with the base finally being completed in 1938 at a cost of £60 million. The base covered 21 square miles and contained the King George VI dry dock, the largest in the world. With its airfields and garrison supposedly able to defend the base for seventy days before the arrival of the main fleet from European and Mediterranean waters, the Singapore base was considered a key bastion of the British Empire in the Far East.

The slow pace of the development of the Royal Navy's strategic vision for Empire and naval dominance took place against the diplomatic backdrop of relations with the United States and Japan. The desire of government to trim the naval estimates in order to help the Exchequer remained a fact of life for the Royal Navy in the 1920s as the service monitored the evolution of diplomatic relations in Asia and the Pacific and the slow pace of development of the strategic infrastructure necessary to support fleet operations on a global basis. Prompted by a steady stream of post–Washington Conference publications on Japan and the Far East, one reviewer for *The Naval Review* took issue with government policy to raise awkward questions about Japanese intentions:

> On Thursday, July 23, 1925, the Prime Minister announced on behalf of the Cabinet that: 'We have found it possible, in view of the peaceful outlook of the world and the absence of any naval antagonism between the Great Powers, very largely to modify the proposals for new construction, which were adumbrated two years ago' (*Hansard*, July 23, 1925). Similar prophecies were made by the

> politicians at the beginning of the year 1914. Their repetition to-day raises the question, what is the answer to the Riddle of Japan? What is the meaning of Japanese naval and military preparations, and on what grounds is based the view of the Cabinet 'of the peaceful outlook and the absence of naval antagonism' so far as it affects the Pacific, where the principal naval Powers are face-to-face?[20]

Unusually for *The Naval Review* the identity of the writer of the review was made clear. It was Geoffrey Drage, former Conservative Party MP and party activist who had worked in Military Intelligence during the First World War.

The issue of naval arms control had not gone away with the signature of the Washington Treaty. An attempt to extend the provisions of the Washington Conference to cruisers, destroyers and submarines, at a conference at Geneva in 1927, foundered as the British and Japanese were unable to accept extension of the 5:5:3 ratio to cruisers. The British considered that they needed a large cruiser force in order to defend the Empire and to ensure the security of Britain's sealines of communication. The abortive Geneva Conference marked a nadir of Anglo-American relations. However, discussions about how naval arms could be limited continued in the late 1920s, with the Wall Street Crash of 1929 and the following Great Depression, clearing the way to a further Naval Conference at London in 1930.[21] Commander Kenworthy later described the British government's preparation and approach to the conference as inadequate and ill-prepared.[22] Amid hopes for a wide-ranging cuts to naval arms, the resulting Washington Naval Treaty signed on 22 April 1930 saw only limited agreement. The treaty established a ratio of 10:10:6 for heavy cruisers and 10:10:7 for light cruisers and destroyers. The tonnage of light cruisers was fixed at 10,000 tons. The prohibition on building capital ships was extended until 1936. These outcomes could probably have been achieved by normal diplomatic means, without the rigmarole and cost of a major international conference.

The true significance of continued Anglo-Japanese-American cooperation at the London Naval Conference in 1930 was highlighted the following year by a crisis over the Chinese province of Manchuria. Staging a bomb blast on the Japanese-controlled South Manchurian railway as a pretext for action, the Imperial Japanese Army took over the capital Mukden, together with the rest of the province. The Japanese claimed a right of self-defence as the Chinese government took the incident to the League of Nations, rather than try to use military force to regain the province. The League investigated the crisis before finally condemning Japan, at which point the Japanese delegation simply walked out of the League of Nations. Manchuria was not restored to Chinese sovereignty until 1945. The crisis resolved a number of outstanding issues affecting British grand strategy in Asia and the Pacific. The lack of an effective response by the League of Nations to the Japanese takeover of Chinese territory highlighted the inadequacies of that organization in the field of peacekeeping and peacemaking. Despite the assurances of British politicians during the 1920s to an electorate sensitized to international issues by the horrors of the First World War, the Manchurian crisis demonstrated that British security would have to depend on the resources of Britain and her Empire. Attempts to work with the Americans to secure a resolution to the crisis came to nothing other than gentle confirmation to the Japanese Navy that it required further expansion to cope with a combined American–British naval threat.

Despite this, and remarkably even after the Manchurian incident, there remained a substantial well pool of respect between the two countries, especially their two navies. As Arthur Marder has commented, 'The old alliance, the traditional friendship of the two navies, memories of the Royal Navy as the teacher of the Imperial Navy, and a profound respect for Nelson and his heirs, all made for a deep-seated tendency in the Imperial Navy, not to want to think seriously about a war with Britain.'[23] However, by the late 1930s, especially after Japan embarked on an all-out war in China in 1937, and events in Europe and Africa demonstrated that three key powers were ready to challenge the post-1918 settlement by force, both Britain and Japan prepared for war.

To some, preparations for war in the late 1930s came as a considerable relief. For the shipbuilders and their workers, naval arms limitation in the 1920s meant hard times and the threat of business failure and the prospect of high unemployment. The award of the contract for HMS *Nelson* to Armstrong Whitworth in 1923 had not brought about a change in the fortunes of the business, or for Tyneside. With limited orders for new merchant ships, and the contract to complete two submarines for Yugoslavia, Armstrong Whitworth had tried to diversify and gain overseas contracts by developing machinery for hydroelectric projects in the Empire. Unfortunately the attempt at diversification had proved to be bad business, and in 1927 Armstrong Whitworth was forced to merge with Vickers to become Vickers Armstrong.[24] The related impacts on employment had been dramatic. In 1914 the company had employed 17,953 at its Elswick works. At the wartime peak in 1917 the works provided 62,895 jobs. By March 1929 just 4,000 people remained at the Elswick works.[25] Armstrong Whitworth was not alone in this misfortune. John Brown's yard, which had employed 9,297 men at the peak in 1920, was down to just 422 care and maintenance staff by late 1932.[26] In the 1930s the company was only saved from insolvency by an order from Cunard to build the *Queen Mary*. Likewise, by 1929 the William Beardmore company, which had built eleven major warships, twenty-one destroyers, plus other warships between 1906 and 1919, but just one cruiser and two submarines in the decade thereafter, faced bankruptcy. The Bank of England stepped in to give National Shipbuilder's Security Ltd. £300,000 to close the Dalmuir yard, which was still the heart of the company despite efforts to diversify into cars, motorcycles and steam engines. Dalmuir was closed and its facilities dismantled.[27] Behind the declines of businesses like Beardmore, Armstrong Whitworth and John Brown lay other figures pointing to joblessness, poverty and despair.[28]

The inability of politicians to respond to the problems affecting the shipbuilding industry was starkly apparent. Even the Liberal Party's supposedly visionary 1928 yellow book on *Britain's Industrial Future* could offer little in the way of practical suggestion and was happy to dispense with the problems of the shipbuilding industry in just a handful of pages.[29] Then in 1929, with the prospect of a new agreement on naval arms which would crystallize into the London Naval Treaty of 1930, remarks by Labour Prime Minister Ramsay MacDonald were sufficient to set alarm bells ringing among the unions. MacDonald's comments in the House of Commons led Vickers to start laying men off on Tyneside, which in turn produced alarming reports in the local media.[30] This resulted in the government receiving two deputations in August and October 1929 which expressed serious concerns at the levels of unemployment on Tyneside and the problems, in particular, of shipbuilding. The first deputation was received on 28 August 1929 by MacDonald together with George Lansbury, First Commissioner of Works, and Oswald Mosley, Chancellor of the Duchy of Lancaster.[31] The deputation had consisted of Union leaders involved in shipbuilding and heavy engineering, together with two of the local Labour MPs, namely J.H. Palin (Newcastle West) and William Whiteley (Blaydon). Palin described the situation on Tyneside as 'little short of panic'. He continued:

> It is impossible to exaggerate the seriousness of the position, not because it is made so much worse at the moment by reason of the slowing down of armaments, but by reason of the fact that we have had so many people unemployed for so long a period. We have people unemployed for ten or twelve years, and we have approximately one family in three existing on unemployment pay, poor relief or private charity.[32]

The August deputation was followed by one from the Amalgamated Engineering Union (AEU) in October 1929. This second deputation was received by the political representatives of the Treasury and Admiralty in Ramsay MacDonald's second ministry. The deputation brought with it a number of resolutions from its different branches, drawing attention to 'the decision of the

Government to cancel or slow down the building of warships' which 'is further increasing unemployment'.[33] Ironically, the Admiralty representative at the meeting was A.V. Alexander, who had been elected as Labour member for one of the Sheffield constituencies in 1922. In office Alexander had swiftly fell in love with the Admiralty and Royal Navy.[34] Leaders of the AEU expressed concern at the likely impact of any new agreement on naval arms. In the Newcastle area 10 per cent of the Union's local membership of 11,900 were unemployed, and the government was urged to find alternative work to naval shipbuilding to help the economy in such areas.[35] This was despite the fact that there had been a dramatic reduction in the number of shipyard workers during the decade. In 1921, 359,000 people had been engaged in shipbuilding, with 129,000 of them unemployed. In the eight years following 150,000 people had 'gone out of the industry' but unemployment remained stubbornly high with the prospect that further naval arms limitation agreements might exacerbate the situation considerably.[36] With approximately half the jobs on Tyneside linked to shipbuilding, and against a backdrop of tough times in the region in the 1920s, the AEU was deeply concerned at the potential impact on their members and the potential damage to local communities. Mr Hutchinson of the AEU put it very bluntly: 'We want to ask what is going to become of a place like Barrow which to all intents and purposes is a self-contained town depending on shipbuilding. There is continued depression on the north east coast, the Clyde and other centres.'[37]

Both the August and October delegations made suggestions as to how the problems on Tyneside could be alleviated, by finding alternative work and by alterations to business conditions and legislation. Significantly comments were made in both meetings that limitation of naval armaments was not the root cause of the problems of the region. For example, in the August meeting one of the union representatives referred to 'The bringing into operation of labour-saving machinery', which he blamed for 'putting men on the streets permanently'.[38] However, for the workers, and thus the majority of the electorate in those areas, it was easier to focus on government policy and pronouncements which might deprive yards of orders, rather than focus on the absence of commercial orders for merchant ships. In other words, it was easier to lay the blame at the door of Westminster than at the board rooms of the merchant shipping companies. Politically the Labour government could not afford to ignore the difficulties of the region and part of what had become its core vote. Economically, though, there was little that could be done other than to leave the depressed areas. As Tom Steel has noted, in relation to the problems of the Scottish economy, in the period 1921 to 1931, 400,000 Scots made new lives for themselves overseas.[39]

Areas which had grown in size and population on the back of the expansion of naval spending before and during the First World War were condemned to decline and to suffer high unemployment in an age of austerity and naval arms limitation. For such areas, the road to the Great Depression began not with American bankers on Wall Street in late 1929 but with the German Armistice and the search for naval arms limitation a decade earlier. For places like Jarrow the hard times of the 1930s were horribly similar to the hard times of the 1920s, and the Jarrow Crusade was effectively just another deputation to Westminster. In 1922 it had been the Lord Mayors. In 1929 it had been the Union Leaders. In 1936 it was the men themselves, without the support of the Labour Party. Stanley Baldwin, Prime Minister for the third time, refused to meet them, and £1 each for the train fare home was the limit of support for the Jarrow unemployed. From 1922 onwards government had turned an increasingly deaf ear to workers in the shipbuilding industry, as the Treasury consistently advised that the room for manoeuvre was sharply limited. Disgust at the government's ineffective response to unemployment in the staple industries led to Oswald Mosley's break with the Labour leadership in 1931 and his pursuit of altogether more radical and dangerous solutions to the problems facing Britain. Naval and diplomatic policy, national and regional identities, the shipbuilding industry and domestic British politics remained firmly linked, and successive governments continued to wrestle with the problems of declining staple industries and the social and economic conditions of the towns, cities and regions which depended on them even as international affairs added further complexities to the relationship.

An attempt in 1935 to hold a second conference on naval arms at London to reach a fresh agreement before the expiration of the capital shipbuilding holiday negotiated in 1922 and 1930 foundered as the Japanese walked out. The only outcome was an agreement between Britain, the United States and France for a six-year ban on the construction of light cruisers of 8,000–10,000 tons. In the same year Britain signed an Anglo-German Naval Agreement allowing the *Kriegsmarine* to build up to 35 per cent of the tonnage of the Royal Navy. In spite of the spirit of the Anglo-German Naval Agreement, with the clouds of war gathering in the late 1930s, the National Government began to consider naval construction policy in the light of the imminent end of the building holiday. In late 1936 a fresh 'Battleship Enquiry' began its deliberations covering much of the same ground as the Bonar Law Enquiry some sixteen years previously.[40] The fact that a fresh enquiry was held, and that it covered broadly similar areas to the Capital Ship Committee of 1920–21, tell us less about naval technology than about divided opinions in naval circles and the reluctance of politicians to spend money on maritime defence even as the danger of a major European war became manifest.

The evidence before the committee suggested a remarkably similar set of conclusions: that updated anti-aircraft weapons and improved anti-torpedo protection made the 'modern' battleship less vulnerable to such weapons than their Jutland-era predecessors. The only problem was that the bulk of the battlefleet, bar *Hood*, *Nelson* and *Rodney*, was of this vintage. Refits and modernization programmes could only improve so far on old designs, tired machinery and inadequate armour and anti-aircraft guns. The findings of the battleship enquiry, which stretched into 1937, were sufficient, along with the menace of Adolf Hitler and especially Japan, to convince the Cabinet to authorize a new programme of battleship construction. As Nicholas Tracy has recognized, at the 1937 Imperial Conference there was considerable unease at the Royal Navy's perceived inability to deploy a Pacific Fleet capable of winning a war against the Japanese.[41] This added to the case for substantial rearmament at sea and in that same year five battleships would be laid down (HMS *King George V*, HMS *Prince of Wales*, HMS *Anson*, HMS *Duke of York*, HMS *Howe*). These vessels, together with HMS *Vanguard*, represented the last of the battleships to be built in Britain, and for the shipbuilders the high point of warship building for the Royal Navy in the interwar period.[42] As George E. Melton has observed, joining the battleships on the slips of British yards was an extensive ensemble of new aircraft carriers, cruisers and destroyers under a programme of naval rearmament in development within the Admiralty since 1935.[43] The first five battleships would be completed before the end of the Second World War, which put into perspective the Admiralty's concerns expressed to the Cabinet in 1920 about the capacity of British shipyards to furnish a substantial capital shipbuilding in the future. Equally significant, as R.A.C. Parker has noted, naval rearmament in the late 1930s was held back by shortages of production in armour plate, gun mountings and optical instruments.[44]

The process of building the last generation of battleships involved powerful reaffirmations of relationships strained by the decline of warship building in the 1920s. As Mark Connelly has noted, launching ceremonies provided important opportunities for displays of local and national pride involving royalty, civic dignitaries, captains of industry and shipyard workers.[45] Such ceremonies celebrated national unity, determination, British power and the success of British industry.

On the eve of the Second World War, opinion within the Royal Navy, and naval circles, was captured in a collection of essays edited by Charles W. Domville-Fife.

In *The Evolution of Sea Power* serving and recently retired officers, together with other maritime experts, offered commentaries on what were considered the key issues affecting the Royal Navy.[46] They reveal a deep sense of distrust towards the direction and outcomes of interwar naval policy and a sense that there had been a failure to resolve a range of critical issues affecting British sea power. The one-power standard was condemned as 'half a power standard' given the far-flung nature of the Empire. In his chapter headed 'Revolution or Evolution', Vice Admiral Usborne, former Director of Naval Intelligence, drew attention to the modernity and speed of the battlefleet allowed to the *Kriegsmarine* under the Anglo-German naval agreement. He contrasted it with the age and slowness of the existing British battleships to suggest that until the completion of the five King George V battleships in 1942 the home fleet might struggle to match a German main fleet capable of operating at speeds in excess of thirty knots.[47] Usborne further considered in a separate chapter on the Far East the dangers posed by an expansionist Japan controlled by 'a military caste indoctrinated with the idea of Japanese ascendancy in the Western Pacific'.[48] Faced with the potential imminence of war, the threat from mine, aircraft and torpedo to capital ship was still under debate in the pages of Domville-Fife's volume.[49] Questions were also raised about the availability of bases and fleet oil reserves to support global operations by the Royal Navy.[50] There was a strong undercurrent of opinion that naval arms limitation in the interwar period had done the Royal Navy no favours, and that the service was about to embark on a renewed naval struggle with a fleet that was inadequate in a series of ways.[51] While naval armaments had been restricted by international treaty for most of the 1920s, there had been no such restriction on the development of land and air armaments. Improvements to the latter were to pose a particular risk to a British battle fleet of First World War vintage. The sea power, on which the security of the British Empire depended, was being eclipsed by other arms.

The concerns underlying the essays in Domville-Fife's book were entirely reasonable, as evidenced by some of the outcomes in the naval conflict between 1939 and 1945. That conflict represents the acid test for what the Royal Navy hoped and tried to achieve in the immediate aftermath of the First World War. Fighting against Germany, Italy and Japan across the oceans of the world, the Royal Navy, with American assistance, was able to preserve Britain and the Empire's sealines of communication. The fight, however, was less than easy and the Admiralty initially struggled to come to terms with the resources available to it following the lean years of the interwar period.[52] At times the Royal Navy found itself short of ships of all classes. In 1940 Churchill began to contemplate sending an incomplete HMS *King George V* to sea with a dummy turret in order to put together a task force to combat a potential breakout into the Atlantic by a force of German capital ships.[53] As Andrew Lambert had argued, by 1941 Britain faced a lack of battleships, partly owing to war losses and partly owing to the Washington Conference and a battleship building holiday that had gone on until 1936.[54] The Royal Navy was unable to defend remote parts of the British Empire in East Asia. The fall of the Singapore naval base in 1942, and the loss of HMS *Prince of Wales* and HMS *Repulse* off the coast of Malaya, demonstrated a fundamental flaw in strategic policy. Yet Britain could afford only one fleet, and its value could be enhanced by strategic bunkering and base facilities around the world to enable it to move and concentrate its forces at any endangered point.

However, when faced with three enemies operating at different points around the globe, one fleet, even a highly mobile one, simply wasn't enough to defend all the vulnerable points of a far-flung empire. As Admiral Sir Herbert Richmond suggested after the Second World War it was simply an 'illusion' to think that a 'Two-Hemisphere Empire' could be protected by 'a One-Hemisphere Navy'.[55] Britain required help from alliance partners, and in 1921 Britain had traded the sure friendship of Japan for the more nebulous hand of a neo-isolationist United States. That was, however, the price for the avoidance of a naval arms race that Britain could not hope to win, and the price of imperial harmony. In the event the attempt to build an Anglo-American relationship foundered on the controversy over cruisers in the late 1920s and the American public's reluctance to be drawn into a potential European conflict in the 1930s. It would take the machinations of President Franklin Roosevelt, and the volatility of the militarists in Japan in the 1940s, to engineer the circumstances and terms for the formation of the special relationship which some Anglo-American navalists had started to champion in 1919.

At least in terms of the wartime record of the fleet fielded by the Royal Navy between 1939 and 1945, there was some validation for the naval policies pursued after the First World War. In fleet-to-fleet actions in the Mediterranean the capital ships of the Royal Navy performed admirably. In the Atlantic, and then in Arctic waters, as the surviving heavy ships of the German Navy were brought to Norwegian waters to threaten the convoys to Russia, British capital ships and cruisers were able to contain and neutralize the larger vessels of the *Kriegsmarine*. The *Bismarck* was battered into a flaming hulk by the British home fleet, and one-by-one from the *Graf Spee* to the *Scharnhorst* the battleships and battlecruisers of the German Navy were eliminated.

HMS *Nelson* and HMS *Rodney*, the two capital ships built under the provisions of the Washington Treaty, were prominent in the fighting. It was with quiet understatement that the Director of Naval Construction, Sir Eustace H.W. Tennyson d'Eyncourt, expressed his satisfaction with their wartime performance in his 1948 memoirs.[56] Despite such successes, losses of British capital ships such as HMS *Royal Oak* (1939) and HMS *Hood* (1941) were shocking events, and they demonstrated that, despite the Admiralty's conclusions about the continued primacy of the capital ship in 1919–21, the battleship was now hugely vulnerable to the torpedo, submarine, mine and airpower as well as to the big gun. The losses of HMS *Royal Oak* and HMS *Hood* were underlined by others: the destruction of HMS *Barham* at the hands of U-331 (25 November 1941); the crippling of HMS *Queen Elizabeth* and HMS *Valiant* by diver laid mines (19 December 1941); severe damage to HMS *Nelson* by mine and air-launched torpedo (4 December 1939 and 27 September 1941); the sinking of HMS *Prince of Wales* and HMS *Repulse* (10 December 1941); and severe damage to HMS *Warspite* by bomb and by guided missile (22 May 1941 and 26 September 1943).[57] The destruction of HMS *Prince of Wales* was perhaps the most shocking event of the lot so far as the confidence of the Royal Navy in its ships was concerned. She was a practically new ship and had been built without impediment of treaty limitations and in the full knowledge of the lessons of Jutland. The loss of HMS *Hood*, HMS *Barham* and others could be put down to old designs and known problems, but not that of HMS *Prince of Wales*. It took just two waves of aircraft and two torpedo hits to turn a capital ship into a broken cripple, listing with her decks awash and only partly able to answer her helm. While it would take further bomb and torpedo attacks to sink her (6 torpedoes and 1 bomb hit), HMS *Prince of Wales*, one of Britain's latest battleships, had been put out of the fight at minimal cost to Japanese forces. By contrast the far older ('pre-lessons of Jutland') HMS *Repulse* was able to survive several waves of Japanese attackers before she too was overcome (by four torpedoes and one bomb hit).[58] Sinkings of capital ships involved the loss of prize military assets that had taken great expense and time to construct. They also involved massive loss of lives (HMS *Repulse* 513 men, HMS *Prince of Wales* 327, HMS *Hood* 1,415, HMS *Barham* 841). Quite apart from the human tragedy of such casualties, the loss of skilled personnel in such numbers was also a serious military blow, and these losses resulted only from the sinking of battleships and battlecruisers.[59]

The losses of capital ships forced the government, yet again, to investigate the future of the capital ship in the light of the threats from torpedo, mine and aircraft. In January 1942 a committee under Mr Justice Bucknill, a vastly experienced High Court judge of the Probate, Divorce and Admiralty Division, began considering the losses of British capital ships in the Far East. Although the committee focussed on the sinkings of HMS *Repulse* and *Prince of Wales*, investigations on the latter raised issues about the other ships of the class. Strikingly the committee found that while improvements to the underwater protection of HMS *Prince of Wales* could have lessened the damage overall the number of torpedo hits suffered by both ships would have immobilized any capital ship no matter how well protected.[60] A separate report by the Director of Naval Construction (DNC) comparing the *King George V* class to the Bismarck backed up some of the conclusions of the Bucknill Committee.[61] The DNC's report found serious flaws in the design of the *King George V* but also raised issues about the training and efficiency of the crew of HMS *Prince of Wales*. That report prompted a fresh enquiry by the Bucknill Committee in April 1942 which addressed wider issues relating to the design of British capital ships. The second Bucknill Committee report widened the areas of interpretation, for example, drawing attention to the point that Bismarck's performance was underpinned by the fact that she was not designed within the limits of the Washington agreement, giving her greater firepower and greater protection than British capital ships. The DNC's report, and that of the Bucknill Committee, demonstrated the extent to which the debate on the obsolescence of the capital ship had broken out afresh. That it was a debate rather than an agreement that the capital ship had reached the end of its useful life as a weapon of war was evidenced by the decision by Dudley Pound, the First Sea Lord, to allow the circulation of the reports.[62] His motive in doing so was 'to restore confidence in the construction of our ships'.[63]

The vulnerability and obsolescence of the battleship was confirmed by experience in the Second World War, and HMS *Vanguard*, laid down in 1941, would be the last battleship to be built in a British yard. Like HMS *Hood* in an earlier era, Vanguard's design was altered to take account of the lessons emerging from the world war. For example, in the light of the sinking of HMS *Prince of Wales* the space between the inner and outer propeller shafts on HMS *Vanguard* was increased from 33.5 to 51.5 feet to prevent a single torpedo hit disabling two shafts. Despite such efforts *Vanguard* went to the breakers yard in 1960. By this stage the earlier generations of battleship had already been scrapped. HMS *Warspite* had run aground on her way to the breaker's yard in 1947, and HMS *Rodney* had gone for scrap in 1948. HMS *Nelson* had followed her the following year. The proponents of airpower were ready to point to the tragedies that had befallen the battleships of all sides during the war, and their demise in the Royal

Navy, as evidence that airpower had finally replaced sea power as the dominant strategic force.

Despite such opinions, and the British capital ship tragedies of the Second World War, the Royal Navy's battleships did have significant value which has been partly overlooked. With the rapid demise of the British capital ship after 1945, the opponents of the big gun ship were reluctant to concede the true strategic significance of the British capital ship during the Second World War. In 1940, it was the prospect of the battleships and battlecruisers of the British home fleet steaming south to intercept a German invasion force that led Hitler to break off plans for Operation Sealion. The need for the *Luftwaffe* to gain control of the skies over the Channel and southern England in the Battle of Britain was necessary to enable the German Air Force to support an invasion landing by the *Kriegsmarine*. Hitler's interest in Sealion decreased as it became steadily apparent that, even if the Luftwaffe managed to defeat the Royal Air Force, the capital ships of the Royal Navy would be able to kill thousands of German soldiers as their invasion fleet came under the guns of the British capital ships and cruisers. The Royal Navy might sustain heavy losses, but the effect on the morale of the German Army might be truly devastating. In effect, the ships of Churchill's Navy in 1940 achieved the same effect as those of Elizabeth in 1588 – the defence of the British Isles from seaborne invasion. Indeed, in 1940 the fleet remained sufficiently powerful to keep the *Kriegsmarine* and Nazi hierarchy from seriously contemplating the venture.

In addition to this very traditional role, and the protection of convoys from enemy surface vessels, later in the war, Allied amphibious landings from the Mediterranean to the coast of Normandy were protected by the big guns of the capital ships. As powerful floating batteries they could support landing forces as they broke through the coastal crust of *Festung Europa* and advanced inland. Gunnery support could interdict forces advancing from the interior and provide a means to deal with stubborn strongpoints. Allied amphibious forces, with British capital ships as an integral part, threatened the German Empire all the way along the coasts of the continent from the Greek and Italian islands to the French coast and beyond to Norway. The battleship had acquired a new role and a new utility as a form of floating mobile artillery operating in support of land forces. In 1939 no one foresaw the growth and importance of amphibious operations, and the pivotal role which the capital ship could play in such strategically telling operations. The capital ship was deadly effective in the role of mobile maritime artillery, which the US Navy would continue to demonstrate until the 1990s as the Iowa class battleships it retained took part in operations in Korea, Vietnam and the Middle East. By the late 1940s in British defence circles the proponents of airpower had won the debate that the effectiveness of aircraft equipped by bomb and missile rendered the battleship an expensive and unnecessary and highly vulnerable weapons platform. After 1945 there would be an unseemly rush to send the last of Britain's battleships to the breakers yard.

Conclusion

> *The rapid rotation of leaders and cabinets hampered the emergence of a national defence consensus. Cabinets which were ill-equipped to debate strategic policy tended to rely on the recommendations of special cabinet committees, the Committee of Imperial Defence, or on the minister heading an important military department.*[1]

In his 2014 study *British Naval Supremacy and Anglo-American Antagonisms, 1914–1930*, Donald J. Lisio comes to a conclusion about the 'failure' of British naval policy which is very different to that of this book. Where he sees discontinuity between the administrations of Lloyd George and his successors in the early 1920s, I would suggest underlying continuity. During this period there was a continuity of personnel within the centre-right elite of British politics (although I would accept that political scientists might take issue with that definition in the fluid circumstances of British politics of the 1920s). It is exactly that fluidity which facilitated continuity. A junior minister in the Lloyd George peacetime government might achieve Cabinet rank in the Conservative administration following the break-up of the coalition. Stanley Baldwin, for example, was appointed as the president of the Board of Trade in 1921, Chancellor of the Exchequer in 1922 and prime minister in 1923 – three different posts in three different administrations. Likewise Leopold Amery could serve in two ministries as under-secretary under Lloyd George before rising to the post of First Lord of the Admiralty in Bonar Law's government. Bonar Law could lead the Conservative Party, the House of Commons and head the Exchequer and the Cabinet Committee on the Capital Ship before becoming the prime minister in November 1922. Figures such as Churchill, the Chamberlains and Lloyd George were among the group of 'big beasts' of British politics who dominated British politics throughout the interwar period and, in some cases, before and/or after that. Political fortunes might rise and fall, and administrations come and go, but the continuities in personnel are striking, as is the depth of experience and knowledge built up in Cabinet ranks as a result of these continuities. Moreover, the continuities within the elite were underpinned by the political outcomes of a stratified British society which fostered a certain commonality of views (only really challenged by the rise of the Labour Party after 1922). Within government, the evolutionary nature of policy was fostered by a professional British Civil Service such as Peter Hennessy identifies, whose job it was to ensure the continuity of good government.[2]

If one accepts this continuity, then the question must inevitably follow: 'Well why was it so difficult to get it right in the field of British naval policy during the early 1920s'? The answer which this book offers is that the issues were so large, and so connected, that their resolution was enormously problematic even though an experienced and able British political elite understood them. In many ways that elite was left facing a difficult set of choices, and a consequent set of risks. Those dangers and risks were well understood and it was down to individual choices as to how the country should 'make the best of a bad lot'.

British naval policy was in crisis (or disequilibrium as Samuel P. Huntingdon would describe it) long before the outbreak of the First World War.[3] The connectedness of naval policy, proposed as a concept in the preface to this book, created a network of relationships. These crossed government, politics, private sector and communities, and made highly difficult the resolution of the series of issues which lay at the heart of this crisis. The period 1919–22 stands as an exemplar of connectedness of naval policy, as the book has shown. A declining economy relative to other powers, the rapid emergence of new technologies that could render existing battle fleets obsolete and the determination of some European states to build naval forces capable of challenging the Royal Navy created a serious problem for Britain with its large seaborne empire and global trading network. Britain was able to meet that problem from 1890 to the outbreak of war in 1914 because the public, marshalled in part by the Navy League, and by politicians friendly to the interests of the Royal Navy, shipbuilders and armaments manufacturers, were willing to provide the tax revenues to sustain a British Fleet substantially larger and more powerful than those of her European rivals. British culture from the stories of Kipling to the art of Wyllie sustained public interest and understanding of maritime and naval matters. The British public understood the role and importance of the Royal Navy and its central role in maintaining imperial and trade security. The issues in British naval policy after 1918 were broadly the same as they had been in 1914: a declining economy, technologies that threatened to render obsolescent the existing battlefleet and states (the United States and Japan) that threatened to outbuild the Royal Navy and end Britain's dominance of the seas. The challenge to Britain's control of the sea lanes was perceived as a major threat to the security, stability and future of a far-flung empire. In trying to meet this threat, naval policy was compromised by failure at the political level as the politicians set strategic goals determined by financial and economic imperatives. In looking ahead the politicians preferred to see national security in terms of what they might be able to afford, rather than worst-case scenarios (such as a global war) which the country could not contemplate.

By the end of the First World War, while the challenges facing the makers of naval policy remained broadly similar, other transformations were turning long-standing issues into a crisis. The Britain of 1919 was a vastly different place to the country which had gone to war in 1914. The self-confidence of the nation, the unquestioned loyalty of the Empire, belief in Britain's economy, society and political leaders had been seriously undermined. Burdened by heavy war debts, with serious social, political and union unrest in some areas, the rise of socialism posed grave challenges to the existing social, economic and political order in Britain. If the working classes remained deferential in most areas, then on Clydeside and Sheffield more open challenges to the political order were emerging. The declining state of the British economy, further evidenced by post-war slump and stubbornly high unemployment, raised grave questions over the long-term health of the British economy and the social and economic order it sustained.

To some on the right and in the centre of British politics, it was a question of 'to be or not to be'. The naval challenge to Britain was serious, but so too were the country's financial problems. Bankruptcy as a nation, defeat on some battlefield of the future or the triumph of socialism at the ballot box, or by the bayonet, all threatened national and imperial disaster with the politicians of the period trying to strike a balance between the imperatives of avoiding each potential outcome.

Beatty and the Admiralty had a rather easier task since their job involved avoidance of only one of the imperatives: defeat on the battlefield. In 1919 Japan was identified as Britain's most likely opponent in a future naval war. The Admiralty framed an appropriate strategy to deal with that eventuality and asked the politicians to provide the personnel and material to deliver that strategy. Those things would not be forthcoming. From very different viewpoints the politicians and admirals of the period pursued policies which they felt were rational and reasonable and in the national interest. Safeguarding national and imperial security from any potential threat was the professional imperative of the Royal Navy. To Conservatives and Liberals, stopping socialism made political sense but it was also a national duty. When Ramsay MacDonald did take office in January 1924, there was considerable surprise in many quarters (and no little disappointment in others) that the social and economic order was not immediately turned upside down.

In many ways defeat on the battlefield was disregarded rather more easily than some of the other threats to Britain. Japan and the United States were seen as unlikely enemies (even if Royal Navy planning had to assume that a threat did exist), and the institution of the ten-year rule into British defence planning in 1919, specifically, excluded the threat of war from government thinking in the short term. That, however, was its purpose. The meeting of the War Cabinet Finance Committee which determined the ten-year rule on 11 August 1919 consisted of just three ministers and Lloyd George.[4] This was a Finance Committee meeting rather than a meeting of the Committee of Imperial Defence, and the prime minister got the outcome he desired as J. Kenneth McDonald noted in his 1971 study.[5] The findings of the Finance Committee were a means to an end – the drastic reduction of public expenditure – rather than a carefully considered analysis of the true state of the strategic balance and likelihood of war. Indeed, given possible rejection of the peace treaties by Germany and Turkey, or the dangers posed by Soviet Russia, the ten-year rule flew in the face of international realities.

In some ways this was a defensible and pragmatic response to the national crisis. Defeat on the battlefield constituted a future potential danger that might be avoided through clever diplomacy, while economic ruin or the possibilities of socialism represented enemies very much at the gates. This left the leadership of the Royal Navy in the 1920s to find new means to request the resources considered necessary for imperial security. As recognized by Orest Babij and John Ferris, perhaps, the real achievement of the admirals and the naval lobby in the post-war period lay in identifying the primary, and domestically focussed, concerns of the leading members of the government and tailoring the naval message accordingly.[6] Even Sir George Barstow was forced to recognize that building battleships could provide a form of unemployment relief and support for declining industries. Tailoring the naval message away from imperial defence and towards new forms of utility was effective in the short term, but in the longer term it perhaps harmed the Royal Navy. It invited questions about the purpose and value of a navy, and whether its essential roles could perhaps be fulfilled in other ways, such as through the application of airpower.

If the process of negotiating the concerns of politicians after 1919 cast a shadow that extended well into the post-1945 period, then the same was also true of the ten-year rule. The ten-year rule was not a major influence on government policy until the late 1920s, but its effects were insidious and long lasting. What was completely indefensible, irresponsible and dangerous about the decision taken in 1919 was that politicians had taken a key strategic decision on the potential threats to the United Kingdom, with little reference to the three services, in order to come to conclusions with one intended outcome: the slashing of military spending. It was a political conjuring trick of the worst order: a politician's equivalent of Nelson's famous conclusion 'I see no signal' as he deliberately placed his telescope to his blind eye at the Battle of Copenhagen in 1801 in order to disobey the order to disengage the Danish Fleet. If the politicians could see no threat in 1919, they would not have to pay to meet it, and the electorate need not be disturbed by the failure to undertake necessary preparations to maintain imperial security. It was dishonest even if it was motivated by a perfectly rational set of considerations about the national finances. It was dangerous because politicians after Lloyd George deluded themselves about the realities of the decision arrived at in 1919. If the Cabinet had concluded that there was no threat, then there was no threat. The decision of 11 August 1919 resulted in British defence policy in the interwar period being compromised, although its poisonous effects would take several years to take effect and become manifest. There was no attempt to frame a strategic assessment or to determine what the Empire required to defend it. As Edward DesRosiers has argued the decision was entirely financial and totally reprehensible, and set a pattern for the administrations which were to follow during the 1920s and early 1930s.[7]

It is questionable whether the malign influence of the ten-year rule continued to weaken British defence policy after the Second World War and perhaps into the twenty-first century. The ten-year rule set a precedent that defence decisions could be taken without an assessment of strategic needs and threats. Even if the rule ceased to operate from the late 1930s, the ten-year rule conjuring trick (strategic decision-making for the purposes of defence cuts) was a political sleight of hand that has remained a feature of British politics since 1945. The Thatcher government's 1981 Defence Review was spectacularly exposed by the outbreak of war over the Falkland Islands in 1982, and the Cameron coalition government was prepared to repeat the game in 2010 to the detriment of a nation facing threats from a resurgent Russia and Islamic fundamentalism in the Middle East and at home. The lesson of the ten-year rule, and the development of naval policy after 1919, is that strategic threat assessments and decisions cannot be compromised by political imperatives. Nor can they be decided in the

Finance Committee of the Cabinet. Dangers must be identified and noted, even if the means to meet them are not immediately to hand.

In the circumstances of 1919, ceding naval parity with the United States was intended to make the danger of defeat in a future naval war still less likely, as were the treaties signed at Washington in 1921–22. The outcomes of the Washington Naval Conference, which opened on 12 November 1921 and concluded on 6 February 1922, resolved a number of dilemmas facing the Royal Navy following the First World War while creating new ones for the policy makers to wrestle with. Britain formally accepted parity in the number of capital ships with the United States in an agreement that would embody Japan as the third largest naval power: securing ongoing good relations with the United States, and the resources to underpin main fleet operations in the Far East against a potential Japanese enemy, would prove much more problematic.

The Washington Conference was a vital moment in the evolution of the lines of strategic policy which the Royal Navy was working towards in the post-war period. That vision, while never fully articulated, is evident in Admiralty memoranda, in conferences and speeches. Effectively the Royal Navy wanted to be a modern force, concentrated in home waters and the Mediterranean but capable of operating on a global basis. Those operations would be underpinned by a network of bases and oiling facilities to allow the main battlefleet to concentrate at any particular point where the interests of a global empire were threatened. The strength of the home nation would be augmented by the further development of dominion naval forces leading, perhaps, to some form of imperial government and a unity of command and direction. Those dominion forces would serve as local defence forces throughout the Empire, being able to fight holding actions until the main fleet arrived. Thereafter dominion units would merge seamlessly with the main fleet in order to defeat the enemy. Overall, the Royal Navy would operate as an informal partner with the US Navy to ensure the security of the sea lanes and to manage world naval armaments: that at least was the hope.

There were alternatives to some of the elements within this strategic vision, although there seems to have been scant consideration of them in the early post-war period. Some contemporary advocates of airpower, utilizing the RAF in Iraq to provide cheap imperial policing, argued that airpower could replace sea power and landpower as a viable means of defence for the whole empire. This was, however, completely impracticable, as Alex Spencer has demonstrated.[8] Britain did not possess the aircraft, the technologies or the network of bases to realize an effective system of imperial defence from the air. Sea power was the only viable option given the technologies of the day and the distances involved. Royal Navy strategy might, however, have been further refined.

The main thrust of Admiralty policy, to create a highly modern and mobile force, was, to some extent, compromised by an emphasis on highly immobile bases and provisioning facilities as the means to provide the necessary infrastructure to support fleet operations. To some extent, this was the automatic reaction of a force that had grown accustomed during five years of war to operating across the short sea stretches across the North Sea, and from a well-established network of bases. It was not until the mid-1930s with the possible vulnerability of naval bases to aerial attack that the Royal Navy began to consider replenishment at sea, and the idea of a mobile fleet train to support distant operations.[9] This was despite the fact that the Royal Navy had first experimented with replenishment at sea in the 1870s, and had considered a number of suggestions in the 1880s. The formation of the Royal Fleet Auxiliary in 1905 (specifically to provide logistical support to the fleet) had marked a further step in the evolution in the idea, and in 1907 RFA *Petroleum* had been used to conduct experiments in ship-to-ship oiling at sea. Further experiments had been undertaken in 1923.[10] When a British Fleet finally operated in the waters of the Pacific in 1945 it was with the support of a full fleet train of auxiliaries, and the cooperation of the United States Navy that had made rather more rapid progress on the practices and technologies of replenishment at sea.[11]

In the development of post-war naval policy the Washington Conference does stand as a landmark event that cast long shadows over the years which followed it. What must also be understood is that the conference exemplifies one particular trend underpinning British naval policy in this period which naval historians have largely overlooked, and which naval officers at the time took almost for granted: the role of diplomacy in maintaining British naval power. To play a truly global role in post-war affairs required more than just a powerful Royal Navy, a global network of oiling facilities, and a naval base at Singapore (the three issues uppermost in the thoughts of the Admiralty). After 1918 there were other threats to Britain's sealines of communication that the Foreign Office took the lead in dealing with. In relations with Spain and Portugal, the keys to the Western end of the Mediterranean, the Foreign Office did what it could to foster stability on the Iberian Peninsula. However, within the Foreign Office there was a strong sense that those efforts were inadequate, especially since the opposition of the Treasury prevented any question of British loans.[12] The Foreign Office, and indeed the Admiralty, did not want to see a hostile power on one of the approaches to the Straits of Gibraltar. The Foreign Office was particularly interested in

Spanish affairs, not least because of the possibility that the development of naval bases in Spain's Moroccan coastal enclaves could threaten passage of ships through the Straits. The port of Tangier was particularly significant in this respect. In a letter of January 1922 Lord Derby, Conservative Party grandee and former Minister of War, noted French ambitions to control the port as a means to establish their own base to project their naval power into the Straits of Gibraltar.[13] The eventual internationalization and neutralization of Tangier in December 1923 was a very effective defence, by diplomatic means, of Britain's sealines of communication.[14] Likewise, at the other end of the Mediterranean Britain was able to respond to the rising tide of Egyptian nationalism, recognize Egypt as an 'independent sovereign state' while maintaining the right to defend the Suez Canal.[15] Beyond the imperial highway through the Mediterranean, the close and harmonious relationship between Foreign Office and Admiralty was evident on other diplomatic issues of relevance to British naval power. In both Iraq and Persia, vital states in terms of the oil reserves of the British Empire, British diplomats and administrators reached accommodations with Arab and Persian nationalism to safeguard access to the oil resources of the region. The defence of Britain's naval interests by diplomacy at the Washington Conference was not a one-off event, but part of a wide-ranging effort to address critical issues threatening the security of Britain's sealines of communication. The diplomats took the lead in this defensive campaign, and at every turn they demonstrated a keen awareness of the country's maritime needs and interests. For the Foreign Office, Britain was a global maritime power and the safety of her sealines of communication was essential to national security.

The diplomatic defence of Britain's maritime interests was backed by determined efforts by the Admiralty to maintain a strong Royal Navy with a modernized fleet. In the aftermath of the Washington agreement, the building of a limited number of new capital ships of no greater than 35,000 tons to replace obsolescent tonnage was exactly what the Royal Navy and Britain's warship builders required. The G-3 and N3 designs envisaged in 1921 were set to produce naval leviathans. The halting of the building of the G-3 class, with the signature of the naval arms limitation agreement, represented a sort of victory for the Royal Navy.[16] The infrastructure problems in British shipbuilding which had become apparent during 1920 and 1921 meant that British industry would struggle to turn out designs of 40,000 or more tons. The 5:5:3 ratio removed, at least for a time, naval arms as a difficult issue in Anglo-American relations and enshrined by treaty a one-power standard for the Royal Navy. Effectively, via diplomatic means, Britain had managed to preserve her position as the leading naval power in the world, and had succeeded in addressing the inadequacy of British shipbuilders to turn out the most modern designs. The orders for two new capital ships were a help to a shipbuilding industry in crisis, to Britain's heavy industries and to the nation's industrial heartlands.

The cost in the short term would be the Anglo-Japanese Alliance, which would be cancelled as a result of the Far Eastern Pact. The Royal Navy's diplomatic victory at Washington was challenged by the imposition of the 'Geddes Axe' on the naval estimates in 1922.[17] The naval estimates for 1923–24 at £58,000,000 did show a decrease of almost £7,000,000 on the previous year.[18] However, this did not prevent the ordering of the two new capital ships allowed under the terms of the Washington Conference. The Admiralty had won its argument thanks to the economic and potential political effects of warship building, and HMS *Rodney* and HMS *Nelson* were ordered in late 1922.[19] Built to the N3 design modified in the light of the Washington restrictions, the ships represented vital orders for British shipbuilders Armstrong-Whitworth and Cammell Laird for the eight years they would take to complete.[20]

The importance of Lee of Fareham's May memorandum on the approach of the Royal Navy to the issues facing it in the post-war period has not been fully appreciated by historians. If there were issues in the Anglo-Japanese relationship that helped to underpin the policy shift in 1921–22, then there were perhaps larger issues in Anglo-American relations that caused a considerable amount of antagonism between the two countries. Ultimately, the British government's decision not to renew the Anglo-Japanese Alliance was based on the naval and Far Eastern security exigencies of the post-war period rather than particular appreciations of Japan and the Japanese. Policy and its tenor did shift quite markedly in 1921. It marked the start of a period of estrangement rather than an outcome of a process substantially underway. To Lord Lee of Fareham the idea of a joined-up approach to the problems facing the Royal Navy represented a moment of deliverance and a decisive moment for the crystallization of policy towards the Anglo-Japanese Alliance. O'Brien captures the sense of desperation felt by policy makers when he describes the 1919–21 period as representing a kind of 'strategic purgatory' for both the Royal Navy and US Navy.[21]

The different strands of policy had been emerging since 1919, but what Lee of Fareham was able to put forward was the idea of a coordinated approach as a means to find a way beyond a Naval and Far Eastern Policy impasse that had dogged the government and Royal Navy for two years. It was a success, even if ultimately the lines of policy which emerged from the Washington Conference would be undermined by the financial problems which continued to dog the

British exchequer in the interwar period and beyond. Those financial problems would prevent the realization of the strategic vision which had been developed within the Admiralty of a modernized but smaller Royal Navy able to operate around the globe thanks to a network of oiling facilities and appropriately placed fleet bases. Within the naval lobby there was a keen understanding of the requirements of global operations. In March 1921 Commander Kenworthy took pains in the House of Commons to explain that grand strategy was more than simply the number of available capital ships: 'If we are to look upon Japan as a possible rival it is no good building ships and having our dockyards and bases in the North Sea and Mediterranean. You have to be prepared to face her in the Pacific, and that means enormous capital expenditure on bases.'[22] Kenworthy was expressing concerns that the need to place orders for capital ships could very easily overshadow strategic thinking as a whole. Ships were not an end in themselves but a means to pursue a given strategy that depended on other things such as the availability of bases in key locations. The financial pressures of the interwar period would seriously hamper the development of the strategic infrastructure to support the main British battlefleet in global maritime operations.

Various factors underlay the agreements reached at Washington, and subsequent policy which was based on the idea that defeat on a future naval battlefield was the least likely of the main threats facing Britain. First there were profound differences of opinion over Britain's future. Should the emphasis of policy be on restoring Britain as a trading, financial or manufacturing power? To what extent should Britain pursue the development of the Empire as an economic, military and political goal? Given the strength of British arms by 1918, should Britain embrace a future where she was the dominant military power in Europe and perhaps the world? Was there a balance to be struck between these competing futures? Different politicians and commentators would have responded differently to these questions, and there was no truly effective forum of debate where Britain's future, and that of the Empire, could be worked out. To men like Eric Geddes and Lord Rothermere, 'sound finances' was the essential goal of government policy after 1919. To Amery and Curzon the imperial future was what really mattered. The leaders of the dominions would have agreed with them, but equally for the political leaders of Australia and New Zealand, Britain had to have the military forces to give them an absolute guarantee of their security.

All of the men charged with the evolution of British naval policy after 1918 had experienced the horrors of the First World War to some extent. Beatty had seen war at first hand, and his famous comment about the quality of British ships at Jutland, with all its bearing on the naval craft which d'Eyncourt would try to produce for the Admiralty after the war, resulted from seeing thousands of men from his Battle Cruiser Force die as their vessels failed them at Jutland.[23] The First Sea Lord knew that in wartime obsolescent and inadequately armoured vessels were little more than expensive coffins for their crews. That an admiral should have such experience of war was perhaps not surprising in any century, and three British admirals had lost their lives between 1914 and 1918, but what marked the First World War out as being so very different to previous wars was the extent to which the civilian leadership was affected by the scale of war losses.[24] Several of those men who formed the navy lobby inside Parliament had operational experience, and the casualty lists featured the names of the sons of the most powerful men in British politics. Bonar Law lost his two eldest sons during the conflict. Second Lieutenant Charles Law, 1/5th Battalion, King's Own Scottish Borderers, was killed at the Battle of Gaza on 19 April 1917 and on September 21, Captain James Kidston Law, Number 60 Squadron Royal Flying Corps, was shot down and killed in France. They were just twenty and twenty-four years of age, respectively. Devastated by these blows Law temporarily stepped down as party leader. Lord Rothermere similarly lost two sons during the war and the majority of families were deeply affected by tragedy as a result of the conflict.

Given the scale of the war losses it was exceptionally difficult for Britain's political leaders to contemplate the thought of another war, and what weapons might be required to fight it. The creation of the League of Nations and the promises made to the electorate about a 'war to end all wars' made a climate in which it was easier to think about disarmament than naval construction programmes. Following the end of the war there was a very real sense that the politicians had failed the electorate in getting the country involved in a war, and not securing victory without such a high 'butcher's bill'. Arguably the politicians failed the electorate again in the post-war period by not emphasizing sufficiently the troubled state of international affairs, and that the League of Nations and collective security could not be relied upon to deal with every emergency which might arise. It was necessary to take other, and financially costly, steps to ensure the security of the nation. National defence, like any insurance policy, is sometimes resented by those who have to pay for it but is deeply welcome when best hopes turn into worst nightmares. For fifteen years the politicians were largely lucky in that the nightmare of war kept away, but by the late 1930s the spectre of renewed conflict was very present and it became politically necessary to address the defence needs which had been neglected over previous years. By that stage many of the armaments firms and factories which had risen to the challenge of war production between 1914 and 1918 had gone out of business.[25] With regard to the Royal Navy, new shipbuilding programmes and refits could only do so much in the months before the outbreak of war in 1939, and a new generation of sailors would have to pay the price of Admiralty.

Afterword

For the policy makers after 1918 the challenges threatening to end British naval superiority were considerable, and particularly difficult to meet, given the connectedness of naval policy. For the senior ranks of the Royal Navy working within the Westminster system to resolve some of these issues, the transition from war to peace during 1918–19 was unexpectedly difficult and painful. This book has charted some of the difficulties and dangers which the Royal Navy sought to negotiate during the years of the Lloyd George coalition. In the post-war period the senior officers and the Admiralty did their best to make the case to the politicians, just as during the First World War the military had done its duty, despite the cost, over years of unrelenting struggle. Arguably the admirals after 1918 failed to make their case sufficiently strongly to convince the politicians. The question is why, especially given the nature of a service imbued with the Nelsonian ethos of 'engage the enemy more closely'.

In large part the answer lies in the concept of the connectedness of naval policy, which this book has advanced, but it also lies within the human dimension of policy-making, which all too frequently is ignored within analyses of naval history. The broadly positive outcomes from the Washington Conference, in providing a way forward for British naval policy, can be ascribed to great powers balancing their interests, to changing considerations of technologies and economies and to the outlook of the new Harding administration. They equally resulted from the desire of Americanophiles like Beatty, and Anglophiles like Sims, wanting to find a way for the Royal Navy and US Navy to avoid a naval-building race.

The tensions, emotions, personalities, prejudices and histories at play among the ranks of the admirals who led the senior service are hard to glimpse in memoranda, public speeches, personal letters and valedictory memoirs. They did, however, have a vital role to play in shaping the response of the post-war Royal Navy to the challenges it faced, and the machinations of the politicians, as the Admiralty tried to put forward naval policy to deliver a coherent strategy for national defence. Beatty, for example, like those around him, was an emotional man, whose response to the issues he faced, especially when dealing with the charismatic and devious Lloyd George, was only partly intellectual and professional. As the senior leadership of the Royal Navy attempted to navigate the twists and turns of the connectedness of naval policy in austerity Britain during 1919–22, the personal level mattered very greatly.

Something of the interpersonal dynamics at work in this world can perhaps be glimpsed in a painting by the celebrated and innovative portrait painter Sir Arthur Stockdale Cope which was commissioned in 1919 and completed in 1921 – the evolution and completion of the painting spanning most of the years of the Lloyd George coalition.[1] A work of art is an unusual focus for analysis in a monograph on naval history, but it captures certain features of the period which cannot be recovered through more 'conventional' sources. When in 1919 the National Portrait Gallery's Trustees commissioned three separate paintings of the generals, admirals and statespersons who had brought Britain to victory in 1918, they found that their preferred artists were happier to paint soldiers and sailors than statespersons.[2] The money was provided by South African businessperson, patriot and cricketer Sir Abraham Bailey, who wanted to celebrate the strength and achievement of a victorious Empire. He had originally intended there to be just one picture covering the military figures of the war, but he was prevailed upon to have two separate pictures covering the Army and Royal Navy. The original idea of a single painting covering the military figures of the war suggests the extent to which the distinctive contribution of the Royal Navy in 1918 had become lost in the public mind.

The painting of the admirals completed in 1921, and exhibited at the Royal Academy summer exhibition in May, bears unusually eloquent testimony to the problems facing the senior leadership of the Royal Navy in the post-war period. The fact that Stockdale Cope was a close friend of Rear Admiral Reginald 'Blinker' Hall (head of Naval Intelligence during the First World War and Conservative MP for West Derby 1919–23) may well have had a bearing on the painter's level of insight into the subjects which he was commissioned to depict.[3]

The painting of the admirals is very different to Sargent's painting of the generals which emphasizes team and equality against a minimal 'classical' backdrop. Stockdale Cope's painting depicted twenty-two admirals (approximately 10 per cent of the admirals who had served in the Royal Navy during 1914–18), including the three killed in action during the war, in the Board Room in the old Admiralty Office in Whitehall. The Board Room, dating from 1725 and remodelled during the nineteenth century, retains many of its original features including its heavy wooden panelling with decorative ornamentation (limewood carvings of nautical instruments and classical columns). The room was heavily damaged by German bombs on 16 April 1941, but restored thereafter.[4] Hanging from the panelling are two paintings depicting sea battles from the age of sail, and a full-length portrait of Nelson by Leonardo Guzzardi. Also built into the panelling is a dial, linked to a weather vane on the roof, which indicates wind direction, and any changes, to those present in the board room. In the days of sail the weather gauge could provide vital intelligence to their Lordships of the Admiralty.

Selecting which admirals would be included in the painting proved to be less than easy as Andrew Lambert has identified.[5] In early December 1918 the National Portrait Gallery turned to Sir Oswyn Murray, secretary to the Admiralty, to advise on which admirals should be included in the painting. Murray suggested the names of twenty officers who had commanded forces at sea during the war, and his selection was taken as the basis of the portrait. This was despite the fact that Sir Eric Geddes, First Lord of the Admiralty, made representations to the National Portrait Gallery for a rather different selection of names. In addition to the twenty names put forward by Murray, two First Sea Lords (Weymss and the Marquess of Milford Haven), who had held that position during the war, were also included in the final painting. That the suggestions of the secretary of the Admiralty should prevail over those of the First Lord underlines the confidence and authority of the Admiralty and Royal Navy in dealing with their political masters.

However, the groupings of the admirals, their juxtaposition, posture and place on the canvas speak volumes about a senior leadership riven by faction and personality. In the centre of the canvas, quite literally at the heart of events, stands the First Sea Lord, David Beatty. Looking into the distance he faces the portrait of Nelson, and Nelson appears to gaze back at him approvingly. Beatty stands next to two naval officers (Tyrwhitt and Keyes) who appear as loyal subordinates, even though their wartime roles meant that they were largely separate from Beatty's immediate command circle in the Battle Cruiser Force and Grand Fleet.[6] Eyes fixed on Beatty, Tyrwhitt and Keyes appear to be waiting on some decision by him. Their submissive attendance suggests the Royal Navy's wider loyalty and belief in the First Sea Lord, and his firm sense that on his shoulders rested the naval security of the Empire and the future of the Royal Navy.

On the left of the painting, by the portrait of Nelson, are three of Beatty's most loyal lieutenants (Alexander-Sinclair, Cowan and de Brock).[7] The physical proximity of Nelson with Beatty's loyal lieutenants again appears to suggest that the First Sea Lord is the heir to Nelson's genius. To the right of the Beatty loyalists, and immediately below the left-hand edge of one of the paintings of a naval battle in the age of sail, stand the three admirals killed in action during the First World War (Arbuthnot, Cradock and Hood). Standing at the back of the room their position suggests that they are receding from view, distant from the present, becoming part of the room and heritage of the naval service in the same way as Nelson. Their inclusion in the portrait was also a neat device to get around the National Portrait Gallery's policy of not displaying paintings of living figures.

On the right-hand third of the painting stands one lone figure and a separate group of two. The lone figure is Wester Weymss, Beatty's immediate predecessor as First Sea Lord. He appears starchy and old fashioned. His relationship with Beatty had been soured particularly by the awkward nature of the transition between the two regimes in 1919. Weymss is depicted sympathetically, standing tall and facing the portrait of Nelson, but he is very firmly alone. To his left are two figures apparently deep in conversation: Jellicoe and Admiral Charles Madden, Jellicoe's loyal chief of staff.[8] Jellicoe sits slumped in a chair, holding papers with charts apparently on the table in front of him, while Madden perches on the edge of a table. Jellicoe appears troubled, ageing rapidly and a man firmly of the past. The papers and charts seem like an allusion to the controversy which has raged over the Battle of Jutland since 1916, the historical interpretation of which firmly divides Beatty and Jellicoe.[9] With arguments raging over which commander did, or signalled what, or made this or that manoeuvre, the charts and papers suggest that Jellicoe is a man mired in the past and limited to fighting battles long behind the Royal Navy. Indeed, the volumes of Jellicoe's papers in the British Library show just how devoted he was in the post-war period to collecting every scrap of information he could on the battle. Beatty, meanwhile, is the man looking to the horizon: he is the future and the hope of the service.

The internal politics of the Royal Navy are evident from the groups and their juxtaposition in the painting, and it is also evident from who is not included by the artist.[10] Lord Fisher and Admiral Sir Henry Jackson both served as First Sea Lord during the First World War. Fisher had done much to prepare the Royal Navy for war and had returned to the Admiralty, coming out of retirement, after a plea by First Lord of the Admiralty, Winston Churchill. Fisher was, however, a difficult personality and unpopular with many of his senior fellow officers. His omission from the painting of the admirals was at his own behest.[11] Quite why Jackson does not appear in the portrait is unclear.

If the painting points to the divisions within the senior ranks of the Royal Navy in the post-war period, then it also points to other unspoken truths. The image is strikingly traditional in tone and composition. The Royal Navy is immersed in its past, perhaps even bound by it. The ghosts of Nelson and the war dead are revered and at the same time hauntingly present. Almost as a reference to the debates raging in 1920–21 about the viability of the battleship, the ships present in the painting are those which by 1919 had been fully obsolete for more than half a century. The technologies referenced in the painting are those of the past as are the materials. The commanders of the Navy of iron and steel are backed by wooden panels: the wooden walls that formed Britain's chief line of defence in the days of sail. Modernity has no place in a board room where the victories of the Napoleonic War were reported and discussed. There is not even a telephone.

The weather gauge, carrying an image of Western Europe, is scarcely discernible behind the admirals, and it points to many things: to obsolescence; to the past; to over-reverence of tradition and heritage; to the fortunes of the Navy, which are perhaps changing; and to the stormier times which are to come. The wind vane points to the North East, across the North Sea and to Germany, Britain's most recent enemy. It does not point to the South West, in line with the direction of the prevailing winds and towards France, Britain's traditional enemy.

The overall image is ambivalent. Beatty looks to the horizon, while his lieutenants discuss the course to the future which must be navigated. There is no triumphalism of victory – no celebration of victory over Germany. There is only worry, debate and guarded hope. Stockdale Cope's painting is a tacit recognition that in the development of post-war naval policy in an age of austerity the Royal Navy faces profound challenges while dealing with legacies of the past. The outcome is uncertain, and the fortunes of the service are no longer dependent on the elements, but on the invisible forces of politics. The closed world of the Admiralty, represented by the board room, no longer guarantees the security of Britain and her Empire. Admirals no longer sit in private cloister, but under scrutiny by the nation, with the viewer acting as representative of the electorate, their political representatives, the people, the taxpayer. Interestingly, a barometer used to hang on the wall of the Board Room, in partnership with the weather gauge, and the fact that Stockdale Cope omits it from his painting seems a deliberate decision not to reference the pressures of the job of First Sea Lord and Admiralty.

Balancing the interests of the diverse constituencies of service, people and politicians is one of the challenges which any First Sea Lord, like Beatty, must face in the modern era. Politicians do things for political reasons, and their timescales are essentially short in nature. Happily the political reasons usually coincide with the national interest. In the formulation of naval policy, admirals work over longer timescales, and a capital ship takes years to build, and may be in service for half a century. In the period 1919 to 1922, broadly speaking, the politicians and admirals arrived at a naval policy that was broadly right, but in many cases only because of the self-confidence of the Admiralty, and senior ranks in putting forward their case, and in cajoling, charming and digging their heels in as appropriate. However, their successors failed to bring to full fruition the strategic vision evolved between 1919 and 1922. As a result Britain would enter the Second World War with a compromised fleet caught between the repercussions of international arms limitation, the concerns of the Treasury, the reluctance of politicians, the problems of British shipbuilders and the hopes and professional opinions of the admirals. In consequence, while Britain would emerge victorious from the Second World War, added to the memorials, alongside the names of thousands of other seamen and officers, would be the names of Admirals Holland and Phillips, both killed in 1941. Poignantly Holland was lost in the explosions that destroyed the dated and unmodernized HMS *Hood*, and Phillips drowned in the loss of HMS *Prince of Wales*, fighting a defensive action against the Japanese north of Singapore in defence of Britain's Asian Empire. Their ghosts would join those of the First World War admirals in haunting the old Admiralty Board Room.

Seventy-five years after the destruction of HMS *Hood* and HMS *Prince of Wales*, in the aftermath the 2015 Defence and Security Review, we await publication of a National Shipbuilding Strategy to ensure the maintenance of a naval industrial infrastructure, and to ensure a controlled flow of orders for new warships.[12] SDSR 2015 marked a vital step on the rebuilding of the Royal Navy, and it may be that the politicians have begun to recognize in policy terms the connectedness of naval policy and the need to align threats to national security to policy, resource (economic and military) and infrastructure. If that is the case, then the ghosts in the old Admiralty Board Room will rest a little easier.

Notes

Preface

1 Letter from head of BAE Systems to Cameron, 2010, cited in 'Cancelling aircraft carriers would have cost taxpayers £690 million', *The Daily Telegraph*, 4 November 2010, http://www.telegraph.co.uk/news/uknews/defence/8111117/Cancelling-aircraft-carriers-would-have-cost-taxpayers-690-million.html (accessed 25 July 2014).

2 'Queen Names New Royal Navy Aircraft Carrier in Rosyth', 4 July 2014, http://www.bbc.co.uk/news/uk-28146412 (accessed 19 July 2014).

3 'Warship sails into defence of the UK', *The Financial Times*, 4 July 2014, http://www.ft.com/cms/s/0/c51be9d6-038e-11e4-8ae4-00144feab7de.html#axzz38UW4dh67 (accessed 25 July 2014).

4 Ibid.

5 *A Strong Britain in an Age of Uncertainty: The National Security Strategy*, Cmd.7953 (London: Her Majesty's Stationery Office, 2010).

6 *Securing Britain in an Age of Uncertainty: The Strategic Defence and Security Review*, Cmd.7948 (London: Her Majesty's Stationery Office, 2010).

7 Till, Geoffrey, 'Great Britain Gambles with the Royal Navy', *Naval War College Review*, vol. 63, no. 1, 2010. pp. 33–60.

8 A National Audit Office Report in 2011 concluded the following in respect to the change to the carrier programme: 'Assessed against the parameters set out in … 2007 …, the Department is delivering a lower scale of carrier capability, later than planned, and at significantly higher cost.' *Ministry of Defence: Carrier Strike*, Report by the Comptroller and Auditor General, HC1092, Session 2010–2012 (London, The Stationery Office, 2011), p. 5.

9 *National Security Strategy and Strategic Defence and Security Review 2015: A Secure and Prosperous United Kingdom*, Cmd.9161 (London: Her Majesty's Stationery Office, 2015).

10 Admiral Sir Henry Leach to Royal United Services Institute, 9 June 1982, reproduced in Speed, Keith, *Sea Change: The Battle for the Falklands and the Future of the Royal Navy* (Bath: Ashgrove Press, 1982), p. 102.

11 'The Lasting Legacy of Shipbuilding', *The Daily Telegraph*, 5 April 2007, http://www.telegraph.co.uk/culture/music/rockandjazzmusic/3664240/The-lasting-legacy-of-Shipbuilding.html (accessed 1 October 2014).

12 Alan Lascelles Diary, 1 December 1944, Hart-Davis, D. (ed.), *King's Counsellor: Abdication and War: The Diaries of Sir Alan Lascelles* (London: Weidenfeld and Nicolson, 2006), p. 274.
13 BBC War Commentary, 28 February 1945, Dickinson, Rear Admiral R.K., *Naval Broadcasts* (London: George Allen & Unwin, 1946), p. 15.
14 Cowling, Maurice, *The Impact of Labour: The Beginning of Modern British Politics* (Cambridge: Cambridge University Press, 2005), p. 1.
15 See J.C.C. Davidson to Bonar Law, 13 January 1922, in Blake, Robert, *The Unknown Prime Minister: The Life and Times of Andrew Bonar Law 1858–1923* (London: Eyre and Spottiswoode, 1955), p. 437.
16 Berghahn, Volker, 'Navies and Domestic Factors', in Hattendorf, John (ed.), *Doing Naval History: Essays Towards Improvement* (Newport, RI: Naval War College Press, 1995), pp. 43–56, 54.
17 Sumida, John, 'Technology, Culture and the Modern Battleship', *Naval War College Review*, vol. 45, no.4, 1992. pp. 82–87, 83.
18 Huntingdon, Samuel P., *The Common Defense: Strategic Programs in National Politics* (New York: Columbia University Press, 1961), p. vi.
19 Edgerton, David, *Warfare State: Britain 1920–1970* (Cambridge: Cambridge University Press, 2006), p. 20. Kennedy, Paul, *The Rise and Fall of British Naval Mastery* (London: Ashfield, 1983).
20 Weir, Gary E., 'Editorial: For the Readers of the IJNH', *International Journal of Maritime History*, vol. 8, no. 3, 2009, http://www.ijnhonline.org/wp-content/uploads/2012/01/editorial_weir_dec09.pdf (accessed 26 December 2014).
21 Ibid.
22 Kipling, Rudyard, 'The Song of the Dead', *English Illustrated Magazine*, May 1893. p. 534.

Introduction

1 For British war plans against Japan in the 1920s see Bell, Christopher M., '"How Are We Going to Make War?": Admiral Sir Herbert Richmond and British Far Eastern War Plans', *The Journal of Strategic Studies*, vol. 20, no. 3, 1997. pp. 123–41.
2 Bell, Christopher M., 'The Royal Navy, War Planning and Intelligence Assessments of Japan between the Wars' in Jackson, Peter and Siegel, Jennifer (eds.), *Intelligence and Statecraft: The Use and Limits of Intelligence in International Society* (Westport, CT: Praeger, 2005), pp. 139–55, 139.
3 Chatfield, Lord, *It Might Happen Again* (London: William Heinemann Ltd, 1947).
4 Cato, *Guilty Men* (London: Victor Gollancz, 1940). Ferris, J.R., *Men, Money and Diplomacy: The Evolution of British Strategic Foreign Policy, 1919–1926* (Ithaca, NY:

Cornell University Press, 1989). Bell, Christopher M., 'Winston Churchill and the Ten Year Rule', *Journal of Military History*, vol. 74, no. 4, 2010. pp. 523–56.

5 Redford, Duncan, 'Review Article from Pre to Post-Dreadnought: Recent Research on the Royal Navy, 1880–1945', *Journal of Contemporary History*, vol. 45, no. 4, 2010. pp. 866–76.

6 'Far Eastern Treaty', January 1922, TNA: CAB24/133.

7 See, for example, Vinson, J.C., 'The Imperial Conference of 1921 and the Anglo-Japanese Alliance', *Pacific Historical Review*, vol. 31, 1962. pp. 257–66.

8 In this book the term 'capital ship' refers to battleship and/or battlecruiser. The term is not static and can equally well be applied to other types of vessels such as aircraft carriers or nuclear submarines. As Geoffrey Till reminds us, 'Admiral Richmond continually urged his colleagues to note the difference between the battleship as a ship and the capital ship as a role.' Till, Geoffrey, 'Airpower and the Battleship in the 1920' in Ranft, Bryan (ed.), *Technical Change and British Naval Policy 1860–1939* (London: Hodder and Stoughton, 1977), p. 122.

9 Edgerton, *Warfare State*, p. 2.

10 Neilson, Keith, 'Greatly Exaggerated: The Myth of the Decline of Great Britain before 1914', *International History Review*, vol. 13, no. 4, 1991. pp. 695–725. Ferris, J.R., 'The Greatest Power on Earth: Great Britain in the 1920s', *International History Review*, vol. 13, no. 4, 1991. pp. 726–50. McKercher, B.J.C., '"Our Most Dangerous Enemy": Great Britain Pre-eminent in the 1930s', *International History Review*, vol. 13, no. 4, 1991. pp. 751–83.

11 Goldstein, Erik, 'The Evolution of British Diplomatic Strategy for the Washington Conference' in Goldstein, Erik, and Maurer, John (eds.), *The Washington Conference, 1921–22: Naval Rivalry, East Asian Stability and the Road to Pearl Harbor* (London: Frank Cass, 1994), p. 4.

12 Ibid., p. 5.

13 McKercher, B.J.C., *Anglo-American Relations in the 1920's: The Struggle for Supremacy* (Basingstoke: Palgrave Macmillan, 1990), p. 5.

14 Fry, M.G., 'The North Atlantic Triangle and the Abrogation of the Anglo-Japanese Alliance', *Journal of Modern History*, vol. 39, no. 1, 1967. pp. 46–64.

15 Best, Anthony, 'The "Ghost" of the Anglo-Japanese Alliance: An Examination into Historical Myth-Making Making', *The Historical Journal*, vol. 49, no. 3, 2006. pp. 811–31.

16 Padfield, Peter, *Maritime Dominion and the Triumph of the Free World: Naval Campaigns That Shaped the Modern World 1852–2001* (London: John Murray, 2009). Wilmott, H.P., *Battleship* (London: Cassell, 2002).

17 Nish, Ian H., *Alliance in Decline: A Study in Anglo-Japanese Relations* (Athlone: University of London, 1972).

18 Roskill, Stephen, *Naval Policy between the Wars*, Volume 1: The Period of Anglo-American Antagonism (London: Collins, 1968).

19 See Gough, Barry, *Historical Dreadnoughts: Marder and Roskill: Writing and Fighting Naval History* (Barnsley: Pen and Sword, 2010), pp. 169–71.
20 Stephen Wentworth Roskill (1 August 1903–4 November 1982), born in London, entered the Royal Navy in 1917, attending both Royal Naval College Osborne and Britannia Royal Naval College. He married Elizabeth van den Bergh in 1930 (they had seven children) and served as gunnery officer on HMS *Eagle* 1933–35; gunnery school HMS *Excellent* 1935–36; gunnery officer HMS *Warspite* 1936–39; Naval Staff 1939–41; executive officer HMNZS *Leander* 1941–44; British Admiralty Delegation Washington, DC, 1944–46; senior British observer Bikini atomic tests 1946; Deputy Director of Naval Intelligence 1946–8; and retired as Captain. He was awarded the DSC in 1943 after HMNZS *Leander* was in action against Japanese forces near Solomon Islands.
21 Roskill, *Naval Policy*, pp. 204–33.
22 Gough, *Historical Dreadnoughts*, pp. 167 and x.
23 Bell, Christopher M., *The Royal Navy, Seapower and Strategy between the Wars* (London: Macmillan, 2000), p. xvi.

Chapter 1

1 See, for example, Ferris, John, 'The Greatest World Power on Earth: Great Britain in the 1920s', *International History Review*, vol. 14, no. 4, 1991. pp. 726–50. Lambert, Andrew, 'The Royal Navy 1856–1914: Deterrence and the Strategy of World Power' in Neilson, K., and Errington, E.J., *Navies and Global Defense: Theories and Strategy* (Westport, CT: Praeger, 1995), pp. 69–92.
2 Paget, John C., *Naval Powers and Their Policy* (London: Longmans and Co, 1876), p. vii.
3 Steevens, G.W., *Naval Policy with Some Account of the Warships of the Principal Powers* (London: Methuen & Co. 1896).
4 Ibid., p. 267.
5 Kennedy, The Rise and Fall of British Naval Mastery, p. 209.
6 Till, Geoffrey, 'Naval Power' in McInnes, Colin, and Sheffield, G.D. (eds.), *Warfare in the Twentieth Century* (London: Unwin Hyman, 1988), p. 81.
7 *Whitaker's Almanack: 1900* (London: Stationery Office, 1899), p. 191.
8 Lambert, Nicholas, *Sir John Fisher's Naval Revolution* (Columbia: University of South Carolina Press, 2002), p. 30. See also Lambert, Andrew, 'Economic Power, Technological Advantage, and Imperial Strength: Britain as a Unique Global Power, 1860–1890', *International Journal of Naval History*, vol. 5, no. 2, August 2006. http://www.ijnhonline.org/wp-content/uploads/2012/01/article_lambert_aug06.pdf (accessed 26 December 2014).

9 Massie, Robert K., *Dreadnought: Britain, Germany and the Coming of the Great War* (London: Vintage, 1992), pp. 832–33.

10 Baer, George, 'That Navy for the Nation: A Shared Responsibility' in Stevens, David, and Reeve, John, *The Navy and the Nation* (Crows Nest, NSW: Allen & Unwin, 2005), pp. 11–22, 11–12.

11 Henry Spenser Wilkinson (1853–1937) was related by marriage to the British diplomat Eyre Crowe (1864–1925). Crowe, especially through his 1907 memorandum on 'The Present State of Relations with France and Germany', played a leading role in shaping British foreign policy towards Germany in the lead up to the First World War.

12 '"The Navy" by RN', *The Times*, 19 December 1893, p. 3. See also Vice Admiral Colomb, P.H., *Essays on Naval Defence* (London: W.H. Allen and Co, 1893).

13 'The Navy' by Samuel W. Baker, *The Times*, 19 December 1893, p. 3.

14 'The Navy League', *The Times*, 23 November 1895, p. 6.

15 See Lawson, Wilfrid (Coalition Liberal, Cockermouth), 6 May 1889, *Parliamentary Debates [Commons]*, vol. 335, cols. 1315–16.

16 Sondhaus, Lawrence, *Naval Warfare, 1815–1914* (New York: Routledge, 2001), p. 161.

17 Sumida, Jon Tetsuro, *In Defence of Naval Supremacy: Finance, Technology and British Naval Policy, 1889–1914* (New York: Routledge, 1993), p. 16.

18 Protheroe, Ernest, *The British Navy: Its Making and Meaning* (London: George Routledge and Sons Ltd, 1914), p. 628.

19 Gordon, W.J., *A Chat about the Navy* (London: Simpkin, Marshall, Hamilton, Kent and Co, 1891), p. 9.

20 Rear Admiral Eardley-Wilmot, S., *The British Navy Past and Present* (London: Navy League, 1904).

21 Bird, Hazel Sheeky, 'Naval History and Heroes: The Influence of U.S. and British Navalism on Children's Writing, 1895–1914', *International Journal of Naval History*, vol. 11, no. 1, July 2014. http://www.ijnhonline.org/2014/07/01/influence-us-british-navalism-childrens-writing/ (accessed 26 December 2014).

22 Clowes, William Laird, *The Royal Navy: A History from the Earliest Times to the Present*, vol. 1 (London: Sampson Low, Marston and Company, 1897), p. iv.

23 Robinson, Commander Charles N., *The British Fleet: The Growth, Achievements and Duties of the Navy of the Empire* (London: George Bell and Sons, 1894).

24 Ibid., p. 7.

25 Williams, Harry, *The Steam Navy of England: Past, Present and Future* (London: W.H. Allen & Co, 1895).

26 Ibid., p. v.

27 Wood, Walter, *Famous British War-ships and Their Commanders* (London: Hurst and Blackett, 1897). See also Mahan, A.T., *Types of Naval Officer Drawn from the*

History of the British Navy (Boston: Little Brown and Company, 1901). Giffard, Edward, *Deeds of Naval Daring: Anecdotes of the British Navy* (London: John Murray, 1910).

28 Clark, Lieutenant Colonel Sir George and Thursfield, James R., *The Navy and the Nation or Naval Warfare and Imperial Defence* (London: John Murray, 1897).

29 Ibid., p. 11.

30 Gibbs, Fred T.M. (ed.), *The Illustrated Guide to the Royal Navy and Foreign Navies* (London: Waterlow Bros. and Layton Ltd, 1896).

31 Ibid., p. vi.

32 'Judson and the Empire' in Kipling, Rudyard (ed.), *Many Inventions* (London: Macmillan, 1893), pp. 327–361.

33 'Steam Tactics' December 1902; 'The Bonds of Discipline' August 1903; 'Their Lawful Occasions' December 1903; 'Mrs Bathurst' September 1904; Kipling, Rudyard, *Traffics and Discoveries* (London: Macmillan,1904).

34 Swinburne, Algernon Charles, *A Word for the Navy* (London: George Redway, 1896).

35 'The Hero of Trafalgar', Royal Maritime Museum Greenwich Catalogue Entry, http://collections.rmg.co.uk/collections/objects/156081.html (accessed 3 August 2014).

36 'The Customary Annual Decoration', *The Times*, 22 October 1904, p. 9.

37 'Lord Charles Beresford on the Navy', *The Times*, 3 May 1897, p. 4.

38 'Lord Charles Beresford on the Navy', *The Times*, 24 May 1897, p. 12.

39 Marder, Arthur J., 'The English Armament Industry and Navalism in the Nineties', *Pacific Historical Review*, vol. 7, no. 3, 1938. pp. 241–53.

40 Ibid., p. 246. Sir Charles Mark Palmer (1822–1907), Palmer's Shipbuilding and Iron Company Limited, Liberal MP North Durham 1874–85 and Jarrow 1885–1907; Sir William Theodore Doxford (1841–1916), shipyard owner, Conservative and Unionist MP Sunderland 1895–1906; and Sir William Alan (1837–1903), engineering works owner, Liberal MP Gateshead 1893–1903.

41 'Lord Charles Beresford on the Navy', 24 May 1897, p. 12.

42 Stenzel, Captain A., *The British Navy* (London: T. Fisher Unwin, 1898), p. 3.

Chapter 2

1 For contemporary evidence see, for example, 'British and Japanese Alliance: Surprise in Europe', *The Maitland Daily Mercury* (New South Wales), 14 February 1902, p. 3. On the scholarship see, for example, Monger, George W., *The End of Isolation: British Foreign Policy, 1900–1907* (London: Nelson, 1963).

2 Seamen, L.C.B., *Post-Victorian Britain* (London: Methuen, 1966), p. 10.

3 Nish, Ian, 'The First Anglo-Japanese Treaty', Symposium at the Suntory Centre (LSE), 22 February 2002, http://eprints.lse.ac.uk/6884/1/Anglo-Japanese_Alliance.pdf (accessed 2 December 2015).
4 See, for example, James O'Kelly (Irish Parliamentary Party, Roscommon), 13 February '1902 on the Anglo-Japanese Agreement–Inclusion of Manchuria', *Parliamentary Debates [Commons]*, vol. 102, col. 1247. Henry Norman (Liberal, Wolverhampton South), 13 February 1902 on the Anglo-Japanese Agreement – Communication to the US Government, *Parliamentary Debates [Commons]*, vol. 102, col. 1246–7.
5 Russell to Neale, 24 December 1862, cited in Russell to Neale, 10 November 1863, printed in *The Times*, 6 February 1864, p. 9.
6 Edward Neale to Japanese Foreign Minister, 24 June 1863, cited in Satow, Sir Ernest, *A Diplomat in Japan* (New York: Muse paperback, 2000), p. 78.
7 The Armstrong gun was introduced in 1858. Lyon, David, *The Ship: Steam Steel and Torpedoes* (London: HMSO, 1980), p. 30.
8 Kuper to Admiralty, 17 August 1863, printed in *The Times*, 31 October 1863, p. 9.
9 Hill, Richard, *War at Sea in the Ironclad Age* (London: Cassell paperback, 2002), p. 55.
10 Earl Russell to Neale, 11 January 1864, printed in *The Times*, 6 February 1864, p. 9.
11 Kuper to Admiralty, 15 September 1864, printed in *The Times*, 19 November 1864, p. 7. Sir Ernest Satow, *A Diplomat*, p. 101.
12 Marder, Arthur J., *Old Friends, New Enemies: The Royal Navy and Imperial Japanese Navy – Strategic Illusions* (Oxford: Oxford University Press, 1981), p. 5.
13 Tarkow-Naamani, Israel, 'The Abandonment of "Splendid Isolation": A Study of British Public Opinion and Diplomacy', 1895–1902, PhD, University of Indiana, 1946.
14 See, for example, 'Dispatches Just to Hand from Japan Report a Terrible Typhoon', *Western Mail* (Cardiff Wales), 20 December 1889, p. 2; 'Japan and Its People', *The Leeds Mercury*, 26 December 1889, p. 3; 'Foreign Trade of Japan', *Glasgow Herald*, 11 June 1890, p. 12.
15 See, for example, 'Japan and the Foreign Powers', *Belfast Newsletter*, 31 July 1890, p. 8.
16 'Japan as a Naval and Military Power', reprinted in the *Birmingham Daily Post*, 8 October 1888. p. 5.
17 Paine, S.C.M., *The Sino-Japanese War of 1894–1895: Perceptions, Power and Primacy* (Cambridge: Cambridge University Press, 2005), p. 7.
18 See 'The Eastern Question', *The Age* (Melbourne, Victoria), 28 October 1895, p. 5.
19 See 'The Premiers Conference – Anglo-Japanese Treaty Objected To', *The Ballarat Star* (Victoria), 6 March 1896, p. 4.
20 Olender, Piotr, *Sino-Japanese Naval War 1894–1895* (Poland: Stratus, 2014), p. 173.
21 Berryman, John, 'British Imperial Defence Strategy and Russia: The Role of the Royal Navy in the Far East, 1878–1898', *International Journal of Naval History*, vol. 1, no. 1, April 2002. http://www.ijnhonline.org/issues/volume-1-2002/apr-2002-vol-1-issue-1/ (accessed 26 November 2014).

22 Macmillan, Margaret, *The War That Ended Peace: How Europe Abandoned Peace for the First World War* (London: Profile Books, 2013), p. 46.
23 See, for example, 'A New Triple Alliance', *The North Queensland Register*, 14 November 1898, p. 13.
24 'The Anglo-American Alliance', *Wagga Wagga Advertiser* (New South Wales), 15 November 1898, p. 2.
25 *The Penny Illustrated Paper and Illustrated Times*, 22 February 1902, p. 116.
26 Steiner, Zara S., *The Foreign Office and Foreign Policy 1898–1914* (Cambridge: Cambridge University Press, 1969), p. 47.
27 Nish, 'The First Anglo-Japanese Alliance', p. 4.
28 Ibid., p. 5.
29 Reynolds, David, *Britannia Overruled: British Policy & World Power in the 20th Century* (London: Longman, 1991), p. 75.
30 See, for example, Corbett, Julian S., *Maritime Operations in the Russo-Japanese War, 1904–1905*, 2 vols. (Annapolis, MD: Naval Institute Press, 2015).
31 Koda, Yoji, 'The Russo-Japanese War: Primary Causes of Japanese Success', *Naval War College Review*, vol. 58, no. 2, 2005. pp. 11–44.
32 Steeds, David, 'The Second Anglo-Japanese Alliance and the Russo-Japanese War', Symposium at the Suntory Centre (LSE), 22 February 2002, p. 19. http://eprints.lse.ac.uk/6884/1/Anglo-Japanese_Alliance.pdf (accessed 31 October 2014).
33 See Clements, Jonathan, *Admiral Tōgō: Nelson of the East* (London: Haus Publishing, 2010).
34 Towle, Philip, 'The Evaluation of the Experience of the Russo-Japanese War' in Ranft (ed.), *Technical Change*, pp. 65–79.
35 'Togo's Great Victory', *The Penny Illustrated Paper and Illustrated Times*, 3 June 1905, p. 340.
36 Chida, Tomohei, Davies, Peter N., *The Japanese Shipping and Shipbuilding Industries: A History of Modern Growth* (London: Bloomsbury, 2012), p. 5.
37 Minutes of the 102nd Meeting of the CID, 29 June 1909, contained in 'Admiralty Memorandum for the War Cabinet', 31 October 1919, TNA: CAB24/92.
38 Minutes of the 102nd Meeting of the CID, 29 June 1909, contained in Admiralty Memorandum for the War Cabinet, 31 October 1919, TNA: CAB24/92.

Chapter 3

1 Marwick, Arthur, *The Deluge* (London: Macmillan, 1973); Winter, J.M., *The Great War and the British People* (London: Macmillan, 1986); McLean, Ian, *The Legend of Red Clydeside* (Edinburgh: John McDonald, 1983); Turner, John, *British Politics*

and the Great War: Coalition and Conflict, 1915–1918 (Newhaven, CT: Yale, 1992); Wohl, R., *The Generation of 1914* (London: Weidenfeld & Nicolson, 1980).

2 Roskill, Stephen, *The Strategy of Sea Power: Its Development and Application* (London: Collins, 1962), p. 109.

3 Protheroe, *The British Navy*, p. 636.

4 'Ex Royal Navy', *The Navy from Within* (London: Hodder and Stoughton, 1914). Hislam, Percival A., *The Navy of To-day* (London: T.C. & E.C. Jack, 1914).

5 Ibid.

6 Cesario, Bradley M., '"Trafalgar Refought": The Professional and Cultural Memory of Horatio Nelson during Britain's Navalist Era, 1880–1914', MA, Texas A & M University, 2011.

7 Breemer, Jan S., 'The Burden of Trafalgar: Decisive Battle and Naval Strategic Expectations on the Eve of World War One', *Journal of Strategic Studies*, vol. 17, no. 1, March 1994. pp. 33–62. See also Rüger, Jan, *The Great Naval Game: Britain and Germany in the Age of Empire* (Cambridge: Cambridge University Press, 2007), p. 256.

8 Marder, Arthur J., *Fear God and Dread Nought: The Correspondence of Admiral of the Fleet Lord Fisher of Kilverstone*, vol. III, *Restoration, Abdication, and Last Years, 1914–1920* (London: Jonathan Cape, 1959), p. 44.

9 Bennett, Geoffrey, *The Battle of Jutland* (Philadelphia: Dufour Editions, 1964), p. 29.

10 See, for example, Thomas, Lowell, *Raiders of the Deep* (Sussex: William Heinemann, 1929).

11 Kennedy, *The Rise and Fall of British Naval Mastery*, p. 251.

12 Long to *Daily Express*, 18 June 1919, Long papers (Swindon and Wiltshire History Centre) 947/690.

13 Weymss to Beatty, 14 November 1918, Lady Weymss, Wester, *The Life and Letters of Lord Wester Weymss* (London: Eyre and Spottiswoode, 1935), pp. 398–99.

14 Long to *Daily Express*, 18 June 1919, Long papers (Swindon and Wiltshire History Centre) 947/690.

15 Warren, Kenneth, *Steel, Ships and Men: Cammell Laird, 1824–1993* (Liverpool: Liverpool University Press, 1998), p. 184.

16 Ibid., p. 189.

17 Navy Estimates 1919–1920, 1 December 1919, www.naval-history.net (accessed 28 November 2013).

18 Kennedy, *The Rise and Fall of British Naval Mastery*, p. 260.

19 Admiral Sir Charles Madden to Jellicoe, 29 November 1918, Jellicoe papers XXI, Add. MSS.49009.

20 Weymss, *The Life and Letters of Lord Wester Weymss*, p. 413.

21 Macmillan, Margaret, *Peacemakers: Six Months That Changed the World* (London: John Murray, 2001), pp. 188–9.

22 See Weymss diary, reproduced in Massie, Robert K., *Castles of Steel: Britain, Germany and the Winning of the Great War at Sea* (London: Jonathan Cape, 2004), p. 788. Admiral Rosslyn Weymss, Baron Wester Weymss (1864–1933) commanded base at Lemnos at the outbreak of war, played a major role in the Dardanelles/Gallipoli campaigns and was appointed First Sea Lord in 1917.
23 Joint note of the Admirals for Council of the Principal Allied and Associated Powers, 27 June 1919, TNA: FO608/248.
24 Preston, Antony and Batchelor, John, *Battleships 1919–77* (London: Phoebus, 1977), p. 5.
25 Gordon, Andrew, *The Rules of the Game: Jutland and British Naval Command* (London: John Murray, 2005), p. 399.
26 Pollen, Arthur, *The British Navy in Battle* (New York: Doubleday Page and Company, 1919). Pollen, Arthur, *The Navy in Battle* (London: Chatto and Windus, 1918), p. 10.
27 Cato, Conrad, *The Navy Everywhere* (New York: E.P. Dutton, 1919).
28 Bartimeus (Captain Sir Lewis Ritchie), *The Navy Eternal* (London: Hodder and Stoughton, 1918). Cope Cornford, L., *The British Navy: The Navy Vigilant* (London: Macmillan, 1918), p. ix.
29 Taffrail (Captain Henry Taprell Dorling), *The Sub: Being the Autobiography of David Munro Sub-Lieutenant Royal Navy* (London: Hodder and Stoughton, 1917).
30 Scott, Admiral Sir Percy, *Fifty Years in the Royal Navy* (New York: George H Doran Company, 1919). Dent, Lieutenant J.M., *The Motor Launch Patrol* (Edinburgh: J.M. Dent and Sons, 1920). Jellicoe, Viscount of Scapa, *The Crisis of the Naval War* (New York: George H. Doran, 1921). See also, Brownrigg, Rear Admiral Sir Douglas, *Indiscretions of the Naval Censor* (New York: Cassell and Company Ltd, 1920).
31 P.H. Kerr to John Dove, 13 July 1920, Kerr papers, Scottish Record Office GD40/17/209.
32 Lambert, Nicholas, 'Economy or Empire?: The Fleet Unit Concept and the Quest for Collective Security in the Pacific, 1909–1914' in Neilson, Keith, Kennedy, Greg (eds.), *Far Flung Lines: Studies in Imperial Defence in Honour of Donald Mackenzie Schurman* (New York: Routledge, 1987), pp. 55–83.
33 'Empire Naval Policy and Co-operation', February 1921, TNA: CAB21/187.
34 Tracy, Nicholas (ed.), *The Collective Naval Defence of the Empire, 1900–1945* (London: Ashgate, 1997), p. xivff.
35 Ibid., p. xxvi.
36 Ibid, pp. xxviii–xxix.
37 Admiralty to Jellicoe, 20 September 1919, TNA: ADM116/1831.
38 Saxon, Timothy D., 'Anglo-Japanese Naval Co-Operation, 1914–18', *The Naval War College Review*, vol. 53, no. 1, Winter 2000, unpaginated. http://digitalcommons.liberty.edu/hist_fac_pubs/5 (accessed 15 October 2014).

39 Report of Admiral of the Fleet Viscount Jellicoe of Scapa on Naval Mission to the Commonwealth of Australia (May–August 1919), vol. IV, p. 229. http://www.navy.gov.au/sites/default/files/documents/Jellicoe_of_Scapa_Vol_IV.pdf (accessed 12 November 2015).

40 Kosukai News Agency, *Anglo-Japanese Alliance* (no place of publication: Japan Times Publishing, 1916).

41 Ibid., p. 1.

42 Lord Lee of Fareham, 'The Japanese as Naval Allies', 17 June 1921, TNA: CAB24/125.

43 C-in-C China Station to their Lord Commissioner of the Admiralty, 5 January 1917, enclosed in Lord Lee of Fareham, 'The Japanese as Naval Allies', 17 June 1921, TNA: CAB24/125.

44 Ibid.

45 Bellamy, Martin, 'Shipbuilding and Cultural Identity on Clydeside', *Journal for Maritime Research*, January 2006 (unpaginated). http://www.jmr.nmm.ac.uk/server/show/ConjmrArticle.210 (accessed 12 November 2015). See also Foster, J., 'Strike Action and Working-Class Politics on Clydeside, 1914–19', *International Review of Social History*, vol. 35, 1990. pp. 33–70.

Chapter 4

1 See, for example, Bulmer-Thomas, Ivor, *The Growth of the British Party System Volume II 1924–1964* (London: John Baker, 1967); Cowling, Maurice, *The Impact of Labour: The Beginning of Modern British Politics* (Cambridge: Cambridge University Press, 2005); Jarvis, David, 'British Conservatism and Class Politics in the 1920s', *The English Historical Review*, vol. 111, no. 440, 1996. pp. 59–84; Keohane, Nigel, *The Party of Patriotism: The Conservative Party and the First World War* (London: Ashgate, 2010); Morgan, Kenneth O., *Consensus and Disunity: The Lloyd George Coalition Government 1918–1922* (Oxford: Oxford University Press, 1986); Powell, David, *British Politics, 1910–1935: The Crisis of the Party System* (London: Routledge, 2004); Rubinstein, David, *The Labour Party and British Society 1880–2005* (Sussex; Sussex Academic Press, 2005); Tanner, Duncan, *Political Change and the Labour Party 1900–1918* (Cambridge: Cambridge University Press, 2003); Thompson, J.A., 'The Historians and the Decline of the Liberal Party', *Albion: A Quarterly Journal Concerned with British Studies*, vol. 22, no. 1, 1990. pp. 65–83.

2 Ball, Stuart, 'Asquith's Decline and the General Election of 1918', *Scottish Historical Review*, vol. 61, 1982. pp. 44–61.

3 Webb, Sidney, *The New Constitution of the Labour Party: A Party of Handworkers and Brainworkers: The Labour Programme and Prospects* (London: Labour Party, 1918). http://webbs.library.lse.ac.uk/124/ (accessed 6 October 2014).

4 Gilbert, Bentley B., 'Lloyd George and the Historians', *Albion*, vol. 11, no. 1, 1979. pp. 74–86, 75.
5 Ibid., p. 85.
6 Ibid., p. 85.
7 Sharp, A.J., 'The Foreign Office in Eclipse 1919–22', *History*, vol. 61, no. 202, 1976. pp. 198–218. With regard to the later historiography, see Maisel, E., *The Foreign Office and Foreign Policy, 1919–1926* (Brighton: Sussex Academic Press, 1994); Bennett, G.H., *British Foreign Policy during the Curzon Period, 1919–1924* (Basingstoke: Macmillan, 1995); Gilmour, David, *Curzon* (London: John Murray,1994); Johnson, Gaynor (ed.), *The Foreign Office and British Diplomacy in the Twentieth Century* (New York: Routledge, 2005); Rose, Inabal *Conservatism and Foreign Policy during the Lloyd George Coalition* (Oxford: Frank Cass, 2013).
8 Huntingdon, *Common Defense*, p. vii.
9 See Balfour to Duke of Buccleuch, 8 December 1916, Balfour papers, vol. XXXIII, Add.MSS.49725.
10 Lady Lee of Fareham diary, 24 February 1921, in Clark, Alan (ed.), '*A Good Innings': The Private Papers of Viscount Lee of Fareham* (London: John Murray, 1974), p. 206.
11 Long to Lloyd George, 10 January 1919, Long papers (Swindon and Wiltshire History Centre) 947/701.
12 See O'Brien, Phillips, *British and American Naval Power: Politics and Policy, 1900–1936* (Westport, CT: Praeger, 1998), p. 140. Rodger, N.A.M., *The Admiralty* (Lavenham (Suffolk): Terrence Dalton Ltd, 1979), p. 147.
13 *Navy Estimates 1920–21* (London: His Majesty's Stationery Office, 1920). TNA: TS27/634. TNA: ADM116/3610.
14 Lloyd George to Bonar Law, 30? January 1922, Bonar Law papers BL/100/1/52.
15 Long to Bonar Law, 9 February 1921, Bonar Law papers BL/100/2/21. Long to Lloyd George, 9 February 1921, Lloyd George papers LG/F/34/1/59.
16 Long to Bonar Law, 10 February 1921, Bonar Law papers BL/100/2/15. See also Lee to Bonar Law, 10 February 1921, Bonar Law papers BL/100/2/16.
17 Lee of Fareham to Lloyd George, 10 February 1921, Lloyd George papers LG/F/31/2/50.
18 'Lord Lee of Fareham: Comes off Noted Naval Family', *Dundee Evening Telegraph*, 27 October 1926, p. 3.
19 See, for example, 'The Government's Naval Policy', Memorandum by the First Lord of the Admiralty, 15 July 1921, TNA: CAB24/126.
20 Roskill, *Naval Policy*, pp. 31–32.
21 Ibid., p. 32.
22 Leopold Stennett Amery (1873–1955) was a journalist, and he was elected in 1911 as Liberal Unionist MP for Birmingham South. During the First World War, he served in intelligence before being appointed as a Parliamentary Under-Secretary.

He also was First Lord of the Admiralty (1922–24) and Colonial Secretary (1924–29). As a prominent critic of appeasement in the 1930s, he played a key role in the Norway debate in May 1940. During the Second World War he served as Secretary of State for India and Burma. He was defeated in his Birmingham South seat in the Labour landslide of 1945.

23 Winston Churchill (Coalition Liberal, Dundee), 3 August 1921, *Parliamentary Debates [Commons]*, vol. 145, cols. 1543–44.
24 Hurd, Sir Archibald, *Who Goes There?* (London: Hutchinson, 1942), p. 139.
25 'The financial situation', 18 July 1919, TNA: CAB24/84.
26 Cabinet minutes, 15 August 1919, TNA: CAB23/15.
27 Ibid., p. 167.
28 Chatfield, *It Might Happen Again*, p. 179.
29 'First Sea Lord: Impending Change Denied', *Daily Standard* (Brisbane, QLD), 27 February 1919, p. 4.
30 Weymss, *Life and Letters*, p. 419.
31 Long to Beatty, 24 February 1919, Long papers (Swindon and Wiltshire History Centre) 947/713/1.
32 Stamfordham to Long, 6 March 1919, Long papers (Swindon and Wiltshire History Centre) 947/713/1.
33 Long to Lloyd George, 7 March 1919, Long papers (Swindon and Wiltshire History Centre) 947/713/1.
34 Stamfordham to Long, 9 March 1919, Long papers (Swindon and Wiltshire History Centre) 947/713/1.
35 Weymss to Long, 10 March 1919, Long papers (Swindon and Wiltshire History Centre) 947/713/1.
36 Long to Lloyd George, 11 March 1919, Long papers (Swindon and Wiltshire History Centre) 947/713/2.
37 Beresford to Long, 10 March 1919, Long papers (Swindon and Wiltshire History Centre) 947/689.
38 Ibid.
39 Armstrong to Long, 8 April 1919 (enclosing Armstrong to Beresford, 8 April 1919), Long papers (Swindon and Wiltshire History Centre) 947/685.
40 Armstrong to Beresford, 8 April 1919, Long papers (Swindon and Wiltshire History Centre) 947/685.
41 Statement by Walter Long (Unionist, Westminster St Georges), 7 May 1919, *Parliamentary Debates [Commons]*, vol. 115, col. 901.
42 Weymss to Long, 28 August 1919, Long papers (Swindon and Wiltshire History Centre) 947/713/2.
43 Beatty to Long, 9 August 1919, and Long to Beatty, 12 August 1919, Long papers (Swindon and Wiltshire History Centre) 947/687.

44 Long to Weymss, 11 October 1919, Long papers (Swindon and Wiltshire History Centre) 947/713/2.
45 Weymss to King George V., undated and reproduced in Weymss, *Life and Letters*, p. 440.
46 The literature on Beatty is extensive and varied. See, for example, Beatty, Charles Robert Longfield, *Our Admiral: A Biography of Admiral of the Fleet Earl Beatty* (London: W.H. Allen, 1980). Chalmers, William S., *The Life and Letters of David Earl Beatty, Admiral of the Fleet, Viscount Borodale of Wexford, Baron Beatty of the North Sea and of Brooksby* (London: Hodder & Stoughton, 1951). Rawson, Geoffrey, *Earl Beatty, Admiral of the Fleet* (London: Jarrolds, 1930). Shaw, Frank Hubert, *The Boy's Life of Admiral Beatty* (London: Hutchinson, 1933).
47 Long to Beatty, 13 March 1919, Long papers (Swindon and Wiltshire History Centre) 947/686.
48 Beatty to Long, 15 March 1919, Long papers (Swindon and Wiltshire History Centre) 946/686.
49 Rodger, *The Admiralty*, p. 146.
50 Lambert, Andrew, 'Sir Julian Corbett and the Naval War Course' in Hore, Peter (ed.), *Dreadnought to Daring: 100 Years of Comment, Controversy and Debate in the Naval Review* (Barnsley: Seaforth, 2012), pp. 37–52, 42.
51 Ranft, Bryan M., 'Admiral David Earl Beatty1919–1927' in Murfett, Malcolm H. (ed.), *The First Sea Lords From Fisher to Mountbatten* (Westport, CT: Praeger Publishers, 1995), pp. 128–29.
52 Long to Beatty, 24 September 1919, Long papers (Swindon and Wiltshire History Centre) 947/713/2. Beatty's acceptance came on 26 September 1919, Long papers 947/713/2.
53 Beatty to Admiralty, 4 April 1919, in Ranft, Bryan M., *The Beatty Papers: Selections from the Private and Official Correspondence and Papers of Admiral of the Fleet Earl Beatty*, vol. II (Aldershot: Scolar Press for the Navy Records Society, 2003), pp. 30–32.
54 Roskill, Stephen, *Admiral of the Fleet Earl Beatty: The Last Naval Hero: An Intimate Biography* (London: Collins, 1980), p. 321.
55 Lambert, Andrew, *Admirals: The Naval Commanders Who Made Britain Great* (London: Faber and Faber, 2008), p. 366.
56 Eric Geddes to Lord Lee of Fareham quoted in Lady Lee of Fareham diary, 7 February 1921, in Clark (ed.), *A Good Innings*, p. 205.
57 Churchill to Lloyd George, 1 May 1919, Lloyd George papers LG/F/38/3/46.
58 Ferris, *Men, Money and Diplomacy*, p. 5.
59 Admiral of the Fleet, First Baron Wester Weymss to Beatty, 28 February 1919, in Ranft, Beatty Papers, pp. 22–24.
60 Minute on Naval Staff Organisation by Beatty, 8 January 1920, ADM116/1803.
61 'Note', *Aberdeen Daily Journal*, 28 February 1921, p. 2.

62 Between 1918 and August 1921 the Admiralty staff reduced from 10,637 to 5,200 with the prospect of a further 20 per cent reduction by December 1921. 'Admiralty Staff', *Aberdeen Daily Journal*, 2 August 1921, p. 5.

63 Kenworthy, Lieutenant-Commander J.M., *Will Civilisation Crash* (London: Ernest Benn, 1927), p. 213.

64 Murray, Lady Oswyn, *The Making of a Civil Servant* (London: Methuen and Co. Ltd, 1940), p. 129.

65 'The Admiralty in War', 5 September 1945, Dickinson, *Naval Broadcasts*, p. 55.

66 Chatfield, Lord, *The Navy and Defence* (London: William Heinemann, 1942), p. 185.

67 Vesey Hamilton, Admiral Sir R., *Naval Administration: The Constitution, Character and Functions of the Board of Admiralty and of the Civil Departments in Directs* (London: George Bell and Sons, 1896).

68 Roskill, *Beatty*, p. 301. Carew, Andrew, *The Lower Deck of the Royal Navy 1900–39: Invergordon in Perspective* (Manchester: Manchester University Press, 1981), p. 78ff. See also TNA: ADM 178/157; ADM 1/8666/159.

69 Statement of the First Lord of the Admiralty explanatory to the Naval Estimates, 1919–20. http://www.naval-history.net/WW1NavyBritishAdmiraltyEstimates1919.htm (accessed 11 June 2014).

70 Chatfield, *It Might Happen* Again, p. 185.

71 Murray, *Making of a Civil Servant*, p. 112.

72 Rear Admiral Murray Sueter (Independent, Hertford), 24 March 1922, *Parliamentary Debates [Commons]*, vol. 152, col. 859.

73 Divine, David, *The Blunted Sword* (London: Hutchinson, 1964), p. 19.

74 Ibid.

75 d'Eyncourt, A Sir Eustace H.W. Tennyson, *A Shipbuilder's Yarn* (London: Hutchinson and Co., 1948), p. 129.

76 Ibid.

77 Chatfield, *It Might Happen Again*, p. 185.

78 Ibid., p. 170.

79 Ibid., p. 186.

80 Jellicoe, *The Crisis*, p. 259.

81 See, for example, 'Crisis of the Naval War – Jellicoe's Book', *The Maitland Daily Mercury* (New South Wales), 30 July 1920, p. 5.

82 See, for example, Rear Admiral Sir William Reginald 'Blinker' Hall to Vice Admiral Keyes (Conservative, West Derby), 17 February 1922, and Keyes to Hall, 20 February 1922, on the issue of a motion that Hall wished to put forward during the debate on the naval estimates. In Halpern, Paul G., *The Keyes Papers: Selections from the Private and Official Correspondence of Admiral of the Fleet Baron Keyes of Zeebrugge, vol. II 1919–1938* (London: George Allen & Unwin, 1980), pp. 39–40, 71–72. Admiral of the Fleet Roger Keyes, First Baron Keyes (1872–1945) served

in China during the Boxer Rebellion (1899–1900) and took part in operations at Gallipoli in 1915. He served as Director of Plans at the Admiralty (1917–18) before taking command of the Dover Patrol. At the end of the war, he was involved in planning and executing the raids on the submarine pens at Ostende and Zeebrugge. In the interwar period he commanded the Battlecruiser Squadron (1919–21), and then as Deputy Chief of the Naval Staff (1921–25), in the latter 1920s, he commanded the Atlantic and Mediterranean Fleets before becoming Commander-in-Chief for Portsmouth (1929–35). He was elected as Conservative MP for Portsmouth North in 1934 before he retired from the Navy in 1935, but during the Second World War he acted as liaison to King Leopold III of Belgium (1940). He played a significant role in the Norway debate in May 1940 which led to the end of Neville Chamberlain's premiership. Desperate to return to active service, he was appointed as the first Director of Combined Operations (1940–41) by Churchill. He was sacked from the post in 1941 and stood down as MP for Portsmouth North in 1943. See TNA: ADM196/43, ADM196/88, ADM196/141.

83 Davison, Robert L., 'Striking a Balance between Dissent and Discipline: Admiral Sir Reginald Drax', *The Northern Mariner*, vol. XIII, no. 2, 2003. pp. 43–57(46). See also Macfarlane, J. Allan C., 'A Naval Travesty: The Dismissal of Admiral Sir John Jellicoe, 1917', PhD, St Andrews, 2014.

Chapter 5

1 Ramsden, J., *The Age of Balfour and Baldwin 1902–1940* (London: Longman, 1978), p. 132. McEwen, J.M., 'The Coupon Election of 1918 and Unionist Members of Parliament', *The Journal of Modern History*, vol. 34, no. 3, 1962. pp. 294–306.

2 Rooth, Tim, 'Britain in the International Economy' in Wrigley, Chris (ed.), *A Companion to Early-Twentieth Century Britain* (Oxford: Blackwell, 2003), p. 215.

3 Ibid., p. 212.

4 Austen Chamberlain to Ida Chamberlain, 21 December 1919, Austen Chamberlain papers, Birmingham University Library AC5/1/46.

5 Tomlinson, B.R., 'The British Economy and the Empire' in Wrigley (ed.), *Companion*, p. 201.

6 Mowat, Charles Loch, *Britain between the Wars 1918–1940* (London: Methuen, 1955), p. 125.

7 Ibid., p. 126.

8 'Rioters trapped', *The Times*, 13 September 1921, p. 10.

9 'Passive Resistance to Short Time', *The Times*, 18 January 1921, p. 11.

10 'Uproar at Woolwich', *The Times*, 13 September 1921, p. 10.

11 'The Unemployed March', *The Times*, 18 November 1922, p. 10.

12 Mowat, *Britain*, p. 126.
13 Ibid., p. 128.
14 David Lloyd George (Liberal, Carnarvon Boroughs), 3 April 1922, *Parliamentary Debates [Commons]*, vol. 152, cols. 1892–95.
15 Arthur Balfour (Conservative, City of London), 12 February 1920, *Parliamentary Debates [Commons]*, vol. 125, cols. 309–11.
16 Curzon of Kedleston (Conservative Peer), 7 February 1922, *Parliamentary Debates [Lords]*, vol. 49, cols. 27–28.
17 Lord Buckmaster (Liberal Peer), 7 February 1922, *Parliamentary Debates [Lords]*, vol. 49, cols. 45–47.
18 George Barker (Labour, Abertillery), 7 March 1922, *Parliamentary Debates [Commons]*, vol. 125, cols. 1167–68.
19 Kirby, M.W., 'The State and the Economy' in Wrigley (ed.), *Companion*, pp. 233–34.
20 Rear Admiral Murray Sueter (Independent, Hertford), 24 March 1922, *Parliamentary Debates [Commons]*, vol. 152, col. 854.
21 See, for example, Ferguson to Keyes, 29 August 1919, in Halpern, *The Keyes Papers*, pp. 39–40.
22 Robert Horne (Conservative, Glasgow, Hillhead), 1 May 1922, *Parliamentary Debates [Commons]*, vol. 153, col. 1024.
23 Rothermere, Viscount, *Solvency or Downfall? Squandermania and Its Story* (London: Longmans, Green, and Co, 1921), pp. viii–ix.
24 On the Harmsworth dynasty, see Bourne, Richard, *Lords of Fleet Street: The Harmsworth Dynasty* (London: Routledge, 2016).
25 Cowling, *Impact of Labour*, p. 56.
26 Bingham, Adrian, 'Enfranchisement, Feminism and the Modern Woman: Debates in the British Popular Press, 1918–1939' in Gottlieb, Julie, and Toye, Richard (eds.) *The Aftermath of Suffrage: Women, Gender and Politics in Britain 1918–1945* (Basingstoke: Palgrave Macmillan, 2013), pp. 87–105, 93.
27 Cronin, James E., *The Politics of State Expansion: War, State and Society in Twentieth Century Britain* (London, Routledge, 1991), p. 79.
28 Mowat, *Britain*, p. 131.
29 See, for example, Taylor, A.J.P., James, Robert Rhodes, Plumb, J.H., Hart, Basil Liddell, and Storr, Anthony, *Churchill: Four Faces and the Man* (London: Book Club Associates, 1969), pp. 91–2; James, Robert Rhodes (ed.), *Memoirs of a Conservative: J.C.C. Davidson's Memoirs and Papers, 1910–37* (London: Macmillan, 1969), pp. 209–10; James, Robert Rhodes, *Churchill: A Study in Failure* (London: Penguin Books, 1970), p. 164; Gretton, Vice Admiral Sir Peter, *Former Naval Person* (London: Cassell, 1968), pp. 244–45; MacGregor, David, 'Former Naval Cheapskate: Chancellor of the Exchequer Winston Churchill and the Royal Navy, 1924–29', *Armed Forces and Society*, vol. 19, no. 3, 1993. pp. 319–33.

30 Bell, 'Winston Churchill and the Ten Year Rule'. Bell, Christopher M., 'Winston Churchill, Pacific Security, and the Limits of British Power, 1921–41' in Maurer, John H. (ed.), *Churchill and Strategic Dilemmas before the World Wars* (London: Frank Cass, 2003), pp. 51–87.

Chapter 6

1 Williams, Andrew J., *France, Britain and the United States in the Twentieth Century 1900–1940: A Reappraisal* (Basingstoke: Palgrave Macmillan, 2014), pp. 94–132. Dobson, Alan P., *Anglo-American Relations in the Twentieth Century: Of Friendship Conflict and the Rise and Decline of Superpowers* (London: Routledge, 1995), pp. 42–55. Lisio, Donald J., *British Naval Supremacy and Anglo-American Antagonisms, 1914–1930* (Cambridge: Cambridge University Press, 2014), pp. 5–15.

2 The historiographic field on Anglo-American relations in the interwar period is vast, and more recent texts have emphasized that contemporary concerns about British weaknesses and difficulties masked underlying continuing strengths. See, for example, Ovendale, Ritchie, *Anglo-American Relations in the Twentieth Century* (New York: St Martins, 1998).

3 Watt, Donald Cameron, *Succeeding John Bull: America in Britain's Place 1900–1975* (Cambridge: Cambridge University Press, 2008), p. 49. See also Rose, *Conservatism*, pp. 108–9.

4 Chatfield, *It Might Happen* Again, p. 164.

5 'British policy as regards the American naval programme', Admiral Sir W.L. Grant, 25 February 1919, TNA: ADM116/3610.

6 Ibid.

7 Maurer, John H., 'Arms Control and the Washington Conference' in Goldstein, and Maurer (eds.), *Washington Conference*, p. 275.

8 Boothe, Leon E., 'A Fettered Envoy: Lord Grey's Mission to the United States, 1919–1920', *The Review of Politics*, vol. 33, no. 1, 1971. pp. 78–94.

9 Mr Lindsay (Washington) to Lord Curzon, 16 August 1919, No. 347, Woodward, E.L. and Butler, Rohan, *Documents on British Foreign Policy*, first series, vol. v (London: HMSO, 1954), p. 986.

10 Letter Curzon to Grey, 9 September 1919, enclosed in Curzon to Grey, 9 September 1919, No. 360, Woodward and Butler, *Documents*, pp. 997–1000, 998.

11 Curzon to Grey, 25 November 1919, No. 411, Woodward and Butler, *Documents*, pp. 1037–38.

12 Grey to Curzon, 26 November 1919, No. 412, Woodward and Butler, *Documents*, pp. 1038–39.

13 Grey to Curzon, 28 November 1919, No. 420, Woodward and Butler, *Documents*, pp. 1046–49.

14 Willmott, H.P., *Battleship* (London: Cassell, 2002), p. 114.

15 Report of Naval Mission to India, March–April 1919, Admiral of the Fleet Viscount Jellicoe of Scapa, Long papers 947/715. Jellicoe papers Add.MSS.49046-49047.

16 See papers relating to his removal from the post see Jellicoe papers Add. MSS.49039.

17 Johnson, Gregory A. and Perras, Galen Roger, 'A Menace to the Country: Perceptions of the Japanese Military Threat to Canada before 1931' in Donaghy, Greg and Roy, Patricia E. (eds.), *Contradictory Impulses: Canada and Japan in the Twentieth Century* (Vancouver, BC: University of British Columbia Press, 2008), p. 68.

18 For the Canadian leg of Jellicoe's tour, see Jellicoe papers, Add MSS 49055–49057.

19 Johnson & Perras, 'A Menace' in Donaghy and Roy (eds.), *Contradictory Impulses*, p. 68.

20 Gow, Ian, 'The Royal Navy and Japan 1900–1920: Strategic Re-Evaluation of the IJN' in Gow, Ian and Hirama, Yoichi (eds.) *The History of Anglo-Japanese Relations, 1600–2000*, volume III (The Military Dimension) (Basingstoke: Palgrave, 2003), p. 48.

21 'Japan and the Pacific: Admiral Jellicoe's Mission' (report on comments by the *New York Sun*), *The Farmer and Settler* (Sydney), *Zeehan and Dundas Herald* (Tasmania), 7 March 1919, p. 4. and p. 3, respectively.

22 Report of Admiral of the Fleet Viscount Jellicoe of Scapa on Naval Mission to the Commonwealth of Australia (May–August 1919), vol. IV, p. 221. http://www.navy.gov.au/sites/default/files/documents/Jellicoe_of_Scapa_Vol_IV.pdf accessed 19/05/2014 (accessed 12 November), Jellicoe papers Add.MSS.49048-49051. For the New Zealand leg of his tour, see Jellicoe papers Add.MSS.49052-49054.

23 Admiral of the Fleet, First Baron Wester Weymss to Long, 31 October 1919, Long papers (British Library) Add.62424.

24 British commitments in the Pacific Ocean, 10 October 1921, TNA: FO412/118.

25 Frank Ashton-Gwatkin (1889–1976) under the pseudonym John Paris wrote a series of novels set in Japan: *Kimono* (1921), *Sayonara* (1924), *Banzai* (1925), *The Island beyond Japan* (1929) and *Matsu* (1932).

26 British Neutrality in the Event of a Japanese-American War, 10 October 1921, TNA: FO412/118.

27 Mackendrick, Lieutenant Colonel W.G., *The Destiny of Britain and America – with an Appendix Who Are the Japanese*? (London: The Covenant Publishing Co. Ltd, 1922), p. 260.

28 Mackendrick, *The Destiny of Britain*, p. 269.

29 Major Hugh O'Neil (Unionist, Mid-Antrim), 4 November 1921, *Parliamentary Debates [Commons]*, vol. 147, cols. 2110–11.

30 See, for example, Admiralty weekly intelligence summary, 20 November 1920, TNA: CAB24/115 reporting on supplementary naval estimates under which two battlecruisers, four light cruisers and twenty-nine destroyers would be laid down in fiscal year 1920–21.

Chapter 7

1 See, for example, Fawcett, H.W. and Hooper, G.W.W., *The Fighting at Jutland: The Personal Experiences of Forty-five Officers and Men of the British Fleet* (London: Hutchinson and Co., 1921).

2 'Some Useful Lessons: Statement by Jellicoe', *The Western Australian* (Perth, WA), 20 December 1920, p. 7.

3 One newspaper commented that the battle of Jutland had been subjected to close scrutiny by those 'striving to forecast their bearing on future battles and the controversy regarding capital ships'. See 'Victory Half Finished: Lessons of Jutland', *Daily Advertiser* (Wagga Wagga, NSW), 21 December 1920, p. 2.

4 Ranft, *Beatty Papers*, p. 417ff.

5 Roberts, John, *Battlecruisers* (London: Caxton, 2003), p. 61.

6 'HMS *Hood* and After', *The Naval Review*, vol. VIII, no. 2, May 1920. pp. 176–82, 178.

7 'Great Ships or Disaster', *The Naval Review*, vol. IX, no. 2, May 1921. pp. 245–47, 247.

8 'The Future of the Battleship', *The Naval Review*, vol. VIII, no. 3, August 1920. pp. 368–69, 369.

9 Marder, Arthur, *From the Dardanelles to Oran: Studies of the Royal Navy in War and Peace* (London: Oxford University Press, 1974), pp. 38–45.

10 Naval Policy and Expenditure, 24 October 1919, TNA: ADM116/1774. Quoted in 'Naval Policy and Construction', Memorandum for the Cabinet by the First Lord of the Admiralty, 22 November 1920, TNA: CAB24/115, ADM116/3610.

11 Ibid.

12 Long to Bonar Law, 8 February 1920, and Long to Bonar Law, 20 February 1920, Bonar Law papers BL/98/7/3 and BL/98/7/11.

13 *Statement of the First Lord of the Admiralty Explanatory of the Naval Estimates of 1920–21*, London, HMSO, 1920. p. 4. See also *The Spectator*, 20 March 1920, p. 3.

14 Ibid.

15 *Newcastle Morning Herald and Miners Advocate*, 10 June 1920, p. 4.

16 'Naval Construction', memorandum for the Cabinet by First Lord of the Admiralty, 23 July 1920, TNA: CAB24/109, ADM116/3610.

17 Sir Clement Kinloch-Cooke (Unionist, Plymouth Devonport), 17 March 1921, *Parliamentary Debates [Commons]*, vol. 139, col. 1831.

18 Sir Frederick Banbury (Unionist, City of London), 17 March 1921, *Parliamentary Debates [Commons]*, vol. 139, col. 1787.

19 Lyon, Hugh, 'The Relations between the Admiralty and Private Industry in the Development of Warships' in Ranft (ed.), *Technical Change*, pp. 37–64.

20 See d'Eyncourt to Beatty, 3 December 1920, in Ranft, *Beatty Papers*, pp. 103–5.

21 'E.H.T. d'Eyncourt Obituary', *Journal of the Institution of Civil Engineers*, 1 April 1951, vol. 36, no. 6. pp. 234–5.

22 'Naval Construction', Admiralty Memorandum for the Cabinet, 14 December 1920, TNA: CAB24/119. John Brown and Company's East Yard contained five slips for battleship building, but only one was capable of handling ships 900 feet in length.

23 See answer of Leo Amery (Parliamentary Secretary to the Admiralty) to question by Sir Clement Kinloch-Cooke (Unionist, Plymouth Devonport), 6 April 1921, *Parliamentary Debates [Commons]*, vol. 140, cols. 249–250.

24 The Production of Armaments: Consideration from the Standpoint of Public Policy, undated, reproduced in Wemyss, *Life and Letters*, pp. 406–8.

25 Taylor, Bruce, *The End of Glory: War and Peace in HMS Hood 1916–1941* (Barnsley: Seaforth, 2012), p. 6.

26 'The King and Queen Watching the Rolling of an Armour Plate at Sheffield', *The Graphic*, 22 July 1905, p. 1.

27 Bell, *The Royal Navy*, pp. 138–61.

28 Comparative naval strengths by 1924 contained in 'Naval Construction', Admiralty Memorandum for the Cabinet, 14 December 1920, TNA: CAB24/119, TNA: ADM116/1775.
Britain – Class A (Post-1916 over 40,000 tons) Ships 9; Class B (30,000 tons) Ships 13; Class C (25,000 tons) 4: Total 26
USA – Class A Ships 12; Class B Ships 11; Class C 4: Total 27
Japan – Class A Ships 8; Class B Ships 4; Class C 4: Total 16 (+ a further 8 by 1928).

29 'Future Provision for Keeping Fully Prepared', memorandum by d'Eyncourt, 8 September 1919, TNA: ADM1/8549/18.

30 'Naval Construction', Admiralty Memorandum for the Cabinet, 14 December 1920, TNA: CAB24/119.

31 Johnman, Lewis and Murphy, Hugh, *British Shipbuilding and the State since 1918: A Political Economy of Decline* (Exeter: University of Exeter Press, 2002), p. 14.

32 Ibid.

33 Ibid.

34 Birkler, J.L. et al., *Differences between Military and Commercial Shipbuilding: Implications for the United Kingdom's Ministry of Defence* (Santa Monica, CA: Rand, 2005), p. xv.

35 Taylor, *End of Glory*, p. 9.

36 'Naval Policy and Construction', Memorandum for the Cabinet by the First Lord of the Admiralty, 22 November 1920, TNA: CAB24/115.

37 See Winston Churchill (Coalition Liberal, Dundee), 17 March 1921, *Parliamentary Debates [Commons]*, vol. 145, cols. 1536–1539.

38 The attention of the Cabinet and the Committee of Imperial Defence was drawn to the implications of the order, 'Admiralty Memorandum for the Cabinet and CID', 16 December 1920, TNA: CAB24/116, TNA: ADM 116/1775.

39 Sir Charles Eliot (Tokyo) to Lord Curzon, No. 384, 11 October 1920, Butler, Rohan and Bury, J.P.T., *Documents on British Foreign Policy*, first series, vol. XIV (London: HMSO, 1966), pp. 152–53.
40 'Admiralty Memorandum for the Cabinet and CID', 16 December 1920, TNA: CAB24/116. The dates of the papers were 12 August 1919, 24 October 1919, 13 February 1920, 23 July 1920 and 22 November 1920. The individual memoranda can be found in ADM116/3610.
41 'Naval Policy and Shipbuilding, Memorandum by the First Lord of the Admiralty, 31 January 1921, TNA: CAB24/119, ADM116/3610.
42 'Naval construction – armour plate', Memorandum by Beatty, 15 December 1920, TNA: ADM116/3610.
43 See, for example, 'Japanese Battleships', *Portsmouth Evening News*, 26 January 1921, p. 2; '3 Warships for Japanese Government', *Lancashire Evening Post*, 8 December 1920, p. 4; 'Japanese Battleships Building In England', *Gloucester Citizen*, 4 January 1921, p. 6.
44 Sir Charles Eliot (Tokyo) to Lord Curzon, No. 384, 11 October 1920, Butler & Bury, *Documents*, pp. 152–53.
45 Note on Lord Curzon to Eliot, No. 352, 14 November 1920, Butler & Bury, *Documents*, p. 174.
46 Lord Curzon to Eliot, No. 352, 14 November 1920, Butler & Bury, *Documents*, p. 174.
47 Roskill, *Naval Policy*, p. 245.
48 Kennedy, Captain Malcolm D., *The Estrangement of Great Britain and Japan* (Manchester: Manchester University Press, 1969), p. 51.
49 Eliot to Curzon, 22 December 1922, TNA: ADM116/3610.
50 Naval attaché (Washington) to First Sea Lord, 11 November 1920, TNA: ADM116/3610.
51 'Empire Naval Policy and Co-Operation', 3 December 1920, TNA: CAB16/37/2.
52 Ibid.
53 Ibid.
54 Ibid.
55 'Naval Shipbuilding Policy – Note by the Secretary of the Cabinet, CID Paper N3', 13 December 1920, TNA: ADM116/3610.
56 'Some notes on Capital Ship Policy', undated, TNA: ADM116/3442.
57 Blake's, *Bonar Law* surprisingly offers no useful commentary on this aspect of the career of his biographical subject.
58 See Long to Lloyd George, 13 December 1920, Lloyd George papers LG/F/34/1/54.
59 'Great Ships Or-?', *The Times*, 7–11 and 13–14 December 1920.
60 'Our Future Naval Policy', *The Times*, 7 December 1920, p. 13.
61 Ibid.
62 See, for example, 'Battleship or Submarine', *The Nottingham Evening Post*, 23 November 1920, p. 3; 'Future of the Battleship', *The Nottingham Evening Post*,

3 December 1920, p. 4; 'Big Navy Plans', *Edinburgh Evening Post*, 7 December 1920, p. 3; 'The Future of the Battleship', *The Evening Telegraph and Post* (Dundee, Scotland), 15 December 1920, p. 3; 'Battleship Problem', *The Nottingham Evening Post*, 15 December 1920, p. 6; 'Sir Percy Scott's Invention', *Hartlepool Northern Daily Mail*, 21 December 1920, p. 8; 'The Value of the Battleship', *The Courier and Argus* (Dundee, Scotland), 4 January 1921, p. 5; 'Testing the Value of the Battleship', *The Evening Telegraph and Post* (Dundee, Scotland), 18 January 1921, p. 2; 'Future of the Big Battleship', *Dundee Courier*, 13 January 1920, p. 4; 'Sir Percy Scott's Prophecy', *Driffield Times*, 17 January 1920, p. 4; 'Use of the Battleship', *The Nottingham Evening Post*, 4 February 1921, p. 5.

63 'Future of the Big Battleship' in *The Courier and Argus* (Dundee, Scotland), 13 January 1920, p. 4.

64 'Must We Build Battleships', *Yorkshire Evening Post*, 7 December 1920, p. 6.

65 See 'Sub-committee of the Committee of Imperial Defence on the Question of the Capital Ship in the Navy 1920–21: Report and Proceedings, vol. 1–3, TNA: CAB16/37/1, CAB 16/37/2, CAB 16/37/3. For the draft report, see TNA: ADM116/3610.

66 See, for example, Beatty to Long, 15 December 1920, Beatty to Long, 3 January 1921, Ranft, *Beatty Papers*, pp. 125–27; 136–37.

67 'The Retention of the Capital Ship', 14 December 1920, TNA: CAB 16/37/2.

68 Till, Geoffrey, 'Naval Power' in McInnes and Sheffield (eds.), *Warfare*, p. 95. Contre Admiral Raoul Castex (1878–1968) entered the French Navy in 1896. He was a prolific author and professor at the École de Guerre Navale. Sir Herbert Richmond (1871–1946) served with the Royal Navy from 1885 to 1931. After retirement from the Navy he sat as Vere Harmsworth Professor of Imperial and Naval History at Cambridge University (1934–36).

69 'Admiralty "Trick": Sir P. Scott "Bearing His Cross"', *Aberdeen Daily Journal*, 5 January 1921, p. 6.

70 Roskill, Stephen, *Churchill & the Admirals* (London: Collins, 1977), p. 74.

71 Reproduced in Rothermere, *Solvency*, pp. 147–8.

72 Cowling, *Impact of Labour*, p. 55.

73 Memorandum for the Finance Committee by the First Lord of the Admiralty, 25 January 1921, TNA: ADM116/3610.

74 Reproduced in Rothermere, *Solvency*, p. 158.

75 Till, Geoffrey, 'Airpower and the Battleship in the 1920's' in Ranft (ed.), *Technical Change*, p. 113.

76 Beatty to Lady Beatty, 15 February 1921, NMM BTY/17/55/9-10.

77 Unknown and undated minute on the undated Draft Report of the Bonar Law Committee, TNA: ADM116/3610.

78 Note by Churchill to Members of the Sub-Committee on the Capital Ship on his rejection of the Draft Report, 13 February 1921, 'Beatty Memorandum to the

Sub-Committee on the capital ship', B. Ranft, *Beatty Papers*, pp. 156–58 and 169–70. Draft report note by Mr Long, 26 February 1921, TNA: ADM116/3610. 'Report of the Sub-Committee of the Committee of Imperial Defence Appointed to Take Evidence on the Question of the Capital Ship in the Royal Navy', 2 March 1921, TNA: ADM116/3610.

79 Roskill, *Beatty*, p. 303.

80 Johnman and Murphy, *British Shipbuilding*, p. 16. The cost of a new 7,500 dead weight ton steamer in 1914 was £54,375; in 1920, £225,000; in 1921 (as the market corrected itself), £97,500; and in 1922, £67,500.

81 Ibid., p. 17.

82 Cammell Laird Annual Reports 1919–21, in Board Minutes, Cammell Laird papers ZCL5/44.

83 Steel, Tom, *Scotland's Story* (London: Harper Collins, 1994), p. 347.

Chapter 8

1 'War with Japan', 4 January 1921, and 'War with the USA', 4 January 1921, Beatty Papers BTY/8/1/8 and BTY/8/1/7.

2 Clark (ed.), '*A Good Innings*'.

3 Lee of Fareham to Lloyd George, 19 March 1921, Lloyd George papers LG/F/31/2/52.

4 Lady Lee of Fareham diary, 2 April 1921, in Clark (ed.), '*A Good Innings*', p. 208.

5 Congressional Record, 66th Congress, 3d Session, vol. LX, part 3, p. 3740. The bill was eventually passed by Congress and received presidential approval on 12 July 1921. See US Senate Document, 66th Congress, 3d Session, XV, 233.

6 Inaugural address by President Warren G. Harding, 4 March 1921, *Inaugural Addresses of the Presidents of the United States*, vol. 2 (Bedford, MA: Applewood Books, 2009), p. 66.

7 'Arrival of Admiral Sims', *The Times*, 24 May 1921. p. 9.

8 Jellicoe, *The Crisis*, p. 116.

9 'The Naval War – Lord Jellicoe's Book', *Northern Star* (Lismore, New South Wales), 31 July 1920, p. 5.

10 Ichihashi, Yamato, *The Washington Conference and After: A Historical Survey* (Stanford, CA: Stanford University Press, 1928), p. 6.

11 'Government Dinner for Admiral Sims', *The Times*, 4 June 1921, p. 10.

12 For example, a lunch in honour of Admiral Sims was held on 26 May at the Hotel Victoria in London. Guests included Lord Beatty (First Sea Lord), Leo Amery (Financial Secretary to the Admiralty), Captain Roger Backhouse (Director of Naval Ordnance), Arthur Shirley Benn (MP) and Captain Curzon (MP). 'Brotherhood of the Sea: Admiral Sims on the Naval War', *The Times*, 27 May 1921, p. 8.

13 'Admiral Sims Impenitent: "I like the British people"', *The Times*, 11 June 1921, p. 7.
14 'The Future of the Battleship', *The Naval Review*, vol. VIII, no. 2, May 1920. pp. 165–75, 175.
15 O'Brien, *British and American Naval Power*, p. 162.
16 'Anglo-Japanese Alliance', Memorandum by First Lord of the Admiralty, 21 May 1921, TNA: CAB24/123.
17 Ibid.
18 Ibid.
19 Ibid.
20 Lady Lee of Fareham, diary entry 22 May 1921, in Clark (ed.), *'A Good Innings'*, p. 209.
21 Ibid.
22 Lady Lee of Fareham diary, 26 May 1921, in Clark (ed.), *'A Good Innings'*, p. 209.
23 Kennedy, *The Rise and Fall of British Naval Mastery*, p. 58.
24 'Empire Naval Policy and Co-Operation: Summary', May 1921, 'Singapore – Development of as Naval Base (note by the Secretary)', 11 June 1921, TNA: CAB34/1.
25 Address by the First Sea Lord to the Imperial Conference, 4 July 1921, TNA: CAB32/2.
26 Tracy (ed.), *Collective*, p. xxix. 'Empire Naval Policy – Brief Summary of the Recommendations of the Admiralty', 11 July 1921, TNA: ADM116/3415. See also Stenographic notes of the 14th Meeting of Representatives of the United Kingdom, the Dominions and India, 4 July 1921, TNA: CAB32/2.
27 Interestingly in April 1921 the Royal Canadian Navy advised its government to renew the alliance as a lever to prevent the Japanese intriguing in India or possibly joining Germany and Russia in an alliance. The government of Arthur Meighen had already formed the opinion that Canada had to oppose renewal of the alliance out of concerns for American opinion and reactions especially in time of war. Johnson, Gregory A. and Perras, Galen Roger, 'A Menace to the Country: Perceptions of the Japanese Military Threat to Canada Before 1931' in Donaghy and Roy (eds.), *Contradictory Impulses*, p. 70.
28 See Mr Hughes (Australia) on the Imperial Conference, 7 April 1921, in Cabinet Memorandum by Churchill, 22 June 1921, TNA: CAB24/125.
29 Curzon to Auckland Geddes (British Ambassador to Washington), 9 July 1921, No. 416, giving account of his conversations with the American Ambassador, 5 July 1921, TNA: FO371/6675.
30 Louis, W.R., *British Strategy in the Far East, 1919–1939* (Oxford: Oxford University Press, 1971), p. 37, p. 81.
31 Note by the Cabinet Secretary, 11 July 1921, enclosing Curzon and Hayashi joint note, 7 July 1921, TNA: CAB24/126.

Chapter 9

1 See, for example, Brown, D.K., *The Grand Fleet: Warship Design and Development 1906–1922* (Barnsley: Seaforth, 2010); Johnston, *Clydebank Battlecruisers*; Johnston, Ian and Buxton, Ian, *The Battleship Builders: Constructing and Arming British Capital Ships* (Barnsley: Seaforth, 2013).
2 Secretary Admiralty to Secretary Treasury, 28 April 1921, TNA: T161/119.
3 Sir George Barstow (1874–1966) was Treasury Clerk from 1909, Controller of Supply Services at the Treasury (1919–27) and Government Director of Anglo-Persian Oil Company (1927–46).
4 Barstow to Chancellor of the Exchequer minute, 4 June 1921, TNA: T161/119.
5 'The Government's Naval Policy', memorandum by the First Lord of the Admiralty, 15 July 1921, TNA: CAB24/126 and T161/119.
6 Lee of Fareham to Lloyd George, 16 July 1921, Lloyd George papers LG/F/31/2/61.
7 Barstow draft memorandum for the Cabinet, 18 July 1921, TNA: T161/119.
8 Ibid.
9 'More Warships: Empire Naval Policy', *The Times*, 5 August 1921, p. 5.
10 Viscountess Astor (Unionist, Plymouth Sutton), 3 August 1921, *Parliamentary Debates [Commons]*, vol. 145, col. 1600.
11 Commander Carlyon Bellairs (Unionist, Maidstone Kent), 3 August 1921, *Parliamentary Debates [Commons]*, vol. 145, col. 1518.
12 Hilton Young to Lloyd George, 28 September 1921, Lloyd George Papers LG/F/28/8/5.
13 'Benefits of Battleship Building: Work for Many Men and Trades', *The Evening Telegraph and Post* (Dundee, Scotland), 20 September 1921, p. 5.
14 'Lord Lee of Fareham', *Western Daily Press*, 24 August 1921, p. 3.
15 Beatrice Webb Typescript Diary, 28 October 1921, pp. 400–1. Passfield Papers 1/2.
16 'Economy Cry', *Western Morning News*, 21 July 1921, p. 5. Plymouth became a single borough in 1914 with the amalgamation of the towns of Plymouth: Stonehouse and Devonport. Up until 1914 Devonport elected two (usually Liberal) Members of Parliament. Conservatives did not tend to fare well in the town. Plymouth, which similarly elected two Members of Parliament after 1832, showed rather more of a balance between the forces of Conservativism and Liberalism, but even here changes in naval policy could make themselves felt in local politics. For example, in the 1906 general election, with the towns experiencing high unemployment as a result of the Conservative government's dockyard economies of 1904–06, the Liberal Party won all four of the Devonport and Plymouth Parliamentary seats. The general elections of 1910, marked by Anglo-German naval antagonism, saw all four seats fall to the Conservatives amid allegations that the Liberals did not have a sufficiently robust naval policy. In 1918 all three

Plymouth seats fell to the Conservatives. In July 1921, seemingly in response to local concerns, the Devonport Dockyard was awarded the contract to build the cruiser minelayer HMS *Adventure*. This helped the Conservatives to win the three Plymouth seats at the 1922 election, although HMS *Adventure* was not laid down until after the election.

17 Admiralty Contracts, *The Daily Telegraph*, 26 October 1921, TNA: T161/119.

18 'Admiralty Contracts', *Aberdeen Daily Journal*, 26 October 1921, p. 6.

19 Jordan, John, *Warships after Washington: The Development of the Five Major Fleets 1922–1930* (Barnsley: Seaforth, 2011), p. xiii.

20 Johnston, *Clydebank Battlecruisers*, pp. 178–79.

21 'General Description of the Vessel', E.H.T. d'Eynecourt, 26 July 1921, TNA: ADM1/2392.

22 Ibid.

23 Jordan, *Warships*, p. 30.

24 Ibid., p. 27.

25 Ibid.

26 Ibid.

27 'See Capital Ship G-3: Submerged Torpedo Tube Experiments', 23 December 1921, TNA: ADM 226/24.

28 'General Description of the Vessel', E.H.T. d'Eynecourt, 26 July 1921, TNA: ADM1/2392.

29 'The Naval Situation in the Pacific', *The Round Table*, vol. XII, no. 45, December 1921, p. 12.

30 'Disarmament', *Western Times*, 9 September 1921, p. 12; 'Labour Leaders on Disarmament', *Dundee Courier*, 9 September 1921, p. 4; 'Labour and Reduction of Armaments', *Aberdeen Journal*, 9 September 1921, p. 6.

31 'Shipbuilding and Unemployment', *Western Morning News*, 10 September 1921, p. 2.

Chapter 10

1 On the Japanese side see, for example, Asada, Sadao, 'Japan's "Special Interests" and the Washington Conference, 1921–1922', *American Historical Review*, vol. 66, no. 1, 1961. pp. 62–70; Asada, Sadao, 'The Revolt against the Washington Treaty: The Imperial Japanese Navy and Naval Limitation, 1921–1927', *Naval War College Review*, vol. 46, 1993. pp. 82–97; Asada, Sadao, 'From Washington to London: The Imperial Japanese Navy and the Politics of Naval Limitation', *Diplomacy & Statesmanship*, vol. 4, no. 3, 1993. pp. 147–91. On the American side see Buckley, Thomas H., *The United States and the Washington Conference, 1921–1922* (Knoxville, TN: Tennessee University Press, 1970); Buell, Raymond,

The Washington Conference, 1922 (New York: Russell & Russell, 1970); Sullivan, Mark, *The Great Adventure at Washington: The Story of the Conference* (New York: Heinemann, 1922); Vinson, J.C., *The Parchment Peace: The United States and the Washington Conference, 1921–1922* (Athens, GA: Georgia University Press, 1955). On the British side see Klein, Ira, 'Whitehall, Washington, and the Anglo-Japanese Alliance, 1919–1921', *Pacific Historical Review*, vol. 41, no. 4, 1972. pp. 460–83. On the minor naval powers see Blatt, J., 'The Parity that Meant Superiority: French Naval Policy towards Italy at the Washington Conference, 1921–22, and Interwar French Foreign Policy', *French Historical Studies*, vol. 12, no. 2, 1981. pp. 223–48. For an overview, see Van Meter, Robert H., 'The Washington Conference, 1921–1922: A New Look', *Pacific Historical Review*, vol. 46, no. 4, 1977. pp. 603–24.

2 Orde, Anne, *The Eclipse of Great Britain* (New York: St Martins, 1996), p. 76.

3 Kennedy, *The Rise and Fall of British Naval Mastery*, p. 321.

4 Kennedy, Malcolm, *The Estrangement of Great Britain and Japan, 1917–1935* (Manchester: Manchester University Press, 1969), pp. 53–56.

5 O'Brien, Philipps, *The Anglo-Japanese Alliance, 1902–1922* (London: Routledge, 2004), p. 281.

6 Roskill, *Beatty*, p. 308.

7 Beatty to King George V, 12 November 1921, Royal Archives RA Geo V O.1735/74.

8 'Sea Power in the Pacific', *The Naval Review*, vol. IX, no. 4, November 1921. pp. 535–41, p. 531.

9 Bywater, Hector C., *Sea-Power in the Pacific: A Study of the American-Japanese Naval Problem* (London: Constable, 1921).

10 Chatfield to Keyes, 28 October 1921, in Halpern, *The Keyes Papers*, pp. 56–57, 57.

11 Minute by Captain Domville, 2 November 1921, TNA: ADM116/3604.

12 Hankey's letters to Lloyd George are in TNA: CAB63/34 and Lloyd George papers LG/F/63/1-15.

13 For the final treaty, see *Papers Relating to the Foreign Relations of the United States: 1922*, vol. 1 (Washington, DC: Government Printing Office, 1922), pp. 247–66.

14 Hawkins, William R., 'Captain Mahan, Admiral Fisher and Arms Control at the Hague, 1899', *Naval War College Review*, vol. 39, no. 1, 1986. pp. 77–91.

15 Ibid.

16 'The Standpoint of Japan', *The Round Table*, vol. XII, no. 45, December 1921. p. 26.

17 *Conference on the Limitation of Armament: Address of the President of the United States* (Washington, DC: Government Printing Office, 1921), pp. 5–7 and 11–15. See also 'Washington Agreement on Capital Ships', *A League of Nations*, vol. IV, no. 5, October 1921. pp. 373–93.

18 Balfour to Lloyd George (Report of 1st Conference of British Empire Delegation to Washington Naval Conference), 13 November 1921, ADM1/8630.

19 Maurer, John H., 'Averting the Great War: Churchill's Naval Holiday', *Naval War College Review*, vol. 67, no. 3, 2014. pp. 25–42.

20 Chatfield to Keyes, 13 November 1921, TNA: ADM116/3417.

21 Keyes to Chatfield, 13 December 1921, in Halpern, *The Keyes Papers*, pp. 67–69.

22 On the issue of submarines at the Washington Conference, see TNA: ADM116/2150.

23 Beatty to Admiralty, 15 November 1921, TNA: ADM116/3445/93.

24 Roskill, *Beatty*, p. 311.

25 Beatty to the Cabinet, 10 December 1921, TNA: ADM 116/1776.

26 Keyes to Chatfield, 13 December 1921, Keyes MSS 7/12.

27 Sadao, 'The Revolt against the Washington Treaty', pp. 82–97, 85.

28 Speech by Balfour, 4th Plenary Session, 10 December 1921, reproduced in Senate (67th Congress), *Document No. 126: Conference on the Limitation of Armaments* (Washington, DC: Government Printing Office, 1922), p. 111.

29 Speech by Balfour, 2nd Plenary Session, 15 November 1921, reproduced in ibid., p. 69.

30 Naval Arms Limitation Treaty, *Papers Relating*, pp. 249–50.

31 Ibid., p. 250.

32 Ibid.

33 Ibid., p. 251.

34 HMS *Commonwealth, Agamemnon, Dreadnought, Bellerephon, St Vincent, Inflexible, Superb, Neptune, Hercules, Indomitable, Temeraire, New Zealand, Lion, Conqueror, Monarch, Orion, Australia, Agincourt, Erin*. At sixteen years of age *Commonwealth* was the oldest vessel and HMS *Erin* and HMS *Agincourt* the newest at seven years of age.

35 Chatfield to Keyes, 13 November 1921, TNA: ADM116/3417.

36 HMS *King George V, Ajax, Centurion* and *Thundrer*, all of which were twelve to thirteen years old.

37 *Papers Relating*, pp. 247–66.

38 In 1934 the twenty-year-old vessels HMS *Iron Duke, Marlborough, Empress of India* and *Benbow* were to be scrapped, and in 1935 HMS *Tiger, Queen Elizabeth, Warspite* and *Barham* (20–21 years old).

39 In 1936 HMS *Malaya, Royal Sovereign* would be scrapped and HMS *Revenge* and *Resolution* in 1937.

40 Willmott, *Battleship*, p. 109.

41 American Government Communique, 10 July 1921, cited in Schofield, B.B., *British Sea Power: Naval Policy in the Twentieth Century* (London: Batsford, 1967), p. 92

42 'The Washington Conference', *The Round Table*, vol. XII, no. 45, December 1921. p. 7.

43 Smith, Dennis, 'The Royal Navy and Japan: In the Aftermath of the Washington Conference, 1922–1926', *Proceedings of the British Association for Japanese Studies*, vol. 3, 1978. pp. 69–86.

44 Mackay, Ruddock F., *Balfour: Intellectual Statesman* (Oxford: Oxford University Press, 1985), p. 332.

45 *Statement of the First Lord of the Admiralty Explanatory of the Naval Estimates of 1921–22* (London: HMSO, 1921). Long papers 947/716/3.
46 Admiralty Board Minute, 17 January 1922, TNA: ADM167/65.
47 'Cancellation of Battleship Orders', *Citizen* (Gloucester, England), 10 January 1922, p. 6.
48 'Lost Battleships Contracts', *The Courier and Argus* (Dundee, Scotland), 11 January 1922, p. 6.
49 Chatfield to Keyes, 29 November 1921, Keyes MSS 7/12.
50 Roskill, Stephen, *Hankey: Man of Secrets, vol. II 1919–1931* (London: Collins, 1972), p. 257.
51 McKercher, B.J.C., *Anglo-American Relations in the 1920's: The Struggle for Supremacy* (Cambridge: Cambridge University Press, 1984), p. 4.
52 See Irwin, Manley R., 'The Naval Policies of the Harding Administration: Time for a Reassessment', *International Journal of Naval History*, vol. 1, no. 1, 2002. http://www.ijnhonline.org/wp-content/uploads/2012/01/pdf_irwin1.pdf (accessed 26 December 2014).
53 Kennedy, *The Rise and Fall of British Naval Mastery*, p. 325. Barnett and Correlli, *The Collapse of British Power* (London: Eyre Methuen, 1972), pp. 271–72. Marder, *Old Friends*, p. 6.
54 Roskill, *Hankey*, p. 257.

Chapter 11

1 Grieves, Keith, *Sir Eric Geddes: Business and Government in War and Peace* (Manchester: Manchester University Press, 1989), p. 82.
2 Willmott, *Battleship*, p. 109.
3 Questionnaire, 13 October 1921, TNA: ADM1/8614.
4 Admiralty Board Minutes, 17 January 1922, TNA: ADM167/65.
5 'Economy Begins at Home', *Sunday Times* (Sydney, New South Wales), 12 February 1922, p. 2.
6 'An Admiralty Criticism', *The Times*, 11 February 1922, p. 12. See also Remarks of the Admiralty on the Interim Report of the Committee on National Expenditure, 1922, Lloyd George papers LG/F/176/11.
7 'The Admiralty Memorandum', *The Times*, 16 February 1922, p. 6.
8 'Admiralty Reply', *The Times*, 11 February 1922, p. 10.
9 'Admiralty up in Arms', *Aberdeen Daily Journal*, 11 February 1922, p. 5. See also 'My Lords of the Admiralty – Condemn the Navy Cut', *The Courier and Argus* (Dundee, Scotland), 11 February 1922, p. 5.
10 'Admiralty's Amazing Reply', *The Evening Telegraph and Post* (Dundee, Scotland), 17 February 1922, p. 6.

11 'Admiralty's "Tact"', *The Nottingham Evening Post*, 13 February 1922, p. 1.

12 'Navy Challenges Report', *The Argus* (Melbourne, Victoria), p. 7. 'The Admiralty', *Advocate* (Burnie, Tasmania), 13 February 1922, p. 1.

13 See, for example, Admiral Osmond de Brock to Keyes, 13 February 1922, Keyes MSS 16/18.

14 Leo Amery diary, 18 February 1922, Barnes, John and Nicolson, David (eds.), *The Leo Amery Diaries, vol 1: 1896–1929* (London: Hutchinson, 1980), p. 277.

15 'New Statement by the Admiralty', *Aberdeen Daily Journal*, 25 February 1922, p. 5.

16 'How They Do Business at the Admiralty', *The Courier and Argus* (Dundee, Scotland), 24 February 1922, p. 5.

17 'A Snub for the Admiralty', *The Courier and Argus* (Dundee, Scotland), 24 February 1922, p. 4.

18 'Aberdeen Sharply Criticised', *Aberdeen Daily Journal*, 22 March 1922, p. 5. See also 'Admiralty Methods in Finance', *The Courier and Argus* (Dundee, Scotland), 22 March 1922, p. 4. 'The Admiralty Rebuked', *Western Gazette*, 24 March 1922, p. 12.

19 It was, for example, one of the issues considered by a committee of the CID headed by Lord Salisbury in March 1923. See Roskill, *Beatty*, p. 316.

20 Leo Amery (Parliamentary Secretary to the Admiralty), 16 March 1922, *Parliamentary Debates [Commons]*, vol. 151, col. 2410.

21 Lieutenant Colonel Burgoyne (Unionist, North Kensington), 16 March 1922, *Parliamentary Debates [Commons]*, vol. 151, col. 2438.

22 *Parliamentary Debates [Commons]*, vol. 152, col. 880–81.

23 Lieutenant Commander Kenworthy (Liberal, Kingston-upon-Hull), 24 March 1922, *Parliamentary Debates [Commons]*, vol. 152, col. 848.

24 Leo Amery (Parliamentary Secretary to the Admiralty), 24 March 1922, *Parliamentary Debates [Commons]*, vol. 152, cols. 860–61.

25 Abandoned Capital Ships (Payments), 8 March 1922, *Parliamentary Debates [Commons]*, vol. 151, col. 1254.

26 New Battleships (Armaments), *27 March 1922, Parliamentary Debates [Commons]*, vol. 152, col. 958.

27 See note by Barstow, 3 November 1922, and accompanying correspondence TNA: ADM1/8626/105.

28 Undated minute by Sir George Barstow, TNA: T161/119.

29 Lieutenant Colonel Ashley (Unionist, Fylde), 24 March 1922, *Parliamentary Debates [Commons]*, vol. 152, col. 842.

30 Rear Admiral Murray Sueter (Independent, Hertford), 24 March 1922, *Parliamentary Debates [Commons]*, vol. 152, cols. 854–55.

31 Lieutenant Commander Kenworthy (Liberal, Kingston-upon-Hull), 24 March 1922, *Parliamentary Debates [Commons]*, vol. 152, col. 851–52.

32 Leo Amery (Parliamentary Secretary to the Admiralty), 16 March 1922, *Parliamentary Debates [Commons]*, vol. 151, col. 2418.

33 Rear Admiral Murray Sueter (Independent, Hertford), 24 March 1922, *Parliamentary Debates [Commons]*, vol. 152, col. 858. See also Leo Amery (Parliamentary Secretary to the Admiralty), 24 March 1922, *Parliamentary Debates [Commons]*, vol. 152, col. 862.

Chapter 12

1 Leo Amery (Parliamentary Secretary to the Admiralty), 16 March 1922, *Parliamentary Debates [Commons]*, vol. 152, col. 2425.
2 Louis, William Roger, *In the Name of God, Go!: Leo Amery and the British Empire in the Age of Churchill* (London: Norton, 1992), p. 86.
3 See, for example, Cammell Laird Board Minutes referring to Roberts and the Rating of Machinery Bill, 8 February 1922, Cammell Laird papers ZCL5/44.
4 'The Modified Programme of Capital Ship Construction: Effect on Unemployment', minutes of a meeting between Lee of Fareham, R.S. Horne and a deputation led by Sir Samuel Roberts MP, 15 March 1922. TNA: T161/119.
5 Ibid.
6 Untitled minutes of the meeting on 15 March 1922, TNA: T161/119.
7 Sir George Barstow minute, 5 May 1922, TNA: T161/119.
8 Ibid.
9 Lee of Fareham to Lloyd George, 22 July 1922, TNA: T161/119, Lloyd George papers LG/F/31/2/70. Letter shown to Leo Amery on 23 July, see Barnes and Nicholson, *Amery Diary*, p. 289.
10 Ibid.
11 Leo Amery Diary, 21 July 1922, Barnes and Nicholson, *Amery Diary*, p. 288.
12 'New Battleship Orders: Clyde Expectant of a Share', *The Courier and Argus* (Dundee, Scotland), 14 August 1922, p. 7.
13 Treasury Solicitor's Department to Treasury Secretary, 9 November 1922, enclosing opinion of the Attorney General, 7 November 1922, TNA: TS27/634.
14 Leo Amery diary, 21 November 1922, Barnes and Nicolson, *Amery Diary*, p. 310.
15 Alex Flint (Admiralty) to Mr Malkin (Foreign Office), 7 October 1922, TNA: TS27/634.
16 Internal review for the Chancellor of the Exchequer, 16 November 1922, TNA: T161/119.
17 Ibid.
18 Amery to Baldwin, 28 November 1922, TNA: T161/119.
19 Jenkins, Roy, *Baldwin* (London: Collins, 1987), p. 71.
20 Amery to Baldwin, 28 November 1922, TNA: T161/119.
21 Ibid.

22 Lord Mayor of Sheffield to Sir Samuel Roberts, 6 July 1922, enclosed in Glasgow Town Clerk to Horne, 11 July 1922, TNA: T161/119.
23 Cook, Chris and Stevenson, John, *A History of British Elections since 1689* (London: Routledge, 2014), p. 125.
24 Ibid., p. 128.
25 Glasgow constituencies: Labour gain from Conservative (Calmachie, Maryhill, St Rollox, Springburn, Tradeston); Labour gain from Liberals (Bridgeton, Cathcart, Shettleston). 'Party gains and Losses', *The Times*, 17 November 1922. p. 10.
26 Diary Monday 23 October to late November 1922, Pottle, Mark (ed.), *Champion Redoubtable: The Diaries and Letters of Violet Bonham Carter 1914–1945* (London: Weidenfeld and Nicolson, 1998), p. 138.
27 McLean, Iain, 'The labour movement in Clydeside politics, 1914–1922', University of Oxford DPhil thesis, 1972. http://ora.ox.ac.uk/objects/uuid:e9100bd8-e0b8-4a62-b81e-9df4d93d4b14 (accessed 11 July 2014), pp. 248–49.
28 See, for example, election manifesto of James Maxton (Glasgow, Bridgeton), 15 November 1922, http://sites.scran.ac.uk/redclyde/redclyde/rc146.htm (accessed 11 July 2014).
29 Blake, *Bonar Law*, pp. 473–74. See 'Close of the Glasgow Campaign', *The Courier and Argus* (Dundee, Scotland), 15 November 1922, p. 5.
30 'Labour Victories', *The Glasgow Herald*, 16 November 1922, p. 3.
31 Josiah C. Wedgwood, *Memoirs of a Fighting Life* (London: Hutchinson & Co Publishers Ltd, 1940), p. 181.
32 Middlemas, Keith, *Thomas Jones: Whitehall Diary, vol. 1 1916–1925* (London: Oxford University Press, 1969), p. 221.
33 Leo Amery diary, 21 November 1922, Barnes and Nicolson, *Amery Diary*, p. 310.
34 Amery to Bonar Law, 5 December 1922, TNA: T161/119.
35 Lord Lee of Fareham, *Parliamentary Debates [Lords]*, vol. 52, col. 314.
36 d'Eyncourt, *A Shipbuilder's Yarn*, p. 143.
37 Ibid., p. 142.
38 Roskill, *Beatty*, p. 316.

Chapter 13

1 Philip Snowden (Labour, Colne Valley), 12 March 1923, *Parliamentary Debates [Commons]*, vol. 161, col. 1114.
2 Ibid.
3 Lambert, *Admirals*, p. 371.
4 Steel, *Scotland's Story*, p. 351. Hutchinson, I.G.C., 'Scottish Issues in British Politics 1900–1939' in Wrigley (ed.), *Companion*, p. 81ff.

5 Kenworthy, *Will Civilisation Crash*, p. 210.
6 Roskill, *Beatty*, p. 340.
7 Roskill, *Naval Policy*, pp. 214–15. Ferris, J.R., *The Evolution of British Strategic Policy, 1919–26* (Basingstoke: Macmillan, 1989), p. xii. Ferris, J.R., 'Treasury Control, the Ten Year Rule and British Service Policies, 1919–1924', *The Historical Journal*, vol. 30, no. 4, 1987. pp. 859–60.
8 Minutes of a meeting of the Committee of Imperial Defence, 22 July 1921, TNA: CAB2/3.
9 Minutes of a meeting of the Committee of Imperial Defence, 28 July 1922, TNA: CAB2/3.
10 Viscount Curzon (Conservative, Battersea South), 24 March 1922, *Parliamentary Debates [Commons]*, vol. 152, col. 868.
11 'Reserve of Oil Fuel for the Navy', memorandum by the Chancellor of the Exchequer, TNA: CAB4/10.
12 Babij, Orest, 'The Royal Navy and Inter-War Plans for War with Japan' in Kennedy, Greg (ed.), *The Merchant Marine in International Affairs 1850–1950* (London: Frank Cass 2000), p. 90.
13 Ibid.
14 Ibid., p. 97.
15 Voyage time to Elphick, Peter, *Singapore the Pregnable Fortress: A Study in Deception, Discord and Desertion* (London: Coronet Books, 1995), p. 25.
16 'Singapore, Proposed Naval Base, 19 February 1923', TNA: CAB24/159. Cabinet minutes, 21 February 1923, TNA: CAB 23/45. McCarthy, J., 'Singapore and Australian Defence 1921–1942', *Australian Outlook*, vol. 25, part 2, 1971. pp. 165–80.
17 Marquand, David, *Ramsay MacDonald* (London: Jonathan Cape, 1977), pp. 316–17. Young, Kenneth, *Baldwin* (London: Weidenfeld & Nicolson, 1976), pp. 69–70.
18 1924 General Election results: Conservatives 46.8 per cent of the vote (7,854,523) and 412 MPs elected; Labour 33.0 per cent of the vote (5,489,077) with 151 MPs elected; Liberals 17.6 per cent of the vote (2,928,747) with 40 MPs elected. On the Liberal failure in 1924, see Douglas, Roy, *The History of the Liberal Party 1895–1970* (London: Sidgwick & Jackson, 1971), pp. 184–85.
19 Buesst, Tristan, 'The Naval Base at Singapore', *Pacific Affairs*, vol. 5, no. 4, 1932. pp. 306–18, 306.
20 'The Riddle of Japan', *The Naval Review*, vol. XIV, no. 1, February 1926. pp. 114–23, 114. Ingram Bryan, J., *Japan from Within* (London: T.F. Unwin Ltd, 1924). The publications included: King Hall, Stephen, *Western Civilisation and the Far East* (London: Methuen, 1924); Kennedy, Captain, *The Military Side of Japanese Life* (London: Cassells, 1924); Longford, J.H., *Japan* (London: Hodder & Stoughton, 1923); Powell, Edward Alexander, *Asia at the Cross Roads* (London: T.F. Unwin Ltd, 1922); Robertson Scott, J.W., *The Foundations of Japan* (London: John Murray, 1922).

21 See McKercher, *Anglo-American*, pp. 171ff.
22 Kenworthy, Lt. Commander J.M., *Sailors, Statesmen – and Others: An Autobiography* (London: Rich & Cowan, 1933), p. 255.
23 Marder, *Old Friends*, p. viii.
24 d'Eyncourt, *A Shipbuilder's Yarn*, pp. 149–50.
25 J.H. Palin, MP (Labour, Newcastle West), to Ramsay MacDonald, 11 August 1929, TNA: BT56/4. Ramsay MacDonald papers GB 133 RMD/1/14/76.
26 Burton, *Rise and Fall*, p. 183.
27 Johnman and Murphy, *British Shipbuilding*, p. 36.
28 Slaven, A., 'A Shipyard in Depression: John Browns of Clydebank 1919–1938' in Davenport-Hines, R.P.T. (ed.), *Business in the Age of War and Depression* (New York: Routledge, 2013), pp. 122–47.
29 *Britain's Industrial Future: Being the Report of the Liberal Industrial Inquiry of 1928* (London: Ernest Benn, 1928), see pp. 31–33 on shipbuilding.
30 Deputation to the Prime Minister, Unemployment on Tyneside, 28 August 1929, TNA: BT56/4.
31 Ibid.
32 Ibid.
33 See, for example, resolution Portsmouth No. 1 Brach (AEU), 23 October 1929, TNA: BT56/4.
34 Kenworthy, *Sailors*, p. 257.
35 Deputation to Chancellor of the Exchequer from Amalgamated Engineering Union, 18 October 1929, TNA: BT56/4.
36 Ibid.
37 Ibid.
38 Ibid.
39 Steel, *Scotland's Story*, p. 351.
40 The papers of the enquiry can be found in TNA: ADM 116/4916.
41 Tracy (ed.), *Collective*, p. 1.
42 Johnman and Murphy, *British Shipbuilding*, p. 55, have calculated the following figures on the displacement tonnages (dt) of warships being built in British yards and Royal dockyards: 1930 - 25,872; 1933 - 10,665; 1934 - 84,975; 1935 - 23,430; 1936 - 86,569; 1937 - 109,369; and 1938 - 83,687. The bulk of these orders were going to private yards. Thus the figure for 1937 is made up of 97,649 dt being built in private yards and 11,720 in the Royal Dockyards.
43 Melton, George E., *From Versailles* to *Mers-el-Kébir: The Promise of Anglo-French Naval Cooperation, 1919–40* (Annapolis, MD: Naval Institute Press, 1993), p. 107.
44 Parker, R.A.C., *Chamberlain and Appeasement: British Policy and the Coming of the Second World War* (Macmillan: Basingstoke, 1993), p. 283.
45 Connelly, Mark, 'Battleships and British Society, 1920–1960', *International Journal of Naval History*, vol. 3, nos. 2–3, August–December 2004, http://www.ijnhonline

.org/wp-content/uploads/2012/01/PDF-Connelly-article.pdf (accessed 26 December 2014).

46 Domville-Fife, Charles W. (ed.), *The Evolution of Seapower: Studies of Modern Naval Warfare and the Effect of Evolution on the Basis and Employment of Sea Power* (London: Rich and Cowan Ltd, 1939).

47 Usborne, Vice Admiral C.V., 'Revolution or Evolution', in Domville-Fife, *Evolution*, p. 107.

48 Usborne, Vice Admiral C.V., 'War in the Pacific', in Domville-Fife, *Evolution*, p. 210.

49 Kerr, Admiral Mark and Harper, Admiral J.E.T., 'Influence of the Air on Sea Power'; Vice Admiral C.V. Usborne, Lieutenant Commander Douglas Dixon 'Influence of the Submarine on Naval Warfare'; Gwynne, Commander A.L., 'The Submarine Mine in Naval Warfare' in Domville-Fife, *Evolution*, pp. 17–33, pp. 34–47, 133–50.

50 Nicolson, Admiral Wilmot, 'The Fuel Problem in Sea Power', and Harper, Vice Admiral J.E.T., 'Naval Bases and Geographical Factor in Sea Power' in Domville-Fife, *Evolution*, pp. 109–23 and 164–85.

51 Baxter, E.H., 'The Capital Ship' in Domville-Fife, *Evolution*, pp. 68–69.

52 Churchill to Sir John Simon, 24 September 1939, Churchill papers 19/2, reproduced in Gilbert, Martin, *The Churchill War Papers, vol. 1, At the Admiralty September 1939-May 1940*, (New York: Norton, 1993), p. 140.

53 Churchill to Admiral Pound, First Sea Lord, 29 January 1940, Churchill papers, 19/6, reproduced in Gilbert, *Churchill War Papers*, pp. 702–3.

54 Lambert, *Admirals*, p. 368.

55 Reproduced without attribution in Marder, *Old Friends*, p. 506.

56 d'Eyncourt, *A Shipbuilder's Yarn*, p. 144.

57 For damage to HMS *Queen Elizabeth,* see plates 4–6, and torpedo damage to HMS *Nelson* plates 1–3, Review of Damage to His Majesty's Ships, 3 September 1941 to 2 September 1942, Part II, BR1886(1) B (Restricted), Naval Construction Department, December 1942 (Britannia Naval College Papers).

58 Marder, *Old Friends*, pp. 491–92. See also 'A Personal Account of the Sinking of HMS Repulse', *The Naval Review*, vol. XXX, no. 3, August 1942. pp. 197–201. Signed K.R.B. the author is probably Lieutenant Commander Kenneth Robertson Buckley (1904–92).

59 In a 1945 Rear Admiral R.K. Dickinson calculated the following: 'From 3rd September, 1939, to VJ Day the price of Admiralty paid by the British Empire was five battleships, eight aircraft carriers, 29 cruisers, 139 destroyers, 74 submarines and more than 500 other war vessels, all sunk. This does not include midget submarines, coastal craft and other small ships.' 'An Instrument of Peace: Address Delivered at University of Oxford', 24 January 1946, Dickinson, *Naval Broadcasts*, pp. 85–86.

60 Bucknill Committee – Interim Findings, TNA: ADM 167/116.
61 Second Report of the Bucknill Committee, 25 April 1942, TNA: ADM 116/4521. Admiral Sir Hugh Binney Papers, Imperial War Museum, IWM/PP/MCR/95.
62 First Sea Lord to Admiralty Board, 29 May 1942, ADM 167/116.
63 Ibid.

Conclusion

1 Lisio, *British Naval Supremacy*, p. 37.
2 Hennessy, Peter, *Whitehall* (London: Pimlico, 2001).
3 Huntingdon, *Common Defense*, pp. 7–14.
4 Cabinet Finance Committee, Second Meeting, 11 August 1919, TNA: CAB 27/71.
5 McDonald, J. Kenneth, 'Lloyd George and the Search for a Postwar Naval Policy, 1919' in Taylor, A.J.P. (ed.), *Lloyd George: Twelve Essays* (London: Hamish Hamilton, 1971), pp. 191–222.
6 Babij, Orest, 'The Royal Navy and the Defence of the British Empire, 1928–1934' and Ferris, John, '"It is Our Business in the Navy to Command the Seas": The Last Decade of British Maritime Supremacy, 1919–1929' in Neilson and Kennedy (eds.), *Far Flung Lines*, pp. 171–89 and 124–70.
7 DesRosiers, Edward, 'The Royal Navy, 1922–1930: The Search for a Naval Policy in an Age of Re-adjustment', MA, McGill University, 1966. pp. 120–21.
8 Spencer, Alex M., 'A Third Option: Imperial Air Defense and the Pacific Dominions', PhD Auburn University, 2008. p. 367.
9 Puddefoot, Geoff, *Ready for Anything: The Royal Fleet Auxiliary 1905–1950* (Barnsley: Seaforth, 2010), p. 128.
10 Ibid., p. 76.
11 Winton, John, *The Forgotten Fleet: The Story of British Pacific Fleet 1944–5* (London: Michael Joseph, 1969), pp. 269–307. History of the Fleet Train, Pacific Fleet: Reports of Proceedings Period May 1945 to January 1946, British TNA: ADM116/5535. Fleet Train, Oiling at Sea, TNA: ADM199/1756. Oiling at Sea by HM Ships, methods, policy, equipment 1938–40, TNA: ADM1/10755. Oiling at Sea, Rubber Hose Method, 1943, TNA: ADM1/15405.
12 See Villiers to Secretary (Admiralty), 7 September 1923, TNA: ADM1/8643. See also minute by Sir Eyre Crowe, 26 October 1921, TNA: FO371/7108.
13 Derby to Howell Gwynne, 12 January 1922, Gwynne Papers 22.
14 On the agreement, see Curzon to Codrington (Tangier), 18 December 1923, TNA: FO371/9467.
15 'Draft Declaration to Egypt', 16 February 1922, TNA: CAB24/133.
16 On 1 April 2011 the *Teeside Gazette* ran an April Fool's story that one of the G-3 battlecruisers being built on the Clyde had in fact been completed in secret, only to

be scrapped in 1931. http://rememberwhen.gazettelive.co.uk/2011/04/teessides-battlecruiserthe-shi.html (accessed 31 May 2014).

17 'Navy Estimates 1922–23: Question of Further Reductions', Memorandum by the Admiralty, 22 February 1922, TNA: CAB24/133.

18 'Navy Estimates 1923–24', Memorandum by the First Lord of the Admiralty 20 February 1923, TNA: CAB24/159.

19 'Lady Lee of Fareham diary, 20 October 1922' in Clark (ed.), *A Good Innings*, p. 231.

20 Cabinet Minutes, 7 December 1922, TNA: CAB23/32.

21 O'Brien, *British and American Naval Power*, p. 149.

22 Lieutenant Joseph Kenworthy (Liberal, Kingston-upon-Hull), 17 March 1921, *Parliamentary Debates [Commons]*, vol. 139, col. 1838.

23 Battle Cruiser Force casualties killed in action 31 May–1 June 1916: *Lion* 99; *Princess Royal* 22; *Queen Mary* 1,266; *Tiger* 24; *Indefatigable* 1,107; *Invincible* 1,026. Roskill, *Beatty*, pp. 164–65.

24 Rear Admiral Christopher Craddock (1862–1914) lost his life while commanding British forces at the Battle of Coronel in 1914 against the cruisers of Admiral von Spee's squadron. Rear Admiral Sir Horace Hood (1870–1916) was killed at Jutland while in action against the German battlecruisers. Rear Admiral Robert Arbuthnot (1864–1916) killed when his cruiser was lost with all hands at Jutland.

25 As James Leasor notes, 'In 1934, out of eleven large concerns which had been active in 1914, only one could still manufacture the heavier munitions, and these only on a small scale.' Leasor, James, *War at the Top: The Experiences of General Sir Leslie Hollis* (London: Michael Joseph, 1959), p. 50.

Afterword

1 Valentine, Helen (ed.), *Art in the Age of Queen Victoria: Treasures from the Royal Academy of Arts Permanent Collections* (London: Royal Academy of Arts, 1999), p. 145.

2 The commissions eventually awarded went to Sir Arthur Stockdale Cope (admirals), John Singer Sargent (generals) and Sir James Guthrie (statesperson).

3 Hart Davis, Duff and Corbeau, Caroline, *Philip de László: Life and Art* (New Haven, CT: Yale, 2010), p. 163.

4 'The Admiralty in War', 5 September 1945, Dickinson, *Naval Broadcasts*, p. 57.

5 Lambert, Andrew, 'Naval Officers of World War I', *Oxford Dictionary of National Biography*, Oxford University Press, http://www.oxforddnb.com/view/theme/106740 (accessed 22 December 2014).

6 Rear Admiral Reginald Tyrwhitt (1870–1951) Commodore and later (1918) Rear Admiral Harwich force. Vice Admiral Roger Keyes (1872–1945), Commander-

in-Chief Submarine Service (1912–15) commanded British naval forces off the Dardanelles (1915) and in 1917 became the director of Plans at the Admiralty.

7 Rear Admiral Edwyn Sinclair Alexander-Sinclair (1865–1945) saw action at Jutland. His signal, on sighting two German destroyers, brought the British Fleet to action. Rear Admiral Walter Henry Cowan (1871–1956) also saw action at Jutland as commanding officer of HMS *Princess Royal*. Rear Admiral Osmond de Beauvoir Brock (1869–1947) saw action at Heligoland Bight, Dogger Bank and Jutland subsequently becoming chief of staff to Beatty while he commanded the Grand Fleet.

8 Admiral Charles Madden (1892–1935), chief of staff to Jellicoe and acting admiral in 1916. Placed in command of the Atlantic Fleet in 1919.

9 For Jellicoe's long-running post-war correspondence with the Admiralty over Jutland, see Jellicoe papers XL, Add. MSS.49028.

10 The other figures in the painting are: Rear Admiral William Goodenough (1867–1945), who fought at Heligoland Bight and Jutland and Vice Admiral Montague Browning (1863–1947), Commander-in-Chief North America and West Indies Station, who was promoted to be the vice admiral in 1917 and later appointed as the president of Allied Naval Armistice Commission. Browning was not a particularly significant naval officer and his inclusion is perhaps because he had lost his hand in a gunnery accident on HMS *Inflexible* in 1889. His artificial hand is a prominent feature of his portrait, perhaps suggesting a link with the thousands of disabled Great War veterans. Vice Admiral John de Robeck (1862–1928) commanded Ninth Cruiser Squadron at outbreak of war, and later the third and subsequently the second battle squadrons, and was appointed as the Commander-in-Chief Mediterranean in 1919. Vice Admiral William Pakenham (1861–1933) commanded Third Cruiser Squadron in 1915 and in 1916 was the Commander-in-Chief Battlecruiser Fleet at Jutland. Admiral Cecil Burney (1858–1929) commanded Channel Fleet in 1914 and then First Battle Squadron of the Grand Fleet and was appointed as an admiral after Jutland and Second Sea Lord thereafter. Vice Admiral Trevylyan Napier (1867–1920) commanded Second and then Third Light-Cruiser squadrons in the first years of the war, saw action at Jutland and second battle of Heligoland Bight in 1917 and was appointed Commander-in-Chief Light Cruisers at the end of the war. Admiral Prince Louis of Battenburg (1854–1921) was First Sea Lord in 1912, resigning in 1914. Vice Admiral Hugh Evan-Thomas (1862–1928) commanded First Battle Squadron in 1914 and Fifth Battle Squadron from 1915 to 1918, fought at Jutland in 1916 and was appointed as the vice admiral in 1917. Admiral Frederick Sturdee (1859–1925) was appointed as the Commander-in-Chief South Atlantic and South Pacific in 1914, and he commanded Fourth Battle Squadron at Jutland. Vice Admiral Arthur Leveson (1868–1929) was appointed as ADC to King George V in 1913

and Commander-in-Chief to the Australian Fleet 1917–18. The inclusions of Leveson and Louis of Battenburg probably reflect the artist's desire to ensure that he continues to enjoy the patronage of King George V and the royal court. Battenburg stares out from the portrait, the only figure to do so. With face set square and eyes meeting those of the viewer, he appears to challenge those who in 1914 forced him out of office by attacking his German origins.

11 Lambert, 'Naval Officers'.

12 *National Security Strategy and Strategic Defence and Security Review 2015: A Secure and Prosperous United Kingdom*, Cmd.9161 (London: Her Majesty's Stationery Office, 2015).

Sources

Unpublished Primary Sources

Britannia Royal Naval College

Review of Damage to His Majesty's Ships, 3 September 1941 to 2 September 1942, Part II, BR1886(1) B (Restricted), Naval Construction Department, December 1942.

Private Papers

Arthur Balfour (British Library)
David Beatty (National Maritime Museum)
Andrew Bonar Law (House of Lords Record Office)
Cammell Laird papers (Wirral Archives)
Austen Chamberlain (Birmingham University Library)
Eustace Tennyson d'Eynecourt (National Maritime Museum)
King George V (Royal Archives, Windsor)
Howell Gwynne (Bodleian Library)
John Jellicoe (British Library)
Philip Kerr, 11th Marquess Lothian (Scottish Record Office)
Roger Keyes (British Library)
David Lloyd George (House of Lords Record Office)
Walter Long (British Library)
Walter Long (Wiltshire and Swindon History Centre)
Ramsay MacDonald (John Rylands University Library)
Sydney and Beatrice Webb (Passfield Papers) (London School of Economics)

National Archives

Admiralty Papers

ADM1/2392
ADM1/8549/18
ADM1/8614
ADM1/8626/105
ADM1/8630
ADM1/8643

ADM 1/8666/159
ADM1/8948
ADM1/9232
ADM1/10755
ADM1/15405
ADM 116/1774–77
ADM116/1831
ADM116/2149–50
ADM116/3165
ADM116/3415
ADM116/3442
ADM116/3445/93
ADM116/3604
ADM116/3610
ADM116/3623
ADM 116/4521
ADM 116/4916
ADM116/5535
ADM167/65
ADM167/116
ADM 178/157
ADM196/43
ADM196/88
ADM196/141
ADM199/1756
ADM226/23–24

Board of Trade Papers

BT56/4

Cabinet Papers

CAB2/3
CAB4/10
CAB16/37/1–3
CAB21/187
CAB23/15
CAB23/32
CAB23/45
CAB24/84
CAB24/92
CAB24/115

CAB24/116
CAB24/123
CAB24/125
CAB24/126
CAB24/133
CAB24/159
CAB 27/71
CAB32/2
CAB34/1

Colonial Office Papers

CO323/844

Foreign Office Papers

FO248/648
FO371/6675
FO371/7108
FO371/9467
FO412/118

Treasury Papers

T161/119
TS27/634

War Office Papers

WO106/5516

Published Primary Sources

Astor, N., *My Two Countries*, London: William Heinemann Ltd, 1923.

Barnes, J. and Nicolson, D. (eds.), *The Leo Amery Diaries, vol 1: 1896–1929*, London: Hutchinson, 1980.

Bartimeus (Captain Sir Lewis Ritchie), *The Navy Eternal*, London: Hodder and Stoughton, 1918.

Bellairs, C., *The Naval Conference and After*, London: Faber and Faber, 1930.

Britain's Industrial Future: Being the Report of the Liberal Industrial Inquiry of 1928, London: Ernest Benn, 1928.

Brownrigg, Rear Admiral Sir Douglas, *Indiscretions of the Naval Censor*, New York: Cassell and Company, 1920.

Butler, R. and Bury, J.P.T., *Documents on British Foreign Policy*, first series, vol. XIV, London: HMSO, 1966.

Bywater, H.C., *Sea-power in the Pacific: A Study of the American-Japanese Naval Problem*, London: Constable, 1921.

Cabinet Office, *A Strong Britain in an Age of Uncertainty: The National Security Strategy*, Cmd.7953, London: Her Majesty's Stationery Office, 2010. https://www.gov.uk/government/uploads/system/uploads/attachment_data/file/61936/national-security-strategy.pdf

Carr-Laughton, L.G., *The British Navy in War*, London: Methuen & Co, 1915.

Cato, C., *The Navy Everywhere*, New York: E.P. Dutton, 1919.

Chaput, R., *Disarmament in British Foreign Policy*, London: George Allen & Unwin, 1935.

Chatfield, Lord, *The Navy and Defence*, London: William Heinemann, 1942.

Chatfield, Lord, *It Might Happen Again*, London: William Heinemann, 1947.

Churchill, W., *The World Crisis*, Toronto: The Macmillan Company of Canada, 1923.

Clark, A. (ed.), *'A Good Innings': The Private Papers of Viscount Lee of Fareham*, London: John Murray, 1974.

Clark, G. and Thursfield, J.R., *The Navy and the Nation or Naval Warfare and Imperial Defence*, London: John Murray, 1897.

Clowes, W.L., *The Royal Navy: A History from the Earliest Times to the Present*, vols. 1–7, London: Sampson Low, Marston and Company, 1897–1903.

Colomb, P.H., *Essays on Naval Defence*, London: W.H. Allen and Co, 1893.

Conference on the Limitation of Armament: Address of the President of the United States, Washington (DC): Government Printing Office, 1921.

Corbett, Julian S., *Maritime Operations in the Russo-Japanese War, 1904–1905*, 2 vols., Annapolis (MD): Naval Institute Press, 2015.

Cornford, L.C., *The British Navy: The Navy Vigilant*, London: Macmillan, 1918.

Dent, J.M., *The Motor Launch Patrol*, Edinburgh: J.M. Dent and Sons, 1920.

Dickinson, Rear-Admiral R.K., *Naval Broadcasts*, London: George Allen & Unwin, 1946.

Domville-Fife, C.W. (ed.), *The Evolution of Seapower: Studies of Modern Naval Warfare and the Effect of Evolution on the Basis and Employment of Sea Power*, London: Rich and Cowan, 1939.

Eardley-Wilmot, S., *The British Navy Past and Present*, London: Navy League, 1904.

'Ex Royal Navy', *The Navy from Within*, London: Hodder and Stoughton, 1914.

Fawcett, H.W. and Hooper, G.W.W., *The Fighting at Jutland: The Personal Experiences of Forty-five Officers and Men of the British Fleet*, London: Hutchinson, 1921.

Gibbs, F.T.M. (ed.), *The Illustrated Guide to The Royal Navy and Foreign Navies*, London: Waterlow Bros. and Layton, 1896.

Giffard, E., *Deeds of Naval Daring: Anecdotes of the British Navy*, London: John Murray, 1910.

Gilbert, M., *The Churchill War Papers, vol. 1, At the Admiralty September 1939–May 1940*, New York: Norton, 1993.

Glasgow, G., *MacDonald as Diplomatist: The Foreign Policy of the First Labour Government in Great Britain*, London: Jonathan Cape, 1924.

Gordon, W.J., *A Chat about the Navy*, London: Simpkin, Marshall, Hamilton, Kent and Co, 1891.

Halpern, Paul, *The Mediterranean Fleet, 1919–1929*, Farnham: Ashgate, 2011.

Halpern, Paul G., *The Keyes Papers: Selections from the Private and Official Correspondence of Admiral of the Fleet Baron Keyes of Zeebrugge, vol. II 1919–1938*, London: George Allen & Unwin, 1980.

Hart-Davis, D. (ed.), *King's Counsellor: Abdication and War: The Diaries of Sir Alan Lascelles*, London: Weidenfeld and Nicolson, 2006.

Hislam, P.A., *The Navy of To-day*, London: T.C. & E.C. Jack, 1914.

Hoare, S., *Empire of the Air: The Advent of the Air Age 1922–29*, London: Collins, 1957.

Hurd, A., *Who Goes There*? London: Hutchinson, 1942.

Ichihashi, Y., *The Washington Conference and After: A Historical Survey*, Stanford (CA): Stanford University Press, 1928.

Inaugural Addresses of the Presidents of the United States, vol. 2, Bedford (MA): Applewood Books, 2009.

Ingram Bryan, J., *Japan from Within*, London: T. Fisher Unwin, 1924.

James, R.R. (ed.), *Memoirs of a Conservative: J.C.C. Davidson's Memoirs and Papers, 1910–37*, London: Macmillan, 1969.

Jellicoe, J., *The Crisis of the Naval War*, New York: George H. Doran, 1921.

Kennedy, Captain, *The Military Side of Japanese Life*, London: Cassells, 1924.

Kenworthy, J.M., *Will Civilisation Crash*, London: Ernest Benn, 1927.

Kenworthy, J.M., *Sailors, Statesmen – and Others: An Autobiography*, London: Rich & Cowan, 1933.

King Hall, S., *Western Civilisation and the Far East*, London: Methuen & Co, 1924.

Kipling, Rudyard, *Many Inventions*, London: Macmillan, 1893.

Kipling, Rudyard, *Traffics and Discoveries*, London: Macmillan, 1904.

Kosukai News Agency, *Anglo-Japanese Alliance*, no place of publication: Japan Times Publishing, 1916.

Long, W., *A Memoir of Brigadier-General Walter Long*, John Murray: London, 1921.

Longford, J.H., *Japan*, London: Hodder & Stoughton, 1923.

Mahan, A.T., *Types of Naval Officer Drawn from the History of the British Navy*, Boston: Little Brown and Company, 1901.

Marder, A.J., *Portrait of an Admiral: The Life and Papers of Sir Herbert Richmond*, London: Alden Press, 1952.

Marder, A.J., *Fear God and Dread Nought: The Correspondence of Admiral of the Fleet Lord Fisher of Kilverstone, vol. III, Restoration, Abdication, and Last Years, 1914–1920*, London: Jonathan Cape, 1959.

Middlemas, K., *Thomas Jones: Whitehall Diary, vol. 1 1916–1925*, London: Oxford University Press, 1969.

Ministry of Defence: Carrier Strike, Report by the Comptroller and Auditor General, HC1092, Session 2010–2012, London: The Stationery Office, 2011.

Minney, R.J. (ed.), *The Private Papers of Hore-Belisha*, London: Collins, 1960.
Murray, O., *The Making of a Civil Servant*, London: Methuen & Co, 1940.
National Security Strategy and Strategic Defence and Security Review 2015: A Secure and Prosperous United Kingdom, Cmd.9161, London: Her Majesty's Stationery Office, 2015.
Paget, J.C., *Naval Powers and Their Policy*, London: Longmans and Co, 1876.
Papers Relating to the Foreign Relations of the United States: 1922, vol. 1, Washington (DC): Government Printing Office, 1922.
Parkes, O., *Ships of the Royal Navy*, London: Sampson Low Marston and Co, 1922.
Pollen, A., *The Navy in Battle*, London: Chatto and Windus, 1918.
Pollen, A., *The British Navy in Battle*, New York: Doubleday Page and Company, 1919.
Pottle, M. (ed.), *Champion Redoubtable: The Diaries and Letters of Violet Bonham Carter 1914–1945*, London: Weidenfeld and Nicolson, 1998.
Powell, E.R., *Asia at the Cross Roads*, London: T. Fisher Unwin, 1922.
Ranft, B.M., *The Beatty Papers: Selections from the Private and Official Correspondence and Papers of Admiral of the Fleet Earl Beatty*, vol. II, Aldershot: Scolar Press for the Navy Records Society, 2003.
Rawson, G., *Earl Beatty, Admiral of the Fleet*, London: Jarrolds, 1930.
Richmond, H., *Sea Power in the Modern World*, London: G Bell & Sons Ltd, 1934.
Robinson, C.N., *The British Fleet: The Growth, Achievements and Duties of the Navy of the Empire*, London: George Bell and Sons, 1894.
Rothermere, Viscount, *Solvency or Downfall? Squandermania and Its Story*, London: Longmans, Green, and Co, 1921.
Satow, E., *A Diplomat in Japan*, New York: ICG Muse paperback, 2000.
Scott, Admiral Sir Percy, *Fifty Years in the Royal Navy*, New York: George H. Doran Company, 1919.
Scott, J.W. Robertson, *The Foundations of Japan*, London: John Murray, 1922.
Securing Britain in an Age of Uncertainty: The Strategic Defence and Security Review, Cmd.7948, London: Her Majesty's Stationery Office, 2010.
Senate [67th Congress], *Document No.126: Conference on the Limitation of Armaments*, Washington, DC: Government Printing Office, 1922.
Shaw, F.W., *The Boy's Life of Admiral Beatty*, London: Hutchinson, 1933.
Snowden, P., *An Autobiography, vol. II 1916–1927*, London: Scolar Press, 1934.
Statement of the First Lord of the Admiralty Explanatory of the Naval Estimates of 1920–21, London: HMSO, 1920.
Steevens, G.W., *Naval Policy with Some Account of the Warships of the Principal Powers*, London: Methuen & Co, 1896.
Stenzel, A., *The British Navy*, London: T. Fisher Unwin, 1898.
Sullivan, M., *The Great Adventure at Washington: The Story of the Conference*, New York: Heinemann, 1922.
Swinburne, A.C., *A Word for the Navy*, London: George Redway, 1896.

Taffrail (Captain Henry Taprell Dorling), *The Sub: Being the Autobiography of David Munro Sub-Lieutenant Royal Navy*, London: Hodder and Stoughton, 1917.
Temple Patterson, A., *The Jellicoe Papers: Selections from the Private and Official Correspondence of Admiral of the Fleet Earl Jellicoe, vol. II 1916–1935*, Greenwich: Navy Records Society, 1968.
Tennyson d'Eyncourt, E.H.W., *A Shipbuilder's Yarn*, London: Hutchinson, 1948.
Thomas, Lowell, *Raiders of the Deep*, Surrey: William Heinemann, 1929.
Tracy, N. (ed.), *The Collective Naval Defence of the Empire, 1900 to 1940*, Aldershot: Scolar, 1997.
Vesey, Hamilton R., *Naval Administration: The Constitution, Character and Functions of the Board of Admiralty and of the Civil Departments in Directs*, London: George Bell and Sons, 1896.
Wedgwood, J.C., *Memoirs of a Fighting Life*, London: Hutchinson, 1940.
Wemyss, W., *The Life and Letters of Lord Wester Weymss*, London: Eyre and Spottiswoode, 1935.
Whitaker's Almanack: 1900, London: Stationery Office, 1899.
Williams, H., *The Steam Navy of England: Past, Present and Future*, London: W.H. Allen & Co, 1895.
Williamson, P., *The Modernisation of Conservative Politics: The Diaries and Letters of William Bridgeman 1904–1935*, London: The Historians Press, 1988.
Wilson Harris, H., *Naval Disarmament*, London: George Allen & Unwin, 1930.
Wood, W., *Famous British Warships and Their Commanders*, London: Hurst and Blackett Ltd, 1897.
Woodward, E.L. and Butler, R. (eds.), *Documents on British Foreign Policy*, first series, vol. v, London: HMSO, 1954.

Newspapers and Journals

Aberdeen Daily Journal.
Advocate (Burnie, Tasmania).
The Age (Melbourne, Victoria).
The Argus (Melbourne, Victoria).
The Ballarat Star (Victoria).
Belfast Newsletter.
Birmingham Daily Post.
The Courier and Argus (Dundee, Scotland).
Daily Advertiser (Wagga Wagga, New South Wales).
Daily Standard (Brisbane, Queensland).
Daily Telegraph.
Driffield Times.
Dundee Evening Telegraph.
Edinburgh Evening Post.

English Illustrated Magazine.
The Evening Telegraph and Post (Dundee, Scotland).
The Farmer and Settler (Sydney).
Glasgow Herald.
Gloucester Citizen.
Hartlepool Northern Daily Mail.
Lancashire Evening Post.
The Leeds Mercury.
The Maitland Daily Mercury (New South Wales).
Northern Star (Lismore, New South Wales).
The Naval Review.
The North Queensland Register.
The Nottingham Evening Post.
The Penny Illustrated Paper and Illustrated Times.
Portsmouth Evening News.
The Round Table: A Quarterly Review of the Politics of the British Commonwealth.
The Spectator.
Sunday Times (Sydney, New South Wales).
Teeside Gazette.
The Times.
Wagga Wagga Advertiser (New South Wales).
The Western Australian (Perth, WA).
Western Daily Press.
Western Mail (Cardiff Wales).
Western Gazette (Yeovil, England).
Western Times.
Yorkshire Evening Post.
Zeehan and Dundas Herald (Tasmania).

Secondary Sources

Books

Abbatiello, J., *Anti-Submarine Warfare in World War 1*, London: Routledge, 2006.
Adams, R.J.Q., *Bonar Law*, London: John Murray Publishers Ltd, 1999.
Adelman, P., *The Decline of the Liberal Party 1910–1939*, London: Addison Wesley Longman Ltd, 1995.
Adelman, P., *The Rise of the Labour Party 1980–1945*, London: Addison Wesley Longman Ltd, 1996.
Arthur, M., *True Glory: The Royal Navy 1914–1939: A Narrative History*, London: Hodder & Stoughton, 1996.

Baer, G.W., *One Hundred Years of Sea Power: The US Navy, 1890–1990*, Stanford, CA: Stanford University Press, 1994.

Ball, S., *Baldwin and the Conservative Party: The Crisis of 1929–1931*, Newhaven, CT: Yale University Press, 1988.

Ballantyne, I., *Warspite*, London: Leo Cooper, 2001.

Barnett, C., *The Collapse of British Power*, London: Eyre Methuen & Co, 1972.

Beasley, W.G., *Japanese Imperialism 1894–1895*, Oxford: Oxford University Press, 1987.

Beatty, C.R.L., *Our Admiral: A Biography of Admiral of the Fleet Earl Beatty*, London: W.H. Allen & Co, 1980.

Bell, C.M., *The Royal Navy, Seapower and Strategy between the Wars*, London: Macmillan, 2000.

Benbow, T., *British Naval Aviation, The First 100 Years*, Farnham: Ashgate, 2011.

Bennett, G., *The Battle of Jutland*, Philadelphia: Dufour Editions, 1964.

Bennett, G.H. *British Foreign Policy during the Curzon Period, 1919–1924*, Basingstoke: Macmillan, 1995.

Best, A., *Britain, Japan, and Pearl Harbor*, London: Routledge, 1995.

Birkler, J.L. et al., *Differences between Military and Commercial Shipbuilding: Implications for the United Kingdom's Ministry of Defence*, Santa Monica (CA): Rand, 2005.

Blake, R., *The Unknown Prime Minister: The Life and Times of Andrew Bonar Law 1858–1923*, London: Eyre and Spottiswoode, 1955.

Bond, B., *British Military Policy between the Two World Wars*, Oxford: Oxford University Press, 1980.

Bourne, Richard, *Lords of Fleet Street: The Harmsworth Dynasty*, London: Routledge, 2016.

Buckley, T.H., *The United States and the Washington Conference, 1921–1922*, Knoxville (TN): Tennessee University Press, 1970.

Buell, R., *The Washington Conference, 1922*, New York: Russell & Russell, 1970.

Bulmer-Thomas, Ivor, *The Growth of the British Party System Volume II 1924–1964*, London: John Baker, 1967.

Burk, K., *War and State: The Transformation of the British Government, 1914–1919*, London: George Allen & Unwin, 1982.

Burk, K., *Britain, America and the Sinews of War, 1914–1918*, Boston (MA): George Allen & Unwin, 1985.

Cable, J., *The Political Influence of Naval Force in History*, London: Macmillan, 1998.

Camrose, Viscount, *British Newspapers and Their Controllers*, London: Cassell & Company, 1948.

Careless, R., *Battleship Nelson: The Story of HMS Nelson*, London: Arms and Armour Press, 1985.

Carew, A., *The Lower Deck of the Royal Navy 1900–39: Invergordon in Perspective*, Manchester: Manchester University Press, 1981.

Chalmers, M., *Paying for Defence: Military Spending and British Decline*, London: Pluto Press, 1985.

Chalmers, W.S., *The Life and Letters of David Earl Beatty, Admiral of the Fleet, Viscount Borodale of Wexford, Baron Beatty of the North Sea and of Brooksby*, London: Hodder & Stoughton, 1951.

Charmley, J., *Churchill: The End of Glory*, London: Hodder and Stoughton, 1993.

Chida, T. and Davies, P.N., *The Japanese Shipping and Shipbuilding Industries: A History of Modern Growth*, London: Bloomsbury, 2012.

Chung, O.C., *Operation Matador: Britain's War Plans against the Japanese 1918–1941*, Singapore: Times Academic Press, 1997.

Clayton, A., *The British Empire as a Superpower, 1919–39*, London: Macmillan, 1986.

Clements, J., *Admiral Tōgō: Nelson of the East*, London: Haus Publishing, 2010.

Cogar, W.B., *New Interpretations in Naval History: Selected Papers from the Twelfth Naval History Symposium Held at the United States Naval Academy 26–27 October 1995*, Annapolis, MD: Naval Institute Press, 1997.

Coles, A. and Briggs, T., *Flagship Hood: The Fate of Britain's Mightiest Warship*, London: Robert Hale, 1985.

Cook, Chris. and Stevenson, John, *A History of British Elections since 1689*, London: Routledge, 2014.

Cowling, Maurice, *The Impact of Labour: The Beginning of Modern British Politics*, Cambridge: Cambridge University Press, 2005.

Cronin, James E., *The Politics of State Expansion: War, State and Society in Twentieth Century Britain*, London: Routledge, 1991.

Darwin, John, *Britain, Egypt and the Middle East: Imperial Policy in the Aftermath of War, 1918–1922*, London: Macmillan, 1981.

Darwin, John, *The End of the British Empire: The Historical Debate*, Oxford: Oxford University Press, 2006.

Dobson, Alan P., *Anglo-American Relations in the Twentieth Century: Of Friendship Conflict and the Rise and Decline of Superpowers*, London: Routledge, 1995.

Doerr, Paul, *British Foreign Policy 1919–1939: Hope for the Best, Prepare for the Worst*, Manchester: Manchester University Press, 1998.

Donaghy, G. and Roy, P.E. (eds.), *Contradictory Impulses: Canada and Japan in the Twentieth Century*, Vancouver (BC): University of British Columbia Press, 2008.

Douglas, R., *The History of the Liberal Party 1895–1970*, London: Sidgwick & Jackson, 1971.

Divine, D., *The Blunted Sword*, London: Hutchinson, 1964.

Edelman, M., *The Mirror a Political History*, London: Hamish Hamilton, 1966.

Edgerton, D., *Warfare State: Britain 1920–1970*, Cambridge: Cambridge University Press, 2006.

Ehrman, J., *Cabinet Government and War 1890–1940*, Cambridge: Cambridge University Press, 1958.

Elphick, P., *Singapore the Pregnable Fortress: A Study in Deception, Discord and Desertion*, London: Coronet Books, 1995.

Evans, D.C. and Peattie, M.R., *Kaigun: Strategy, Tactics & Technology in the Imperial Japanese Navy, 1887–1941*, Annapolis, MD: Naval Institute Press, 1997.

Ferris, J.R., *Men, Money and Diplomacy: The Evolution of British Strategic Foreign Policy, 1919–1926*, Ithaca (NY): Cornell University Press, 1989.

Field, A., *Royal Navy Strategy in the Far East, 1919–1939: Preparing for War against Japan*, London: Frank Cass, 2004.

Ford, D., *Britain's Secret War against Japan, 1937–1945*, New York: Routledge, 2006.

Franklin, G., *British Anti-Submarine Capability 1919–1939*, London: Frank Cass, 2003.

Friedman, N., *British Carrier Aviation: The Evolution of the Ships and Their Aircraft*, London: Conway, 1988.

Gilmour, David, *Curzon*, London: John Murray, 1994.

Glyn, S. and Oxborrow, J., *Interwar Britain: A Social and Economic History*, London: George Allen & Unwin, 1976.

Goldstein, E., *Winning the Peace: British Diplomatic Strategy, Peace Planning, and the Paris Peace Conference, 1916–1920*, Oxford: Oxford University Press, 1991.

Goldstein, Erik and Maurer, John (eds.), *The Washington Conference, 1921–22: Naval Rivalry, East Asian Stability and the Road to Pearl Harbor*, London: Frank Cass, 1994.

Gordon, A., *The Rules of the Game: Jutland and British Naval Command*, London: John Murray, 2005.

Gordon, G.S., *British Seapower and Procurement between the Wars*, Cambridge: Cambridge University Printing House, 1965.

Gough, B., *Historical Dreadnoughts: Marder and Roskill: Writing and Fighting Naval History*, Barnsley: Pen and Sword, 2010.

Gow, I. and Hirama, Y. (eds.), *The History of Anglo-Japanese Relations, 1600–2000*, volume III, Basingstoke: Palgrave, 2003.

Green, E.H.H.,*The Crisis of Conservatism: The Politics, Economics and Ideology of the British Conservative Party, 1880–1914*, London: Routledge, 1995.

Greene, J. and Massignami, A., *The Naval War in the Mediterranean 1940–1943*, Annapolis, MD: United States Naval Institute Press, 2002.

Gretton, Peter., *Former Naval Person*, London: Cassell, 1968.

Grieves, Keith, *Sir Eric Geddes: Business and Government in War and Peace*, Manchester: Manchester University Press, 1989.

Grigg, J., *Nancy Astor: Portrait of a Pioneer*, London: Sidgwick & Jackson, 1980.

Grove, Eric, *The Royal Navy since 1815: A New Short History*, Basingstoke: Palgrave Macmillan, 2005.

Haggie, P., *Britannia at Bay: The Defence of the British Empire against Japan 1931–1941*, Oxford: Clarendon Press, 1981.

Hamilton, C.I., *The Making of the Modern Admiralty: British Naval Policy-Making 1805–1927*, Cambridge: Cambridge University Press, 2011.

Hart Davis, Duff and Corbeau, Caroline, *Philip de László: Life and Art*, New Haven, CT: Yale, 2010.

Hattendorf, John (ed.), *Doing Naval History: Essays towards Improvement*, Newport (RI): Naval War College Press, 1995.

Henig, Ruth, *Versailles and After, 1919–1933*, London: Routledge, 1995.

Hennessy, Peter, *Whitehall*, London: Pimlico, 2001.

Hill, R., *War at Sea in the Ironclad Age*, London: Cassell paperback, 2002.

Hinsley, F.H., *Command of the Sea: The Naval Side of British History from 1918 to the End of the Second World War*, London: Christophers, 1950.

Hore, P., *Dreadnought to Daring: 100 Years of Comment, Controversy and Debate in the Naval Review*, Barnsley: Seaforth, 2012.

Hughes, M., *British Foreign Secretaries in an Uncertain World, 1919–1939*, Oxford: Routledge, 2006.

Huntingdon, Samuel P., *The Common Defense: Strategic Programs in National Politics*, New York: Columbia University Press, 1961.

Hyatt, A.M.J., *Dreadnought to Polaris: Maritime Strategy since Mahan – Papers from the Conference on Strategic Studies at the University of Western Ontario, March 1972*, Annapolis, MD: Naval Institute Press, 1973.

James, R.R., *Churchill: A Study in Failure*, London: Penguin Books, 1970.

Jenkins, Roy, *Baldwin*, London: Collins, 1987.

Johnman, Lewis and Murphy, Hugh, *British Shipbuilding and the State since 1918: A Political Economy of Decline*, Exeter: University of Exeter Press, 2002.

Johnson, G., *The Foreign Office and British Diplomacy in the Twentieth Century*, Oxford: Routledge, 2009.

Johnston, Ian, *Clydebank Battlecruisers: Forgotten Photographs from John Brown's Shipyard*, Barnsley: Seaforth, 2011.

Johnston, Ian and Buxton, Ian, *The Battleship Builders: Constructing and Arming British Capital Ships*, Barnsley: Seaforth, 2013.

Jordan, G., *Naval Warfare in the Twentieth Century 1900–1945: Essays in Honour of Arthur Marder*, Crane, New York: Russek & Company, 1977.

Jordan, John, *Warships after Washington: The Development of the Five Major Fleets 1922–1930*, Barnsley: Seaforth, 2011.

Kennedy, Greg, *The Merchant Marine in International Affairs 1850–1950*, London: Frank Cass, 2000.

Kennedy, Greg (ed.), *British Naval Strategy East of Suez 1900–2000: Influences and Actions*, London: Frank Cass, 2005.

Kennedy, Malcolm, *The Estrangement of Great Britain and Japan*, Manchester: Manchester University Press, 1969.

Kennedy, Paul, *The Rise and Fall of British Naval Mastery*, London: Ashfield, 1983.

Keohane, Nigel, *The Party of Patriotism: The Conservative Party and the First World War*, London: Ashgate, 2010.

Kitching, C.J., *Britain and the Problems of International Disarmament 1919–1934*, London: Routledge, 1999.

Kitching, C.J., *Britain and the Geneva Disarmament Conference*, Basingstoke: Palgrave Macmillan, 2003.

Lambert, Nicholas, *Sir John Fisher's Naval Revolution*, Colombia (SC): University of South Carolina Press, 2002.

Lambert, Antony, *Admirals: The Naval Commanders Who Made Britain Great*, London: Faber and Faber, 2008.

Laybourn, Keith, *The Labour Party 1881–1951*, Stroud: Alan Sutton Publishing, 1988.

Layman, R.D., and McLaughlin, S., *The Hybrid Warship: The Amalgamation of Big Guns and Aircraft*, London: Conway Maritime Press, 1991.

Leasor, J., *War at the Top: The Experiences of General Sir Leslie Hollis*, London: Michael Joseph, 1959.

Lindsay, T.F. and Harrington, M., *The Conservative Party 1918–1979*, London: Macmillan, 1979.

Lisio, Donald J., *British Naval Supremacy and Anglo-American Antagonisms, 1914–1930*, Cambridge: Cambridge University Press, 2014.

Llewellyn-Jones, M., *The Royal Navy and Anti-Submarine Warfare, 1917–49*, London: Routledge, 2006.

Louis, W.R., *British Strategy in the Far East, 1919–1939*, Oxford: Oxford University Press, 1971.

Louis, W.R., *In the Name of God, Go!: Leo Amery and the British Empire in the Age of Churchill*, London: Norton, 1992.

Lyman, R.W., *The First Labour Government 1924*, London: Chapman & Hale, 1957.

Lyon, D., *The Ship: Steam Steel and Torpedoes*, London: HMSO, 1980.

Mackay, R.F., *Fisher of Kilverstone*, Oxford: Oxford University Press, 1973.

Mackay, R.F., *Balfour: Intellectual Statesman*, Oxford: Oxford University Press, 1985.

Maisel, E., *The Foreign Office and Foreign Policy, 1919–1926*, Brighton: Sussex Academic Press, 1994.

Macmillan, M., *Peacemakers: Six Months That Changed the World*, London: John Murray, 2001.

Macmillan, M., *The War That Ended Peace: How Europe Abandoned Peace for the First World War*, London: Profile Books, 2013.

Marder, Arthur J., *From the Dreadnought to Scapa Flow: The Royal Navy in the Fisher Era, 1904–1919*, 5 vols., London: Oxford University Press, 1961–70.

Marder, Arthur J., *From the Dardanelles to Oran: Studies of the Royal Navy in War and Peace 1915–1940*, London: Oxford University Press, 1974.

Marder, Arthur J., *Old Friends, New Enemies: The Royal Navy and Imperial Japanese Navy: Volume 1: Strategic Illusions 1936–1941*, Oxford: Oxford University Press, 1981.

Marder, Arthur J., *Old Friends, New Enemies: The Royal Navy and Imperial Japanese Navy: Volume 2: The Pacific War, 1942–45*, Oxford: Oxford University Press, 1990.

Marquand, David, *Ramsay MacDonald*, London: Jonathan Cape, 1977.

Massie, R.K., *Dreadnought: Britain, Germany and the Coming of the Great War*, London: Vintage, 1992.

Massie, R.K., *Castles of Steel: Britain, Germany and the Winning of the Great War at Sea*, London: Jonathan Cape, 2004.
Maurer, J.H. (ed.), *Churchill and Strategic Dilemmas before the World Wars*, London: Frank Cass, 2003.
McBeth, B.S., *British Oil Policy, 1919–1939*, London: Frank Cass, 1985.
McInnes, C. and Sheffield, G.D. (eds.), *Warfare in the Twentieth Century*, London: Unwin Hyman, 1988.
McIntyre, D.W., *The Rise and Fall of the Singapore Naval Base, 1919–1942*, London: Macmillan, 1979.
McKercher, B.J.C., *Anglo-American Relations in the 1920's: The Struggle for Supremacy*, Cambridge: Cambridge University Press, 1984.
Medlicott, W.N., *British Foreign Policy since Versailles, 1919–1963*, London: Methuen & Co, 1968.
Melton, George E., *From Versailles* to *Mers-el-Kébir: The Promise of Anglo-French Naval Cooperation, 1919–40*, Annapolis (MD): Naval Institute Press, 1993.
Monger, George W., *The End of Isolation: British Foreign Policy, 1900–1907*, London: Nelson, 1963.
Moretz, J., *The Royal Navy and the Capital Ship in the Inter-War Period: An Operational Perspective*, London: Routledge, 2002.
Morgan, Kenneth O., *Consensus and Disunity: The Lloyd George Coalition Government 1918–1922*, Oxford: Oxford University Press, 1986.
Morison, E.E., *Admiral Sims and the Modern American Navy*, Boston: Houghton Mifflin, 1942.
Mowat, C.L., *Britain between the Wars 1918–1940*, London: Methuen & Co, 1955.
Murfett, M.H., *The First Sea Lords from Fisher to Mountbatten*, Westport, CT: Praeger Publishers, 1995.
Neilson, K. and Errington, E.J. (eds.), *Navies and Global Defense: Theories and Strategy*, Westport, CT: Praeger, 1995.
Neilson, K. and Kennedy, G. (eds.), *Far Flung Lines*, London: Frank Cass Publishers, 1996.
Nish, I.H., *Alliance in Decline: A Study in Anglo-Japanese Relations*, Athlone: University of London, 1972.
Northedge, F.S., *The Troubled Giant: Britain among the Great Powers*, New York: Praeger, 1966.
O'Brien, Philipps, *British and American Naval Power: Politics and Policy, 1900–1936*, Westport, CT: Praeger, 1998.
O'Brien, Philipps (ed.), *Technology and Naval Combat in the Twentieth Century and Beyond*, London: Frank Cass Publishers, 2001.
O'Brien, Philipps, *The Anglo-Japanese Alliance, 1902–1922*, London: Routledge, 2004.
Olender, P., *Sino-Japanese Naval War 1894–1895*, Poland: Stratus, 2014.
Orde, Anne, *The Eclipse of Great Britain*, New York: St Martins, 1996.
Ovendale, Ritchie, *Anglo-American Relations in the Twentieth Century*, New York: St Martins, 1998.

Padfield, Peter, *The Battleship Era*, London: Hart Davis, 1972.
Padfield, Peter, *Maritime Dominion and the Triumph of the Free World: Naval Campaigns That Shaped the Modern World 1852–2001*, London: John Murray, 2009.
Paine, S.C.M., *The Sino-Japanese War of 1894–1895: Perceptions, Power and Primacy*, Cambridge: Cambridge University Press, 2005.
Parker, R.A.C., *Chamberlain and Appeasement: British Policy and the Coming of the Second World War*, Basingstoke: Macmillan, 1993.
Parkes, O., *British Battleships: Warrior 1860 to Vanguard 1950: A History of Design, Construction and Armament*, London: Seeley Service, 1957.
Partridge, M.S., *Military Planning for the Defense of the United Kingdom*, 1814–1870, New York: Greenwood Press, 1989.
Peden, G.C., *British Rearmament and the Treasury, 1932–1939*, Edinburgh: Scottish Academic Press, 1979.
Poirier, P.P., *The Advent of the Labour Party*, London: George Allen & Unwin, 1958.
Pollard, S., *The Development of the British Economy 1914–1950*, London: Edward Arnold Ltd, 1962.
Powell, David, *British Politics, 1910–1935: The Crisis of the Party System*, London: Routledge, 2004.
Preston, A. and Batchelor, J., *Battleships 1919–77*, London: Phoebus, 1977.
Puddefoot, G., *Ready for Anything: The Royal Fleet Auxiliary 1905–1950*, Barnsley: Seaforth, 2010.
Ramsden, John, *The Age of Balfour and Baldwin 1902–1940*, London: Longman, 1978.
Ranft, Brian M. (ed.), *Technical Change and British Naval Policy 1860–1939*, London: Hodder and Stoughton, 1977.
Raven, A., *British Battleships of World War Two: The Development and Technical History of the Royal Navy Battleships and Battlecruisers from 1911–1946*, London: Arms and Armour Press, 1976.
Reynolds, David, *Britannia Overruled: British Policy & World Power in the 20th Century*, London: Longman, 1991.
Richardson, D., *The Evolution of British Disarmament Policy in the 1920s*, London: Pinter Publishers, 1989.
Robbins, K., *Sir Edward Grey: A Biography of Lord Grey of Fallodon*, London: Cassell, 1971.
Roberts, J., *Battlecruisers*, London: Caxton, 2003.
Rodger, N.A.M., *The Admiralty*, Lavenham (Suffolk): Terrence Dalton Ltd, 1979.
Rose, Inabal, *Conservatism and Foreign Policy during the Lloyd George Coalition*, Oxford: Frank Cass, 2013.
Roskill, Stephen, *The Strategy of Sea Power: Its Development and Application*, London: Collins, 1962.
Roskill, Stephen, *Naval Policy between the Wars, vol. 1: The Period of Anglo-American Antagonism*, London: Collins, 1968.
Roskill, Stephen, *Hankey: Man of Secrets, vol. II 1919–1931*, London: Collins, 1972.
Roskill, Stephen, *Churchill & the Admirals*, London: Collins, 1977.

Roskill, Stephen, *Admiral of the Fleet Earl Beatty: The Last Naval Hero: An Intimate Biography*, London: Collins, 1980.
Rubinstein, David, *The Labour Party and British Society 1880–2005*, Sussex: Sussex Academic Press, 2005.
Rüger, J., *The Great Naval Game: Britain and Germany in the Age of Empire*, Cambridge: Cambridge University Press, 2007.
Schofield, B.B., *British Sea Power: Naval Policy in the Twentieth Century*, London: Batsford, 1967.
Seamen, L.C.B., *Post-Victorian Britain*, London: Methuen & Co, 1966.
Smith, P.C., *Great Ships Pass*, London: William Kimber, 1977.
Smith, P.C., *Hit First, Hit Hard: HMS Renown 1916–1948*, London: William Kimber, 1979.
Sondhaus, L., *Naval Warfare, 1815–1914*, New York: Routledge, 2001.
Spector, R., *At War at Sea: Sailors & Naval Warfare in the Twentieth Century*, London: Penguin Books Ltd, 2001.
Speed, Keith, *Sea Change: The Battle for the Falklands and the Future of the Royal Navy*, Bath: Ashgrove Press, 1982.
Starkey, D.J. and Jamieson, A.G. (eds.), *Exploiting the Sea: Aspects of Britain's Maritime Economy since 1870*, Exeter: Exeter University Press, 1998.
Steel, T., *Scotland's Story*, London: Harper Collins, 1994.
Steiner, Zara S., *The Foreign Office and Foreign Policy 1898–1914*, Cambridge: Cambridge University Press, 1969.
Sumida, J.T., *In Defence of Naval Supremacy: Finance, Technology and British Naval Policy, 1889–1914*, New York: Routledge, 1993.
Tanner, Duncan, *Political Change and the Labour Party 1900–1918*, Cambridge: Cambridge University Press, 2003.
Tarrant, V.E., *Battleship Warspite*, London: Arms and Armour Press, 1990.
Taylor, A.J.P. (ed.), *Lloyd George: Twelve Essays*, London: Hamish Hamilton, 1971.
Taylor, A.J.P., James, R.R., Plumb, J.H., Liddell Hart, B. and Storr, A., *Churchill: Four Faces and the Man*, London: Book Club Associates, 1969.
Taylor, B., *The End of Glory: War and Peace in HMS Hood 1916–1941*, Barnsley: Seaforth, 2012.
Thompson, F.M.L., *The Rise of Respectable Society: A Social History of Victorian Britain*, Harvard: Harvard University Press, 1989.
Till, G., *Airpower and the Royal Navy*, London: Macdonald and Jane's, 1979.
Towle, P., *From Ally to Enemy: Anglo-Japanese Military Relations, 1900–45*, Cambridge: Global Oriental Ltd, 2006.
Valentine, Helen (ed.) *Art in the Age of Queen Victoria: Treasures from the Royal Academy of Arts Permanent Collections*, London: Royal Academy of Arts, 1999.
Vinson, J.C., *The Parchment Peace: The United States and the Washington Conference, 1921–1922*, Athens (GA): Georgia University Press, 1955.

Warren, K., *Steel, Ships and Men: Cammell Laird, 1824–1993*, Liverpool: Liverpool University Press, 1998.
Watt, D.C., *Succeeding John Bull: America in Britain's Place 1900–1975*, Cambridge: Cambridge University Press, 2008.
Watts, D., *Stanley Baldwin and the Search for Consensus*, London: Hodder and Stoughton, 1996.
Williams, Andrew J., *France, Britain and the United States in the Twentieth Century 1900–1940: A Reappraisal*, Basingstoke: Palgrave Macmillan, 2014.
Williamson, P., *Stanley Baldwin: Conservative Leadership and National Values*, Cambridge: Cambridge University Press, 1999.
Wilmott, H.P., *Battleship*, London: Cassell, 2002.
Winton, J., *The Forgotten Fleet: The Story of British Pacific Fleet 1944–5*, London: Michael Joseph, 1969.
Wrigley, C. (ed.), *A Companion to Early-Twentieth Century Britain*, Oxford: Blackwell, 2003.
Young, G.M., *Stanley Baldwin*, London: Rupert Hart-Davis, 1952.
Young, K., *Baldwin*, London: Weidenfeld & Nicolson, 1976.

Articles and Book Chapters

Asada, Sadao, 'Japan's "Special Interests" and the Washington Conference, 1921–1922', *American Historical Review*, vol. 66, no. 1, October 1961. pp. 62–70.
Asada, Sadao, 'The Revolt against the Washington Treaty: The Imperial Japanese Navy and Naval Limitation, 1921–1927', *Naval War College Review*, vol. 46, Summer 1993. pp. 82–97.
Asada, Sadao, 'From Washington to London: The Imperial Japanese Navy and the Politics of Naval Limitation', *Diplomacy & Statesmanship*, vol. 4, no. 3, 1993. pp. 147–91.
Baer, George, 'That Navy for the Nation: A Shared Responsibility' in Stevens, David and Reeve, John (eds.), *The Navy and the Nation*, Crows Nest (NSW): George Allen & Unwin, 2005, pp. 11–22.
Ball, Stuart, 'Asquith's Decline and the General Election of 1918', *Scottish Historical Review*, vol. 61, 1982. pp. 44–61.
Bell, Christopher M., '"Our Most Exposed Outpost": Hong Kong and British Far Eastern Strategy', *Journal of Military History*, vol. 60, no. 1, January 1996. pp. 76–81.
Bell, Christopher M., '"How Are We Going to Make War?": Admiral Sir Herbert Richmond and British Far Eastern War Plans', *The Journal of Strategic Studies*, vol. 20, no. 3, September 1997. pp. 123–41.
Bell, Christopher M., 'Winston Churchill and the Ten Year Rule', *Journal of Military History*, vol. 74, no. 4, October 2010. pp. 523–56.
Bell, Christopher M., 'The Royal Navy, War Planning and Intelligence Assessments of Japan between the Wars' in Jackson, P., and Siegel, J. (eds.), *Intelligence and Statecraft:*

The Use and Limits of Intelligence in International Society, Westport, CT: Praeger, 2005, pp. 139–55.

Bellamy, Martin, 'Shipbuilding and Cultural Identity on Clydeside', *Journal for Maritime Research*, January 2006 (unpaginated). http://www.jmr.nmm.ac.uk/server/show/ConjmrArticle.210 (accessed 10 March 2010).

Bennett, G.H., 'Lloyd George, Curzon and the Control of British Foreign Policy 1919–22', *Australian Journal of Politics and History*, vol. 45, no. 4, 1999. pp. 467–82.

Berryman, John, 'British Imperial Defence Strategy and Russia: The Role of the Royal Navy in the Far East, 1878–1898', *International Journal of Naval History*, vol. 1, no. 1, April 2002. http://www.ijnhonline.org/issues/volume-1-2002/apr-2002-vol-1-issue-1/ (accessed 26 November 2014).

Best, Anthony, 'The "Ghost" of the Anglo-Japanese Alliance: An Examination into Historical Myth-Making Making', *The Historical Journal*, vol. 49, no. 3, 2006. pp. 811–31.

Bingham, Adrian, 'Enfranchisement, Feminism and the Modern Woman: Debates in the British Popular Press, 1918–1939' in Gottlieb, Julie, and Toye, Richard (eds.) *The Aftermath of Suffrage: Women, Gender and Politics in Britain 1918–1945*, Basingstoke: Palgrave Macmillan, 2013, pp. 87–105.

Bird, Hazel Sheeky, 'Naval History and Heroes: The Influence of U.S. and British Navalism on Children's Writing, 1895–1914', *International Journal of Naval History*, vol. 11, no. 1, July 2014. http://www.ijnhonline.org/2014/07/01/influence-us-british-navalism-childrens-writing/ (accessed 26 December 2014).

Birn, Donald S., 'Open Diplomacy at the Washington Conference of 1921–22: The British and French Experience', *Comparative Studies in Society and History*, vol. 12, no. 3, 1970. pp. 297–319.

Blatt, J., 'The Parity That Meant Superiority: French Naval Policy towards Italy at the Washington Conference, 1921–22, and Interwar French Foreign Policy', *French Historical Studies*, vol. 12, no. 2, 1981. pp. 223–48.

Boothe, Leon E., 'A Fettered Envoy: Lord Grey's Mission to the United States, 1919–1920', *The Review of Politics*, vol. 33, no. 1, 1971. pp. 78–94.

Breemer, Jan S., 'The Burden of Trafalgar: Decisive Battle and Naval Strategic Expectations on the Eve of World War One', *Journal of Strategic Studies*, vol. 17, no. 1, 1994. pp. 33–62.

Buesst, Tristan, 'The Naval Base at Singapore', *Pacific Affairs*, vol. 5, no. 4, 1932. pp. 306–18.

Carlton, David, 'Great Britain and the Coolidge Naval Disarmament Conference of 1927', *Political Science Quarterly*, vol. 83, no. 4, 1968. pp. 573–98.

Connelly, Mark, 'Battleships and British Society, 1920–1960', *International Journal of Naval History*, vol. 3, nos. 2–3, August–December 2004. http://www.ijnhonline.org/wp-content/uploads/2012/01/PDF-Connelly-article.pdf (accessed 26 December 2014).

Davison, Robert L., 'Striking a Balance between Dissent and Discipline: Admiral Sir Reginald Drax', *The Northern Mariner*, vol. XIII, no. 2, 2003. pp. 43–57.

'E.H.T. d'Eyncourt Obituary', *Journal of the Institution of Civil Engineers*, vol. 36, no. 6, 1951. pp. 234–5.

Ferris, J.R., 'Treasury Control, the Ten Year Rule and British Service Policies, 1919–1924', *The Historical Journal*, vol. 30, no. 4, 1987. pp. 859–60.

Ferris, J.R., 'The Greatest Power on Earth: Great Britain in the 1920s', *International History Review*, vol. 13, no. 4, 1991. pp. 726–50.

Ferris, J.R., '"It Is Our Business in the Navy to Command the Seas": The Last Decade of British Maritime Supremacy, 1919–1929' in Neilson, K., and Kennedy, G. (eds.), *Far Flung Lines: Studies in Imperial Defence in Honour of Donald Mackenzie Schurman*, London: Frank Cass, 1997, pp. 124–71.

Ford, Douglas, 'A Statement of Hopes? The Effectiveness of US and British Naval War Plans against Japan, 1920–1941', *The Mariner's Mirror*, vol. 101, no. 1, 2015. pp. 63–80.

Foster, J., 'Strike Action and Working-Class Politics on Clydeside, 1914–19', *International Review of Social History*, vol. 35, 1990. pp. 33–70.

Fry, M.G., 'The North Atlantic Triangle and the Abrogation of the Anglo-Japanese Alliance', *Journal of Modern History*, vol. 39, no. 1, 1967. pp. 46–64.

Fry, M.G., 'The Pacific Dominions and the Washington Conference, 1921–22', *Diplomacy & Statecraft*, vol. 4, no. 3, 1993. pp. 60–101.

Gilbert, Bentley B., 'Lloyd George and the Historians', *Albion*, vol. 11, no. 1, 1979, pp. 74–86.

Goldstein, Erik, 'The Evolution of British Diplomatic Strategy for the Washington Conference', *Diplomacy & Statecraft*, vol. 4, no. 3, 1993. pp. 4–34.

Hamilton, C.I., 'The Childers Admiralty Reforms and the Nineteenth-Century "Revolution" in British Government', *War in History*, vol. 5, no. 1, 1998. pp. 37–61.

Hamilton, C.I., 'Expanding Naval Powers: Admiralty Private Secretaries and Private Offices, 1800–1945', *War in History*, vol. 10, no. 2, 2003. pp. 126–56.

Harrington, Ralph, '"The Mighty Hood": Navy, Empire, War at Sea and the British National Imagination, 1920–60', *Journal of Contemporary History*, vol. 38, no. 2, 2003. pp. 171–85.

Hawkins, William R., 'Captain Mahan, Admiral Fisher and Arms Control at the Hague, 1899', *Naval War College Review*, vol. 39, no. 1, 1986. pp. 77–91.

Irwin, Manley R., 'The Naval Policies of the Harding Administration: Time for a Reassessment', *International Journal of Naval History*, vol. 1, no. 1, April 2002.

Jarvis, David, 'British Conservatism and Class Politics in the 1920s', *The English Historical Review*, vol. 111, no. 440, 1996, pp. 59–84.

Kennedy, Gregory C., 'Britain's Policy Making Elite, the Naval Disarmament Puzzle and Public Opinion, 1927–1932', *Albion*, vol. 26, no. 4, 1994. pp. 623–43.

Klein, Ira, 'Whitehall, Washington, and the Anglo-Japanese Alliance, 1919–1921', *Pacific Historical Review*, vol. 41, no. 4, 1972. pp. 460–83.

Koda, Yoji, 'The Russo-Japanese War: Primary Causes of Japanese Success', *Naval War College Review*, vol. 58, no. 2, 2005. pp. 11–44.

Lambert, Andrew, 'The Royal Navy 1856–1914: Deterrence and the Strategy of World Power' in Neilson, K. and Errington, E.J. (eds.), *Navies and Global Defense: Theories and Strategy*, Westport, CT: Praeger, 1995, pp. 69–92.

Lambert, Andrew, 'Economic Power, Technological Advantage, and Imperial Strength: Britain as a Unique Global Power, 1860–1890', *International Journal of Naval History*, vol. 5, no. 2, August 2006. http://www.ijnhonline.org/wp-content/uploads/2012/01/article_lambert_aug06.pdf (accessed 12 November 2015).

Lambert, Nicholas A., 'British Naval Policy, 1913–14: Financial Limitation and Strategic Revolution', *The Journal of Modern History*, vol. 76, no. 3, 1993. pp. 595–626.

MacGregor, David, 'Former Naval Cheapskate: Chancellor of the Exchequer Winston Churchill and the Royal Navy, 1924–29', *Armed Forces and Society*, vol. 19, no. 3, 1993. pp. 319–33.

Marder, Arthur J., 'The English Armament Industry and Navalism in the Nineties', *Pacific Historical Review*, vol. 7, no. 3, 1938. pp. 241–53.

Maurer, John H., 'Averting the Great War: Churchill's Naval Holiday', *Naval War College Review*, vol. 67, no. 3, 2014. pp. 25–42.

McEwen, J.M., 'The Coupon Election of 1918 and Unionist Members of Parliament', *The Journal of Modern History*, vol. 34, no. 3, 1962. pp. 294–306.

McKercher, B.J.C., 'Belligerent Rights in 1927–1929: Foreign Policy versus Naval Policy in the Second Baldwin Government', *The Historical Journal*, vol. 29, no. 4, 1986. pp. 963–74.

McKercher, B.J.C., 'A Sane and Sensible Diplomacy: Austen Chamberlain, Japan and the Naval Balance of Power in the Pacific Ocean, 1924–1929', *Canadian Journal of History*, vol. XXI, 1986. pp. 193–200.

McKercher, B.J.C., 'Wealth, Power, and the New International Order: Britain and the American Challenge in the 1920s', *Diplomatic History*, vol. 12, no. 4, 1988. pp. 411–41.

McKercher, B.J.C., '"Our Most Dangerous Enemy": Great Britain Pre-eminent in the 1930s', *International History Review*, vol. 13, no. 4, 1991. pp. 751–83.

Neilson, Keith, 'Greatly Exaggerated: The Myth of the Decline of Great Britain before 1914'. *International History Review*, vol. 13, no. 4, 1991. pp. 695–725.

Nish, Ian, 'The First Anglo-Japanese Alliance', Symposium at the Suntory Centre (LSE), 22 February 2002, p. 4. http://eprints.lse.ac.uk/6884/1/Anglo-Japanese_Alliance.pdf (accessed 31 October 2014).

Parkinson, Jonathan, 'HIJMS *Wakamiya* and the Early Development of Japanese Naval Air Power', *The Mariner's Mirror*, vol. 99, no. 3, 2013. pp. 312–22.

Redford, Duncan, 'Review Article from Pre to Post-Dreadnought: Recent Research on the Royal Navy, 1880–1945', *Journal of Contemporary History*, vol. 45, no. 4, 2010. pp. 866–76.

Saxon, Timothy D., 'Anglo-Japanese Naval Co-Operation, 1914–18', *The Naval War College Review*, vol. 53, no. 1, Winter 2000, unpaginated. http://digitalcommons.liberty.edu/hist_fac_pubs/5 (accessed 15 October 2014).

Sharp, A.J., 'The Foreign Office in Eclipse 1919–22', *History*, vol. 61, no. 202, 1976. pp. 198–218.

Silverlock, Gerald, 'British Disarmament Policy and the Rome Naval Conference, 1924', *War in History*, vol. 10, no. 2, 2003. pp. 184–205.

Slaven, A., 'A Shipyard in Depression: John Browns of Clydebank 1919–1938', in Davenport-Hines, R.P.T. (ed.), *Business Kin the Age of War and Depression*, New York: Routledge, 2013. pp. 122–47.

Smith, Dennis, 'The Royal Navy and Japan: In the Aftermath of the Washington Conference, 1922–1926', *Proceedings of the British Association for Japanese Studies*, vol. 3, 1978. pp. 69–86.

Steeds, David, 'The Second Anglo-Japanese Alliance and the Russo-Japanese War', Symposium at the Suntory Centre (LSE), 22 February 2002, p. 19. http://eprints.lse.ac.uk/6884/1/Anglo-Japanese_Alliance.pdf (accessed 31 October 2014).

Sumida, John, 'Technology, Culture and the Modern Battleship', *Naval War College Review*, vol. 45, no. 4, 1992. pp. 82–7.

Thompson, J.A., 'The Historians and the Decline of the Liberal Party', *Albion: A Quarterly Journal Concerned with British Studies*, vol. 22, no. 1, 1990, pp. 65–83.

Till, Geoffrey, 'Great Britain Gambles with the Royal Navy', *Naval War College Review*, vol. 63, no. 1, 2010. pp. 33–60.

Van Meter, Robert H. 'The Washington Conference, 1921–1922: A New Look', *Pacific Historical Review*, vol. 46, no. 4, 1977. pp. 603–24.

Vinson, J.C., 'The Imperial Conference of 1921 and the Anglo-Japanese Alliance', *Pacific Historical Review*, vol. 31, no. 3, 1962. pp. 257–66.

Weir, Gary E., 'Editorial: For the Readers of the IJNH', *International Journal of Maritime History*, vol. 8, no. 3, December 2009. http://www.ijnhonline.org/wp-content/uploads/2012/01/editorial_weir_dec09.pdf (accessed 26 December 2014).

Unpublished Theses

Cesario, Bradley, '"Trafalgar Refought:" The Professional and Cultural Memory of Horatio Nelson during Britain's Navalist Era, 1880–1914', MA, Texas A&M University, 2011.

DesRosiers, Edward, 'The Royal Navy, 1922–1930: The Search for a Naval Policy in an Age of Re-adjustment', MA, McGill University, 1966.

Gibson, Martin William, *British Strategy and Oil, 1914–1923*. PhD , Glasgow University, 2012.

Hall, Michael, 'Anglo-American Naval Relations and Naval Policy, 1919–1930', PhD, McGill University, 1990.

Macdonald, J. Kenneth, 'British Naval Policy and the Pacific and Far East: From Paris to Washington, 1919–1922'. DPhil, Oxford University, 1977.

Macfarlane, J. Allan C., 'A Naval Travesty: The Dismissal of Admiral Sir John Jellicoe, 1917', PhD, St Andrews, 2014.

McLean, Iain, 'The Labour Movement in Clydeside Politics, 1914–1922', DPhil thesis, University of Oxford, 1972.

Neate, James, 'The Royal Navy and the Royal Air Force in Anti-Submarine Warfare Policy, 1918–1945', MPhil, Birmingham University, 2012.

Pattee, Phillip G., 'A Great and Urgent Imperial Service: British Strategy for Imperial Defense during the Great War, 1914–1918', PhD, Temple University, 2010.

Scully, Jon Christopher, 'From Alliance to Enmity: Anglo-Japanese Relations, 1930 to 1939', MPhil, Birmingham University, 2011.

Spencer, Alex M., 'A Third Option: Imperial Air Defense and the Pacific Dominions', PhD, Auburn University, 2008.

Tarkow-Naamani, Israel, 'The Abandonment of "Splendid Isolation": A Study of British Public Opinion and Diplomacy, 1895–1902', PhD, University of Indiana, 1946.

Websites

Election manifesto of James Maxton (Glasgow, Bridgeton), 15 November 1922, http://sites.scran.ac.uk/redclyde/redclyde/rc146.htm (accessed 11 July 2014).

Lambert, Andrew, 'Naval Officers of World War I', *Oxford Dictionary of National Biography*, Oxford University Press, http://www.oxforddnb.com/view/theme/106740 (accessed 22 December 2014).

'Queen Names new Royal Navy Aircraft Carrier in Rosyth', 4 July 2014, http://www.bbc.co.uk/news/uk-28146412 (accessed 19 July 2014).

Report of Admiral of the Fleet Viscount Jellicoe of Scapa on Naval Mission to the Commonwealth of Australia (May–August 1919), vol. IV, p. 229. http://www.navy.gov.au/sites/default/files/documents/Jellicoe_of_Scapa_Vol_IV.pdf (accessed 10 December 2013).

Sidney Webb, *The new constitution of the Labour Party: a party of handworkers and brainworkers: the Labour programme and prospects*, London: Labour Party, 1918. http://webbs.library.lse.ac.uk/124/ (accessed 6 October 2014).

'The Hero of Trafalgar', Royal Maritime Museum Greenwich Catalogue Entry, http://collections.rmg.co.uk/collections/objects/156081.html (accessed 3 August 2014).

'Warship sails into defence of the UK', *The Financial Times*, 4 July 2014, http://www.ft.com/cms/s/0/c51be9d6-038e-11e4-8ae4-00144feab7de.html#axzz38UW4dh67 (accessed 25 July 2014).

Index

Note: The letters 'n' and 't' following locators refer to notes and tables.

Lightning Source UK Ltd.
Milton Keynes UK
UKHW01f1313140818
327204UK00004B/394/P